CEASE FIRING

BY MARY JOHNSTON

D0180517

THE JOHNS HOPKINS UNIVERSITY PRESS
BALTIMORE AND LONDON

Foreword © 1996 The Johns Hopkins University Press
All rights reserved
Printed in the United States of America on acid-free paper

Originally published in a hardcover edition by Houghton Mifflin Company,
Boston and New York, 1911
Johns Hopkins Paperbacks edition, 1996
05 04 03 02 01 00 99 98 97 96   5 4 3 2 1

The Johns Hopkins University Press
2715 North Charles Street
Baltimore, Maryland 21218-4319
The Johns Hopkins Press Ltd., London

Library of Congress Cataloging-in-Publication data will be found at the end
of this book.

A catalog record for this book is available from the British Library.

ISBN 0-8018-5525-X (pbk.)

Since its original publication, this work has taken its place among other
classics of a region and an era. While our knowledge and awareness has
increased and many social attitudes have changed, we the publisher believe
that the value of such books as literary and historical perspectives on our
culture remains undiminished.

CEASE FIRING

FOREWORD

Whaten *The Long Roll* was published in 1911, an advertisement announced that it was the "first of two volumes dealing with the war between the states. With illustrations in color by N. C. Wyeth." Thus the reader of *The Long Roll* began with the awareness that this novel was only part of the whole, that the two books were meant to be linked together (or would be, for no date was mentioned for the next, untitled volume) by subject matter and by design and, as well, by the use of illustrations in color by the same artist. The reader was also being warned that whatever closure occurred in *The Long Roll,* its ending could not be taken as final, but must point ahead to the next novel.

What followed, a year later, was the publication of *Cease Firing.* Where *The Long Roll* is concerned with the early campaigns in the Shenandoah Valley and in and around Richmond and—among other things—follows the fighting career of Thomas Jonathan ("Stonewall") Jackson from the outset of the war until his death at Chancellorsville in 1863, *Cease Firing* begins in the West, as the siege of Vicksburg is about to commence, and continues, swiftly alternating between the West and the Virginia campaigns, following the inexorable decline of the South's fortunes and ending just before the final events at Appamottox. In addition to detailed accounting of far-flung battlefields—Gettysburg, Chickamauga, Missionary Ridge, The Wilderness, Atlanta, Franklin—we are given brief and vivid scenes set in hospitals, prison camps, the cabins of the poor, and the houses of the well-to-do. As in *The Long Roll,* prominent historical figures on both sides appear, speak (usually in their own words), and interact amid the confusion of events. Just so, the fictional characters who dominated the first volume reappear and change before our eyes, as events replace innocence and ignorance with brutal knowledge. It is to Mary

Johnston's special credit that all of her characters, the "real" as well as the fictional, see what they see and do what they do without breaking the spell of contemporaneity. Not one is a prophet able to transcend the limits of the moment. Some of them, the best and the brightest, learn something and can make some sense out of what has happened to them, and can even share that knowledge with others; but none knows what we, the readers, know. We are deftly led into their world and share their consciousness, gradually divesting ourselves of the sure and certain knowledge of where and how things will end.

This transition is the one great advantage of using fictional characters, each with his or her own story, in a book that aims to tell the whole story of the Civil War in two volumes. For, as *Cease Firing* implacably demonstrates, it is the large story of the war that Johnston wants to tell, rather than using it, as it so often was and still is, as a kind of theatrical background against which personal stories are played out. Her fictional characters, linking together the two volumes, have lively, interesting stories, well plotted and executed; but they seem to exist mainly to give the narrative of the war a human scale and some human significance.

All are wounded, one way or another, by their experience. Some, including the principal characters, Désirée Gaillard and Edward Cary, die. Their story ends in rape and murder. Others endure. And the end of things includes a happy, if somewhat shabby, wedding, and a major personal act of forgiveness and reconciliation. Not all goes badly for the survivors. There is every indication that life will go on, not as if the horrors of the war had never happened, but certainly in spite of the worst that had to be endured. As we follow the lives of the fictional characters, we are invited to suppose that justice, as we wish for it, is a hit-or-miss prospect, and that Providence, though it may be at the heart of history, is much too subtle and mysterious to comprehend.

As the last bits and pieces of the "historical romance" disappear and more and more the war itself becomes the principal character of these novels, Mary Johnston uses a variety of narrative voices to tell the tale. These are often the actual voices taken from documents, memoirs, and transcripts. There is the voice of the overall, omniscient narrator, godlike, who can shift from the large and abstract picture to the sentient level of a single soldier. Present also are little scenes, like a chorus, where nameless soldiers banter with one another and brood over the shapes of what has been. There are moments of poetic narration in which the narrator comes close to creating a prose equivalent to what we would now recognize as cinematic montage:

> The bells tolled loud in the South, tolled for the women in the night-time, tolled for the shrunken armies, tolled for the cities that waited, a vision before their eyes of New Orleans, Atlanta, Savannah, tolled for the beleaguered places where men watched in the trenches, tolled for the burned farmhouses, the burned villages, the lonely, blackened country with the gaunt chimneys standing up, tolled for famine, tolled for death, tolled for the broken-hearted, tolled for human passions let loose, tolled for anger, greed and lust, tolled for the shrunken good, tolled for the mounting ill, tolled for war! Through the South they tolled and tolled. (Pp. 416–17)

At times, in the midst of a battle scene, Mary Johnston goes beyond her already vividly realistic rendition of combat to edge into a kind of surrealism. Here she summons up the "Bloody Angle," using Wyeth's facing illustration (present as a color plate in the 1912 edition) functionally as an outward and visible image and a base for her own narrative poetry:

> Billy fired, bit a cartridge, loaded, fired, loaded, fired, loaded, fired, and all over and over again, then, later used his bayonet, then clubbed his musket and struck with it, lifted, struck, lifted, struck. Each distinct action carried with it a more or less distinct thought. "This is going to be hell here, presently," thought the first cartridge. "No guns and every other Yank in creation coming jumping!" *"Thunder Run!"* thought the second; *"Thunder Run, Thunder Run, Thunder Run!"* Thought the third, "I killed that man with the twisted face." Thought the fourth, "I forgot to give Dave back his tin cup." The fifth cartridge had an irrelevant vision of the schoolhouse and the water-bucket on the bench by the door. The sixth thought, "That man won't go home either!" Down the line went the word, *Bayonets!* and he fixed his bayonet, the gun bore burning his fingers as he did so. The breastwork here was log and earth. Now other bayonets appeared over it, and behind the bayonets blue caps. "I have heard many a fuss," said the first bayonet thrust, "but never a fuss like this!" "Blood, blood!" said the second. "I

am the bloody Past! Just as strong and young as I ever was! More blood!" (Pp. 302–3)

Johnston's careful, thoughtful imagination set her free to write some of the best combat scenes in American literature. How does her work stand up in comparison with other Civil War fiction? For ambition and scope—the attempt to tell the whole story of the war in two volumes—the books' chief rival, really, is not fiction at all. Shelby Foote's *The Civil War: A Narrative* does not use anything fictional, though its techniques of telling are often novelistic. *The Civil War* deliberately limits itself to hard facts and real people in their words and deeds. It aims to cover all of the war's events, east and west, on land and at sea, and it succeeds admirably. There is no place in Foote's scheme for the vestiges of "historical romance" and no need for fictional characters to humanize his tale. Foote had already written a Civil War novel, *Shiloh* (1952), equally rooted in fact, and setting an example that would be followed by other writers dealing with the subject—limiting the range and focus of the story to the one major battle or event. For *The Civil War,* Foote took as his models and ideals the great classical historians Tacitus and Thucydides, and above all the *Iliad*: "Richmond Lattimore's translation put a Greekless author in close touch with his model." Mary Johnston had no such end in view, though she certainly sought the means to tell the story of the whole war as truly as possible in fictional terms. If, in the process, she did not shatter the conventions of the "historical romance" once and for all, she did do a better job of testing them against reality than many writers before or since her time.

In the banner literary year of 1929, the year that saw the publication of William Faulkner's *The Sound and the Fury,* Thomas Wolfe's *Look Homeward, Angel,* and Ernest Hemingway's *A Farewell to Arms,* Evelyn Scott brought out *The Wave,* a novel covering the whole of the Civil War that deployed a huge cast of historical and fictional characters in a sequence of discreet events and actions related to one another only as minute parts of a panoramic portrait of the war. "War itself is the only hero of the book," Scott said. (See Peggy Bach, "On Evelyn Scott's *The Wave,*" in *Classics of Civil War Fiction,* ed. David Madden and Peggy Bach [Jackson: University Press of Mississippi, 1991].) The differences from Mary Johnston's books are, first, that here no element of the popular historical romance remains, and second, that Scott is much less interested in evoking and depicting the truths about combat. By that time, with a world war behind them, readers did not need to be forcefully reminded that war is hell.

Before Johnston's time, there had been plenty of examples of good, bad, and indifferent books dealing with the Civil War. Most of the popular fictional works were unabashed and sentimental "historical romances." On the positive side, there were exemplary poets and poems of the war—Whittier, Whitman, and Herman Melville, among others. There is every reason to believe that the avid reader Mary Johnston was familiar with their works. And in the year 1895, just as she was beginning to move toward writing her own first novel, there was the shining example of Stephen Crane's *The Red Badge of Courage: An Episode of the American Civil War*. This unique short novel, marked by its poetic language, structure, and profound psychological insight, as well as by a deliberate vagueness of time and place—almost the opposite of Johnston's gritty specificity—has more in common with the poetry of the war than its fictional representations. But it must have been an inspiration to Johnston if only in the sense that it proved that one did not need to be an actual veteran of the Civil War to write accurately about the experience, that imagination was capable of summoning up reality.

Perhaps more pertinent and useful was the example of Johnston's friend Ellen Glasgow, and her Civil War novel *The Battle-Ground*. Glasgow, like Johnston and Scott, undertook to follow the whole war, beginning to end. Deliberately not a romance, indeed, written (like Mary Johnston's books a decade later) against the grain of the conventions of the popular "historical romance," *The Battle-Ground* is as concerned with the lives of women and children as it is with the lives—and deaths—of fighting men. Again, what Johnston brought to the subject that was distinctly different was her factual and imaginative knowledge of the experience of combat, something that no other writer—except, perhaps, Shelby Foote in *Shiloh* and *The Civil War*—has demonstrated. Moreover, Glasgow and Johnston were starting at different points of departure, Glasgow as the very young author of three novels, two of them—*The Descendant* (1897) and *Phases of an Inferior Planet* (1898)—clearly in the naturalistic tradition; Johnston as an already established author of several highly successful "historical romances." There was an element of self-sacrifice involved in Johnston's bold attempt to bring life into a literary form. Certainly it was a risky enterprise.

Since that time, throughout our century, there has been no diminution in the fascination, shared by writers and readers, with the Civil War as subject or setting. Some of our finest novelists have written major works dealing with the Civil War. There are too many examples to be named, but surely any list of these works would include William Faulkner's *Absalom, Absalom!* (1936), which ironically appeared in the same year Margaret Mitchell's *Gone with the Wind,* and William Faulkner's *The Unvanquished* (1938). Also from the 1930s came John Peale Bishop's *Many Thousands Gone* (1931), Stark Young's *So Red the Rose* (1934), Andrew Lytle's *The Long Night* (1936), Carolyn Gordon's *None Shall Look Back* (1937), and Allen Tate's *The Fathers* (1938).

Since World War II there have been many visions and versions of the Civil War, both popular and literary, sometimes both. Besides Shelby Foote's aforementioned triumph, the three volumes of *The Civil War: A Narrative* (1958–1974), there are such outstanding examples as Foote's own *Shiloh* (1952), Mary Lee Settle's *Know Nothing* (1960), Robert Penn Warren's *Wilderness* (1961), and Stephen Becker's masterpiece, *When the War Is Over* (1969). What is noteworthy about all these works is how they focus on the war from odd and sometimes limited angles. No longer—at least in fiction—the grand epic scope. The larger story is reflected or suggested in smaller stories. We start always with a human scale. *Shiloh* is the story of a single battle. Warren's *Wilderness* has as its protagonist Adam Rosenweig, an idealistic German Jewish immigrant who finds himself working as a peddler in the midst of the battle of the Wilderness in 1863. Mary Lee Settle's *Know Nothing,* part of her Beulah Quintet, follows the lives of a number of characters in the years leading up to the war, ending just as the war itself begins. Becker's story is based on the historical execution by firing squad of one Thomas Martin (May

11, 1865), a young Confederate. It brings inextricably together "real" and fictional characters in a small bitter tragedy.

It would be extravagant to claim (which she never did) that Mary Johnston's *The Long Roll* and *Cease Firing* radically changed the way fiction about the Civil War was written. But it is not too much to say (perhaps not enough) that her two novels are of great importance in the tradition of American fiction about the Civil War; that, except for Evelyn Scott, she is one of the last to try to encompass the experience of the whole war in fiction; and that as a story of war—any war—*The Long Roll* and *Cease Firing* give the reader a powerful sense of being there physically during the fully imagined combat scenes. These books have earned their rediscovery, and one may hope that readers will be led to seek out other works by this gifted author.

George Garrett

CONTENTS

CONTENTS

To the Memory of

JOHN WILLIAM JOHNSTON

MAJOR OF ARTILLERY, C. S. A.

AND OF

JOSEPH EGGLESTON JOHNSTON

GENERAL, C. S. A.

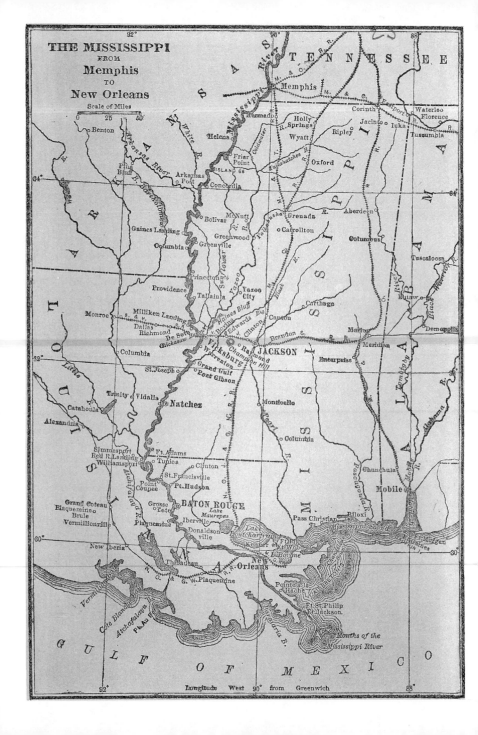

THE MISSISSIPPI
FROM
Memphis
TO
New Orleans

Scale of Miles
0   25   50

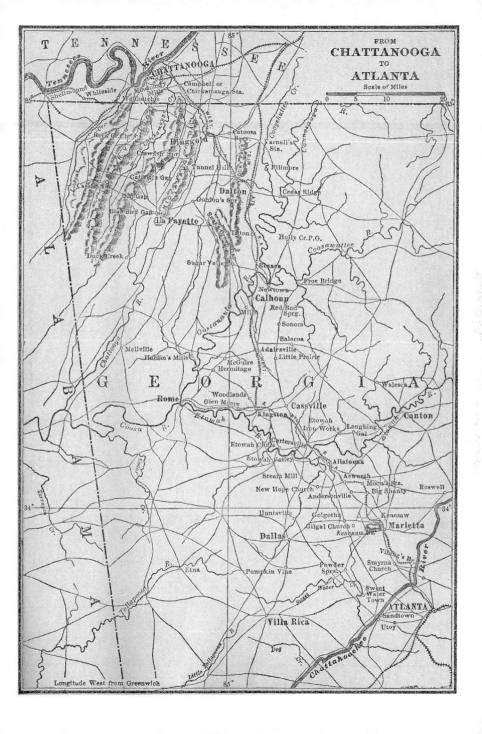

FROM
CHATTANOOGA
TO
ATLANTA
Scale of Miles

0   5   10   20

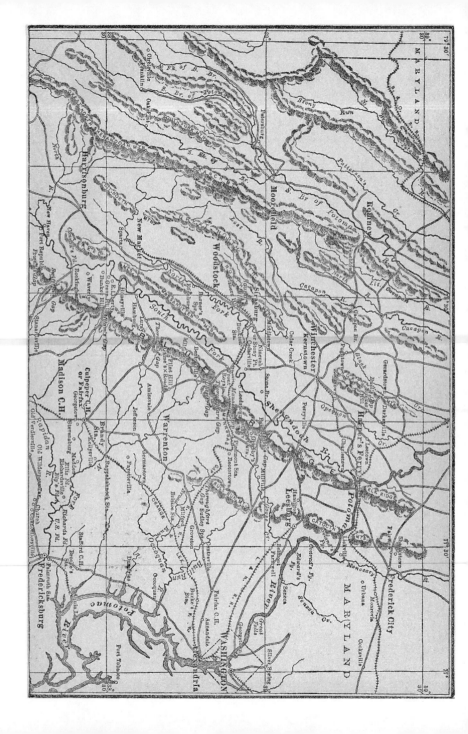

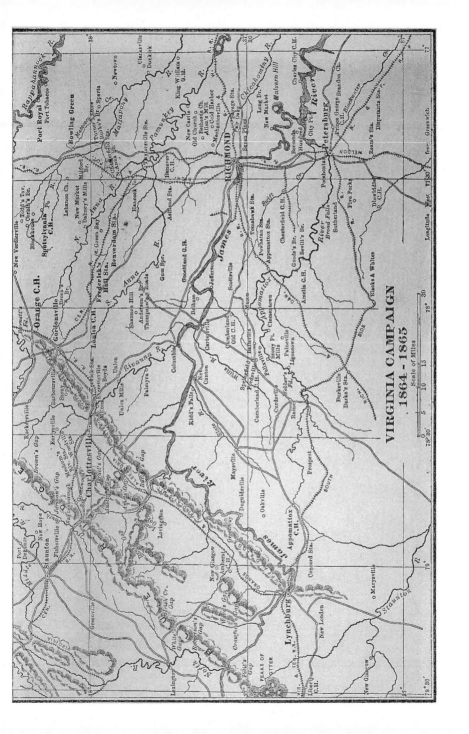

VIRGINIA CAMPAIGN
1864 - 1865

Scale of Miles

CEASE FIRING

CEASE FIRING

CHAPTER I

THE ROAD TO VIDALIA

THE river ran several thousand miles, from a land of snow and fir trees and brief summers to a land of long, long summers, cane and orange. The river was wide. It dealt in loops and a tortuous course, and for the most part it was yellow and turbid and strong of current. There were sandbars in the river, there were jewelled islands; there were parallel swamps, lakes, and bayous. From the border of these, and out of the water, rose tall trees, starred over, in their season, with satiny cups or disks, flowers of their own or vast flowering vines, networks of languid bloom. The Spanish moss, too, swayed from the trees, and about their knees shivered the canebrakes. Of a remarkable personality throughout, in its last thousand miles the river grew unique. Now it ran between bluffs of coloured clay, and now it flowed above the level of the surrounding country. You did not go down to the river: you went up to the river, the river caged like a tiger behind the levees. Time of flood was the tiger's time. Down went the levee — widened in an instant the ragged crevasse — out came the beast! —

December, along the stretch of the Mississippi under consideration, was of a weather nearly like a Virginian late autumn. In the river towns and in the plantation gardens roses yet bloomed. In the fields the cotton should have been gathered, carried — all the silver stuff — in wagons, or in baskets on the heads of negroes, to the ginhouses. This December it was not so. It was the December of 1862. Life, as it used to be, had disintegrated. Life, as it was, left the fields untended and the harvest ungathered. Why pick cotton when there was nowhere to send it? The fields stayed white.

The stately, leisurely steamers, the swan-like white packets, were gone from the river; gone were the barges, the flatboats and freight boats; gone were the ferries. No more at night did there come looming — from up the stream, from down the stream — the giant shapes, friendly, myriad-lighted. No more did swung torches reveal the long wharves, while the deep whistle blew, and the smokestack sent out sparks, and the negro roustabouts sang as they made her fast. No more did the planter come aboard, and the planter's daughter; no more was there music of stringed instruments, nor the aroma of the fine cigar, nor sweet drawling voices. The planter was at the front; and the planter's daughter had too much upon her hands to leave the plantation, even if there had been a place to go to. As it happened there was none.

Farragut, dressed in blue, ruled the river upward from the Gulf and New Orleans to Baton Rouge. Porter, dressed in blue, ruled it downward from Cairo to Grand Lake. Their steam frigates, corvettes, and sloops-of-war, their ironclads, tinclads, gunboats, and rams flew the Stars and Stripes. Between Grand Lake and Baton Rouge the river was Confederate, unconquered yet, beneath the Stars and Bars. They flew from land and water defences at Vicksburg, from the batteries up the Yazoo, from Natchez and the works on the Red River, and the entrenchments at Port Hudson. They flew from the few, few remaining grey craft of war, from the transports, the cotton-clads, the Vicksburg, the De Soto, the gunboat Grand Duke, the ram Webb. Tawny and strong ran the Mississippi, by the Stars and Stripes, by the Stars and Bars.

It had rained and rained. All the swamps were up, the bayous overflowing. The tiger, too, was out; now here, now there. That other tiger, War, was abroad, and he aided in breaking levees. On the Mississippi side, on the Louisiana side, bottom lands were brimming. Cottonwood, red gum, china trees, cypress and pine stood up, drenched and dismal, from amber sheets and eddies, specked with foam. The clouds hung dark and low. There was a small, chill, mournful wind. The roads, trampled and scored by eighteen months of war, were little, if any, better than no roads.

A detachment of grey infantry and a section of artillery, coming up on the Louisiana side from the Red River with intent to cross at

Vidalia and proceed from Natchez to Vicksburg, found them so. In part the detail was from a regiment of A. P. Hill's, transferred the preceding month from Fredericksburg in Virginia to Vicksburg in Mississippi, sent immediately from Vicksburg toward Red River, it being rumoured that Farragut meant a great attack there, and almost immediately summoned back, Secret Service having determined that Grant at Oxford meant a descent upon Vicksburg. The detachment was making a forced march and making it through a Slough of Despond. The no-roads were bottomless; the two guns mired and mired; the straining horses could do little, however good their will. Infantry had to help, put a shoulder to wheel and caisson. Infantry was too tired to say much, but what it said was heartfelt, — "Got the right name for these States when they called them *Gulf* States! If we could only telegraph to China they might pull that gun out on that side!" — "O God! for the Valley Pike!" — "Don't say things like that! Homesickness would be the last straw. If anybody's homesick, don't, for the Lord's sake, let on! . . . Get up, Patsy! Get up, Pansy! Get up, Sorrel!" . . . "Look-a-here, Artillery! If it's just the same to you, we wish you'd call that horse something else! You see it kind of brings a picture up. . . . This identical minute 'Old Jack's' riding Little Sorrel up and down before Burnside at Fredericksburg, and we're not there to see! . . . Oh, it ain't your fault! You can't help being Mississippi and Louisiana and bringing us down to help! You are all right and you fight like hell, and you've got your own quality, and we like you first-rate! If we weren't Army of Northern Virginia, we surely would choose to be Army of Tennessee and the Southwest — so there's no need for you to get wrathy! . . . Only we would be obliged to you if you'd change the name of that horse!"

The clouds broke in a bitter downpour. "Ooooh-h! Country's turned over and river's on top! *Get up, Patsy! Get up, Pansy! Get up* — This ain't a mud-hole, it's a bayou! God knows, if I lived in this country I'd tear all that long, waving, black moss out of the trees! It gives me the horrors." — "*Get on, men! get on!*" — "Captain, we can't!"

Pioneers came back. "It's a bayou — but there's a corduroy bridge, not more than a foot under water."

Infantry crossed, the two guns crossed. Beyond the arm of the bayou the earth was mere quaking morass. The men cut canes, armfuls and armfuls of canes, threw the bundles down, and made some sort of roadbed. Over it came those patient, famished, piteous soldiers, the horses, and behind them, heavily, heavily through the thickened mire, guns and caissons. Gun and wheel and caisson were all plastered with mud, not an inch of bright metal showing. The horses, too, were all masked and splashed. The men were in no better case, wet through, covered from head to foot with mud and mire, the worn, worn uniforms worsened yet by thorn and briar from the tangled forest. The water dripped from the rifles, stock and barrel, the water dripped from the furled and covered colours. The men's shoes were very bad; only a few had overcoats. The clouds were leaden, the rain streamed, the comfortless day was drawing down. The detachment came into a narrow, somewhat firmer road set on either hand with tall cypresses and water oaks, from every limb of which hung the grey moss, long, crêpe-like, swaying in the chill and fretting wind. "For the Lord's sake," said Virginia in Louisiana, "sing something!"

A man in the colour guard started "Roll, Jordan, roll" —

"I want to get to Heaven when I die, —
To hear Jordan roll!"

The line protested. "Don't sing about a *river!* There's river enough in ours now! — That darkey, back there, said the levees were breaking."

"Moses went up to de mountain top —
Land of Canaan, Canaan Land,
Moses went up to de mountain top —"

"Don't sing that either! We're nine hundred miles from the Blue Ridge and Canaan Land. . . . Sech a fool to sing about mountains and home!"

"Well," said Colour Guard, "that was what I was thinking about. If anybody knows a cheerful hymn, I'll be glad if he'll line it out —"

"Don't sing a hymn," said the men. "Sing something gay. Edward Cary, you sing something."

"All right," said Edward. "What do you want?"

"Anything that'll light a fire in the rain! Sing us something funny. Sing us a story."

"There was a ram of Derby,"

sang Edward —

> "As I have heard it said,
> That was the fattest ram, sir,
> That ever had a head —"

The cypress wood ended. They came out into vast cotton-fields where the drowning bolls, great melancholy snowflakes, clung to the bushes, idle as weeds, careless of famine in mill-towns oversea. The water stood between the rows, rows that ran endlessly, cut from sight at last by a whirling and formless grey vapour.

> "The fleece that grew on that ram, sir,
> It grew so mighty high,
> The eagles built their nest in it,
> For I heard the young ones cry.
> And if you don't believe me,
> Or think I tell a lie,
> Why, just look down to Derby
> And see as well as I!"

The land was as flat as Holland, but the rank forest, the growth about the wandering arms of bayous breathed of another clime. The rain came down as in the rainy season, the wind was mounting, the wings of the dusk flapping nearer.

"Get on, men, get on! We're miles from Vidalia."

> "The horns that grew on that ram, sir,
> They grew up to the moon,
> A man went up in December
> And did n't come down till June!

"Look out, Artillery! There's water under those logs!"

The horses and the first gun got across the rotting logs roofing black water, infantry helping, tugging, pushing, beating down the cane.

"Shades of night, where are we anyhow? Cane rattling and the moss waving and water bubbling — is it just another damned bayou or the river? . . . And all the flat ground and the strange trees . . . My head is turning round."

"It's Bayou Jessamine," volunteered an artilleryman. He spoke in a drawling voice. "We are n't far from the river, or the river is n't far from us, for I think the river's out. It appears to me that you Virginians grumble a lot. There is n't anything the matter with this country. It's as good a country as God's got. Barksdale's men and the Washington Artillery are always writing back that Virginia can't hold a candle to it . . . Whoa, there, Whitefoot! Whoa, Dick!"

The second gun had come upon the raft of logs. A log slipped, a wheel went down, gun and caisson tilted — artillery and infantry surged to the aid of the endangered piece. A second log slipped, the wheel beneath the caisson went down, the loaded metal chest jerked forward, striking forehead and shoulder of one of the aiding infantrymen. The blow was heavy and stretched the soldier senseless, half in the black water, half across the treacherous logs. Amid ejaculations, oaths, shouted orders, guns and caisson were righted, the horses urged forward, the piece drawn clear of the bayou. Down came the rain as though the floodgates of heaven were opened; nearer and nearer flapped the dusk. . . .

Edward Cary, coming to himself, thought, on the crest of a low wave of consciousness, of Greenwood in Virginia and of the shepherds and shepherdesses in the drawing-room paper. He seemed to see his grandfather's portrait, and he thought that the young man in the picture had put out a hand and drawn him from the bayou. Then he sank into the trough of the sea and all again was black. The next wave was higher. He saw with distinctness that he was in a firelit cabin, and that an old negro was battling with a door which the wind would not let shut. The hollow caught him again, but proved a momentary prison. He opened his eyes fully and presently spoke to the two soldiers who hugged the fire before which he was lying.

"You two fellows in a cloud of steam, did we lose the gun?"

The two turned, gratified and congratulatory. "No, no, we did n't lose it! Glad you've waked up, Edward! Caisson struck you, knocked you into the bayou, y' know! Fished you out and brought you on till we came to this cabin. Company had to march away. Could n't wait — dark coming and the Mississippi gnawing holes out of the land like a rat out of a cheese! The boys have been gone twenty minutes. Powerful glad you've come back to us! We'd have missed you like sixty! Captain says he hopes you can march!"

Edward sat up, then lay down again upon the pallet. "I've got a singing head," he said dreamily. "What's involved in my staying here?"

His comrades laughed, they were so glad to hear him talking.

"Told Kirk you could n't march yet awhile! You got an awful
blow. Only, we can't stay with you — that's involved! Captain's
bent on making Vidalia. Orders are to bring you on if you can
march, and if you can't to double-quick it ourselves and catch
up! Says Grant's going to invest Vicksburg and he can't spare even
Kirk and me. You're to come on as quick as you can, and rejoin
wherever we are. Says nobody ever had a better headpiece than
you, and that you'll walk in somewhere that is n't at the end of the
procession!"

The night descended. Edward lay half asleep upon the pallet,
in the light of the pine knots with which the negro fed the fire. The
rushing in his head was going, the nausea passing, the warmth was
sweet, bed was sweet, rest, rest, rest was sweet! The old negro went
to and fro, or sat upon a bench beside the glowing hearth.

After his kind he communed with himself half aloud, a slow stream
of comment and interrogation. Before long he took from some mysterious press a little corn meal and a small piece of bacon. The meal
he stirred with water and made into thin pones, which he baked upon
a rusty piece of tin laid on a bed of coals. Then he found a broken
knife and cut a few rashers of bacon and fried them in an ancient
skillet. The cabin filled with a savoury odor! Edward turned on the
pallet. "Uncle, are you cooking for two?"

The meal, his first that day, restored him to himself. By now it
took much to kill or permanently disable a Confederate soldier. Life
forever out of doors, the sky for roof, the earth for bed, spare and
simple diet, body trained and exercised, senses cleared and nerves
braced by danger grown the element in which he moved and had his
being, hope rising clear from much reason for despair, ideality intact
in the midst of grimmest realities, a mind made up, cognizant of
great issues and the need of men — the Confederate soldier had no
intention of dying before his time. Nowadays it took a bullet through
heart or head to give a man his quietus. The toppling caisson and the
bayou had failed to give Edward Cary his.

The young white man and the old negro shared scrupulously between them the not over-great amount of corn bread and bacon. The
negro placed Edward's portion before him on a wooden stool and took
his own to the bench beside the hearth. The wind blew, the rain
dashed against the hut, the flames leaped from resinous pine knot to
pine knot.

Supper finished, talk began. "How far from the river are we?"

"Ef you'll tell 'Rasmus, sah, 'Rasmus'll tell you! En rights hit oughter be two miles, but I's got er kind ob notion dat de ribber's done crope nigher."

Edward listened to the wind and rain. "What's to hinder it from coming nigher yet?"

"Nothin', sah."

The young man got up, somewhat unsteadily, from the pallet, and with his hand against the wall moved to the door, opened it, and looked out. He shivered, then laughed. "Noah must have seen something like it when he looked out of the Ark!" He closed the door with difficulty.

Behind him, the negro continued to speak. "Leastways, dar's only de Cape Jessamine levee."

"Cape Jessamine?"

"De Gaillard place, sah."

With a stick he drew lines in the ashes. "Bayou heah. Ribber heah. De Cun'l in between — only right now he way from home fightin' de Yankees — he en' Marse Louis. De Gaillard place — Cape Jessamine. Hope dat levee won't break!"

Edward came back to the fire. "Do you belong to the place?"

"No, sah, I'se free. Ol' marster freed me. But I goes dar mos' every day en' takes advice en' draws my rations. No, sah, I don' 'zactly belong, but dey're my white folks. De Gaillards 's de finest kind dar is. Dar ain't no finer."

Old man and young man, dark-skinned and light, African and Aryan, the two rested by the fire. The negro sat, half doubled, his hands between his knees, his eyes upon the floor by the door. Now he was silent, now he muttered and murmured. The glare from the pine knots beat upon his grey pate, upon his shirt, open over his chest, and upon his gnarled and knotted hands. Over against him half reclined the other, very torn and muddy, unshaven, gaunt, and hollow-eyed, yet, indescribably, carrying his rags as though they were purple, showing through fatigue, deprivation, and injury something tireless, uninjured, and undeprived. He kept now a somewhat languid silence, idle in the warmth, his thoughts away from the Mississippi and the night of storm. With the first light he would quit the cabin and press on after his company. He thought of the armies of the Far South, of the Army of Tennessee, the Army of the Trans-Mississippi, and he thought of the fighting in Virginia, of the Army of Northern Virginia, the army he had quitted but a few weeks before. He, too, that afternoon, had felt homesick for it, lying there behind the hills to the south of Fredericksburg, waiting for Burnside to cross the Rappahannock! . . . The soldier must go where he is sent! He thought of his own people, of his father, of Fauquier Cary, of Greenwood, and his sisters there. He should find at Vicksburg a letter from Judith. From the thought of Judith he moved to that of Richard Cleave. . . . Presently, with an impatient sigh, he shook himself free. Better think, to-night, of something else than tragedies and mysteries! He thought of roses and old songs, and deep forests and sunny childhood spaces. He put attention to sleep, diffused his mind and hovered in mere warmth, odors, and hues of memory and imagination. He set faint silver bells to ringing, then, amid slow alternating waves of red and purple, a master violin to playing. Lulled, lulled in the firelight, his eyelids drooped. He drew sleeper's breath.

"*De water's comin' under de doah! De water's comin' under de doah!*"
The violin played the strain for a moment, then it appeared that a string broke. Edward sat up. "What's the matter? — Ha, the levee broke, did it?"

"Hit ain't de river, hit am de bayou! De bayou's comin' out, en' ef you don' min', sah, we's obleeged ter move!"

Edward rose, stretching himself. "Move where?"

"Ter Cape Jessamine, sah. Bayou can't git dat far, en' dey sho' ain't gwine let de river come out ef dey kin help hit!"

The floor was ankle deep in yellow water. Suddenly the door blew open. There entered streaming rain and a hiss of wind. The negro, gathering into a bundle his meagre wardrobe and bedding, shook his head and made haste. Edward took his rifle and ragged hat. The water deepened and put the fire out. The two men emerged from the cabin into a widening lake, seething and eddying between the dark trees. Behind them the hut tilted a little upon its rude foundation. The negro looked back. "Liked dat house, en' now hit's er-gwine, too! Bayou never come out lak dat befo' dishyer war!"

Out of the knee-deep water at last, they struck into something that to the feet felt like a road. On either hand towering cypresses

made the intense night intenser. It was intense, and yet out of the
bosom of the clouds, athwart the slant rain, came at times effects of
light. One saw and one did not see; there was a sense of dim revela-
tions, cloudy purposes of earth, air, and water, given and then withdrawn before they could be read. But there was one thing heard
plainly, and that was the voice of the Mississippi River.

They were going toward it, Edward found. Once, in the transient
and mysterious lightening of the atmosphere, he thought that he saw
it gleaming before them. The impression was lost, but it returned.
He saw that they were at the base of a tongue of land, set with
gigantic trees, running out into the gleaming that was the river.
The two were now upon slightly rising ground, and they had the
sweep of the night before them.

"Fo' Gawd!" said the negro; "look at de torches on de levee!
River's mekkin' dem wuhk fer dey livin' to-night at Cape Jessamine!"

CHAPTER II

CAPE JESSAMINE

THE two came from beneath the dripping trees out upon the cleared bank of the Mississippi, and into a glare of pine torches. The rain had lessened, the fitful wind beat the flames sideways, but failed to conquer them. There was, too, a tar barrel burning. The light was strong and red enough, a pulsing heart of light shading at its edges into smoky bronze and copper, then, a little further, lost in the wild night. The river curved like a scimitar, and the glare showed the turbulent edge of it and the swirling cross-current that was setting a tooth into the Cape Jessamine levee.

'Rasmus spoke. "Dis was always de danger place. Many er time I've seen de Cun'l ride down heah, en' stand er-lookin'!"

There seemed as many as a hundred negroes. They swarmed about the imperilled point; they went to it in two converging lines. Each man was bent under a load of something. He swung it from his shoulder, straightened himself, and hurried, right or left, back to shadowy heaps from which he lifted another load. "Dey sho' gwine need de sand bags dishyer night!" said 'Rasmus.

In the leaping and hovering light the negroes looked gigantic. Coal black, bending, lifting, rushing forward, set about with night and the snarl of the tiger, they had the seeming of genii from an Eastern tale. Their voices came chantingly, or, after a silence, in a sudden shout. Their shadows moved with them on the ground. Edward glanced around for the directing white man. "Dar ain't none," said 'Rasmus. "De haid oberseer when he heah dat New Orleans been taken he up en' say dey need mo' soldiers than dey do oberseers, en' he went ter Baton Rouge! En' de second oberseer dat come up en' tek he place, en' is er good man, las' week he broke he hip. En' dar wuz two-three others er-driftin' erroun, doin' what dey wuz tol' ter do, en' dey gone too. When hit wants ter, de river kin pull 'em in en' drown 'em en' tek 'em erway, but dishyer war's de wust yet! Yaas, sah, dishyer war's er master han' at eatin' men! No, sah, dar ain't no white man, but dar's a white woman —"

Then Edward looked and saw Désirée Gaillard. She was standing high, beneath her heaped logs, behind her the night. She had clasped around her throat a soldier's cloak. The wind raised it, blew it outward, the crimson lining gleaming in the torchlight. All the red light beat upon her, upon the blowing hair, upon the deep eyes and parted lips, the outstretched arm and pointing hand, the dress of some bronze and clinging stuff, the bent knee, the foot resting upon a log end higher than its fellows. The out-flung and lifted cloak had the seeming of the floating drapery in some great canvas, billowing mantle of heroine, saint, or genius.

"Saintly," however, was certainly not the word, and Désirée would not have called herself heroine or genius. She was simply fearless and intent, and since, to keep the negroes in courage and energy, it was needful to keep them in good spirits, she was, also, to-night, cheerful, humorous, abounding in praise. Her voice rang out, deep and sweet. "Good man, Mingo! Mingo's carrying two to everybody else's one! Lawrence is doing well, though! So is Hannah's Tom! —

'Levee! levee! lock your hands hard!
Levee, levee! keep the river from my home! —'

Par ici, François! Christopher, Harper, Sambo, Haiti, Mingo Second, make a line! Big Corinth, throw them the sacks! Work hard — work hard! You shall have rest to-morrow, and at night a feast! Look at Mingo, how he works! He is n't going to let the river cover Cape Jessamine! When the Colonel comes home he is going to say, 'Good boy, Mingo!' To-morrow night all the banjos playing, and good things to eat, and the house-servants down at the quarters, and a dance like Christmas! — Mingo, Mingo, put ten sacks just there —"

When she saw the soldier beside her her eyes opened wide in a moment's query, after which she accepted him as an item of the storm and the night. All the land was in storm, and the stream of events rapid. From every quarter and from distant forests the wind blew the leaves. Sometimes one knew the tree from which they came, sometimes not. On presumption, though, if the leaf were grey, the tree was a proper tree, humble, perhaps, in its region and clime, but sound at heart and of a right grain. When Private Edward Cary, gaunt, ragged, muddy, unshaven, asked what he could do, she considered him gravely, then gave him Mingo Second and thirty men, with whom he set to strengthening a place of danger not so imminent. From where he worked he heard at intervals her clear voice, now *insouciante*, now thrilling. There came a moment of leisure. He turned and saw her where she stood, her knee bent, her hand and arm outstretched against the river, the horseman's cloak blown backward and upward into a canopy, the red light over all, strong and clear upon her face and throat and bronze-sheathed body — saw her and loved her.

The December night, already well advanced, grew old. Always the river attacked, always the land opposed. The yellow current sucked and dragged, but the dyke held and the dyke grew stronger. The rain ceased; far up in the sky, through a small, small rift peered a star. The wind died into a whisper. By three o'clock there came a feeling that the crisis had passed. 'Rasmus, working well with Edward's detachment, gave it voice. "Cape Jessamine's done stood heah sence de flood, en' I specs dat's two hundred yeahs! Yaas, Lawd! En' when Gabriel blow he trump, Cape Jessamine gwine up en' say, 'Heah I is, sah!'"

And at that moment there came running through the fields a wild-eyed negro, panic in his outstretched hands. "De levee by de backwoods — de levee by de backwoods — de levee what nobody eber thinks ob, hit's so safe! De ribber done swing ergin hit — de ribber done gouge er hole big ez de debbil! De yerth's er-tumblin' in, en' de ribber's comin' out —"

Through the last half-hour of the night, up a broad avenue between water oaks, Edward found himself hurrying with Désirée. Before them raced the negroes, some upon the road, others streaming through the bordering fields. Désirée ran like a huntress of Diana's. Her soldier's cloak, blown by the wind, impeded her flight. She unclasped it as she ran, and Edward took it from her.

"Will the house go?" he asked. "How great is the danger?"

She shook her head. "I don't think we are in danger of our lives. I don't think the water can get to the house. It is not as though the levee had broken where we were working. What would happen then does n't stand contemplating. This other is but an arm of the river

— not deep nor strong. I think that the house quarters are safe and the stables. But we must get the women and children and the old men from the lower quarter. And the cattle in the fields —" She ran faster.

In the pallor of the dawn the house of Cape Jessamine rose before them. Winged, with columns and verandahs, it loomed in the grey light above leisurely climbing wide lawns and bosky garden. At the house gates, — iron scroll and tracery between brick pillars, antique, graceful, — they were met by the younger, less responsible of the house servants.

"O my Lawd! O Lawd Jesus! O my Lawd, Missy! de ribber's out! O my Lawd, my sins! What we gwine ter do?"

"We're going to stand a siege," said Désirée. "Have they brought Mr. Marcus in?"

"No'm. Dey waitin' fer you ter tell dem —"

She pushed the cluster aside and ran on up the broad path, Edward following. They mounted the steps, passed between the pillars, entered, and sped through a wide panelled hall and came out upon another verandah commanding a grassy space between house and offices. At a little distance, upon the same level, straggling away beneath pecan and pine and moss-draped oak, could be seen the house quarter.

The negroes came crowding, men and women, big and little. "De ribber, Missy! De ribber, Missy! I don' climb er tree en' see hit! I see hit er-comin' en' er-eatin' up de cotton en' de cane! O my Lawd, hit er comin' lak er thief in de night-time! O my Lawd, hit er comin' lak er ha'nt!"

Désirée stood on the verandah steps and issued her orders. "Mingo, you take four men and go to the overseer's house. Tell Mr. Marcus that I say he's not to trust to the water not coming high in his house. Tell him I *order* him to come to the big house. Take him up on his mattress and bring him. Hurry, now, hurry! Mingo Second, Lawrence, Adolph, Creed, Lot, — six more of you! Try what you can do for the cattle in the lower fields! Try hard! If you bring them in, you shall have everything double to-night! — Haiti, Sambo, Hannah's Tom, all of you men on this side, — yes, you too, soldier, if you will! — we'll go now and bring the women and children and old men from the lower quarter!"

They were brought in — brought the last part of the distance through the knee-deep flood. When they got to the rising ground and the house quarter the water was close behind them. Yellow now in the strengthening light, beneath a tempestuous morning sky, it washed and sucked and drew against the just-out-of-reach demesne.

When the crippled overseer had been laid in a wing of the house, and the lower-quarter people had been disposed of in the house quarter and the innumerable out-buildings, when the cattle Mingo Second brought in had been stalled and penned, when with great iron keys Désirée had opened smokehouse and storehouse and given out rations, when fires had been kindled on cabin hearths, and old Daddy Martin had taken his banjo, and the house servants had regained equanimity and importance, and "Missy" had lavishly praised everybody, even the piccaninnies who had n't cried — the plantation, so suddenly curtailed, settled under a stormy yellow sunrise into a not unpleasurable excitement and holiday feeling — much like that of an important funeral.

Désirée stood at last alone but for Edward, and for two or three house servants, hovering in the doorway. She had again about her the scarlet-lined cloak; her throat, face, and head were drawn superbly against the lighted east.

She pushed back her wind-blown hair and laughed. "It might have been worse! — which is my habitual philosophy! We will have fair weather now, and the water will go down."

"I am strange to this country," said Edward. "How can I find the road to Vidalia?"

He stood illumined by the morning glow, his rifle beside him where he had leaned it against the pillar. Now and again, through the past hours, his voice had been in her ear. In the first hearing it, in the moil and anxiety, she had at once the knowledge that this chance soldier possessed breeding. In this time and region the "private" before the "soldier" had the slightest of qualificatory value. University and professional men, wealthy planters, sons of commanding generals — all sorts and conditions were private soldiers. This one was, it appeared from his voice, of her own condition. But though she had noted his voice, by torchlight or by daybreak she had scarce looked at him. Now she did so; each looked into the other's eyes.

"Vidalia ? The road to Vidalia is covered. You must wait until the water goes down."

"How long will that be ? "

"Three days, perhaps. . . . You gave me good help. Permit me now to regard you as my guest."

"You are all goodness. If you will give yourself no concern — I am Edward Cary, private in the ——th Virginia Infantry, lately transferred South. An accident, yesterday evening, left me behind my company on the road to Vidalia. I must follow as soon as it is at all possible."

"It is not so yet. My father is with General Beauregard. My brother is at Grenada with General Van Dorn. I am Désirée Gaillard. We Louisianians know what soldiers are the Virginia troops. Cape Jessamine gives you welcome and says, 'Be at home for these three days.'"

She turned and spoke. The old butler came forward. "Etienne, this gentleman is our guest. Show him to the panelled room, and tell Simon he is to wait upon him." She spoke again to Edward. "Breakfast will be sent to you there. And then you must sleep. — No, there is nothing we can do. The danger to the main levee has passed for this time, I am sure. — Yes, there is still food. We can only fold our hands and wait. I am used to that if you are not. Refresh yourself and sleep. Supper is at seven, and I hope that you will take it with me."

The panelled room, with a lightwood fire crackling upon the hearth, with jalousied windows just brushed against from without by a superb magnolia, with a cricket chirping, with a great soft white bed — ah, the panelled room was a place in which to sleep! The weary soldier from Virginia slept like the dead. The day passed, the afternoon was drawing toward evening, before he began to dream. First he dreamed of battle; of A. P. Hill in his red battle-shirt, and of an order from "Old Jack" which nobody could read, but which everybody knew must be immediately obeyed. In the midst of the whole division trying to decipher it, it suddenly became perfectly plain, and the Light Division marched to carry it out, — only he himself was suddenly back home at Greenwood and Mammy was singing to him

"The buzzards and the butterflies."

He turned upon his side and drifted to the University, and then turned again and dreamed of a poem which it seemed he was writing, — a great poem, — a string of sonnets, like Petrarch or Surrey or Philip Sidney. The sonnets were all about Love. . . . He woke fully and his mind filled at once with the red torchlight, the wild river beyond the levee, and the face and form of Désirée Gaillard.

The door gently opened and Simon entered the panelled room, behind him two boys bearing great pitchers of heated water. The lightwood fire was burning brightly; through the jalousies stole the slant rays of the sinking sun; the magnolia, pushed by the evening wind, tapped against the window frame. Simon had across his extended arm divers articles of wearing apparel. These he laid with solemnity upon a couch by the fire, and then, having dismissed the boys and observed that Edward was awake, he bowed and hoped that the guest had slept well.

"Heavenly well," said Edward dreamily. "Hot water, soap, and towels."

"I hab tek de liberty, sah," said Simon, "ob extractin' yo' uniform from de room while you slep'. De mud whar we could clean off, we hab cleaned off, en' we hab pressed de uniform, but de sempstress she say 'scuse her fer not mendin' de tohn places better. She say dat uniform sut'n'y seen hard service."

"She's a woman of discernment," said Edward. "The tatters are not what troubles me. No end of knights and poets have appeared in tatters. But I do feel a touch when it comes to the shoes. There's nothing of the grand manner in your toes being out. And had it ever occurred to you, Simon, before this war, how valuable is a shoestring?" He sat up in bed. "At this moment I would give all the silken waistcoats I used to have for two real shoestrings. — What, may I ask, could you do for the shoes?"

"King Hiram de cobbler, sah, he hab de shoes in han'. He shake he haid, but he say he gwine do all he kin. De sempstress, too, she say she gwine do her natchul bes'. But Miss Désirée, she say dat perhaps you will give Marse Louis, what am at Grenada wif Gineral Van Dorn, de pleasure ob sarvin' you? She say de Mississippi River all 'roun' Cape Jessamine fer three days, en' nobody gwine come heah less'n dey come in gunboats, en' you kin wear yo' uniform away de third day —" Simon, stepping backward, indicated with a gesture the apparel spread upon the sofa. "You en' Marse Louis, sah, am erbout ob er height en' make. Miss Désirée tol' me so, en' den I see fer myself. Marse Louis's evening clothes, sah, en' some ob his linen, en' a ruffled shu't, en' er pair ob his pumps dat ar mighty ol', but yet better than yo' shoes. — Dat am de bell-cord ober dar, sah, en' ef yo' please, ring when you ready fer me ter shave you."

Downstairs the last roses of the west tossed a glow into the Cape Jessamine drawing-room. It suffused the high, bare, distinguished place, lay in carmine pools upon the floor, glorified the bowls of late flowers and made splendid the silken, heavy, old-gold skirt of Désirée Gaillard. There was a low fire burning on the hearth. She sat beside it, in an old gilt French chair, her hands resting upon the arms. Folding doors between room and hall were opened. Désirée could see the spacious, finely built stairs from the gallery landing down; thus she had fair benefit of Edward Cary's entrance. The candles had been lighted before he came. Those in the hall sconces gave a beautiful, mellow light. Désirée had made no effort to explain to herself why all the candles were lighted, and why she was wearing that one of her year-before-last Mardigras dresses which she liked the best. She rarely troubled to explain her actions, to herself or to another. All her movements were characterized by a certain imperial sureness, harmony. If she merely wished — the Southern armies being held in passionate regard by all Southern women — to do a ragged Virginia private honour; if she wished, delicately, fleetingly, half-ironically to play-act a little in the mist of flood and war; if she wished, or out of caprice or in dead earnest, to make a fairy oasis — why, she wished it! Whatever had been her motive, she possibly felt, in the moment of Edward Cary's appearance on the stair, that gown and lights were justified.

He was a man eminently good to look at. Louis Gaillard, it appeared, knew how to dress; at any rate, the apparel that Edward wore to-night became him so well that it was at once forgotten. He was clean-shaven, and Simon had much shortened the sunburnt hair.

Down the stair and across hall and drawing-room he came to her side. "Did you ever get through the thorny wood and the briar hedge in the fairy story? That's what, without any doubt, I have done!"

Désirée smiled, and the room seemed to fill with soft rose and golden lights. "*I* don't call it a thorny wood and a briar hedge. I always see a moat with a draw-bridge that you have to catch just at the right moment, or not at all —"

At table they talked of this or that — which is to say that they talked of War. War had gripped their land so closely and so long; War had harried their every field; War had marked their every door — all their world, when it talked of this and that, talked only of some expression on some one of War's many faces. It might be wildly gay, the talk, or simple and sad, or brief and grave, with tragic brows, or bitterer than myrrh, or curiously humorous, or sardonic, or angry, or ironic, or infinitely touching, or with flashing eyes, or with a hand that wiped the drop away; but always the usual, customary talk into which folk fell was merely War. So Désirée and Edward talked War while they ate the delicate, frugal supper.

But when it was eaten, and he followed her back into the drawing-room, they sat on either side the hearth, the leaping red and topaz flame between them lighting each face, and little by little forgot to talk of this and that.

It appeared that save for the servants she had had few to talk to for a long, long while. There was a relief, a childlike outpouring of thought and fancy caged for months. It was like the awakened princess, eager with her dreams of a hundred years. They were dreams of a distinction, now noble, now quaint, and always somewhat strange. He learned a little of her outward life — of her ancestry, half French, half English; of her mother's death long ago; of her father, studious, courteous, silent, leaving her to go her own way, telling her that he, not she, was the rapier in action, the reincarnated, old adventurousness of his line. He learned that she idolized her brother; that, save for a year once in France and six weeks each winter in New Orleans, she rarely left Cape Jessamine. He gathered that here she reigned more absolute than her father, that she loved her life, the servants, and the great plantation. It was as large almost as a principality, yet even principalities had neighbours up and down the river! He gathered that there had been visiting enough, comings and goings, before the war. Other principalities had probably come a-wooing — he hoped with passion to no purpose! He also was of the old, Southern life; he knew it all, and how her days had gone; she was only further South than his sisters in Virginia. He knew, too, how the last eighteen months had gone; he knew how they went with the women at home.

They sat by the jewelled fire and talked and talked — of all things but this and that. War, like a spent thunder-cloud, drifted from their minds. They did not continuously talk; there were silences when they looked into the exquisite flame, or, with quiet, wide eyes, each at the other. They were young, but their inner type was ancient of days; they sat quiet, subtle, poised, not unlike a Leonardo canvas. Before ten o'clock she rose and said good night and they parted. In the panelled room Cary opened the window and stood gazing out. There was a great round moon whitening a garden, and tall, strange trees. He saw an opaline land of the heart, an immemorial, passion-pale Paradise, and around it all the watery barrier of the flood . . . Désirée, in her own room, walked up and down, up and down, then knelt before her fire and smiled to find that she was crying.

The next morning, although he was up early, he did not see her until eleven o'clock. Then he came upon her as she quitted the wing in which had been laid the crippled overseer. All around was an old, formal garden, the day grey pearl, a few coloured leaves falling. The two sat upon the step of a summer-house, and at first they talked of the recession of the water and the plantation round which had kept her through the morning. Then, answering her smiling questions, he told her of his home and family, lightly and readily, meaning that she should know how to place him. After this the note of last evening came back, and with its thrilling sound the two fell silent, sitting in the Southern sunshine, gazing past the garden upon the lessening crescent of the flood.

Late in the afternoon, as he sat in a dream before an excellent old collection of books, the door opened and she appeared on the threshold, about her the cloak of the other night. He rose, laying down an unopened book.

"I am going," she said, "to walk down the avenue to look at the levee."

They walked beneath the slant rays, through the deepening shade. Before them was the great river; turn the head and they saw, beyond the rising ground and the house gleaming from the trees, the encroaching backwater, the two horns of that sickle all but touching the main levee. When they came upon this, out of the long avenue, the cypresses behind them were black against the lit west, unearthly still and dark against the gold. The river, too, was gold, a red gold, deep and very wide and swift.

They stood upon the levee, and even his unaccustomed eye saw that the danger and strain of the other night was much lessened, but that always there was danger. — "The price of safety hereabouts is vigilance."

"Yes. To keep up the levees. Now and then, before the War, we heard of catastrophes — though they were mostly down the river. Then, up and down, everything would be strengthened. But now — neglect because we cannot help it, and tremor in the night-time! Below Baton Rouge the Yankees have broken the levees. Oh, the distress, the loss! If Port Hudson falls and they come up the river, or Vicksburg and they come down it, Cape Jessamine will be as others." She drew her cloak close for a moment, then loosened it, held her head high and laughed. "But we shall win, and it will not happen! . . . If we walk to the bend yonder, we shall see far, far! — and it is lovely."

At the bend was a bench beneath a live-oak. The two sat down and looked forth upon vast levels and shining loops of the river. From the boughs above hung Spanish moss, long and dark, like cobwebs of all time, like mouldered banners of some contest long since fought out. The air was an amethyst profound.

For some minutes she kept the talk upon this and that, then with resolution he made it die away. They sat in a silence that soon grew speech indeed. Before them the golden river grew pale, the vast plain, here overflowed, there seamed with huge, shaggy forests, gathered shadow; above day at its latest breath shone out a silver planet.

Désirée shivered. "It is mournful, it is mournful," she said, "at Cape Jessamine."

"Is it so? Then let me breathe mournfulness until I die."

"The water is going down. Mingo says it is going down fast."

"Yes. I could find it in my heart to wish it might never go down."

"It will. I am not old, but I see how what — what has been pleasant, dwindles, lessens — The road to Vidalia lies over there."

"Yes. In the shadow, while the light stays here."

Silence fell again, save for a bird's deep cry in some canebrake. Presently she rose and set her face toward the house. They hardly spoke, all the way back, beneath the cypresses.

In a little while came night and candlelight. He found her in the dress of the evening before, by the jewelled flame, ruby and amber. They went into the next room, where there were tall candles upon the table, and ate of the delicate, frugal fare. There was some murmured dreamy talk. They soon rose and returned to the drawing-room. There was a chess-table, and she proposed a game, but they played languidly, moving the pieces slowly. Once their hands touched. She drew back; he lifted his eyes, then lowered them. It is probable that they did not know which won.

Again at ten, she said good night. Standing within the door he watched her slowly mount the stair — a form all wrapped in gold, a haunting face. At the turn of the stair there came a pause. She half turned, some parting courtesy upon her lips. It died there, for his upward look caught hers. Her face changed to meet the change in his, her body bent as his strained toward her; so they stayed while the clock ticked a quarter-minute. She was the first to recover herself. She uttered a low sound, half cry, half singing note, straightened herself and fled.

The next morning again solitude and the drift of leaves in the garden walks. He did not see her until the middle of the day, and then she was somewhat stately in her courtesy, dreamy and brief of speech.

"Would he excuse her at dinner? There was a woman ill at the quarter —"

"I asked you to let me give you no trouble. Only the day is flying and to-morrow morning I must be gone."

"The water is not down yet!"

"Yes, it is, or all but so. I have been to see. I must go, you know that — go at dawn."

"I will be in the garden at four."

But in the garden, she said it was sad with the cold, dank paths and the fading roses. They came up upon the portico and passed through a long window into the drawing-room. She moved to the hearth and sat in her great, gilt chair, staring into a deep bed of coals above which, many-hued, played the flames. There was in the room a closed piano. "No; she did not use it. Her mother had." He opened it, sat down and sang to her. He sang old love-songs, old and passionate, and he sang as though the piano were a lute and he a minstrel knight, sang like Rudel to the Lady of Tripoli.

When he made an end and rose, she was no longer by the fire. She had moved to the end of the room, opened the long window, and was out in the sunset light. He found her leaning against a pillar, her eyes upon the narrow, ragged, and gleaming ribbon into which had shrunk the flood at Cape Jessamine.

For a moment there was silence, then he spoke. "Nice customs curtsy to great kings," he said, "and great love knows no wrong times and mistaken hours. Absence and the chance of war are on their way. I dare hold my tongue no longer. Moreover, you, too, — I believe that you, too, know what this is that has come upon us! The two halves of the whole real world must in some fashion know each other — I love you, Désirée Gaillard — loved you when I saw you first, there on the river bank —"

He put out his hands. Hers came to them, unhesitatingly. She uttered the same sound, half cry, half singing note, with which she had turned upon the stair the night before. In a moment they had embraced.

CHAPTER III

VICKSBURG

SEVERAL days later, having crossed at Vidalia and passed
through Natchez, he came to Vicksburg. "The ——th Virginia?"

"Camped, I think, in a vacant lot near the Court-House. Fine
regiment!"

"Yes, fine regiment. Why is the town so dressed up? I have
not heard so many bands since General Lee reviewed us on the
Opequon."

"Similar occasion! The President and General Johnston are here.
They came from Jackson yesterday. This morning they inspect the
defences, and this afternoon there will be a review."

"Give me all the news. I have been in another world."

"Grant and Sherman are preparing to swoop. The first is at
Oxford with fifty thousand men, the second has left Memphis. He
has thirty-five thousand, and the Gunboat Squadron. We're in
for it I reckon! But the town's taking it like a birthday party. —
When I was a boy my father and mother always gave me a birthday
party, and always every boy in town but me was there! Can't skip
this one, however! — They say Forrest is doing mighty good work
east of Memphis, and there came a rumour just now that Van Dorn
had something in hand. — You're welcome!"

The fair-sized town, built up from the riverside and over a shady,
blossomy plateau, lay in pale sunshine. The devious river, yellow,
turbid, looping through the land, washed the base of bluff and hill.
Gone was the old clanging, riverside life, the coming and going of
the packets, laughter and shouting of levee and wharf, big warehouses looking benignantly on, manœuvres of wagons and mules
and darkies; gone were the cotton bales and cotton bales and cotton
bales rolling down the steep ways into the boats; gone the singing
and singing and casual sound of the banjo! There was riverside life
now, but it partook of the nature of War, not of Peace. It was the

life of river batteries, and of the few, few craft of war swinging at anchor in the yellow flood. Edward Cary, climbing from the waterside, saw to right and left the little city's girdle of field-works, the long rifle-pits, the redoubts and redans and lunettes. All the hillsides were trenched, and he saw camp-fires. He knew that not more than five thousand men were here, the remainder of the Army of the West being entrenched at Grenada, behind the Yallabusha. Above him, from the highest ground of all, sprang the white cupola of the Court-House. Around were fair, comfortable houses, large, old, tree-embowered residences. The place was one of refinement of living, of boundless hospitality. Two years ago it had been wealthy, a centre of commerce.

Edward came into a wider street. Here were people, and, in the distance, a band played "Hail to the Chief." Every house that could procure or manufacture a flag had hung one out, and there were garlands of cedar and the most graceful bamboo vine. In the cool, high, December sunlight everything and everybody wore a holiday air, an air of high and confident spirits. Especially did enthusiasm dwell in woman's eye and upon her lip. There were women and children enough at doors and gateways and on the irregular warm brick pavement. There were old men, too, and negro servants, and a good sprinkling of convalescent soldiers, on crutches or with arms in slings, or merely white and thin from fever. But young men or men in their prime lacked, save when some company swung by, tattered and torn, bronzed and bright-eyed. Then the children and the old men cheered and the negroes laughed and clapped, and the women waved their handkerchiefs, threw their kisses, cried, "God bless you!" East and west and north and south, distant and near, from the works preparing for inspection, called the bugles.

Edward, moving without haste up the street, came upon a throng of children stationed before what was evidently a schoolroom. A boy had a small flag — the three broad stripes, the wreath of stars. He held it solemnly, with a thin, exalted face and shining eyes. The girl beside him had a bouquet of autumn flowers. Upon the doorstep stood the teacher, a young woman in black.

The group pressed together a little so that the soldier looking for his regiment might pass. As with a smile he made his way, his hand now on this small shoulder, now on that, the teacher spoke.

"It's a great day, soldier! They must all remember it, must n't they?"

"Yes, yes!" said Edward. He paused beside her, gazing about him. "I am of the Virginia troops. We passed through Vicksburg a fortnight ago, but it was at night. — Well! the place wears its garland bravely, but I hope the siege will not come."

"If it does," said the young woman, "we shall stand it. We stood the bombardment last summer."

The boy nearest her put in a voice. "Ho! that was n't anything! That was just fun! There was n't more 'n a dozen killed and one lady."

"An' the house next ours burned up!" piped a little girl. "An' a shell made a hole in the street before my grandma's door as big as — big as — big as — big as the moon!"

All the children began to talk. "It was awful —"

"Ho! it was n't awful. I liked it."

"We got up in the middle of the night an' it was as light as day! An' the ground shook so it made your ears ring, an' everybody had to shout so 's they 'd be heard —"

"An' it was n't just one night! It was a whole lot of nights an' days. Old Porter an' old Farragut —"

"An' Miss Lily used to give us holiday —"

"Huh! She would n't give it less'n the noise got so loud she had to scream to make us hear! When we could honest-Injun say, 'Miss Lily, we can't hear you!' then she 'd give it — "

"We had a whole lot of holiday. An' then old Porter an' old Farragut went away —"

The boy who held the banner had not spoken. Now he waved it once, looking with his brilliant eyes up and out, beyond the river. "The damn-Yankees went away, and if the damn-Yankees come any more, they can go away over again —"

"Gordon! don't use injurious epithets!" said Miss Lily, very gently.

Edward laughed and said good day. Farther on, keeping step for a moment with a venerable old gentleman, he asked, "What, sir, are all those small excavations in the hillsides, there, beyond the houses —"

"They are refuges, sir, for the women and children and sick and helpless. We made them when Farragut came up the river and Porter came down it and poured shot and shell in upon us every few days for a month or two! If signs may be trusted, it is apparent, sir, that we shall find use for them again."

"I am afraid it is. I am not sure that it is correct to try to hold the place."

The old gentleman struck his cane against the ground. "I am no strategist, sir, and I do not know a great deal about abstract correctness! But I am not a giver-up, and I would eat mule and live in a rat-hole for the balance of my existence before I would give up Vicksburg! Yes, sir! If I were a two-year-old, and expected to live as long as Methuselah, those would be my sentiments! Damn the outrageousness of their presence on the Mississippi River, sir! Our women are heroic, sir. They, too, will eat mule and live in rat-holes for as long a time as may be necessary! — No, sir; the President may be trusted to see that the town must be held!"

"Will General Johnston see it so?"

The old gentleman wiped his forehead with a snowy handkerchief. "Why should n't he see it so? He's a good general. General Pemberton sees it so. Why should n't General Johnston see it so?"

Edward smiled. "Evidently you see it so, sir. — Yes; I know that except for Port Hudson, it 's the only defensible place between Memphis and New Orleans! We won't cross swords. Only our forces are n't exactly as large as were Xerxes'!"

"Xerxes! Xerxes, sir, was an effete Oriental! — I gather from your accent, sir, that you are from Virginia. I don't know how it may be with Virginia, — though we have heard good reports, — but *our* people, sir, — our people are determined!"

"Oh," said the other, with a happy laugh. "I like your people mighty well, sir! Do you happen to know where the ——th Virginia is camped?"

The old gentleman waved his hand toward another and still broader street. Cary, passing into it, found more banners, more garlands, more people, and in addition carriages and civic dignitaries. In front of him, before a dignified, pillared residence, was an open place with soldiers drawn up. He gathered that this was the vacant lot for which he was searching, but nearer approach failed to reveal the ——th Virginia. A lieutenant stood beneath a tree, pondering his forming company. Edward saluted, begged for information.

"——th Virginia? Ordered off at dawn to Grenada. Something's up over that way. Grant making a flourish from Oxford, I reckon. Or maybe it's Van Dorn. Do you belong to the ——th Virginia?"

The major came up. "Are you looking for the ——th Virginia? Yes? Then may I ask if you are Edward Cary? Yes? Then I promised Captain Carrington to look out for you. He was worried — he said that you must have been hurt worse than he thought —"

"I was not badly hurt, but a levee broke and flooded that region, and I could not get by."

"I am glad to see you. It's not only Carrington — I 've heard a deal about you from a brother of mine, in your class at the University, Oliver Hébert."

"Oh, are you Robert ?"

"Yes. Oliver's in Tennessee with Cleburne. I hope you'll dine with me to-day? Good! Now to your affair. The regiment's going on to-morrow to Grenada with the President and General Johnston. You'd best march with us. We're waiting now for the President — detachment's to act as escort. He'll be out presently. He slept here last night."

The company, whose first line had opened to include Edward, moved nearer the pillared house. Orderlies held horses before the door, aides came and went. Down the street sounded music and cheering. An officer rode before the waiting escort.

"*Attention !*"

"That's Old Joe they're cheering," said the private next Edward. "Glad Seven Pines could n't kill him! They say he's got a record for wounds — Seminole War — Mexican War — little scrimmage we're engaged in now! — always in front, however. I was at Seven Pines. Were you ?"

"Yes."

"Awful fight! — only we've had so many awful fights since — There he is! — *General Johnston ! General Johnston ! General Johnston !*"

Johnston appeared, spare, of medium height, with grizzled hair, mustache and imperial, riding a beautiful chestnut mare. But recently recovered from the desperate wound of Seven Pines, recently appointed to the command of the Department of the West, the bronze of the field had hardly yet ousted the pallor of illness. He rode very firmly, sitting straight and soldierly, a slight, indomitable figure, instinct with intellectual strength. He lifted his hat to the cheering lines and smiled — a very sweet, affectionate smile. It gave winsomeness to his quiet face. He was mingled Scotch and English, — somewhat stubborn, very able.

Beside him rode General Pemberton, commanding the forces at Vicksburg and Grenada. The two were speaking; Edward caught Johnston's quick, virile voice. "I believed that, apart from any right of secession, the revolution begun was justified by the maxims so often repeated by Americans, that free government is founded on the consent of the governed, and that every community strong enough to establish and maintain its independence has a right to assert it. My father fought Great Britain in defence of that principle. Patrick Henry was my mother's uncle. Having been educated in such opinions, I naturally returned to the State of which I was a native, joined my kith and kin, the people among whom I was born, and fought — and fight — in their defence."

He reached the broad steps and dismounted. As he did so, the door of the house opened and the President, a number of men behind him, came out upon the portico. Tall and lean as an Indian, clearcut, distinguished, theorist and idealist, patriot undoubtedly, able undoubtedly, Jefferson Davis breathed the morning air. Mississippi was his State; Beauvoir, his home, was down the country. He looked like an eagle from his eyrie.

Johnston having mounted the steps, the two met. "Ah, General, I wish that *I* were in the field with this good town to defend!"

"Your Excellency slept well, I trust — after the people would let you sleep?"

"I slept. General Pemberton, good morning — What are your arrangements?"

"In a very few moments, if your Excellency pleases, we will start. The line of works is extensive."

"Haynes Bluff to Warrenton," said Johnston. "About fifteen miles."

"It is not expected," said Pemberton, "that his Excellency shall visit the more distant works."

Mr. Davis, about to descend the steps, drew a little back. Between his brows were two fine, parallel lines. "You think, General Johnston, that the lines are too extensive?"

"Under the circumstances — yes, your Excellency."

"Then what is in your mind? Pray, speak out!"

"I think, sir, that one strong work should be constructed above the town, at the bend in the river. It should be made very strong. I would provision it to the best of our ability, and I would put there a garrison, say of three thousand. The remainder of General Pemberton's forces I would keep in the field, adding to them —"

"Yes? Pray, be frank, sir."

"It is my custom, your Excellency. I hesitated because I have already so strongly made this representation that I cannot conceive . . . Adding to them the Army of the Trans-Mississippi."

"I cannot consent to rob Peter, sir, to pay Paul."

"I conceive, sir, that it is neither Peter nor Paul that is in question, but the success of our arms. The enemy's forces are uniting to invade. Equally ours should unite to repel. General Holmes and his army are doing little in Arkansas. Here they might do much. — If we had the strong works and garrison I speak of —"

"You would abandon all the batteries up and down the river?"

"A giant properly posted will guard the Mississippi better than will your long line of dwarfs."

"Pray, sir, do not say *my* line of batteries. They are not mine."

"I will say, then, your Excellency, General Pemberton's."

"You, sir, and not General Pemberton, are in command of the Department of the West."

"So, when it is convenient, it is said. I have, then, sir, authority to concentrate batteries and a certain proportion of troops at the bend of the river?"

"We will take, sir, your ideas under consideration."

The President moved to the steps, the others following. The line was still between Mr. Davis's brows. All mounted, wheeled their horses, moved into the street. The aides came after, the escort closed in behind. With jingle and tramp and music, to salutes and cheering, the party bent on inspection of the Vicksburg defences moved toward its object.

The words upon the portico had not of course floated to the ears of the soldiers below. But the Confederate soldier was as far removed from an automaton as it is conceivable for a soldier to be. Indeed, his initiative in gathering knowledge of all things and moods governing the Board of War was at times as inconvenient as it was marked. His intuition worked by grapevine.

"What," asked the soldier nearest Edward, "made the quarrel?"

"Old occasions, I believe. Now each is as poison to the other."

The inspection of water batteries and field-works was over, the review of the afternoon over. Amid cheering crowds the President left Vicksburg for Grenada, with him General Johnston and General Pemberton. The regiment which had given Edward Cary hospitality made a night march.

In the cold December dawn they came to a stream where, on the opposite bank, a cavalry detail could be made out watering its horses. There was a bridge. Infantry crossed and fraternized.

"What's the news? We had a big day in Vicksburg yesterday! The President and Old Joe —"

"Have you heard about the raid?"

"What raid?"

"Boys, they haven't heard! — Oh, I see our captain over there telling it to your colonel."

"That's all right! We'll get it from the colonel. But you fellows might as well tell — seeing that you're dying to do it! What raid?"

"Van Dorn's raid — our raid! Raid on Holly Springs! Raid round Grant! *Yaaaih! Yaaiih! Yaaaaih!*"

A tall and strong trooper, with a high forehead, deep eyes, and a flowing black beard, began to speak in a voice so deep and sonorous that it boomed like a bell across the water. "Van Dorn's a jewel. Van Dorn loves danger as he might love a woman with a temper. When she's smiling she's so white-angry, then he loves her best. Van Dorn rides a black thoroughbred and rides her hard. Van Dorn, with his long yellow hair —"

"Listen to Llewellen chanting like the final bard! — Well, he is handsome, — Van Dorn!"

"He ain't tall, but he's pretty. Go on, Llewellen!"

"Van Dorn riding like an Indian —"

"He did fine in the Comanche War. Did you ever hear about the arrow?"

"Van Dorn and two thousand of us — two thousand horse!"

"Dead night and all of them fast asleep!"

"Holly Springs — Grant's depot of supplies — three months' stores for sixty thousand men —"

"Burnt all his supplies — cut his lines of communication — captured the garrison! — Hurrah!"

"Ulysses S. Grant's campaign's deranged —"

"Reckon Vicksburg's safe for this time! Reckon he'll have to trot Sherman back to Memphis —"

"Reckon he'll have to clear out of Mississippi himself!"

"Light as hell in the dead night and all of them scampering! Hurrah! Van Dorn and two thousand horse — "

"'Now, men,' says Van Dorn,'I want Glory with a capital letter, and I reckon we're most of us built the same way! Well, Glory Hallelujah is growing round Grant's army like tiger lilies round a beehive — '"

"Van Dorn and two thousand horse — took 'em like a thunderclap! Burned three months' supplies for sixty thousand men — cut their lines —"

"Toled danger away from Vicksburg —"

"Van Dorn and —"

Fall in! Fall in!

That evening the infantry regiment bivouacked within sight of Grenada. The next morning, early, it swung out toward the Yallabusha. Passing a line of ragged sentries it presently came to a region of ragged, huge fields with cotton all ungathered, ragged, luxuriant forest growth, ragged, gully-seamed, low hills. From behind one of these floated the strains of "Dixie" played by ragged Confederate bands. The regiment climbed a few yards and from a copse of yellow pine looked down and out upon a ragged plain, an almost tentless encampment, and upon a grand review of the Army of the West.

Halt! In place! Rest!

The regiment, leaning on its muskets, watched through a veil of saplings. Officers and men were vividly interested and comment was free, though carried on in low tones. Not far below waved the colours marking the reviewing-stand. The music of the massed bands came from the right, while in front a cluster of well-mounted men was moving down the great field from division to division. A little in advance rode two figures. "The President and General Johnston," said the colonel and the major and the captains. "Old Joe and the President," remarked the men.

The day was bright and still and just pleasantly cold. A few white clouds sailed slowly from west to east, the sky between of the clearest azure. A deep line of trees, here bare or partly bare, here evergreen, marked the course of the Yallabusha. The horizon sank away in purple mist. The sun came down and glinted brightly on sixteen thousand bayonets, and all the flags glowed and moved like living things. The trumpets brayed, the drums beat; there stood out the lieutenant-general, Pemberton, the major-generals, Loring and Dabney Maury and Earl Van Dorn, the latter laurel-crowned from as brilliant a raid as the War had seen. Back to the colours fluttering beneath a live-oak came the reviewing party. Brigade by brigade, infantry, cavalry, and artillery, the army passed in review.

Past the President of the Confederacy went an array of men that, in certain respects, could only be matched in the whole earth by the other armies of that Confederacy. They were of a piece with the Army of Tennessee now operating near Chattanooga, and with the Army of Northern Virginia now watching Burnside across the Rappahannock, and with other grey forces scattered over the vast terrain of the War.

It emerged at once how spare they were and young and ragged. There were men from well-nigh every Southern State; from Georgia, Alabama, Mississippi, Louisiana, Missouri, Texas, Kentucky, the Carolinas; — but whether they came from lands of cotton and cane, or lands of apple and wheat, they were alike lean and bronzed and ragged and young. Men in their prime were there, and men past their prime; there did not lack grey-beards. Despite this, the impression was overwhelmingly one of youth. Oh, the young, young men, and lean as Indians in winter! Brigade by brigade, — infantry, cavalry, artillery, — with smoke-stained, shot-riddled colours, with bright, used muskets, with the guns, with the war-horses, with the bands playing "Dixie," they went by Mr. Davis and General Johnston beneath the live-oak.

Toward noon the regiment from Vicksburg found its chance to

report, and a little later Edward Cary rejoined his command. The command was glad to see him; not all his comrades understood him, but they liked him exceedingly. That night, the first lieutenant, with whom at the University, he had read George Sand and the dramas of M. Victor Hugo, found him seated under a yellow pine with a pine stump for table, and a pine torch for lamp, slowly covering with strong, restrained handwriting, several sheets of bluish Confederate paper.

The lieutenant threw himself down upon the pine needles. "Writing home?"

"No. Not to-night."

Two letters lay addressed in their envelopes. The lieutenant, weary and absent-minded, took them up, fingering them without thinking. Edward drew the letter he was writing into the shadow, guarded it with his arm, and, smiling, held out the other hand.

<blockquote>
Colonel Henry Gaillard,
—— Louisiana Cavalry,
Mobile,
Alabama.
</blockquote>

<blockquote>
Captain Louis Gaillard,
—— Louisiana,
Barton's Brigade ——
</blockquote>

read the lieutenant. He dropped the letters. "I am sure I beg your pardon, Cary! I did n't in the least think what I was doing!"

"There's no harm done, Morton." He repossessed himself of the letters, struck the torch at another angle, and turned from the forest table. "Morton, I'm going in for promotion."

The lieutenant laid down his pipe. "Well, if you go in for it, I'll back you to get it, but I thought you said —"

"I did."

"What do you want it for? Vain-glory?"

Edward locked his hands behind his head. "No; not for vain-glory — though it 's remarkable how brothers and fathers and kins-folk generally like the *clang* of 'Colonel' or 'Brigadier'! After the Merrimac and Monitor I would n't take promotion, but I did get a furlough. . . . Morton, I 'm going in for furloughs and a lieutenant-colonelcy. Back me up, will you ?"

"Oh, we 'll all do that !" quoth Morton. "You might have entered as captain and been anything most by now —"

"I did n't care to bother. But now I think I will."

"All right!" said Morton. "I gather that presently there will be chances thick as blackberries."

CHAPTER IV

CHICKASAW BAYOU

For ages and ages, water, ceaselessly streaming, ceaselessly seeping, through and over the calcareous silt, had furrowed the region until now there was a medley and labyrinth of narrow ravines and knife-blade ridges. Where the low grounds opened out it was apparently only that they might accommodate bayous, or some extension of a bayou, called by courtesy a lake. Along these the cane was thick, and backward from the cane rose trees and trees and trees, all draped with Spanish moss. It had been a rainy winter, a winter of broken banks and slow, flooding waters. Sloughs strayed through the forest; there was black mire around cypress and magnolia and oak. The growth in the ravines was dense, that upon the ridges only less so. From Vicksburg, northward for several miles, great clearings had recently been made. Here, from the Upper Batteries above the town to Haynes Bluff on the Yazoo, stretched grey field-works, connected by rifle-pits.

Chickasaw Bayou, sullen and swollen, curved away from the scarped hills and the strip of forest. On the other side of Chickasaw, and of that width of it known as McNutt's Lake, there was shaking ground — level enough, but sodden, duskily overgrown, and difficult. This stretched to the Yazoo.

Down the Mississippi from Memphis came Sherman with thirty thousand blue infantry. They came in transports, in four flotillas, and in front went Porter's Gunboat Squadron. Grant had planned the campaign. With the forces which had been occupying southwestern Tennessee, he himself was at Oxford. He would operate by land, overwhelming or holding in check Pemberton's eighteen thousand at Grenada. In the mean time Sherman, descending the Mississippi to the mouth of the Yazoo, some miles above Vicksburg and its river batteries, should ascend that stream, flowing as it did not far to the northward of the doomed town; — ascend the Yazoo, disembark the thirty thousand, and with a sudden push take Vicksburg in the rear. It was known that there were but five thousand troops in the place.

The plan was a good plan, but Van Dorn disarranged it. Grant, his base of supplies at Holly Springs captured and all his stores destroyed, was compelled to fall back toward Memphis. He sent an order to Sherman, countermanding the river expedition, but Sherman had started and was well down the vast yellow stream, the gunboats going ahead.

On the twenty-third of December these entered the Yazoo, to be followed, three days later, by four flotillas. There ensued several days of Federal reconnoitring. The Yazoo, not so tortuous as the great stream into which it flowed, was yet tortuous enough, and in places out of banks, while the woods and swamps on either side were confusing, wild, and dark. Necessary as it may have been, the procedure militated against taking a city by surprise. The grey had notice of the gunboats, and of the trail of flotillas.

Pemberton acted with promptness and judgment. Grant was not so far away that the forces at Grenada could be utterly weakened, but the brigades of Barton, Vaughn, and Gregg were detached at once for Vicksburg. There, on the line from the sandbar north of the town to Haynes Bluff, they joined the provisional division of Stephen D. Lee. The position was strong. The grey held the ridges crowned by field-works and rifle-pits. Before them spread the dark, marsh-ridden bottom land, crept through, slow and deep, by Chickasaw Bayou. They had greatly the advantage of position, but there were, on the strip between the Yazoo and the Walnut Hills, four men in blue to one in grey. At the last moment, in answer to a representation from General Martin Luther Smith, commanding the defences at Vicksburg, an additional regiment was despatched from Grenada. It chanced to be the ——th Virginia Infantry.

The night was cold, very dark, and pouring rain. Vicksburg had been reached at dusk. There seemed no soldiers here. "Everybody's out toward McNutt's Lake. Reckon you're wanted there, too!" The ——th Virginia found at last the man to report to, upon the heels of which event, without having tasted supper or experienced warmth, it discovered itself on the road to Chickasaw Bayou. "On the road" is merely a figure of speech. The regiment concluded that some time in the Bronze Age there might have been a road, but that since then it had been washed away. This was the Mud Age.

In the pitchy dark, the chill, arrowy rain, the men stumbled along. Except for an occasional order, an occasional exclamation, impatient groan, long-drawn sigh, there was silence. They had some miles to go. To keep step was out of the question.

Edward Cary, closing his file, moved with a practised, light steadiness. His body was very supple, fine, with long clean lines. From head to heel he was in order, like a Greek runner. Spare and worn and tired like all the rest, he kept at all times a certain lift and poise as though there were wings upon his cap.

He was not like Richard Cleave. He had little innate feeling for War, intuitive understanding of all its phases. Being with all his people plunged deep, deep within it, he played his part there bravely enough. He served his native land, and her need and woe dwelt with him as it dwelt with all his world, both men and women. Much of him, perforce, was busy with the vast and mournful stage. But he found himself not truly at home with the war-drums and the wailing, with smell of blood and smoke, weight of shot-riddled banners, trampled faces. He was born for beauty and her worship, for spacious order and large harmony, and for months now there had been war and agony and smell of blood and sight of pale, twisted faces — for long months only that. And then somehow, accidentally it seemed, he had rubbed the lamp. Only ten days ago — oh, light and warmth and harmony! Oh, the strange and sweet in combination! Oh, serene spaces for the mind! Oh, golden piping and beckoning to emotions not stern! Oh, the deepest, oldest wine! Oh, by the oddest, simplest chance, sudden as a wind from Heaven, intimacy warm and fragrant with the Only-Dreamed-Of, the Never-Found-Before! Oh, in a word, the love of Désirée Gaillard!

He was marching through the dark night, the mire, the cold, the wet. Certain centres of consciousness, no doubt, knew them all, — knew hunger, cold, weariness. But the overman, the Lover, moved through rose-scented dusk, through intricate, sweet thoughts, in some imaged Vale of Cashmere. Only not at all, not at all could he banish anxiety as to the Beloved's well-being.

About him, in the night, was the tramp, tramp of other weary feet, the dim sight and sound of other weary bodies, cold, wet, thinly clad. Most of these men in the darkness thought, perhaps, of beings far away from these labyrinthine ridges and hollows. Many a soldier warmed his heart by the fires of home, dreamed as he marched of lover, wife, or child. But the thoughts were shot with pain and the dreams were bitter sweet. No man in a Southern army could take comfort in the thought that whatever of want and strain and boding might obtain where he moved, ragged, through the darkness, all was well at home — comfort there, warmth and food there, ease of heart there! Many knew that at home there was immediate suffering; others, that while the board was spread to-night, yet the dark sail of privation grew larger and larger. All knew that there was little, little ease of heart. Marching through the rainy night they carried with them, heavier than musket and haversack, the ache of all at home, as, upon this night, all at home felt cold and gaunt with the marching, marching armies. Yet the South at home managed to keep a high head and a ready smile, and the South in the field managed a jest, a laugh, a song. At home and in the field vast need and stress lifted the man, lifted the woman, lifted the child. Some one in the ——th Virginia, moving out to Chickasaw Bayou, began to sing jerkily —

> "Old Dan Tucker!
> You too late to get your supper —"

The regiment climbed another of the innumerable mole-hills, all stumps of recently felled trees, and between, tenacious and horrible mud. The far side was worse than the near, and the bottom land, when finally they slipped and slid and wavered down upon it, proved mere quagmire. Here they found, deeply mired, two sections of artillery, bound as they were bound and struggling with the night. Gun wheels were sunken above the axle-tree; it seemed a mud burial, a question of never getting out. One heard straining gun teams, chattering negro drivers. There were torches, saffron blurs of light, hissed against by the rain, moving up and down like dejected will-o'-the-wisps.

Infantry came up. "Halfway to China, are n't you ? Want us to lend a hand ?"

"Thank you, boys! William, tell those mules to pull harder."

"What are you doing with mules ? Has it come to mule artillery?"

"Well, it's coming to so many things! — We're Army of Tennessee — Stevenson's division — come down to help hold the

Mississippi River. Right big eel, is n't it ? Rushed through — two sections, Anderson's battery — from Jackson. Horses yet on the road. Impressed mules. — Lieutenant Norgrove, tell those darkies there's a watermelon field in front of them and 'paterollers' behind! — Pull there! pull!"

The howitzer came slowly up from halfway to China, the Napoleon followed, infantry encouraging. "You've trained your mules quick! That gun came from the Tredegar, did n't it ? Artillery 's a mighty no-account arm, but you sort of somehow grow fond of it —"

"Are n't you all Virginia ?"

"Yes; ——th Virginia. Are n't you all —"

"Of course we are! Botetourt. Anderson's battery. — What's the matter, Plecker ?"

"Firing ahead, sir, and those negroes are getting ready to stampede —"

There broke and increased a wild night-time sputter of minies. Panic took the chance medley of negroes. They sprang from the horses, paid no heed to appeal or threat, twisted themselves from clutching hands, and vanished into darkness. Artillery, infantry helping, got the guns on somehow. Amid a *zip — zip — zip* of minies both arms came to a grey breastwork where Stephen D. Lee was walking up and down behind a battery already placed.

The dull light and rattle of skirmishes in the night died away. With it died, too, the rain. The dawn came spectrally, with a mist over McNutt's Lake. One of Sherman's division commanders had received orders to bridge this water during the night. Over the mournful, water-logged land the pontoons were brought from the Yazoo. Standing in the chill water, under the sweep of rain the blue engineers and their men worked courageously away, but when dawn came the pale light discovered the fact that they had not bridged the lake at all, but merely a dim, Briareus arm of the bayou, wandering off into the forest. They took up the pontoons, moved down the shore to the widening of the water, and tried again. But now the water was too wide. There were not boats enough, and while they were making a raft, the wood across McNutt's filled with men, grey as the dawn. Tawny-red broke the flames from the sharpshooters' rifles. A well-placed Confederate battery began, too, to talk, and the lake was not bridged.

Barton's brigade had come down to occupy the wood. When the bridge builders were driven away, it fell back to the high ground crested with slight works, seamed with rifle-pits, where were Vaughn and Gregg and Stephen D. Lee. Across the bayou the blue began to mass. There was a strip of corduroy road, a meagre bridge spanning the main bayou, then a narrow encumbered front, muck and mire and cypress stumps, and all the felled trees thrown into a grey abatis. The blue had as many divisions as the grey had brigades, but the grey position was very strong. On came the dull, December day, — raw, cold, with a lowering sky.

The blue, assaulting force, the blue reserves, the division commanders, drew shoulders together, brows together, and looked across and upward doubtfully enough at the bluffs they were expected to take. Wade the bayou, break through the cane, cross that narrow front of brush and morass, attack at the apex of a triangle whose base and sides were held by an unknown number of desperate Rebels defending Vicksburg, a place that had got the name for obstinacy! — the blue troops and their generals, however hard they tried, could not at all visualize success. All the prospect, — the opposite height and the small grey batteries, the turbid, winding waters and the woods so strange to Northern eyes, — all was hostile, lowering. Indiana, Ohio, Illinois, Iowa drew uneasy breath, it was so sinister a place!

An officer came from Sherman to the senior division commander. "General Sherman says, sir, that you will order the assault."

"It 's a bad place —"

"Yes. He says we will lose five thousand men before we take Vicksburg and that we might as well lose them here as anywhere."

"All right. We'll lose them all right. Tell him I'll give the signal."

A grey rifle-pit, dug along the face of the hill, had received since dawn the attention of blue sharpshooters stationed in a distant row of moss-draped trees. The bottom of the long trench was all slippery mud, the sides were mud, the out-thrown, heaped earth atop was mud. Rest a rifle barrel upon it and the metal sank as into water. The screen of scrub along the forward rim was drenched, broken, insufficient. Through it the men in the pit looked out on a sodden world. They saw a shoulder of the hill where, in the early light, the caisson of an isolated gun had been exploded by a Federal shell. Horses and men lay beside it, mangled. Farther away yet, and earlier yet, they had seen a reconnoitring party enter a finger of land crooking toward the Federal lines, and beyond the cover of the grey guns. The blue, too, had seen, and thrusting forward a regiment cut off the grey party. The bulk of the latter hewed its way through, back to the shelter of the grey Parrotts, but there were officers and men left wounded in the wood. — The day was gloomy, gloomy! The smoke from Stephen Lee's guns and from the answering Federal batteries hung clogged and indiffusible, dark and hard.

"Somebody's going to get hurt this day," said the men in the rifle-pits. "There ain't any joke about this place."

"Do you know I think they're going to charge us? Just as brave as they are foolish!"

"I don't think much of Sherman's capacities as a general. Grant's the better man."

"They're getting ready. — Well, I always did hate waste, whatever colour it was dressed in!"

"My God! Even their bugles don't sound cheerful! —

> *Chickasaw — Chickasaw Bayou*
> *The death of you — the death of you!* "

Edward Cary, loading his rifle, had the cartridge knocked from between his fingers by the swaying against him of the man on the right. He moved, and the corpse slid softly down upon the miry bottom of the pit.

The man on the left began to talk, a slow, quiet discourse not at all interfering with eye or hand. "Western troops, I reckon! They've always the best sharpshooters. — Is he dead? I'm sorry. I liked Abner. He had an application in for furlough. Wife ill after the baby was born, and the doctor writing that there might be a chance to save her mind if she could see Abner. Told me last night he was sure he'd get the furlough. — Can you see for those damned bushes? There's a perfectly hellish fuss down there."

"The guns echo so. Here they come! And God knows I am sorry for them — for Abner here and Abner there! Martin, I hate War."

"It ain't exactly Christian, and it's so damned avoidable. — The baby died, and I reckon his wife — and she was a sweet, pretty girl — 'll go to the Asylum at Williamsburg —"

"Here they come! — Here they come! — Here they come!" . . .
Fire!

. . . At last the dreadful repulse was over. Shattered, disorganized, in sullen and horrible confusion, Sherman's brigades, the four that had charged, sank downward and back, a torn and beaten blue wave, into the dark forest beyond the bayou, the bayou whence they had come. In the water, in the mire and marsh and swamp, beside the sloughs in the forest, through the wild tangle of the abatis, over the narrow cleared ground, at the foot of the bluffs they had tried to storm, lay thick the dead and wounded. They did not number Sherman's "five thousand," but then neither was Vicksburg taken. The blue had charged without order, all formation broken, forced together in a narrow space, and they had rolled, a broken flood, back upon the dark bayou. As the rain had fallen in the night-time, so now fell the grey shot and shell, and they were beaten down like wheat beneath hail. The chill air was filled with whistling. The pall of the smoke added itself to the pall of the clouds. It was like fighting under a great and dingy tent with the stark cypress trees for tent poles. By the closing-down of day the desperately defeated had rolled back toward the Yazoo. Their dead and dying strewed the tent floor.

If there was relief and exultation on the heights it found no strenuous voice. The dreariness of the day and place, the streaming wet and sighing wind somehow forbade. The grey loss was slight enough — two hundred men, perhaps, in killed and wounded. Some lay within or below the rude works, some upon the hillside and the low ground where there had been a countercharge, some down by the abatis, fallen before the pursuit was recalled. It had been idle really to pursue. Sherman had thirty thousand, and the gunboats. A detachment or two streamed down, over the fatal and difficult ground, dislodging from a momentary shelter some fragment of the blue wave, cutting off and taking prisoner. Occasional thunder came from a battery, or a crack of rifles shook the clinging gloom. But the atmosphere deadened the sound, and the rain came down again fine and cold, and though the grey soldiers had reason for cheer and tried their best, it was but a makeshift glee. They had known hot joy in battle and would know it again, but it did not haunt the fight of Chickasaw Bayou.

There were yet the wounded that the reconnoitring party had left behind in the twilight wood. Volunteers were called for to bring them in. The wood crooked toward the enemy's lines, might at any moment be overflowed by the blue. Edward was among those who stood forward. The lieutenant of the other night beside the Yallabusha raised his brows. "Don't volunteer too often," he said. "There's no promotion in a trench with a hundred others! Furloughs can be too long."

In the dusk the platoon went zigzagging down into the wood by the bayou. It went through the zone of Federal wounded. "*Oh, you people! take us up; take us out of this! O God — O God — O God! Water!*" To the last cry neither grey nor blue in this war failed to answer when they could. Despite all need for haste and caution there were halts now, canteen or cup held to thirsty lips, here or there a man helped nearer to muddy pool or stream. "*Take us up — take us out of this!*"

The grey shook their heads. "Can't do that, Yanks. We would if we could, but we're sent to get our own. Reckon your side'll be sending a flag of truce directly and gather you up. Oh, yes, they will! We would if we could. You charged like hell and fought first-rate!"

"Silence, men! Get on!"

It was dusk enough in the wood which they finally reached. The bayou went through it crookedly, and from the other side of the water came the hum of Sherman's troubled, recriminatory thousands. They were so close that orders might be heard and the tread of the sentries. The men in grey broke rank, moved, two and two, cautiously through the cane looking for the wounded. The cane grew thick, and for all it was so sodden wet might be trusted here or there for a crackling sound. The trees grew up straight from black mud. They were immensely tall and from their branches hung yards and yards of moss, like tatters of old sails or like shrivelled banners in a cathedral roof. Large birds sat, too, upon the higher limbs, watching. Beneath lay killed and wounded, a score or so of forms half sunk in the universal swamp. The searchers left the dead, but where there was life in a figure they laid hold of it, head and feet, and bore it, swiftly and silently as might be, out of the wood, back to the rising, protected ground.

Edward and the man with him found an officer lying between huge knees of cypress. The cane walled him in, a hand and arm hung languid in the dark water. Kneeling, Edward felt the heart. "He's far and far away, but there's a chance, perhaps. Take the feet."

Half an hour later, by a great camp-fire behind a battery, surgeons and helpers took these wounded from the hands of the men who had gone after them.

Stephen D. Lee and General Seth Barton were standing by. "Thank God," said the former, "for a small field hospital! After Sharpsburg — ugh!"

A major of Wither's brigade walked slowly between the rows. "It was the ——th Louisiana cut off in the wood. There's an officer or two missing —"

"This is an officer, sir," said Edward. "He was living when we lifted him —"

General Barton came across. "He is not living now. A handsome man! . . . He lies there so stately. . . . A captain."

Edward held out his hand — in it an envelope. "This fell from his coat, sir. The bullet went through it —" The movement brought hand and letter into the ruddy light. Involuntarily he uttered an exclamation. "It is addressed to me!"

The major rose from his knees. "Quite dead. . . . And you would have called him Fortune's favorite. It is Louis Gaillard from down the river — Cape Jessamine."

CHAPTER V

FORT PEMBERTON

Van Dorn's raid and the battle of Chickasaw Bayou made of naught the December '62 — January '63 push against Vicksburg. Grant fell back to Memphis. McClernand, Sherman's superior, withdrew the thirty thousand column from before the Walnut Hills, to the Yazoo and down it, into the Mississippi and up that vast and turbid stream. His forces reunited, Grant, a stubborn, good soldier, studied in his quiet fashion, a cigar between his teeth, the map of the region. His instinct was always to strike out straight before him. The river, for all its windings, was the directest road to Vicksburg. Late in January he brought a great army down the Mississippi and landed it on the Louisiana side, some miles above the town that must be taken. Here, too, above the line of danger from the grey river batteries, he anchored his ships-of-war.

During the past summer the Federal General Williams had conceived the project of canalling the tongue of land opposite Vicksburg, the almost islanded sliver of Louisiana soil. Cut through this thumblike projection, fill your great ditch from the river, let your fleet enter at Tuscumbia Bend, and hey, presto! emerge again upon the bosom of the Mississippi *below* Vicksburg, the grey river batteries sweetly ignored; in a word all the grey defences of the Mississippi above Grand Gulf circumvented! The canal seemed worth digging, and so, in the summer, the blue had digged. But the summer was dry and the river low; it refused to enter the prepared by-path, and after a series of disappointments the digging had been discontinued. Now the season was wet, and the river brimming. With a large force of engineers and sappers, Grant began again upon the canal. But now there was too much moisture as before there had been too little. The water was so high that it ran into a hundred paths beside the one which the blue were digging. It turned the flat Louisiana shore into lake and quagmire. Impossible to trench with the semi-liquid stuff flowing in as fast as it was thrown out! — impossible to keep an army encamped in a morass! Again there was a withdrawal.

From higher ground and reaches of the river far above Vicksburg, Grant, the cigar between his teeth, parallel lines showing across his forehead, studied flank movements. . . . The Yazoo again! — though it seemed a stream of ill omen. Not that Grant thought of omens. He was not superstitious. A plain, straightforward, not over-imaginative, introspective, or sophisticated person, he did not so much plan great campaigns as take, unswervingly, the next common-sense step. His merit was that, in the all-pervading fog of war, it was usually upon firm ground that he set his step. Not always, but usually. The Yazoo. . . . It flowed southward from the Tennessee line. There it was called the Coldwater. Farther down, in northern Mississippi it became the Tallahatchie, into which flowed the Yallabusha. Lower yet it was named the Yazoo, and so flowed into the Mississippi. Throughout its course it drained a vast, flat, egg-shaped lowland, overshot by innumerable lesser streams, lakes, and bayous, rising into ridge and bluff at the southern end of the egg. Named the Valley of the Yazoo, it was reported to be enormously fertile and a storehouse from which Vicksburg and all the exaggerated grey armies in Tennessee and Mississippi were fed. Moreover, at Yazoo City, where the three-named stream became finally the Yazoo, there existed, said Secret Service, a big Confederate navy yard where gunboats were rapidly hatching. To get into that valley from the northern end, come down those rivers, surprise Yazoo City and spoil the nest of gunboats, then on like a swooping hawk and take Vicksburg in the rear! . . . Grant put out his hand for another cigar. *But* the Valley of the Yazoo was said to be in effect roadless, and though the Yazoo from Yazoo City downwards was navigable, the Tallahatchie and the Coldwater were not. Then came in Admiral Porter with a well-considered plan, though an audacious one and ticklishly dependent upon a thousand circumstances.

Some distance below Memphis there was a point where the Mississippi and the Coldwater came within calling distance of each other. Between was only the Yazoo Pass — and Yazoo Pass was a bayou which anciently had connected the two. Anciently, not now; for years before a levee had been built, shutting off bayou from river, and preventing untoward floods in the upper Yazoo Valley. Assemble a fleet over against Yazoo Pass, cut the levee, and so lift the water in the Coldwater and the Tallahatchie, then proceed down those streams with the vessels-of-war and as many transports as needed, take Yazoo City, enter the Yazoo, and so on triumphantly! Grant chewed the end of his cigar, then nodded acquiescence.

On the third of February, after much time spent in digging, they laid and exploded a mine. The levee broke in rout and ruin. Like a tiger from the jungle out leaped the Mississippi, roaring down to the bayou. Yazoo Pass became a furious yellow torrent, here spume and eddy, here torn arms of trees, an abatis in motion. The Coldwater received the flood and bore it on to the Tallahatchie. But so angry were the churning waters by the gate in the levee that days passed before the ironclads DeKalb and Chillicothe, the rams Fulton and Lioness, the tinclads Forest Rose, Marmora, Rattler, Romeo, Petrel, and Signal, and all the transports in the rear could attempt that new-made passage. At last they did enter the Yazoo Pass and made slow way to the Coldwater, only presently to find that the grey troops had felled the tall, tall trees on either bank and thrown them into the stream. There, arms interlocked, they made for miles an effective barrier, removed only after slow days and days of effort. The stream wound like a tortured serpent. There presented themselves strange currents, pits, and shoals. The bed was unknown, save that it possessed a huge variety of snag, bar, and obstacle. The flood was narrow, and the thick overhanging forest obscured and fretted. Every turn presented a fresh difficulty. The fleet made three miles a day. Behind it crept, crept the transports, forty-five hundred men under Generals Ross and Quinby. There was much sickness and the fret, fret of utter delay. It was late February before the expedition entered the Coldwater, early March before it approached the Tallahatchie. Here it encountered afresh felled trees like endless bundles of jackstraws, thrown vigorously, crossed under water at every imaginable angle. A little later the blue scouts brought news of Fort Pemberton.

The Southern spring was at hand, a mist of young leaf and bloom, a sound of birds, a sapphire sky, a vapour, a warmth, a rhythm. Edward Cary loved it, and said that he did so, lying after supper, on the bank of the Tallahatchie, under the cotton-bale rampart of the cotton-bale fort that was to keep the enemy out of the Yazoo. The rest of the mess agreed — lovely spring, lovely evening! They lit corn-cob pipes and clay pipes and fig-stem pipes, and stretched themselves on a meagre bit of dry earth, beside a clump of Spanish bayonet. The sun dipped behind the woods across the river, leaving air and water an exquisite coral. There were seven men — five privates, a corporal, and a sergeant-major. All were tall and all were lean and none was over thirty. One bore an old Huguenot name and the forbear of one was a Highland chief. The others were mainly of English stock, names of Devon, Surrey, and Sussex. Two were university men, sons of great planters, born into a sunny and settled world that after their majority overclouded. Three had less of that kind of fortune and had left for the war a lawyer's office, a tobacco warehouse, and an experiment in mining. The sergeant-major was of the yeoman type, a quiet man with little book learning and a name in the regiment for courage and resource. The seventh man, very young, a grown-up-anyhow bit of mortality, who until he came to handle steel had worked in iron, stood next, perhaps, to Edward Cary in the affections of the mess. Dreadful as was this war, it had as a by-product the lessening of caste. Men came together and worked together as men, not as conventions.

"Yes, it is lovely," said the warehouse man. "I used to think a deal about beauty."

"Woman's beauty?"

"No. Just plain beauty. Cloud or sea or face or anywhere you found it. At the end of every furrow, as Jim might say."

Jim, who was the sergeant, shook out rings of smoke. "It ain't only at the end of the furrow. I've seen it in the middle."

The worker in iron stretched his thin body, hands under his young head. "I like fall better'n spring. Late fall when it's all red and still, and at night there are shooting stars. Spring makes me sad."

"What are you doing with sadness?" asked Edward. "You had as well talk of Jack-o'-Lantern being sad! — I like all seasons, each with its proper magnificence! Look at that pine, black as wrath —"

"Look at the pink water about the old Star of the West —

' The charmed water burnt alway
A still and awful red.'"

"I hated to see the Star sunken. After all her fighting — Sumter and all —"

"Well, we've put her where she'll fight again! It's a kind of Valhalla ending to lie there across Grant's path."

"You can see a bit of spar. And the rosy water all around — rosy as hope. Do you hear that bird over there in the swamp? Boom — boom — boom! Mournful as a whip-poor-will. . . . Heavens! if I could hear the whip-poor-wills in Virginia! — Have you got any tobacco?"

The soldier from the lawyer's office sat up. "Grand Rounds? No. It's the General by himself! Heard him say once he had a taste for sunsets."

Loring, one-armed since Mexico, impatiently brave, with a gift for phrases, an air, and a bearing, came down the threadlike path through the palmetto scrub. With three guns and fifteen hundred men he held this absurd structure called Fort Pemberton, and from hour to hour glanced up the Tallahatchie with an experienced and careless eye. If he expected anything more than a play flotilla of cock-boats, his demeanour did not show it. In practice, however, he kept a very good drill and outlook, his pieces trained, his earthworks stout as they might be in the water-soaked bottom lands, and he had with discretion sunk the Star of the West where she lay, cross channel, above the fort. He was very well liked by his soldiers.

The seven on the river bank rose and saluted. He made the answering gesture, then after a moment of gazing up the Tallahatchie walked over to a great piece of driftwood and seated himself, drawing his cloak about him with his one hand.

"I want to study that water a bit. Go on with your pipes, men. — I thought I smelled coffee."

"It was made of sweet potato, sir," said the sergeant-major regretfully, "and I'm afraid we didn't leave a drop. We're mighty sorry, sir."

"Well," said Loring amicably, "I don't really like sweet potato coffee, though I'd drink brimstone coffee if there were no other kind of coffee around. That's one of the things I never could understand about General Jackson — he never drinks coffee. The time we could all have sold our souls for coffee was that damned Bath and Romney trip . . . Ugh!" He gazed a moment longer on the rosy, narrow stream and the violet woods across, then turned his eyes. "You're ——th Virginia? There is n't one of you a Cary by chance?"

"I am Edward Cary, sir."

"Come across," said Loring; and when he came gave him a knotted arm of the driftwood. "I heard from Fauquier Cary not long ago, and he said you were down this way and to look out for you. He said he did n't know whether you were a survival or a prophecy, but that anyhow your family idolized you. He said that from all he had read and observed War had an especial spite against your kind — which, perhaps," said Loring, "is not a thing to tell you."

Edward laughed. "As to War, sir, the feeling is reciprocal. He's of those personalities who do not improve on acquaintance. — Dear Fauquier! The family idolizes him now, if you like!"

"Yes, he's of the finest. I knew him in Mexico. Gallant as they make them! — He has lost an arm."

"Yes — at Sharpsburg."

"It's no little loss," said Loring. "By the way — you knew Maury Stafford?"

"Yes."

"The word 'Sharpsburg' brought him up. He was taken prisoner there — unfortunate fellow! There has been no exchange?"

"I have heard of none. They will not exchange."

"Infernal tactics!"

"It's all infernal. I have grown to see no sense in this war. North and South, we surely might have been wiser."

"That may be," said Loring. "But we are in it now and must act according to tradition. — Maury Stafford! — He was with me during that wretched, abortive, freezing, and starving Romney expedition. I was very fond of him. It aches me to think of him in prison."

Edward sighed. "Yes, I am sorry, too."

"Was he not," asked Loring, "was he not engaged to your sister?"

"No."

"Indeed? I thought some one told me so. . . . He has a fine nature."

"In many ways — yes."

"Well, we may be talking of the dead. No one seems to have

heard. It's like a tomb — prison! North and South, they die like flies. . . . Damn it all, such is war!"

"Yes, sir. . . . I beg your pardon, but is n't there something moving on the river — very far up, beyond that line of purple ? "

Loring whipped out his field-glass, looked, and rose from the driftwood. "Gunboats!" A bugle blew from the earth-and-cotton-bale fort, drums began to roll. "Get to your places, men! If Grant thinks I am going to let him get by here, he 's just mistaken, that 's all!"

With three guns and fifteen hundred men and cotton-bale walls and the sunken Star of the West, Loring made good his words — though it was not Grant in front of him, but Grant's lieutenants. Two ironclads, two rams, seven tinclads crept up that night, anchoring above the sunken Star. Behind them came slowly on the transports with the forty-five hundred infantry. Dawn broke, and the gunboats, feeling their way, found the Star. Vexation and delay! They undertook to blow her up, and while they sank torpedoes the transports nosed along the river bank trying to find firm landing in a bottom country flooded alike by the spring rains and the far-away broken levee. They could not find it, and on board there was restlessness and complaining. The Star of the West was hard to raise. She clung fast, fought stanchly still for the Stars and Bars. . . . The third day the Chillicothe and DeKalb got by, steamed down to the fort, and began a raking fire. The rams, too, and several of the tinclads came wriggling through the clearance in the channel. There followed a three days' bombardment of the crazy fort, all hastily heaped earth and cotton bales, rude trenches, rough platforms for the guns, all squat in the marshy land, wreathed with cannon smoke, musket smoke, topped by the red square with the blue and starry cross! Behind the screen of the gunboats the transports sought continuously for some *terra firma* where the troops might land. They could not find it. All was swamp, overflowing waters, half-submerged trees. Above waved Spanish moss, swung vines spangled with sweet-smelling, satiny yellow bloom.

The smoke from the river, the smoke from Loring's three guns and fifteen hundred muskets met and blended, and, spreading, roofed out the cerulean, tender sky. Looking up, his men saw Loring, mature, imposing, standing high on the cotton-bale parapet, his empty sleeve pinned to his coat, gesturing with the remaining arm, about him the grey battle breath, above him the flag.

"Give them blizzards, boys! Give them blizzards!" roared Loring.

The most daring of the transports put a party ashore. But what to do? They struck out toward the fort and plunged waist deep into a mocking slough of the forest. Out of this they crossed a bank like mud turtles, and came into the wide overflow of a bayou. Beyond was a tangle of cane and vine, and here they began to feel the bullets of hidden grey sharpshooters. Beyond the cane was a cypress swamp, impossible twisted roots, knees, and hummocks; between, deep threads of water and bottomless black mire. Miserable and useless fight with an earth like this! The party turned, got back — torn, bemired, panting with fatigue — to the transports, ranged behind the gunboats and the cloud of smoke and the thunder of the iron men. Night came down, the smoke parted, stars shone out.

Dawn came, and the battle renewed itself. Red flashes tore the mist on the Tallahatchie and the roaring sound made the birds flee the woodland. The gunboats worked hard, all unsupported by the blue infantry. The officers of the last stamped upon the transports' decks. So near and yet so far! After weeks of tortoise crawling! Try again! Boats were lowered, filled, sent up bayous, along creeks spiralling like unwound thread, or brought alongside some bit of bank with an air of firmness. Vain! The bit of bank gave and gave under the cautious foot; the bayou spilled out upon plains of black mire in which you sank to the middle; the creeks corkscrewed away from Fort Pemberton. . . . In the afternoon the Chillicothe got a shell through her sides. The day went down in thunder and sulphurous cloud, the fleet belching broadsides, Fort Pemberton loudly replying, Loring on the ramparts shouting, "Give them blizzards, boys! Give them blizzards!"

In the morning the Rattler turned and went back to the Coldwater, Yazoo Pass, and the Mississippi, in her cabin Watson Smith commanding the expedition, ill for days and now like to die. His second took command and the third day's struggle began. But the Chillicothe again was roughly handled, and certain of the tinclads were in trouble. A ram, too, had lost her smokestack and carried a ragged hole just above her water line. And the infantry could not land, — gave up the attempt. All day the boats on the Tallahatchie and the courtesy fort crouched on her eastern bank roared and tugged. *"Yaaih! Yaaaii! Yaaihh!"* rose the grey shouting through the rolling smoke. Loring, slightly wounded, came out of a crazy tent at the back of the enclosure, crossed the encumbered space, and mounted again the cotton bales. The men cheered him loud and long. "Old Blizzard! Old Blizzard! Yes, sir! Yes, sir! We're going to give them snow, rain, hail, and sleet!"

The day weltered by, the rays of the sunset struck through powder-stained air. Then came silence, and a thinning of smoke, and at last the stars. On the DeKalb was held a council of war. The Chillicothe badly hurt, the commander of the expedition ill, sent back upon the Rattler, Quinby's men not yet up, Ross's quite unable to land, sickness, tedium, dissatisfaction, Heaven knew what going on in the Mississippi while they had been lost for endless weeks in a no-thoroughfare of half earth, half water, overhung by miasmas! The boats alone could not reduce this fort, and infantry that could not land was no better than infantry in the moon! Go back without anything gained? Well, the knowledge was gained that Vicksburg could n't be taken this way — and the guns had probably blown out of existence some scores of rebels! That much was gained. Sick and sore, the talk pulled this way and that, but in the end it was deter-mined to put back. In the stillness before the dawn gunboats and rams and tinclads weighed anchor and steamed away, slowly, slowly up the difficult reaches of the Tallahatchie and Coldwater, back to Yazoo Pass and so out into the Mississippi. Behind them trailed the transports. At the mouth of Yazoo Pass they met with a scouting party and learned of a second expedition.

Porter, fertile in expedients, was conducting this in person. With five Eads gunboats he was winding southward by way of innumer-able joined streams, — Steele's Bayou, Black Bayou, Deer Creek, Rolling Fork, finally the Sunflower which empties into the Yazoo, — while accompanying him on the land crept and mired from swamp to swamp troops of Sherman's. Infantry and Eads flotilla, they reached at last Rolling Fork, but here they met grey troops and a determined check. Infantry proved as helpless in the swamps of the Sunflower as infantry had proved in the swamps of the Tallahatchie. Moreover detached grey parties took to felling trees and crossing them in the stream behind the gunboats. Porter saw himself becoming the eel in the bottle, penned in grey toils. Nothing for it but to turn, figuratively to back out — the region being one of all the witches!

The Tallahatchie expedition, the Sunflower expedition, returned to the Father of Waters. Here, on the western bank, they found Grant, cigar in mouth, lines across brow, studying the map between Vicksburg and Port Hudson. Upon the grey side Loring waited at Fort Pemberton until his scouts brought news of the clearance of the Yazoo Valley, but he waited with only half his force, the other moiety being withdrawn to Vicksburg.

Edward Cary, marching with these troops, marched into Vicksburg on an April day, — Vicksburg indomitable; Vicksburg with a wretchedly inadequate number of picks and spades extending her lines of breastworks, forming salients, mounting batteries, digging trenches, incidentally excavating refuges — *alias* "rat-holes" — for her non-combatant citizens; Vicksburg extremely busy, with an air of gaiety not altogether forced! Life, nowadays, had always and everywhere a deep organ bass, but that was no reason the cymbals and castanets should not come in if they could.

That afternoon, in an encampment just below the town, he came into possession of an accumulation of mail, home letters, letters from comrades in various commands, other letters. It was a time of rest after arduous marching. All around him, on the warm spring earth, lay the men of his company. They, too, had letters and long-delayed newspapers. They read the letters first, mused over them a little, with faces wistful or happy or tragically anxious as the case might be, then turned with avidity to the papers, old though they were. A little man with a big, oratorical voice had got a Richmond *Examiner* of a none-too-recent date. Sitting cross-legged on a huge magnolia stump he read aloud to a ring of listeners, rolling out the items like a big bass drum.

"News from the Mississippi —"

"That's us!"

"'As we go to press it is reported that Grant has met at Fort Pemberton a worse repulse than did Sherman at Chickasaw Bayou, the gallant Loring and his devoted band inflicting upon the invaders a signal defeat. Thousands were slain —'"

"Hm! Old Blizzard's gallant all right, and we're devoted all right, and they're invaders all right, and we certainly made them clear out of the Yazoo Valley, but somehow I did n't see those thousands slain! Newspapers always do exaggerate."

"That's true. Nature and education both. North and South — especially North. That New York paper, for instance, that we got from the picket at Chickasaw —"

"The one that said we tortured prisoners?",

"No. The one that said we mutilated the dead. They're all Ananiases. Go on, Borrow."

"'Farragut has succeeded in running the batteries at Fort Hudson. The mouth of the Red River —'"

"We know all that. What 're they doing in Virginia?"

"Marse Robert and Stonewall seem to be holding south bank of Rappahannock. Fighting Joe Hooker on the other side's got something up his sleeve. He and 'the finest army on the planet' look like moving. The paper says Sedgwick's tried a crossing below Fredericksburg, but that General Lee's watching Ely and Germanna fords. Here's an account of Kelly's Ford and the death of Pelham —"

"Read that," said the men.

Edward left them reading, listening, and making murmured comment. At a little distance rose a copse overrun with yellow jessamine. Entering this, he sat down at the foot of a cedar and, laying by the home letters and the letters from comrades, opened one written on thin, greyish paper, in a hand slender yet bold: —

My Heart, —

I am glad that it was you who found him. *O Louis, Louis, Louis!* . . . I am not going to write about him. . . . I loved him, and he loved me. . . . Oh, we give, we give in this war!

I hear from my father, broken-hearted for his son, tender and loving as ever to his daughter. I hear, too, from your father — a letter to keep forever, praising you to me so nobly! And Judith Cary has written. I shall love her well, — oh, well!

Where are you this stormy night? I sit before the fire, in the gilt chair, and the magnolia strikes against the window pane, and I hear, far off, the thunder and shouting, and if I could I would stay the bullets with my hands.

The enemy is cutting the levees on this side, up and down the river. If they cut a certain one, it will be to our disaster at Cape Jessamine. The negroes grow frightened, and now every day they leave. I did not mean to tell you all this. It is nothing.

Where are you this night of rainy wind? I look into the fire which is low at this hour, and I see ranged cannon, and banners that rise and fall. And may the morning — and may the morning bring me a letter!

Thine, all thine,

DÉSIRÉE GAILLARD.

A week later, having been granted the furlough for which he asked, he found himself below Natchez, bargaining with two black ferrymen to take him across the river.

CHAPTER VI

THE RIVER

THE two men were strong, magnificently formed negroes, one middle-aged, one young. "It ain't easy, marster," said the first. "River's on er rampage. Jes' er-look how she's swirlin' an' spittin' an' sayin' things! An' erbout every day now dar's er crevasse! Yankees make them befo' breakfast. When dishyer river tuhns sideways an' shakes down de land a boat ain' so safe as ef 't was er mountain-top."

"Dat's so!" said the other. "Hit's wuth twenty-five dollars, Confederate money."

Edward produced and held between thumb and forefinger one gold dollar.

"Git the oars, Daniel!" said the elder negro. "Yes, sah, we certainly will git you ercross an' down the river the best we kin!"

Out pushed the boat into the yellow, sullen river. It was running swift and rough. Edward sat with his chin in his hand, his eyes upon the farther shore, bathed in a golden, shimmering, spring-time light. It was slow rowing across this stream, and the shore far off.

The negroes began to sing.

"I'se gwine tell you ob de comin' ob de Saviour!
    Far' you well! Far' you well!
Dar's er better day er comin',
    Far' you well! Far' you well!
When my Lord speaks ter his Father,
    Far' you well! Far' you well!
Says, 'Father, I'm tired of bearin','
    Far' you well! Far' you well!
'Tired of bearin' fer pore sinners,'
    Far' you well! Far' you well! —"

The Louisiana shore came softly nearer. It was a jewelled and spangled April shore, that sent out sweet breath from flowers without number. Viewed at a little distance it seemed a magic green curtain, rarely embroidered; but when it came nearer its beauty was seen to be shot with the sinister, the ghostly, even, vaguely, with the terrible. Hereabouts rose a great forest through which deep bayous crept to join the river, into which, too, the river ran an inlet or so like a Titan's finger. The boat with the two negroes and the soldier turned its head downstream, following the loops of the river and the scalloped shore. To-day, indeed, there seemed no proper shore. The shore had turned amphibian. White cypress, red cypress, magnolia, live-oak, in and out between them sucked the dark water. Vines and the wild festoons of the grey moss mirrored themselves within it; herons kept watch by rotting logs over dusk pools swept by the yellow jessamine; the water moccasin slipped beneath perfumed thickets, under a slow, tinted rain of petals. At intervals there opened vast vistas, an endless and mournful world of tall cypress trunks propping a roof that was jealous of the sun. In the river itself were islets, magically fair, Titania bowers, a loveliness of unfolding leaf, delicate and dreamlike enough to make the tears spring. It was past the middle of the day; heat and golden haze in the sun, coolness and cathedral gloom where the enormous woodland threw its shadow.

Now the negroes were silent and now they were talkative, passing abruptly from one mood to the other. Everything in their range of speech was dwelt upon with an equal volubility, interest, and emphasis. A ruined eagle's nest, a plunging fish-hawk, the slow-sailing buzzards, difficulties with the current, the last duel between gun-boats, the latest dash of a Confederate ram, the breaking levees, a protuberance on a bar of black slime and mud which, on the whole, they held to be a log, until with a sudden dull gleaming it slid into the water and proved to be a turtle — all things received an equal dole of laughter with flashing teeth, of amiable, vivid, childlike discussion. Sometimes they appealed to the white man, and he, friendly minded, at home with them, gave in a word the information or settled with two the dispute. "That's so! that's so!" each agreed. "I done see hit that-er-way, too! That's right, sir! Quarrelling is powerful foolish — jes' as foolish as gittin' drunk!"

Any swiftness of work was, in these parts, for the river alone. The boat moved slowly enough, here caught by an eddy, here travelling among snags and bars, doubling with the river, following the wave line of the water-logged shore. The sun's rays began to fall slantingly. Through the illimitable forest, down between the cypress trunks, came flights of golden arrows.

"We are not far from Cape Jessamine ?"

"No, marster. Not very far."

Silence fell again. They turned a horn of land, all delicate, flowering shrubs, and ran beneath a towering, verdurous bank that rained down odours. It laid, too, upon the river, a dark, far-reaching shadow.

The younger negro spoke with suddenness. "I belongs to Cape Jessamine."

Edward turned. "Do you? — Why were you up the river and on the other side?"

"Hit ain't safe any mo' at Cape Jessamine. But I ain't no runaway, sah. Miss Désirée done tol' us to go." He felt in his shirt, took out a piece of bandanna, and unwrapped from it a piece of paper which he held out to Edward. "Dar's my pass, all right, sah! She done tol' us to go, an' she say she don' know that she'll ever call us back. She say she mighty fond of us, too, but all things er-comin' down an' er-changin' an' er-changin'! Hit ain't never any more gwine be lak hit was."

"How many have gone?"

"Mos' everybody, sah. Yankees come an' tek de cattle an' de meal, an' dar wa'n't much to eat. An' ef er man or er yaller gal step in er rain puddle dey wuz took with er shakin'-fit, cryin' out dat de river was er-comin'! She say we better go. De Fusilier place — way back an' crosst the bayou where de river could n't never git — she done sont de women an' chillen dar, an' Madam Fusilier she say she tek care ob dem des ez long ez dar's anything in de smokehouse an' de meal ain' stolen —"

"The overseer — did he get well?"

"No, sah. He hurt he hip, an' ole Brer Fever come er-long an' he died."

"Then who *is* at Cape Jessamine with — ?"

"Dar's her mammy, sah, who would n't go. An' 'Rasmus an' Mingo an' Simon. . . . Plantation beg Miss Désirée to come away, too, but she say 'No,' we go, but she's got er responsibility — an' she doubt ef de river come anyway. Yes, sah. She say she got her post, but dat hit's all right for us to go, de meal givin' out an' all. An' she say she certain'y is fond of us, every one, an' she come down de great house porch steps an' shake hands all round —" He took the slip of paper and wrapped it carefully in the bandanna. "When de war's over I'se gwine right back."

Edward spoke to the older man. "How real is the danger?"

"Of the river coverin' Cape Jessamine, sah? Well, they've cut a powerful heap of levees. It's lak this." He rested on his oars and demonstrated with his hands. "Cape Jessamine's got water mos' all around it anyhow. It comes suckin' in back here, suckin' and underminin'. The Mississippi's er powerful, big sapper an' miner — the biggest kind of er one! It might be workin' in the cellar like under Cape Jessamine this very minute. And then ergain it might not. Ain' nobody kin really tell. Though nowadays it's surely lucky to expect the worst. Yes, sah, the Mississippi's er bigger sapper an' miner than any they've got in the army!"

They went on, by the dense woodland, beneath the low sun. A cypress swamp ran back for miles. In this hour the vast, knotted knees, dimly seen, innumerable, covering all the earth, appeared like sleeping herds of an ancient monster. The wash of the water was like the breathing of such a host. All the country here was very low, and over it there began to be drawn a purple veil. It was as still as a dream. The boat passed between two islets covered with a white flower, and came into sight of a point of land.

"Cape Jessamine!" said the young negro.

It lay painfully fair, an emerald breadth with groups of trees, seen through the veil like a fading dream which the mind tries to hold, and tries in vain, it is so fair! There was magic in the atmosphere; to look down the river was to look upon a vision. Edward looked, bent forward, his eyes steady and wide.

"Row fast!" he said in his friendly voice. "I want to go back now."

They rowed fast, by monstrous white cypresses, under boughs hung with motionless banners of moss, by fallen trees, decaying logs, grotesquely twisted roots. The boat kept in the shadow, but the light was on Cape Jessamine. Presently they could see the lofty pillars of the house, half veiled in foliage, half bare to the sinking sun. They were now not half a mile away. The distance lessened. . . .

They were skirting a muddy shore, rowing amid a wild disorder of stumps that rose clear from the water, of dead and fallen trees, dead and far-flung vines. There came to the boat a slight rising and fall-ing motion.

"What's dat?" said the young negro.

His fellow turned and stared. "Lak er swell from er steamer, only there ain't any steamer on the Mississippi these days —"

"O my Lawd, what dat sound?"

The boat rocked violently. "Oh, Destruction, not there!" cried Edward Cary.

Cape Jessamine went down, down. They saw and heard; it was before their eyes; the bending pillars, the crashing walls, the trees that fell, the earth that vanished, the churned and horrible water. . . . They saw the work of the river, the sapper who worked with a million hands. . . . Shrieking, the negroes drove the boat head into the muddy shore, leaped up and caught at the overhanging boughs. Their frail craft was stayed, resting behind a breakwater of dead limbs. "O God-er-moughty! O God-er-moughty!" wailed the young negro.

Edward stood like marble. It had been there celestially fair — his port and haven and the wealth it held. It was gone — gone like a mirage. The red sun sank and left the wild world a wide waste. . . . The darkness, which, in this latitude, followed at once, was unwel-come only because it closed the door on search, hopeless and im-possible as would search have been in that cauldron of earth and water. The inner darkness was heavier than that which came up from the east. Through it all the long night throbbed like a dark star, now despair, now hope against hope.

They fastened the boat with a rope to a great projecting piece of Spanish bayonet. For a while, despite the sheltered spot into which they had driven, it rose and fell as though it were at sea, but this passed with the passing hours. At last the excited negroes fell quiet, at last they lay asleep, head pillowed on arms. As best he might Cary wore out the darkness.

It was not yet dawn when he roused the negroes. The boat lay quiet now; the river was over its disturbance of the evening be-fore. Since its origin deep in past ages the river had pulled down too many shores, swallowed too many strips of land to be long con-cerned over its latest work. Yellow and deep and terrible, on it ran, remorseless and unremembering. The boat on the edge of the swamp, in the circle of projecting root and snag, lay quiet. Above and around it hung lifeless from the boughs the grey moss. Bough and moss, there was made a vast tracery through which showed the primrose sky, cold, quiet, infinitely withdrawn. Looking down the stream, all that was missed was Cape Jessamine. The yellow water rolled over that.

"There was a bayou a mile or two back," said Edward. "The one on which stood 'Rasmus's house. It ran north and south and the road went across it. Can we get to that bayou?"

"Yes, sah. Hit's haid ain' far from here. But we'd have to leave de boat."

"It is fastened and hidden. You will find it again."

The elder negro looked doubtful. "We's poor men, marster. Ain't anybody to look after us now —"

"I ain' er-carin' how poor I is," broke in the younger. "I'se gwine. Ef dey got warnin' dey might hab took to de bayou, crosst hit, an' went on to de Fusilier place. But hit don' look ter me lak de river give any warnin'."

"That's what we've got to see," said Edward. He touched the shoulder of the elder black. "You're a good man, like Daniel here! Leave the boat and come on."

In the deep wood, among the cypresses, the light was faint enough. The three crept over the purple brown hummocks, the roots like stiffened serpents. Now and again they plunged into water or black mire. Edward moved in silence, and though the negroes talked, their voices were subdued to the place. It was slow, slow going, walking among traps. An hour passed. The cypresses fell away and cane and flowering vines topped by giant magnolias took their place.

"Haid of bayou," said Daniel.

They found an old dugout half full of water, bailed it out, and began to pole down the narrow, winding water, that ran two miles in the wood behind the lost Cape Jessamine.

"If she had even an hour —" said Edward.

"Miss Désirée des' er-sa'nter er-long," said Daniel, "but what she wan' ter do, hit gets done lak er bolt ob lightnin' runnin' down de sky! Dar' ain' any tellin'. Ef she saw hit er-comin' she sholy mek 'em move —"

On either hand the perfumed walls came close. Far overhead the trees mingled their leaves and through the lace roof the early light came stilly down. The water was clear brown. Each turn brought a vista, faintly lit, tapering into mist, through which showed like smoked pearl mere shapes of trees. They went on and on, to a low and liquid sound. A white crane stood to watch them, ghostly in its place. Isolation brooded; all was as still as the border of the world.

Turning with the turning water they found another reach with pearl grey trees. A boat came toward them out of the mist, a dugout like their own, with a figure, standing, poling. In the greyness and the distance it was not immediately to be made out; then, as the boat came nearer, they saw that it was a woman, and another minute told her name.

The young negro broke into a happy babbling. "Miss Désirée ain' gwine let de river drown her! — no, nurr her mammy, nurr Mingo, nurr Simon, nurr 'Rasmus! She got mo' sence dan de river. 'Ho!' she say, 'you ol' river! You can tek my house, but you can't tek me! I des walk out lak de terrapin an' leave you de shell!'"

She came out of the mist into the morning light, into the emerald and gold. She rowed bareheaded, standing straight, slender, and fine as Artemis. The elder negro dipped the oar strongly, the distance lessened with swiftness. When she saw Edward, she gave the singing cry he knew as though he had known it always. . . .

'Rasmus's cabin, it seemed, had been rebuilt. Here were mammy and 'Rasmus himself and Mingo and Simon, and a little bag of meal and a little, little coffee. Everybody had breakfast while the birds sang and the trees waved, and the honey bees were busy with all the flowers of the Southern spring. Later, there was held a council between General Cary and General Gaillard, sitting gravely opposite each other, he on a cypress stump and she on a fallen pine. The Fusilier place? Yes, the servants had best go there. Mammy, at any rate, must go. She was old and feeble, a little childish — and Madam Fusilier was a true saint who gave herself to the servants. Five miles down the road lived an old man who had a mule and a cart. Désirée had an idea that they had not been taken. The Fusilier place was fourteen miles away. They might get mammy there before night.

"And you?"

"I will take her there, of course."

"Madam Fusilier will insist upon caring for you, too."

"Undoubtedly. But I do not wish to stay at the Fusilier place. It is in the back country. News never comes there. You could not hear even the firing on the river. It is a cloister, and she is old and always on her knees. I would beat against the cage until I died or beat it down."

"Désirée, would you come with me? We could marry at Natchez, and the women are not leaving Vicksburg. . . . Oh, I cannot tell if I am giving you good counsel!"

"It is a counsel of happiness."

"And of danger —"

"I will take the danger. . . . Oh, that is so much better than the Fusilier place!"

Two days later they left the friendly boatmen on the Mississippi side. An old family carriage which they overtook, creeping along the spring-time road, in it a lady, her little girl, and a maid, gave them a long lift upon the way. At the last they came into Natchez in an ambulance sent up from Port Hudson, in friendly company with a soldier with a bandaged leg and a soldier with a bandaged head and arm. In Natchez they were married.

Three days passed and they entered Vicksburg. His furlough would expire the next morning. She knew people in this town, old friends of her mother's, she said. She and Edward found the house and all was well. Her mother's friends kissed her, laughed and cried and kissed her again, and then they shook hands warmly with her husband, and then they gave the two a cool high room behind a cascade of roses, and sent them cake and sangaree.

As the evening fell, they sat together by the window, in the fair stillness, and relief of a place all their own.

"The town is full of rumours," he said. "There is news of a bombardment of Charleston, and we have had a success in Tennessee, a great raid of Forrest's. Longstreet is being attacked south of the James. The armies on the Rappahannock appear to be making ready —"

"And here?"

"There is a feeling that we are on the eve of events. Grant is starting some movement, but what it is has not yet developed.

There will be fighting presently —" He put out his hand and drew within the room a bough of the Seven Sisters rose. "Look, how they are shaded! Pale pink, rose, crimson."

He had letters from home which he presently took up from the table, opened, and read aloud. They were sprinkled with gracious references to his happiness and messages of love for Désirée at Cape Jessamine.

"Oh, Cape Jessamine — oh, Cape Jessamine!"

"This is from Molly. 'Will you be able to see her before the war is over? They say it will be over this summer.'"

"Molly is the little one? And I am here! We see each other, though the war is not over. Oh, there is no cup that has not the pearl dropped in —"

"If you think this rose light comes only from the roses —"

The dusk deepened to night, the night of the sixteenth of April, 1863. A perfumed wind blew through the town, the stars shone, the place lay deep in sleep, only the sentries walking their beat. From river battery to river battery, patrolling the Mississippi, went pickets in rowboats. They dipped their oars softly, looking up and down and across the stream. Toward the middle of the night they drew together in a cluster, and now they looked upstream. Then they separated and went in different directions, rowing no longer with slow strokes, but with all their strength of arm. The most made for the nearest shore battery, but others shot across to the small settlement of De Soto on the Louisiana bank. That which they did here was to fire a number of frame buildings near the water's edge. Up soared the red pillars, illuminating the river. Across the water a signal shot boomed from the upper batteries. Up and down the bugles were heard. Lights sprung out, the wind filled with sound. Down the Mississippi, into the glare thrown by the burning houses came at full speed Porter's ironclads, meaning this time to get by. The Benton, Lafayette, and Tuscumbia, the gunboats Carondelet, Pittsburg, Louisville, Mound City, the ram General Price, the transports Forest Queen and Silver Wave and Henry Clay — one by one they showed in the night that was now red. The transports were protected by bulwarks of cotton bales, by coal barges lashed to their sides. From the smokestacks of all rushed black clouds with sparks of fire. *Go ahead! Go ahead!*

Vicksburg, that was to dispute the ownership of the Mississippi, had with which to do it twenty-eight guns. She was hardly a Gibraltar — Vicksburg; hardly ironclad and invulnerable, hardly fitted with ordnance sufficient for her purpose. The twenty-eight guns upon the bluffs above the river might be greatly served, they might work tirelessly and overtime, but it remained that they were but twenty-eight. Now in the midnight of the sixteenth of April, they opened mouth. At once the blue ironclads answered.

The excited town came out of doors. On the whole it was better to see the shells than to hear them where you sat in dark rooms. The women had a horror of being caught within falling walls, beneath a roof that was on fire; they, too, preferred to meet death and terror in the open. Not that they believed that death was coming to many to-night, or that they could have been called terrified. Vicksburg was growing used to bombardments. The women gathered the children and came out into the streets and gardens. There had been that evening a party and a dance. The signal gun boomed hard upon its close; young girls and matrons had reached home, but had not yet undressed. They came out of doors again in their filmy ball gowns, with flowers in their hair. As the guns opened mouth, as the blue shells rose into the night, each a swift, brilliant horror, the caves were suggested, but the women of Vicksburg did not like the caves and only meant to use them when the rain was furious. Not all came out of doors. The young wife of a major-general was afraid of the night air for her baby, and stayed quietly by its cradle, and others kept by the bedridden. Vicksburg, no more than any other Southern town, lacked its sick and wounded.

The signal shot had awakened Désirée and Edward. Before he was dressed there came the sound of the beaten drum in the streets below.

"The long roll!" he said. "I must hurry. The regiment is camped by the river."

He bent over her, took her in his arms. "Good-bye, love! good-bye, love!"

"Good-bye, love; good-bye, good-bye!"

He was gone. With a sob in her throat she fell back, lay for a moment outstretched on the bed, face down, her hands locked above her head. The house shook, a light came in the window, there were hurried voices through the house and in the garden below. She rose and dressed, braiding her long hair with flying fingers, her eyes upon the red light in the sky. When she had done she looked around her once, then went out, closing the door behind her, and ran down into the garden.

CHAPTER VII

PORT GIBSON

THE twenty-eight guns sent out continuously shot and shell against the blue ironclads, the gunboats, the transports. The blue returned the fire with fervency. Not before had the shores rocked to such sound, the heavens been filled with such a display. The firing was furious, the long shriek and explosion of crossing shells, bluff and river screaming like demons. All the sky was lit. The massed smoke hung huge and copper red, while high and low sprang the intense brightness of the exploding bomb. The grey guns set on fire several transports. These burned fiercely, the coal barges, the cotton bales that made their shields betraying them now, burning high and burning hard. The village of De Soto was aflame. The Mississippi River showed as light as day, a strange red daylight, stuffed with infernal sound. Through it steadily, steadily, the blue fleet pushed down the river, running the gauntlet of the batteries. All the boats were struck, most were injured. A transport was burning to the water's edge, coal barges were scattered and sunk. Firing as it went, each ironclad a moving broadside, the fleet kept its way. The twenty-eight did mightily, the gunners, powder-grimed automata, the servers of ammunition, the officers, the sharpshooters along the shore — all strove with desperation. Up and down and across, the night roared and flamed like a Vulcan furnace. The town shook, and the bluffs of the river; the Mississippi might have borne to the sea a memory of thunders. Less a sunken transport, less one burning low, less scattered and lost small craft, the fleet — scarred and injured though it was — the fleet passed! It ran the gauntlet, and at dawn there was a reason the less for holding Vicksburg.

Two nights later other ironclads got by. Grant had now a fleet at New Carthage, on the Louisiana shore, halfway between Vicksburg and Grand Gulf. He proceeded to use it and the transports that had passed. The sky over the grey darkened rapidly; there came a feeling of oppression, of sultry waiting, of a storm gathering afar, but moving. Sherman again threatened to approach by the Yazoo, but that was not felt to be the head of the storm. From La Grange, in Tennessee, southward, Grierson was ruining railroads and burning depots of supplies, but that was but a raid to be avenged by a raid. In the cloud down the river was forging the true lightning, the breath of destruction and the iron hail. Vicksburg held its breath and looked sideways at small noises, then recovered itself, smiled, and talked of sieges in history successfully stood by small towns. On the twenty-ninth, Porter's squadron opened fire on the Confederate batteries at Grand Gulf, and that night, under a fierce bombardment, ironclads, gunboats, and transports ran this defence also of the Mississippi. At dawn there was another reason the less for confining few troops in small places.

On the thirtieth of April, Grant began to ferry his army across from the Louisiana shore. Brigade by brigade, he landed it at Bruinsburg, nine miles below Grand Gulf, sixty below Vicksburg. At Grand Gulf was Bowen with five thousand grey soldiers with which to delay Grant's northward march. Between Bruinsburg and Grand Gulf ran Bayou Pierre, wide and at this season much swollen, but with an available bridge at Port Gibson. Bowen's three brigades took the road to the last-named place, and Bowen telegraphed to Pemberton at Vicksburg for reinforcements. Pemberton sent Tracy's Alabama brigade of Stevenson's division, and with it Anderson's Battery, Botetourt Artillery. The ——th Virginia, figuring in this story, marched also.

They broke camp at dusk. "Night march!" quoth ——th Virginia. "Double time! Old Jack must have come down from Virginia!"

The colonel heard. "Old Jack and Marse Robert are looking after Fighting Joe Hooker to-day. I saw the telegram. They're moving toward the Wilderness."

"Well, we wish we were, too," said the men. "Though the Mississippi is mighty important, we know!"

There existed a road, of course, only it had not been in condition for a year. No roads were kept up nowadays, though occasionally some engineer corps momentarily bettered matters in some selected place in order that troops might pass. Troops had gone up and down this road, and the feet of men and horses, the wheels of wagons and gun-carriages had added force to neglect, making the road very bad, indeed. It was narrow and bad, even for Southern roads in wartime. To the aid of neglect and the usage of hoof and wheel had come the obliterating rains. Bayous, too, had no hesitation in flinging an arm across. It was a season when firm ground changed into marsh and marsh into lake and ordinary fords grew too deep for fording. Miles of the miserable road ran through forest — no open, park-like wood whereon one might travel on turf at the sides of the way, but a far Southern forest, impenetrable, violent, resenting the road, giving it not an inch on either hand, making raids and forays of its own. Where it could it flung poisoned creepers, shot out arms in thorn-mail, laid its own dead across that narrow track. It could also blot out the light, keep off the air.

At midnight the Big Black River was reached. Oh, the reinforcements for Bowen were tired and worn! The night was inky, damp, and hot. The ——th Virginia, closing Tracy's column, must wait and wait for its turn at the crossing. There was a long, old-type ferryboat, and many men and horses swam the stream, but it took time, time to get the whole brigade across! Broken and decaying wood was gathered and a tall fire made. Burning at the water's edge, it murkily crimsoned landing and stream, the crowded boat slow passing from shore to shore, and the swimming, mounted men. Above it, on the north side, the waiting regiments threw themselves down on the steaming earth, in the rank and wild growth. The ——th Virginia, far back on the road, had a fire of its own. Behind it yet were the guns accompanying Tracy.

As the fire flamed up Artillery drew near, drawn by the genial glow. "May we? Thank you! If you fellows are as wet as we are, you are wet, indeed. That last bayou was a holy terror!"

"In our opinion this entire night's a holy terror. Have n't we met you before? Are n't you the Botetourt Artillery?"

"Yes. We've met a lot of people in this war, some that we liked and some that we did n't! You look right likable. Where —"

"Going out to Chickasaw Bayou. Pitch black night like this, only it was raining and cold. Your mules could n't pull —"

"Oh, now we remember!" said Artillery. "You're the ——th Virginia that helped us all it could! Glad to meet you again. Glad to meet anything Virginian."

"You've been out of Virginia a long time?"

"Out of it a weary year. Tennessee, Cumberland Gap, Kentucky, and so forth. We sing 'most everything in this army, but the Botetourt Artillery can't sing 'Carry me back to Old Virginny'! It chokes up. — What's your county?"

Company by company, regiment by regiment, Tracy's brigade got over the Big Black. Foot by foot the troops in the rear came nearer the stream; minute by minute the dragging night went by. Half seated, half lying on the fallen trunk of a gum, Edward Cary watched the snail-like crossing. When one dead tree burned down, they fired another. There was light enough, a red pulsing in the darkness through which the troops moved down the sloping bank to the ferryboat. The bank was all scored and trampled, and crested by palmetto scrub and tall trees draped with vines. The men stumbled as they went, they were so stiff with fatigue. Their feet were sore and torn. There was delay enough. Each man as he passed out of the shadow down to the boat had his moment of red light, a transitory centre of the stage.

Cary watched them broodingly, his elbow on the log, his hand covering his mouth. "A bronze frieze of the Destined. Leaves of the life tree and a high wind and frost at hand." An old man stood his moment in the light, the hollows in his cheeks plain, plain the thin and whitened hair beneath a torn boy's cap. He passed. The barrel of his musket gleamed for an instant, then sank like a star below the verge. A young man took his place, gaunt, with deep circles about his eyes. The hand on the musket stock was long and thin and white. "Fever," thought Edward. "Disease, that walks with War." The fever-stricken passed, and another took his place. This was a boy, certainly not more than fifteen, and his eyes were dancing. He had had something to eat, Edward thought, perhaps even a mouthful of whiskey, he carried himself with such an impish glee. "Is it such fun? I wonder — I wonder! You represent, I think, the past of the human species. Step aside, honourable young savage, and let the mind of the world grow beyond fifteen!"

On and down went the column, young, old, and in between. Two years earlier a good observer, watching it, would have been able fairly to ascribe to each unit his place in life before the drum beat. "A farmer — another — a great landowner, a planter

— surely a blacksmith — a clerk — a town-bred man, perhaps a banker — another farmer — a professional man — a student — Dick from the plough —" and so on. Now it was different. You could have divided the columns, perhaps, into educated men and uneducated men, rough men and refined men, as you could have divided it into young men and old men, tall men and men not so tall. But the old stamp had greatly worn away, and the new had had two years in which to bite deep. It was a column of Confederate soldiers, poorly clad and shod, and, to-night, hungry and very tired. Soldier by soldier, squad, company, regiment, on they stumbled through prickly and matted growth down to the water of the Big Black and the one boat. The night wore on. One and two and three o'clock went by before the last of the ——th Virginia was over. Edward, standing in the end of the boat, marked the Botetourt Artillery move forward and down to the stream. There was a moment when the guns were drawn sharply against the pallor of the morning sky. There came into his mind an awakening at dawn on the battle-field of Frayser's Farm, and the pale pink heaven behind the guns. But, indeed, he had seen them often, drawn against the sky at daybreak. There was growing in this war, as in all wars, a sense of endless repetition. The gamut was not extensive, the spectrum held but few colours. Over and over and over again sounded the notes, old as the ages, monotonous as the desert wind. War was still war, and all music was military. Edward and his comrades touched the southern shore of the Big Black, and the boat went back for the Botetourt Artillery.

The reinforcements for Bowen made no stop for breakfast for men or for horses, but pushed on toward Grand Gulf. The day was warm, the forest heavily scented, the air languid. All the bourgeoning and blossoming, the running sap, the upward and outward flow, was only for the world of root and stem, leaf and bud. The very riot and life therein seemed to draw and drain the strength from the veins of men. It was as though there were not life enough for both worlds, and the vegetable world was forcing itself uppermost. All day Tracy's column moved forward in a forced march. The men went hungry and without sleep; all day they broke with a dull impatience thorn and briar and impeding cane, or forded waist-deep and muddy bayous, or sought in swamps for the lost road. They were now in a region of ridge and ravine, waves of land and the trough between, and all covered with a difficult scrub and a maze of vines.

A courier from Grand Gulf met the head of the column. "General Bowen says, sir, you'll have to cross Bayou Pierre at Port Gibson. The bridge is there. Yes, sir, make a détour — yonder's the road."

"That turkey track?"

"Yes, sir. General Bowen says he surely will be obliged if you'll come right on."

Sundown and Bayou Pierre were reached together. At the mouth of the bridge at Port Gibson waited an aide on horseback.

"General Tracy?"

"Yes, sir."

"General, we're in line of battle across the Bruinsburg road, several miles from here! McClernand's corps is in front of us and he's got at least four divisions. General Bowen says he knows your men are tired and he's sorry, but you must move right out. They'll attack at dawn at latest. We are n't but five thousand."

The reinforcements from Vicksburg moved out. At ten o'clock they got into line of battle — a hot, still, dark night, and the soft blurred stars swimming before the men's eyes. When the order was given, the troops dropped down where they stood, lay on their arms, and slept like the dead.

At two in the morning of the first of May the pickets began firing. Up rose the reinforcements. They looked for breakfast, but breakfast was scant indeed, a stopgap of the slightest description. Presently came the order, "Move to the left and support General Green."

Missouri formed Bowen's left, and Missouri fought bravely at Port Gibson. It had to face treble its numbers, artillery and infantry. It faced them so stubbornly that for a time it bade fair to outface them. On that hot May day, on that steaming Southern battle-field, occurred strong fighting, grey and blue at grips, Victory shouting now here, now there, Defeat uncertain yet into which colour finally to let fly the deadly arrow. The battle smoke settled heavily. The bright colours, the singing-birds fled the trees and bushes, the perfume of flowers was smothered and vanished.

Artillery on both sides became heavily engaged. The ——th Virginia, during one of those sudden and mysterious lulls coming suddenly in battle as in other commotions of the elements, found itself, after hard fighting, with nothing to do but to watch that corner of the fight immediately before it. The corner was but a small, smoke-shrouded one. Only general officers, aides, and couriers ever really saw a battle-field. The ——th Virginia gazed with feverish interest on what it could see and guessed that which it could not. It could guess well enough that for the grey the struggle was growing desperate.

All this field was up and down, low ridge and shallow ravine. The ——th Virginia held a ridge. Over against it was a blue battery, and beyond the battery there might be divined a gathering mass of infantry. The ——th Virginia looked to its cartridge boxes. "Wish we had some guns! There won't be much of this left — What's that? Praise the Lord!" At a gallop, out of the smoke to the right, came a section of a grey battery, the guns leaping and thundering. Red-nostrilled, with blood-shot eyes up strained the horses. At the ridge-top, with an iron clang, all stopped. At once the gunners, grey wraiths in grey smoke, were busy; busy also at once the shapes upon the opposite ridge, blue wraiths in grey smoke. There was shouting, gesturing, then the flare and shriek of crossing shells. The ——th Virginia, still in possession of its spare moment, watched with an interest intense and critical. "Hello!" it said. "That's the homesick battery! That's the Botetourt Artillery!"

Out of the haze in front, above the opposing crest, came a glint of bayonets, the blue infantry, coveting the grey ridge, moving forward under artillery support. The ——th Virginia handled its rifles. *Ready — take aim — fire!* The blue failed to acquire the coveted ridge. The ——th Virginia, at rest once again in its corner of the field, looked sideways to see what the homesick battery was doing. There was a silence; then, "Give them a cheer, men!" said the colonel. "They're dying fast, and it always was a brave county!"

The shells from the many blue cannon came many and fast. It was necessary to clear the ridge of that grey section which stood in the way of a general advance. The gunners fell, the gunners fell, the officers, the horses. Dim in the universal cloud, from the left, a force was seen approaching. "Grey, I think," said the lieutenant commanding this section of the Botetourt Artillery. "J. J. Smith, climb up on the roof of that cabin, and see what you can see!"

J. J. Smith climbed. "Lieutenant Norgrove! Lieutenant Norgrove! they're damn-Yankees —"

Out of the smoke came a yellow light and a volley of lead. Gunner
Number 8, J. J. Smith, fell from the roof of the cabin, desperately
wounded. "Double canister!" shouted Norgrove.

An orderly came up the back side of the ridge. The ——th Virginia was needed to cover a break in the line to the right. Off perforce went the regiment, with one backward look at the homesick
battery, left without infantry support. An aide dashed up, rose in his
stirrups, and shouted, "Move your guns to the ridge in your rear!"
He was gone; Botetourt looked and shook its head. The horses were
all killed. "Put your hands to them, men!" ordered Norgrove —
and they tried. But the scrub was thick, the ground rough; there
burst a frightful fire, shell and musketry, and on came the blue wave
hurrahing. "All right! We can't!" shouted Norgrove. "*Load!*
This hill's Botetourt County — *Take aim!* — and we don't propose
to emigrate! *Fire!*"

The blue guns threw death. Deep, many-atomed, resistless, up
roared the blue wave. It struck and went over Botetourt County,
and, taking the two guns, turned them on the Botetourt men. There
were few Botetourt men now, Botetourt was become again the
wilderness. Norgrove jerked the trail from a gun, a man in blue
calling on him all the time to surrender. He made at the man, who
lifted his rifle and fired. Norgrove fell, mortally wounded, fell by the
side of J. J. Smith. He put his arms about the gunner, "Come on!
Come on!" he cried. . . . The wave swept over Botetourt County,
the dead and the dying.

The ——th Virginia, fighting strongly in another quarter of the
field, came in mid-afternoon to a stand between charges. All knew
now that the day was going against them. The smoke hung thick, a
dark velvet in the air, torn in places by the lightning from the guns.
Grey and blue — all was dimly seen. The flags looked small and distant, mere riddled and blood-stained rags. The voice of War was
deep and loud. The ——th Virginia, looking up from a hollow between the hills, saw two grey guns, stolid in the midst of wreck and
ruin. The plateau around had a nightmare look, it was so weighted
and cumbered with destruction. There was an exploded caisson, a
wreck of gun-carriages. Not a horse had been spared. The agony of

them was ghastly, sunk in the scrub, up and down and on the crest of the ridge. . . . A few grey gunners yet served the grey guns.

A captain, young, with a strong face and good brown eyes, stood out, higher than the rest, careless of the keening minies, the stream of shells. "A habit is a habit, men! This battery's got a habit of being steadfast! Keep it up — keep it up!"

"Captain Johnston — Captain Johnston! They've killed Lieutenant Douthatt —"

"Lay him in the scrub and fight on. How many rounds, Peters? — Two? — All right! You can do a good deal with two rounds —"

"It's the rest of the homesick battery," said the ——th Virginia, "*Botetourt Artillery! Botetourt Artillery!*"

There rushed a blue, an overpowering, a tidal wave — out of the smoke and din, bearing with it its own smoke and din, overmasteringly strong, McClernand's general advance. At the same moment, on the left, struck McPherson. When the roar that followed the impact died, the blue had won the field of Port Gibson; the grey had lost.

At sunset, Bowen's retreating regiments re-crossed Bayou Pierre. The exhaustion of the troops was extreme. There was no food; the men sank down and slept, in the whispering Southern night, in the remote light of other worlds. At dawn began the slow falling-back upon Vicksburg.

Lieutenant-General Pemberton telegraphed the situation to General Johnston in Tennessee, adding, "I should have large reinforcements."

In Tennessee, Rosecrans lay menacingly before Bragg. Johnston telegraphed to Pemberton, "Reinforcements cannot be sent from here without giving up Tennessee. Unite all your forces to meet Grant. Success will give you back what you abandoned to win it."

Pemberton, personally a brave and good man, looked out south and east from Vicksburg over the sparsely settled, tangled country. He looked west, indeed; but it was too late now to gather to him the Army of the Trans-Mississippi. His mind agreed that perhaps it should have been done in December . . . The troops in Vicksburg and north of Vicksburg, the troops at Jackson, the troops falling back from Grand Gulf — leaving out the garrison at Port Hudson, one might count, perhaps, thirty thousand effectives. Unite all

these, but not at Vicksburg . . . move out from Vicksburg, manœuvre here and manœuvre there, and at last take Grant somewhere at disadvantage. . . . General Johnston's plan as against
the President's. . . . Leave Vicksburg defenceless, to be taken by
some detached force, by Sherman, by the Federal men-of-war that
could now march up and down the Mississippi. . . . Pemberton
looked out at the batteries that had been built, all the field-works,
all the trenches. Most useless of all considerations moved him, the
consideration of the pity, of the waste of all these. He looked at the
very gallant town; he thought of the spirit of an old gentleman and
prominent citizen to whom he had talked yesterday. "Before God,"
said Pemberton, "I am not going to give up Vicksburg!"

The third day after Port Gibson the——th Virginia came again to
its old camp above the river, just without the town. Here, the next
morning, Edward Cary received an order to report to his colonel.
He found the latter at Headquarters and saluted — the colonel being an old schoolmate and hopelessly in love with his sister Unity.
"Cary," said the colonel, "we're poorer than the Ragged Mountains, but apparently we are considered highly presentable, a real
crack command, dandies and so forth! The War Department wants
a word-of-mouth description of Mississippi conditions. In short,
there's an embassy going to Richmond. The general came down and
asked if my uniform was whole and if I could muster two or three
men in decent apparel. Said I thought I could, and that there was
a patch, but I did n't think it would show. I am going to take you
as my orderly. The train for Jackson leaves at midday."

"Yes, sir. It is ten now. May I have the two hours?"

"Yes. I'll take you on now. Tell your captain."

Outside he heard the news of the battle of Chancellorsville.

"It was a victory!" said the men, sore from Port Gibson. "A big
victory! We're having them straight along in Virginia."

"It ain't a victory to have Stonewall Jackson wounded."

"Telegram said he'd get well. Old Jack is n't going to leave us.
God! We'd miss him awful!"

Edward and Désirée had one hour together. They spent it in the
garden, sitting beneath a flowering tree.

"How soon are you coming back? Oh, how soon are you coming
back?"

"As soon as we may. It must be soon, for the fighting will begin now. Port Gibson was but the opening gun."

"We have been making the cave for this house larger. A siege. . . ."

"I do not believe that we should pen ourselves up here. Grant can bring, if needed, a hundred thousand men. He is a dogged, earnest man. I think that we should concentrate as rapidly as possible and move from behind these walls. The odds are not much greater than they were in the Valley, or during the Seven Days."

"We have not General Jackson and General Lee."

"No, but the Government should give General Johnston free hand. He is the third."

"Oh, War! — When will it end and how ? "

"When we have fought to a stand-still. There is a Trojan feel to it all. . . . How beautiful you are! — fighter of floods, keeper of home! warrior and sufferer more than I am warrior and sufferer! I do not know how to say good-bye."

He had in Virginia three days. There was no time nor leave for Greenwood. His father was upon the Rappahannock, but in Richmond he saw Fauquier Cary. He had in Richmond two days.

The town lay in May sunshine, in bloom of the earliest roses. They mantled the old porches, the iron balconies, while above the magnolias opened their white chalices. The town breathed gladness for the victory in the Wilderness, and bitter grief for the many dead, and bitter grief for Stonewall Jackson. Edward heard in Richmond the Dead March for Jackson and watched him borne through the sighing streets. He heard the minute guns, and the tolling bells, and the slow, heroic music, and the sobbing of the people. He saw the coffin, borne by generals, carried into the Capitol, upward and between the great white Doric columns, into the Hall of the Lower House, where it rested before the Speaker's chair. He was among the thousands who passed before the dead chieftain, lying in state among lilies and roses, shrouded in the flag of Virginia, in the starry banner of the Confederate States. All day he heard the tolling of the bells, the firing of the minute guns.

On the morrow began the return journey to the Mississippi, long and slow on the creeping, outworn train, over the road that was so seldom mended. On the train crept, for many hundred miles, until just within the boundaries of Mississippi, at a crowded station, the passengers heard grave news. Jackson, the capital of the State, was in Federal hands!—there had been a desperate and disastrous battle at Baker's Creek, as desperate and more disastrous than Port Gibson! — there had been a Confederate rout at Big Black Bridge. . . . The colonel of the ——th Virginia, and the three or four officers and men with him, left the train, impressed horses, struck north, and then west and south. After three days they came upon a grey picket line, passed, and entered Vicksburg, where they found Pemberton with something over twenty thousand effectives, — the troops that had met defeat at Baker's Creek, with others not engaged, — all under orders from Richmond to hold Vicksburg at all hazards.

On the eighteenth, the Federal forces appeared on the Jackson and Grapevine road, east of the town. The two following days were spent by the blue in making their lines of circumvallation. The grey and the blue lines were about eight hundred yards apart. On the twenty-second, the ironclads came up the river from Grand Gulf. When they opened fire on the town and its defences, which they did almost immediately, the siege of Vicksburg was formally begun.

CHAPTER VIII

IN VIRGINIA

THIRTY guns of the horse artillery moved into position — not for battle, but for a splendid review. Right and left, emerging from the Virginia forest and the leafy defiles between the hills, came with earth-shaking tread the cavalry, a great force of cavalry, Jeb Stuart's splendid brigades! In the misty, early morning they moved into line, having come up from Brandy Station to a plain north of Culpeper Court-House. It was the eighth of June, something more than a month after Chancellorsville.

Beckham's Horse Artillery, that had been John Pelham's, having got into position, proceeded to take interest in the forming cavalry. There was so magnificently much of cavalry; it was so rested, so recuperated, so victorious, so proud of its past and determined as to its future, so easy, so fine, so glorious, so stamped, in short, with the stamp of Jeb Stuart, that to watch it was like watching a high and gay pageant! The sound of its movement, its jingle and clank, was delightful; delightful the brave lilt of voices, the neighing of impatient horses, delightful the keen bugles! The mist being yet heavy, there was much of mere looming shapes, sounds out of a fogbank. The plain was far spread, the review meant to be a noble one. There was a sense of distant gaiety as of near. The mist hid panoplied war, and far away bugles rang with an elfin triumph.

A certain company of the horse artillery was beautifully placed on a small, clear knoll, above it the fine leaves, the drooping, sweet bloom of a solitary locust. The guns were ranged in order, the horses in harness, cropping the wet grass where they stood. But it was early yet and the battery men had not received the order, *To your pieces!* They were clustered in groups, watching the gathering cavalry. Lean and easy and powerful, bronzed and young, they cheerfully commented upon life in general and the scene below.

"Jeb is n't here yet! He bivouacked last night at Beverly Ford. Orderly, riding by, heard the banjo."

"Is this review his notion or Marse Robert's ? "

"I reckon I can answer that. I was at headquarters. Jeb came out of that lovely little cabin he's got with a letter in his hand which he read to Heros von Borcke —"

"Yes ?"

"And he said in it that he did n't believe there ever had been in this sinful world a finer cavalry force, and would n't the greatest general on earth come over with some of his friends and review the greatest body of horse —"

"Sounds like him."

"And he gave the letter to Heros von Borcke, who went off with it. And then I was at headquarters again —"

"You sound like the Old Testament! Well, you were at head-quarters again — ?"

"And Heros von Borcke brought an order from Marse Robert — Jeb and all of us to come over and be reviewed on the plain north of Culpeper. Marse Robert said he 'd be there with 'some of his friends' —"

"Longstreet, I reckon. A. P. Hill's still at Fredericksburg."

"And they say Ewell's going toward the Valley —"

To right and left there sprang a rustling. The sun strengthened, the mist began to lift, a number of bugles blared together. Into the very atmosphere sifted something like golden laughter. A shout arose — *Jeb Stuart! Jeb Stuart! Jeb Stuart!*

Out of the misty forest, borne high, a vivid square in the sea of pearl, came a large battle-flag. Crimson and blue and thirteen-starred, forth it paced, held high by the mounted standard bearer. The horse artillery saluted as it went by, going on to a sentinelled strip of greensward where stood three ancient and weather-beaten tents. Here it was planted, and here in the June wind it streamed outward so that every star might be seen. The mist yet held on the farther side of the plain, but all the nearer edge was growing light and sunny. The bugles rang. *Jeb Stuart! Jeb Stuart!* shouted the plain above Culpeper.

Stuart, followed by his staff, trotted from the forest. He wore his fighting jacket and his hat with the plume, he was magnificently mounted, he stroked his wonderful, sunny beard, and he laughed with his wonderful, sunny, blue eyes. He had more *verve* than any

leader in that army; he was brave as Ney; the army adored him!
The victory of Chancellorsville was his victory no less than it was
that of Stonewall Jackson and of Robert Lee. All knew it, and the
victory was but five short weeks ago. The glory of the great fight
hung about him like a golden haze, a haze that magnified, and yet
that, perhaps, did not magnify overmuch, for he was a noble cavalry
leader. Suddenly, —

" Old Joe Hooker, won't you come out of the Wilderness ? "

chanted the hosts about him.

He lifted his hat. The horse, that had about his arching neck a
great wreath of syringa and roses, pranced on to the colours and
stopped. Staff drew up, bugles blew, there came a sound of drum
and fife, mist began rapidly to lift. "Oh," breathed Horse Artillery,
getting into place, "most things have a compensatory side!"

From the misty middle of the plain came with tramp and jingle
another mounted party. One rode ahead on a grey horse. Noble of
form and noble of face, simple and courteous, he came up to the
great flag and grandeur came with him. *General Lee! General Lee!*
shouted Cavalry, shouted Horse Artillery.

Stuart, who had dismounted, came forward, saluting.

"Ah, General," said Lee. "I am going to review you with much
pleasure, and I have taken you at your word and brought with me
some of my friends."

Stuart beamed upon Longstreet, commander of the First Corps,
and upon several division generals.

"Oh, I have brought more than these!" said Lee. "Look how the
sun is drinking up the mist!"

As he spoke the sun finished the draught. The rolling plain north
of Culpeper lay bare. All the dewy, green middle waited for the
cavalry evolutions, for the march past, but the farther side, up and
down and over against Jeb Stuart's flag, was already occupied
and not by cavalry. Troops and troops and troops, like a grey wall
pointed with banners! — Horse Artillery, from its place of vantage,
stared, then softly crowed. "Great day in the morning! Marse
Robert has brought the whole First Corps!"

Now here, now there, on the plain, went in brilliant manœuvres the cavalry. The horse artillery came into line, manœuvred and thundered as brilliantly. The massed infantry cheered, the reviewing general stood with a grave light in his eyes. Jeb Stuart shifted his place like a sunbeam. Oh, the blowing bugles; oh, the red and blue flag outstreaming; oh, the sunlight and the clear martial sounds and the high, high hopes on the plain north of Culpeper! June was in the heart of most; doubly, doubly was it the Confederacy's June, this month! Great victories in Virginia lay behind it: in the Far South there had been disasters, but Vicksburg — Vicksburg was heroically standing the siege. And in front lay, perhaps, the crossing of the Potomac and the carrying the war into Africa! June, June, June! it sang in the blood of the grey. Long and horrible had been the war, and many were the lost, and tears had drenched the land, but now it was summer and victory would come before the autumn. The North was tired of spilling blood and treasure; there sounded a clamour for peace. One or two other great victories, and peace would descend and the great Confederacy would stand! The march past raised its eyes to the crimson banner with the thirteen stars, and June was in every soldier's heart.

The march past was a thing to have seen and to remember. By the starry banner, by Robert Edward Lee, went the cavalry brigades of his son, "Roony" Lee, of his nephew, Fitzhugh Lee, of Beverly Robertson, of W. E. Jones, of Wade Hampton. They lifted their sabres, the sun made a dazzle of steel. June, June, June! sang the bugles, sang the birds in the woods back of the warm-hearted, the admiring infantry. Past went the horse artillery, the thirty guns, the proud battery horses, the easy and bronzed cannoneers, the grave young officers. . . . *General Lee! General Lee!* shouted Cavalry, shouted Artillery! The dust rose from the plain, all grew a shimmering blur. . . .

It was over, the great cavalry review. The day descended; the troops drew off toward hidden bivouacs. Lee and Longstreet and Stuart rode together awhile, under the sunset sky. Staff, behind them, understood that great things were being spoken of — marches toward Maryland, perhaps, or a watch on Joe Hooker, or the, of late, vastly increased efficiency of the enemy's cavalry. Staff had its own opinion as to this. "They always could fight, and now they've learned to ride! Pity!"

"I don't call it a pity. I'd rather meet them equal. Pleasanton's all right."

"We've had a beautiful review and we've also made a lot of noise, to say nothing of a dust cloud like the Seven Days come back. Double pickets to-night, I should say. We are n't a million miles from Hooker."

"That's true enough. — *Halt!* General Lee's going back."

Under a great flush of sunset coral and gold above the trees, Lee and his cavalry leader parted. The one smiled, the other laughed, they touched gauntleted hands, and Lee turned grey Traveller. Longstreet joined him and they rode away, staff falling in behind, out of the June-time forest, back to the encampment at Culpeper. A moment and their figures were drowned in the violet evening. Jeb Stuart, singing, plunged with his staff into the woods. His headquarters were at Brandy Station.

The starry night found this village filled with troops. They bivouacked, moreover, all about it, on Fleetwood Hill and toward St. James Church. There were outposts, too, toward the Rappahannock; a considerable troop tethered its horses on the bank above Beverly Ford. Others went toward Providence Church and Norman's Ford, others toward Kelly's. Eight thousand horse bivouacked beneath the stars. Camp-fire saw camp-fire, and the rustling night wind and the murmuring streams heard other voices than their own, heard voices full of cheer.

The horse artillery prepared to spend the night in a grassy field beside the Beverly Ford road. In front was a piece of thick woods. The battery horses, tethered in a long line, began to crop the grass. The guns, each known and loved like an old familiar, were parked. The men gathered dry wood for their supper fires, fried their bacon, baked their corn-meal pones, brewed their "coffee" — chiccory, rye, or sweet potato, as the case might be. There was much low laughter and crooning, and presently clouds of tobacco smoke. Beautiful review — beautiful day — rest to-night — march to-morrow — Jeb lovely as ever — going to end this blessed war — pile on the pine knots so we can read the letters from home! . . .

Toward midnight, on the farther edge of the wood, a post of the horse artillery relieved its pickets. The sound of the retiring steps died away and the fresh sentinels took cognizance of their positions.

The positions were some distance apart, between them wood and uneven ground and the murmurous night. Each picket was a lonely man, with the knowledge only that if he raised his voice to a shout he would be heard.

The moon shone brightly. It silvered the Beverly Ford road and made a frosted wall of the forest left and right, and bathed with the mildest light the open and undulating country. Somewhere a whip-poor-will was calling. *Whip-poor-will! Whip-poor-will!*

Beside the road sprang a giant sycamore. From beneath it Philip Deaderick, once Richard Cleave, standing picket, watched the night. He stood straight and still, powerfully knit, his short rifle in the hollow of his arm. He stood grave and quiet, a wronged but not unhappy man. The inner life, the only life, had marched on. A gulf had opened and certain hopes and happinesses had fallen therein, but his life was larger than those hopes and happinesses. The inner man had marched on. He had marched even with a quickened step in this last month. "What did it matter?" reasoned Cleave. "Those whom I love know, and I am not cut off from service, no, nor from growth!" Around, above, below the sharpened point of the moment he was aware enough of the larger man. The point might ache at times, but he knew also impersonal freedom. . . . Things might be righted some day or they might not be righted. He could wait. He looked from the shadow of the sycamore out upon the lovely, moonlit land. Tragedy, death, and sorrow through all the world, interpretations at grips, broken purposes, misunderstandings, humanity groping, groping! He ached for it all — for the woman sleepless on her pillow, for the prisoner in prison. The spirit widened; he stood calm under all, quiet, with suspended judgment. *Whip-poor-will! Whip-poor-will!* He looked up and studied the stars between the silver branches of the sycamore, then dropped his gaze and leaned slightly forward, for he heard the tread of horses on the road.

Two horsemen, one in front, the other a little way behind, came quietly up the silver streak.

"Halt!" said Deaderick.

The two drew rein. "All right!" said the one in advance. "A friend. Colonel of Cary's Legion, with an orderly."

"Advance, friend, and give the countersign."

"*Ivry.*"

"Correct, *Ivry.* Pass!"

The officer, with a motion of his hand to the orderly to stay where he was, came closer to the picket. "Before I do so," he said, and his tone was a strange one, "tell me your name."

"Philip Deaderick."

"You are trying to disguise your voice. . . . *Richard !*"

"Don't, Fauquier! I am Philip Deaderick, gunner in —— 's battery, horse artillery."

"How long ?"

"Since Groveton. Don't betray me."

"Who knows ? Does Judith know ?"

"Yes. She and my mother."

The other covered his eyes with his hand, then spoke, much moved. "Richard, if ever this war gives us time we might reopen matters. We surely have influence enough —"

"I know, Fauquier. But there is no time now to be given nor stress to be laid on private matters. Somehow they have sunk away. . . . Perhaps a day will come, and perhaps it will not come. . . . In the mean time dismissal from the army has not worked. I am back in the army."

"And are not unhappy? You do not sound unhappy."

"No. I am not unhappy. Only now and then. . . . Be careful, will you ? If I were known I should be unhappy soon enough!"

"You may trust me." He leaned from the saddle and put his hand on the other's shoulder. "Richard, you're a true man. I've always honoured you, and I honour you more than ever! Truth will out! You be sure of that."

"I am at times reasonably sure of it, Fauquier. And if it does not appear, I am reasonably sure that I can endure the darkness. I told you that I was not unhappy." He laid an affectionate touch on the other's hand. "I was sorry enough to hear about the arm, Fauquier."

"Oh," said Cary, "I have learned to use the left. I had rather it was the arm than the leg, like dear old Ewell! . . . Richard, meeting you like this moves me more than I can well let show. I've got so much of my mother in me that I'd like to kiss you, my dear —" He bent as he spoke and touched with his lips the other's broad, uplifted brow, which done, with a great handclasp they parted. Cary, turn-

ing, called to the orderly who came up. The two rode on toward
Brandy Station, and Deaderick resumed his watch.

Another time passed. The moon rode high, the forest rustled, the
road lay a silver streak. Deaderick, still and straight beneath the
sycamore, presently turned his head and regarded the line of woods
upon his left. He had caught a sound — but it was some distance
away. It had been faint, but it was like a horse being pushed
cautiously through undergrowth. Now there was no more of it.
He stood listening, with narrowed eyes. The bushes a hundred feet
away parted and a man and horse emerged. They stopped a moment and the man rose in his stirrups and looked about him. Then,
with a satisfied nod, he settled to the saddle again and the two came
through the thin growth down to the road.

"Halt!" said Deaderick, cocking his rifle.

The horseman came on. "Halt! or I fire."

The horse was stopped. "Don't waste your bullets on me!" said
the rider coolly. "Save them for the Yankees."

"Dismount before you advance."

"I have the countersign. I am Lieutenant Francis, bearing an
enquiry from General Lee."

"Dismount before you advance."

The officer dismounted. He was a tall man, wrapped, though the
night was warm, in a grey horseman's cloak. "You are tremendously careful to-night! I suppose my horse may follow me? He
does n't stand well."

"Fasten him to the sapling beside you. — Advance and give the
countersign."

The tall man came up, revealing, beneath a grey hat pulled low, a
tanned countenance with long mustaches. "*Ivry.* I'll tell General
Stuart that you are about the most cautious picket he's got. I
remember having to convince just such another when I was in
Texas in '43 —"

"Did you convince him?"

"I did. The word is *Ivry.* Allow me to pass."

"Be so good first as to open your cloak. It is too warm to wear
it so."

"My man, you are on your way to the guardhouse. Messengers
from General Lee are not accustomed — *What is that?*"

"Nothing. I was humming a line of an old carol. Do you remember the road to Frederick?"

Dead silence, then a movement of Marchmont's hand beneath the cloak. Cleave divined, and was upon him. Not so tall, but more powerfully built and a master wrestler, the tug of war was a short one. The pistol, wrenched from the Englishman's grasp, fell to the ground and was kicked away. The two struggling figures swung round until Marchmont was nearer the sycamore, Cleave between him and the horse. Another fierce instant and the Englishman was thrown — the picket's rifle covered him.

"I regret it," said Cleave, "but it can't be helped. I wish that some other had been sent in your place." He raised his voice to a shout. "Picket two! A prisoner. Send guard!" There came back a faint "All right! Hold on!"

Marchmont sat up and picked the leaves from his clothing. "Well, I have thought of you more than once, and wished that we might meet again! Not precisely under such auspices as these, but under others. I was obliged to you, I remember, that day at Front Royal."

"It was a personal matter then, in which I might indulge my own inclination. To-night I regret that it is not a personal matter."

"Exactly. Well, I bear you no grudge. 'Fortune of war!' At Front Royal you were a colonel leading a charge — may I ask why I find you playing sentry?"

"That is a long story," said Cleave. "I am sorry that I should be your captor, and it is entirely within your right to deny the request I am going to make. I am Philip Deaderick, a private soldier. I ask you to forget that I ever had another name."

"All right, Philip Deaderick, private soldier!" said Marchmont. "Whatever may be your reasons, I won't blab. I liked you very well on the road to Frederick, and very well that day at Front Royal. — To-night was just a cursed fanfaronade. Knew you must all be hereabouts. Crossed over to see what I could see, got the word and this damned cloak and hat from a spy, and ambled at once into the arms of a man who could recognize me! Absurd! And here comes the guard."

Guard came up. "What is it, Deaderick? Deserter? Spy?"

"It's not a deserter," said Deaderick. "It's somebody in a blue
uniform beneath a grey cloak. I don't think he's an accredited spy
— probably just an officer straying around and by chance hearing
the word and acting on the spur of the moment. You'd better take
him to the captain back on the road."

Another hour passed and he was relieved. Back with the outpost
he lay down upon the summer earth and tried to sleep. But the
two encounters of the night had set the past to ringing. He could
not still the reverberations. Greenwood! Greenwood! — the place
and one within it — and one within it — and one within it! . . .
And then Marchmont, and the hopes and ambitions that once
Richard Cleave had known. "A colonel leading a charge" —
and the highest service in sight — and a man's knowledge of his
own ability. . . . Philip Deaderick turned and lay with his face to
the earth, his arm across his eyes. He fought it out, the thousandth
inner battle, then turned again and lay, looking sideways along the
misty night.

In the distance a cock crew. The chill air, the unearthly quiet told
the hour before dawn. The east grew pale, then into it crept faint
streaks of purple. The birds in the woodland began incessantly to
cheep! cheep! The mist was very heavy. It hid the road, swathed all
the horizon. Reveille sounded: the bugler, mounted on a hill behind
the guns, looked, in the moody light, like some Brocken spectre.
Far and wide, full at hand, thin and elfin in the distance, rang
other reveilles. They rang through the streets of Brandy Station
and through the surrounding forests, fields, and dales, waking Jeb
Stuart's thousands from their sleep.

Horse Artillery stood up, rubbed its eyes, and made a speedy
toilet. In the shortest possible time the men were cooking breakfast. Cooking breakfast being at no time in the Army of Northern
Virginia a prolonged operation, they were to be found in an equally
short space of time seated about mess-fires eating it. It was yet dank
and chilly dawn, the east reddening but not so very red, the mist
hanging heavy, closing all perspectives. Horse Artillery lifted its tin
cup, filled with steaming mock-coffee, to its lips — *Crack! crack!*
came the rifle shots from the Beverly Ford woods. Horse Artillery
set down its cup. "What's that? What are all those pickets firing
that way for? Good Lord, if there's going to be a surprise, why

could n't they wait until after breakfast? *Get the horses and limber up !* — All right, Captain —"

Vedettes, driven in, came galloping up the road. "Blue cavalry! No end of blue cavalry! Column crossing, and a whole lot of them up in the woods! Nobody could see them, the mist was so heavy! You slow old Artillery, you'd better look out!"

Beckham came up. "Captain Hart, draw a piece by hand down into the road! Get hitched up there, double-quick! Into position on the knoll yonder! — Oh, here comes support!"

The Sixth Virginia Cavalry had been on picket; the Seventh Virginia Cavalry doing grand guard. Alert and in the saddle, they had seen and heard. Now from toward Brandy Station up they raced, like a friendly whirlwind, to the point of danger. A cheer from the artillery welcomed them, and they shouted in return. Flournoy and the Sixth dashed down the Beverly Ford road and deployed in the woods to the right. Marshall and the Seventh followed and deployed to the left. Artillery limbered up and took to the high ground near St. James Church. Up galloped Eleventh and Twelfth Virginia and fell into line behind the guns.

Jeb Stuart, in the saddle on Fleetwood Hill, his blue eyes upon the Beverly Ford situation, found a breathless aide beside him.

"General! General! They're crossing below at Kelly's Ford! Two divisions —'artillery and infantry behind! They've got us front and rear!"

Stuart's eyes danced. He stroked his beard. "All right! All right! I'll send Robertson and Hampton — Here's W. F. H. Lee — Cary, too! This is going to be the dandiest fight!"

A brigadier galloped up. "General, shall we detach regiments to guard all approaches?"

"Too many approaches, General! We'll keep concentrated and deliver the blow where the blow is due! Will you listen to that delightful fuss? — Dabney, you go tell General Hampton to place a dismounted battalion by Carrico Mills."

The clang and firing in the Beverly Ford woods grew furious — the Sixth and Seventh fighting with the Eighth New York and the Eighth Illinois. On pushed the Federal horse, many and bold, Buford's Regulars, trained, efficient. The forward surge, the backward giving, brought all upon the edge of the wood. There was charge and countercharge, carbine firing, sabring, shouts, scream of horses, shock and fire, hand-to-hand fighting. Back and upward roared the surge, up and over the hill where were the guns, the guns that were trained, but could not be fired, so inextricably was friend intertwined with foe. The shouting blue laid hold of the guns; the cannoneers fought hand-to-hand, with pistol muzzle and pistol butt, dragging at the horses' reins, striking men from the saddle, covering the guns, wrenching off the blue clutch. Then came like a jubilant whirlwind the supporting grey, Hampton and Lee.

"Isn't it beautiful?" asked Jeb Stuart on Fleetwood Hill. "Oh, ho! They're coming thick from Kelly's Ford!"

"General Robertson reports, sir, that there's artillery and infantry on his front. The cavalry, in great strength, is sweeping to the right —"

"Fine! They're all coming to Fleetwood Hill. Go, tell Major Beckham to send any guns that he can spare."

Beckham sent two of McGregor's. Artillery was in straits of its own. Charges from the Beverly Ford woods might be repelled, but now arose the dust and thunder of the advance from Kelly's. Impossible to stay before St. James Church and become grain between the upper and nether millstones! Artillery fell back, first to Pettis's Hill, then to Fleetwood, and fell back with three pieces disabled. Before they could get into position, Buford's regiments charged again. There followed a mêlée. The cannoneers, too, must deal with that charge. They had pistols which they used, they had sponge staff and odd bits of iron. As soon as it was humanly possible, they got a gun into service — then two. The shells broke and scattered the shouting blue lines.

Through Brandy Station charged regiment after regiment, — blue, magnificent, shouting, — Gregg and Duffie's divisions up from Kelly's Ford. A dismounted squadron of Robertson's broke before them; they fell upon a supporting battery and took the guns. On they roared, through Brandy Station, out to Fleetwood Hill. Jeb Stuart swung his hat. "Now, Cavalry of the Army of Northern Virginia! Now, Cavalry of the Army of Northern Virginia!"

There followed a great cavalry fight. Squadron dashed against squadron. All was gleaming and dust and shouting, carbine smoke

and wheeled lightning of sabres. June stood a-tiptoe; the earth
seemed to rock; a hundred brilliant colours went in sparkles before
the eyes, the ears rang. There was a mad excitement in which,
whether time plunged forward like a cataract, or stood still like an
arrested hearkener to the last trump, none in that abandonment
could have told. It was a gay fight, shrieking with excitement, the
horses mad as the riders, the air shaking like castanets. The squad-
rons crashed together, the sabres swung, the pistols cracked! Down
went men and horses, biting the dust, gaiety going out like a blown
candle. Without, air and sunshine and wild animal exultation;
within, pain, smothering, and darkness, darkness. . . . The guns
were taken, the guns were retaken; the grey gave back, the blue
gave back. The battle lines wheeled and charged, wheeled and
charged. There was shock and fire and a mad mêlée — a staccato
fight, with cymbal and quick drum. And ever in front tossed the
feather of Stuart.

To and fro, through the hot June weather, the battle swung.
Though no one could tell the time, time passed. The blue gave
back — slowly. Slowly the grey pressed them eastward. A train
shrieked into Brandy Station, and grey infantry came tumbling out.
Loud blew Pleasanton's bugles. "Leave the fight a drawn fight, and
come away!"

With deliberation the blue, yet in battle front, moved eastward
to the fords of the Rappahannock. After them pressed the grey.
An aide, dust from head to foot, rode neck by neck with Stuart.
"General! we are being hard put to it on the left — Buford's
Regulars! General Lee has a wound. We've got a battery, but
the ammunition's out —" The feather of Stuart turned again to
the Beverly Ford road.

W. H. F. Lee's troops, re-forming, charged again, desperately,
brilliantly. Munford, commanding Fitzhugh Lee's brigade, had
been up the river at Wellford's Ford. Now, bringing with him
Breathed's battery, he fell upon the blue flank. Buford gave way;
the grey came on with a yell. Down through the Beverly woods,
past the spot where, at dawn, there had been outpost fighting, down
to the ford again, rolled the blue. The feather of Stuart went by in
pursuit.

Philip Deaderick, resting after a hard fight, leaning against a yet smoking gun, watched with his fellows the retreat of the tide that had threatened to overwhelm. The tide was finding outlet by all the fords of the Rappahannock. It was streaming back from all the region about Brandy Station. It went in spirits, retiring, but hardly what one might call defeated. It had been, in sooth, all but a drawn battle — a brilliant cavalry battle, to be likened, on an enormous scale, to some flashing joust of the Middle Ages.

Deaderick, watching, leaned forward with a sound almost of satisfaction. Below him passed two men, riding double, blue gallopers toward Beverly Ford. The one behind, without cloak or hat, saw him, waved his arm and shouted, "*Au revoir*, Lieutenant McNeil!"

CHAPTER IX

THE STONEWALL

FIVE days before the fight at Brandy Station, Ewell and the
Second Corps, quitting the encampment near Fredericksburg
and marching rapidly, had disappeared in the distance toward
the Valley. Two days after the fight, Hooker, well enough aware
by now that grey plans were hatching, began the withdrawal of the
great army that had rested so long on the northern bank of the Rappahannock. A. P. Hill and the Third Corps, watching operations
from the south bank, waited only for the withdrawal from Falmouth
of the mass of the enemy. When it was gone, Hill and the Third,
moving with expedition, joined Lee and Longstreet at Culpeper
Court-House.

Stuart and his thousands rested from Brandy Station and observed
movements. All day the grey infantry moved by, streaming toward
the Blue Ridge. Cavalry speculated. "Jeb knows, of course, and
the brigadiers I reckon, and I suppose Company Q knows, but I wish
I did! Are we going to Ohio, or Maryland, or Pennsylvania, or just
back to the blessed old Valley? I don't hold with not telling soldiers
things, just because they don't have bars on their collars or stars or
sashes! We've got a *right* to know —"

"What's in those wagons — the long white ones with six horses?"

"Danged if I know!"

"Boys, *I* know! Them's pontoons!"

"*Pontoons!* We're going to cross the Potomac!"

On went the infantry, over country roads, through the forest,
over open fields. There were no fences now in this region, and few,
few standing crops. All day the infantry streamed by, going toward
the Blue Ridge. Before sunset blew the trumpets of Stuart. "Boot
and saddle!" quoth the men. "Now we are going, too!"

Ewell and the Second Corps, far in advance of the First, the Third
and the cavalry, pierced the Blue Ridge at Chester Gap. "Old Dick"
had left a leg at Groveton, but he himself was here, going ahead of

his troops, a graver man than of old, but irascible yet, quaintly lovable yet and well loved.   Behind him he heard the tramp of his thousands, Jubal Early's division, Edward Johnson's division, the division of Rodes.   They were going back to the Valley, and they were going to take Winchester, held by Milroy and eight thousand.

The Stonewall Brigade, led now by Walker, was numbered in Edward Johnson's division.   It marched near the head of the column, and it gazed with an experienced eye upon the wall of the Blue Ridge.   How many times, O Mars, how many times!   Up, up the June heights wound the column, between leafy towers, by running water, beneath a cloudless sky.   The Sixty-fifth Virginia, Colonel Erskine, broke into song.

> "Should auld acquaintance be forgot,
> An' never brought to mind . . .
> For auld lang syne, my dear,
> For auld lang syne —"

Allan Gold was not marching with the Sixty-fifth.   He was half a day ahead, scouting. Around stretched the rich woods of the western slope of the Blue Ridge, below lay the wooded valley of the Shenandoah.   He saw the road to Front Royal, and before him the Massanuttens closed the view.   He had been travelling since sun-up, and now, at noon, he was willing enough to camp awhile.   He chose the bottom of a knife-blade ravine where was a trickle of water beneath laurels in bloom.   The sun came down between leaves of ash and hickory; the topmost branches just stirred, bees buzzed, birds sang far and wide.   He was quite alone with the earth.   First he set his rifle against a hickory, and then he gathered a very small heap of twigs and dead leaves, and then he set fire to these.   From his haversack he took a metal plate, one side of a burst canteen.   It made a small but splendid griddle and he set it on the coals.   Then out came a fragment of bacon and two pieces of hard-tack.   He fried the bacon, then crumbled the hard-tack in the gravy and made "coosh."   Then, with slow enjoyment, he ate the bacon and the coosh.   When the last atom was gone, he lifted the griddle, handling it with a thick glove of leaves, plunged it in the streamlet, washed it clean, and restored it, sun-dried, to his haversack.   This done, he took out a small bag of tobacco and his pipe, filled the latter, and with his back against the hickory began to smoke.   He was happy, alone with the earth whom he understood. Long and blond and strong, the grey of his clothing weatherbeaten until it was like in hue to the russet last year's leaves on which he lay, he looked a man of an old-time tale, Siegfried, perhaps, quiet and happy in the deep, deep forest.

When the pipe was empty, he cleaned it and restored it to his pocket. This done, he routed out the side of the haversack devoted to apparel, comb, toothbrush, and — when he could get it — soap, together with other small articles. He had a little New Testament in which he conscientiously read at least once a week. Now he took this up. Between its pages lay an unopened letter. He uttered an exclamation. It had come to him at Fredericksburg, an hour before marching. He had had no time to read it then, and he had put it here. Then had come the breaking camp, the going ahead — he could hardly tell whether he had forgotten it or had simply taken up the notion that it had been read. He laughed. "Well, Aunt Sairy, it never happened before!" He opened it now, settled his shoulders squarely against the hickory, and read —

"DEAR ALLAN: — It's Tom's turn to write, but he says I do it because his hand's took to shaking so. The doctor says it's just eagerness — he wants to know all the time and at the right identical minute what's happening. And even the newspapers don't know that, though Lord knows they think they do! But it's just as bad to be sick with eagerness as to be sick with anything else. It's sickness just the same as if it was typhoid or pleurisy. Yes, Allan, I'm anxious enough about Tom, — though, of course, I did n't read that out to him. He's sitting in the sunshine holding the toll-box, and there ain't anything in it — and there never will be until you all stop this fool war. The doctor says — Yes, Tom! . . . Allan, you just straighten this letter out in your own head."

Oh, it straightened out well enough in Allan's head! He let the hand that held it drop upon the leaves, and he looked up the knife-blade ravine to where the green rim of the mountain touched the blue. He saw Thunder Run Mountain, and he heard, over the murmur of surrounding trees, the voice of Thunder Run. He saw with the inner eye the toll-house, the roses and the pansies and the bees. It was not going well with the toll-house — he knew that. Tom failing, and no toll taken, the county probably paying nothing. . . . Where was the money with which it could pay? Sairy fighting hard — he saw her slight, bent old figure — fighting hard now with this end, now with that, to make them meet. He knew they would never meet now, not while this war lasted. It was one of the bitter by-products — that never meeting. There was nothing to send — he himself had had no pay this long while. Pay, in the Southern armies, was a vanishing quantity.

The wood blurred before Allan's eyes. He sighed and took up the letter again.

"The school-house is most fallen down. They told me so, and I went up the Run one evening and looked at it. It's so. It looked like a yearning ghost. Christianna tried to teach the children awhile this spring, but Christianna never was no bookworm. An' then she had to do the spring ploughing, for Mrs. Maydew went down into the Valley to nurse the smallpox soldiers. Mrs. Cleave went, too, from Three Oaks. I have n't got much of a garden this year, but the potatoes and sparrowgrass look fine. The wrens have built again in the porch. They're company for Tom, now that there's so little other company. He's named the one Adam and the other Eve — Lord knows they're wiser than some Adams and Eves I know! — Tom's calling! —

"It was n't anything. He thought it was a wagon coming up the road. If this war don't stop soon, some of us won't be here to see it stop. And now he says if he just had a little something sweet to eat — and there ain't no sugar nor nothing in the house!

"Lord sake, Allan, I did n't mean to write like this! I know you've got your end to bear. Tom is n't really so sick, and I'm jest as right as ever I was! The sun's shining and the birds are singing, and the yellow cat's stretching himself, and the gourd vine's got a lot of flowers, and I bet you'd like to hear Thunder Run this minute! Steve Dagg's still here and limping — when he thinks anybody's looking. Rest of the time he uses both feet. He's making up to Christianna Maydew —"

Allan's hand closed on the paper. "Steve Dagg making up to Christianna Maydew! Why — damn him —" He was not a swearing man, but he swore now, rising from the ground to do so. He did not pause to analyze his feeling. A cool-blooded, quiet-natured man, he found himself suddenly wild with wrath. He with the balance of the Sixty-fifth had fully recognized Steve Dagg as the blot on their 'scutcheon — but personally, the blot had until now only amused and disgusted him. Quite suddenly he found the earth too small for both Allan Gold and Stephen Dagg.

Standing in the deep and narrow ravine and looking upward he had a vision. He saw Thunder Run Mountain, and high on the comb of it, the log house of the Maydews. He saw the ragged mountain garden sloping down, and the ragged mountain field. All about was a kind of violet mist. It parted and he saw Christianna standing in the doorway.

Allan Gold sat down upon a stone beside the brook. He leaned forward, his clasped hands hanging below his knees. The clear, dark water gave him back his face and form. He sat so, very still, for some minutes, then he drew a long, long breath. "I have been," he said, "all kinds of a fool."

Sairy's letter offered but a few more words. He read them through, folded the paper thoughtfully and carefully, and laid it between the leaves of the Testament. Then he stood up, carefully extinguished with his foot the fire of leaves and twigs, took his rifle, and turned his face toward the Shenandoah.

Thirty-six hours later found him waiting, a little east of Front Royal, for the column. It appeared, winding through the woods, Ewell riding at the head, with him Jubal Early and J. B. Gordon. Allan stood out from the ferny margin of the wood and saluted.

"Hello!" said Old Dick. "It's the best scout in the service!"

Allan gave his information. "General, I've been talking to an old farmer and his wife, refugeeing from the Millwood section. They believed there was a considerable Yankee force at Berryville. So I went on for a few miles, and got three small boys and sent them into Berryville on a report that there was a circus in town. They got the news all right and came back with it. McRennolds is there with something like fifteen hundred men and a considerable amount of stores."

"Is he?" quoth Old Dick. "Then, when we get to Cedarville

I'll send somebody to get that honey out of the gum tree! Now you go on, Gold, and get some more information."

The column marched through Front Royal. All of Front Royal that was there came out and wept and laughed and cheered, and dashed out to the ranks to shake hands, to clasp, to kiss. "Oh, don't you remember, little more'n a year ago — and all the things that have happened since! The North Fork — and the burnt bridge — and Ashby at Buckton. . . . *Oh, Ashby!* . . . and the fight with Kenly — and the big charge — and Stonewall Jackson. . . . '*My father, my father, the chariot of Israel and the horsemen thereof!*'"

The column crossed the Shenandoah and came to Cedarville, where it rested for the night. Here there reported to Ewell Jenkins's cavalry brigade. In the morning Old Dick sent this body of horse, together with Rodes's division, across country to Berryville with instructions to capture or disperse McRennolds's command, and then to press on to Martinsburg. Ewell himself, with Early and Edward Johnson's divisions, took the road that led by Middletown and Nineveh to the Valley Pike.

At Nineveh Allan Gold again appeared. "General, I've been almost into Winchester. Milroy has breastworks all around, and he's well off in artillery. The hills west and northwest of the town command his works."

"All right, all right!" said Ewell. "Winchester's going to see another battle."

On the morning of the thirteenth the column divided. Edward Johnson, with Nounnan's cavalry force, keeping on upon the Front Royal and Winchester road, while Early's division struck the Valley Pike at Newtown.

The Valley Pike! The Valley soldiers — of whom there were a number in this division, though more in Edward Johnson's — the Valley soldiers had last seen the Valley Pike in October — and now it was June. They had seen it in a glory of crimson and gold, and a violet haze of Indian summer, and then they had left it, Stonewall Jackson riding ahead. . . . and then had come Fredericksburg . . . and then had come the Wilderness.

"Howdy, Valley Pike!" said the soldiers. "It's been long that we've been away! Did you miss us, old girl? We've missed you. A lot of us did n't come back, but here's some of us!"

Through the hot afternoon Jubal Early and his troops moved down the pike toward Winchester. Near Bartonsville, in position upon a low hill, they found the First Maryland Infantry and the Baltimore Artillery.

Colonel Herbert of the First reported. "They 've got a force, sir, at Kernstown, and a battery on Pritchard's Hill. We 've been skirmishing off and on all day."

"All right!" swore Old Jube. "I 'll send the Louisiana Brigade and dislodge that battery."

Hays and the Louisianians went, crossing the meadow and skirting the ridge, marching where had marched the Army of the Valley on the old field of Kernstown. The blue battery removed from Pritchard's Hill; they took that eminence without difficulty. Hays sent back tidings of Federal infantry massing to the left. Early ordered Gordon forward. That dashing officer and brave and handsome man swung by with his brigade. Joining Hays, the two, Georgia and Louisiana, drove the blue detachment over field and ridge and Abraham's Creek to Bowers's Hill. This, infantry and artillery, the blue seized and held through the night. The brigades of Hoke and Smith arrived, but it was twilight and a drenching summer rain. The grey bivouacked on the field of Kernstown.

Dawn came up, hot and still, and with it Old Dick to confer with Old Jube. Council over, Gordon was moved forward, the Maryland troops with him, and left to skirmish with, amuse, and distract the enemy. Hays and Hoke and Smith with some artillery plunged into the woods. "Flank movement!" said the men. "It 's fun to flank and it 's hell to be flanked. That 's the road to Romney over there."

They came to the lower slopes of Little North Mountain, to the Pughtown road. On high ground to the south was a ruined orchard and a ruined house called Folk's Old House; while on high ground to the north lay a ruined cornfield, part of Mrs. Brieley's land. Both points overlooked the fortifications. Old Jube divided Jones's Artillery. Twelve pieces were posted in the ruined orchard, eight in the ruined cornfield. The Fifty-seventh North Carolina kept guard in the direction of the Pughtown road, and Hoke and Smith were drawn up in the rear of Hays. It was late in the day; intensely hot, and the men suffering greatly from thirst. The twenty pieces opened on the blue earthworks crowning the hills in front. Harry Hays and the Louisianians moved forward, climbing the hill, through felled brushwood, to the assault. They took the height and six guns upon it. It overlooked and commanded the main works of the blue, and the grey brought up and trained the guns. But the hot night fell, and the soldiers lay on their arms till daybreak. When the dawn came, pink over the distant Blue Ridge, it was found that the Federals had evacuated all fortifications on this side of Winchester. Before the earth was well lit, scouts brought news that they were in retreat upon the Martinsburg Pike.

While on the thirteenth, Early advanced upon Winchester by the Valley Pike, Edward Johnson's division, Nounnan's cavalry going ahead, kept to the Front Royal and Winchester road. Two miles from the town they made a line of battle and began to skirmish. There was a blue battery upon the Millwood road, and to meet it Carpenter's guns were brought up. A dozen blue pieces upon this side of Winchester opened fire and for hours there went on a slow cannonade. On the morning of the fourteenth the division moved forward, the Stonewall leading, and renewed the skirmishing. In the afternoon they heard the roar of Early's guns.

The Fifth Virginia was thrown forward, across the Millwood road to the low hills fronting the town. The blue held in some strength the scrubby crest of this ridge. The Fifth had sharp skirmishing. Behind it came two companies of the Sixty-fifth, turned a little to the left, and began sharpshooting from a screen of pine and oak.

"Sergeant Maydew," said a captain, "take six men and go occupy that scrub-oak clump down there. Watch that ravine and pick them off if they come up it."

Billy Maydew and the six fairly filled the tuft of bushes halfway down the hill. "Jest as snug as a bug in a rug!"

"They'll get it hot if they come up that gully! It's a beautiful — what did Steve use to call it ? — 'avalanche'!"

"I kind of miss Steve. He had his uses. He'd keep up even a yaller dog's self-esteem. Even a turkey-buzzard could say, 'I am better than thou.' Every time I got down in the mouth and began to think of my sins I just looked at Steve and felt all right."

"Reckon the army'll ever get him again ? Reckon his sore foot'll ever get well ?"

"He'd better not come back to the Sixty-fifth," said Sergeant

Billy Maydew. He spoke with slow emphasis. "The day Steve Dagg comes back to the Sixty-fifth Billy Maydew air goin' to be marched to the guardhouse for killing a polecat."

The six smiled, smiled with grimness. "Ef you do it, Sergeant, reckon the Sixty-fifth, from the colonel down,'ll appear for you and swear you did a public service!"

Dave Maydew moved his head aside, then softly raised his rifle. The others did likewise. There was a pause so utter that they heard each other's breathing and the dry *Zrrrr!* of a distant grasshopper.

Dave lowered the rifle. "I see now! 'T wa'n't nothing but a squirrel."

"Reckon 't won't do to shoot him? Squirrel stew —"

"Don't you dar!" said Billy. "There air to be no firing out of this oak clump ex-cept upon the enemy."

The skirmish line of the Fifth swept past them, driving the blue. The fighting was now nearer town; they knew by the slight change in sound that there were houses and stone walls. The afternoon wore on, — hot, hot in the clump of bushes! Litter bearers came by, carrying a wounded officer. " Colonel of the Fifth — Colonel Williams. They came against our right! They've got ten of our men. But then did n't we drive them!"

Litter and bearers and escort went on. "Ain't anybody, less'n it's a crittur with fur, comin' up that ravine!"

"An old mooley cow might come up."

"Where'd she come from? They're all slaughtered and eaten. Nothing 's left of anything."

"That's right! Egypt and the locusts —"

"Lieutenant Coffin's signalling to rejoin. Reckon Sixty-fifth's going on, too!"

Forward! March!

Just before night the general commanding sent an order to Edward Johnson. "Move with three brigades by right flank to the Martinsburg Turnpike at a point above Winchester. If enemy evacuates, intercept his retreat. If he does not, attack him in his fortifications from that direction." Johnson started at once with Steuart's and Nicholls's brigades, and Dement's, Raines's, and Carpenter's batteries, Snowden Andrews commanding. Their way lay across country on a dark night, by the Jordan Springs road.

The objective was Stephenson's, several miles above Winchester, where a railroad cut hidden by heavy woods almost touched the Martinsburg Pike. Off marched Steuart and Nicholls and the artillery. The Stonewall Brigade, nearest to the enemy, was ordered to advance skirmishers to conceal the movement, and then to follow to Stephenson's. There was some delay in the receipt of the order. The Stonewall advanced its skirmishers, ascertained on this side the position of the enemy, but did not till midnight take the road by which the two brigades had gone.

It was a pitch black night after a hot and harassing day. The "foot cavalry" marched as Stonewall Jackson had taught it to march, but all country and all roads were now difficult, scarred, trenched, broken, and torn by war. This was like a dream road, barred, every rood, by dream obstacles. The Sixty-fifth sighed. It was too tired to make any other demonstration. In the hot, close night it was damp with perspiration. The road was deeply rutted and the drying mud had a knife-like edge. The shoes of the Sixty-fifth were so full of holes! The bruise from the chance stone, the cut of the dried mud helped at least in keeping the regiment awake. The Sixty-fifth's eyes were full of sleep: it would have loved — it would have loved to drop down in the darkness and float away — float away to Botetourt and Rockbridge and Bedford . . . float away — float away, just into nothingness!

Behind the Stonewall the sky began, very faintly, to pale. The native of the country who was guiding spoke briefly. "We're near the pike. Stephenson's not far on the other side." Down the dark line, shadows in the half light, rang an order like a ghostly echo. "Press forward, men! Press forward!" The "foot cavalry" made a sound in its throat, then did its best.

The east grew primrose, the rolling country took form. It was now a haggard country, seamed, burned over, and ruined, differing enough from what it once had been. There came a gleam of the Valley Pike, then with suddenness a heavy sound of firing. "They're attacking! They're attacking!" said the Stonewall. "Hurry up there! — hurry up — *Double-quick !*"

So thick was the fog that it was difficult to distinguish at any distance shape or feature. A mounted man appeared before the head of the column, all grey in grey mist. "It's Captain Douglas,

General, from General Johnson! The enemy's evacuating Winchester. We're holding the railroad cut over there, but they're in strength and threaten to flank us! Ammunition's almost out. Please come on as fast as you can!"

The Stonewall felt the Valley Pike beneath its feet. Through the fog, a little to the west of the road, they saw a body of troops moving rapidly. In the enveloping mist the colour could not be told. "Grey, are n't they? — Can you see the flag — ?" "No, but I think they're ours — Steuart or Nicholls . . ." "They're not Steuart and they are not Nicholls," said Thunder Run. "They're blue."

"It's the Yankee flanking body! . . . *Fire!*"

The dew-drenched hills and misty woods echoed the volley. It was answered by the blue, but somewhat scatteringly. The blue were in retreat, evacuating Winchester, moving toward the Potomac. They were willing to attack the grey regiments known to be holding the railroad cut, but a counter-attack upon their own rear and flank had not entered into their calculations. In the fog and in the smoke it could not be told whether it was one grey brigade or two or four. Soldiers, grey or blue, might be stanch enough, but in this, as in all wars, the cry, "We're flanked!" stirred up panic. The constitutionally timid, in either uniform, were always expecting to be flanked. They often cried wolf where there was no wolf. This morning certain of the blue cried it lustily. And here, indeed, was the wolf, grey, gaunt, and yelling! The blue, bent on flanking the two brigades and the artillery in and around the railroad cut, found themselves, in turn, flanked by the Stonewall Brigade. They were between Scylla and Charybdis, and they broke. There was a wood. They streamed toward it, and the Stonewall came, yelling, on their tracks. At the same moment at the railroad cut, Nicholls's Louisiana regiments, Dement's and Raines's and Carpenter's guns, came into touch with and routed the blue cavalry and infantry moving to the left. The cavalry — most of it — escaped, Milroy on a white horse with them. The infantry were taken prisoner. From the centre, where it, too, was victor, rose the jubilant yell of Steuart's brigade.

The Stonewall reached the rim of the wood. It was filled with purple, early light and with the forms of hurrying men. The charging line raised its muskets; the Stonewall's finger was on the trigger. Down an aisle of trees showed a white square, raised and shaken to and fro. Out of the violet light came a voice. "Don't fire! We surrender!"

Steuart and Nicholls and the Stonewall and the artillery took, above Winchester, twenty-three hundred prisoners with arms and equipments, one hundred and seventy-five horses, and eleven stands of colours. Back in Winchester and the surrounding fortifications there fell into Early's hands another thousand men in blue, other horses, twenty-five pieces of artillery, ammunition, and three hundred loaded wagons and stores. The remainder of Milroy's command, evacuating the town early in the night, had passed the danger-point on the Martinsburg Pike in safety. Now it was hurrying toward the Potomac, after it Jenkins's cavalry.

"Dear Dick Ewell" with his crutches, Jubal Early with his eccentricity, his profanity, his rough tongue, his large ability, and heroic devotion to the cause he served, behind them Hays and Gordon and Hoke and Smith, and all the exultant grey officers, and all the exultant grey men passed in the strengthening sunlight through happy Winchester. It was a scarred Winchester, a Winchester worn of raiment and thin of cheek, a Winchester that had wept of nights and in the daytime had watched, watched! *Sister Anne, Sister Anne, what do you see?* This June morning Winchester was happy beyond words.

Out on the Martinsburg Pike, Ewell and Early met Edward Johnson and his brigadiers. "Rodes is at Martinsburg. His courier got to us across country. He's taken the stores at Berryville and now at Martinsburg,—five pieces of artillery, two hundred prisoners, six thousand bushels of grain. The enemy's making for the river, Jenkins behind them. They'll cross at Williamsport. I've sent an order to General Rodes to press on to the Potomac. We'll rest the men for two hours and then we'll follow."

The next day, the fifteenth of June, Rodes crossed to Williamsport in Maryland, Jenkins going forward to Chambersburg. Jubal Early with his division took the Shepherdstown road, threatening, from that vicinity, Harper's Ferry. Edward Johnson and his division crossed at Shepherdstown and encamped near the field of Sharpsburg.

On the fifteenth, Longstreet and the First Corps left Culpeper, and marched along the eastern base of the Blue Ridge toward Ashby's

Gap. At the same time A. P. Hill and the Third Corps took the road for the Valley already traversed by Ewell and the Second. Stuart and the cavalry moved to cover Longstreet's front. Fighting Joe Hooker had left the Rappahannock, but he yet hovered in Virginia, on the south side of the Potomac.

June seventeenth, June nineteenth, June twenty-first saw the second tilt of this month between Pleasanton and Stuart, the running cavalry fight through the Loudoun Valley, between the spurs of the Bull Run Mountains, by Middleburg and the little town of Aldie. The tournament was a brilliant one, with charge and counter-charge, ambuscade, surprise, wheelings here and wheelings there, pourings from dark mountain passes, thundering dashes through villages quivering with excitement, fighting from the saddle, fighting dismounted, incursions of blue infantry and artillery, hairbreadth escapes, clank and din and roll of drum, dust cloud and smoke cloud, mad passage of red-nostrilled, riderless horses, appeal of trumpet, rally and charge. It was a three-days' fight to stir for many a year to come the blood of listening youth, but it was not a fortunate fight — not for the grey South! The honours of the joust itself were evenly enough divided. Stuart lost five hundred men, Pleasanton eight hundred. But before the trumpets rang *Halt!* the blue horsemen pushed the grey horsemen across the Loudoun Valley from Bull Run Mountains to Blue Ridge. In itself the position was well enough. Stuart, jocund as a summer morning, extricated with skill brigade after brigade, plunged with them into the dark passes, and, the fight drawn, presently marched on to the Potomac. But Pleasanton's patrols, winding upward, came out upon the crest of Blue Ridge. Here they reined in their horses and gazed, open-mouthed. Far below, travelling westward, travelling northward were troops on the roads of the great Valley — troops and troops and troops; infantry, artillery, cavalry, wagon trains and wagon trains. The vedettes stared. "The Confederacy's moving north! The Confederacy's moving north!" They turned their horses and went at speed back to Pleasanton. Pleasanton sent at speed to Fighting Joe Hooker. Hooker at once pushed north to the Potomac, which he crossed, on the twenty-fifth, at Edwards's Ferry.

CHAPTER X

THE BULLETIN

MISS LUCY opened the paper with trembling fingers. "'A great cavalry fight at Brandy Station! General Lee's telegram. Killed and wounded.'" Her three nieces came close to her. "It's not a long bulletin. . . . Thank God, there's no Cary!"

She brushed her hand across her eyes, and read on. "We have few particulars as yet. The fighting was severe and lasted all day. The loss on both sides is heavy. Our loss in officers was, as usual, very considerable. Among those killed we have heard the names of Colonel Hampton, brother of General Wade Hampton. Colonel John S. Green, of Rappahannock County, and Colonel Williams, of the Eighteenth North Carolina. The latter was married only one week ago. General W. H. F. Lee, son of General Lee, was shot through the thigh. Colonel Butler, of South Carolina, is reported to have lost a leg. From the meagre accounts we already have we are led to conclude that the fight of Tuesday was one of the heaviest cavalry battles that has occurred during the war, and perhaps the severest ever fought in this country."

Molly drew a long breath. "Let's turn the sheet, Aunt Lucy, and look for Vicksburg."

"A moment!" said Judith. "I saw the word 'artillery.' What does it say about the horse artillery?"

"Just that it made a brilliant fight. A few casualties — there are the names."

Judith bent over and read. "You always want to know about the horse artillery," said Molly. "I want to know about everybody, too, but until you've heard about the artillery your eyes are wide and startled as a fawn's. Is there somebody whom *you* like —"

"Don't, Molly!" spoke Miss Lucy. "Don't we all want to know about every arm? God knows, it is n't just our kith and kin for whom we ache!"

"Of course not!" said Molly. "I just wanted to know —"

Judith looked up, steady-eyed again. "So did I, Molly! I just
wanted to know. The paper says it was a brilliant fight, and everybody did well — those who've ridden on, and those who are lying
on the leaves in the woods. And it gives the names of those who are
lying there, and we don't know them — only that they are names of
our brothers. Vicksburg, read about Vicksburg, Aunt Lucy!"

Miss Lucy read. "We have received the Jackson *Mississippian* as
late as the twenty-seventh, since when there has been no reliable information from the besieged city. We have, however, from prisoners, Northern papers as late as June the first. We quote from them.

"'*Washington, June first. Midnight. Up to one o'clock to-night no
additional intelligence had been received from General Grant's army
later than the previous dispatches of the twenty-eighth, when it was stated
that Grant's forces were progressing as favourably as could be expected,
and Grant had no fears of the result.*'"

"Well, I hope that he may yet acquire them," said Unity.

"'*Chicago, June first. A special dispatch to the Times dated,* "*Headquarters in the Field. Near Vicksburg. May twenty-third,*" *says,* "*But
little has been effected during the last thirty-six hours. Over a hundred
pieces of field artillery and several siege guns rained shot and shell on
the rebels' works yesterday. The mortar fleet took position behind De
Soto Point and bombarded the city during the entire day.*"'"

"Oh," cried Molly. "Oh!"

"'*On the right General Sherman has pushed Steele's division squarely
to the foot of the parapets. Our men lay in a ditch and on the slope of a
parapet, inside one of the principal forts, unable to take it by storm, but
determined not to retire. The Federal and Rebel soldiers are not twenty-
five feet apart, but both are powerless to inflict much harm. Each
watches the other and dozens of muskets are fired as soon as a soldier
exposes himself above the works on either side —*'"

"Oh, I hope that Edward thinks of Désirée and all of us!"

"If there's need to expose himself he will do it — and Désirée
and none of us would say, 'Think of us!' — Go on, Aunt Lucy."

"'*Nearly the same condition of things exists in McPherson's front,
and his sharpshooters prevent the working of the enemy's pieces in one or
two forts. A charge was made yesterday (Friday) morning on one of
them by Stephenson's brigade, but was repulsed. Two companies of one
brigade got inside, but most of them were captured. The forts are all*

filled with infantry. Our artillery has dismounted a few guns and damaged the works in some places, but they are still strong —'"

"O may they stay so!"

"'General Joe Johnston is reported to be near the Big Black River in our rear, with reinforcements for the besieged army. General Grant can detail men enough for the operations here to keep Johnston in check.'"

"Oh, always their many, many troops!"

"'General McClernand was hard pressed on the left yesterday, and sent for reinforcements. General Quinby's division went to his assistance at four o'clock. The contest continued until one of our flags was planted at the foot of the earthworks on the outside of a rebel fort, and kept there for several hours, but the fort was not taken.'"

"Thank God!"

"'McClernand's loss yesterday is estimated at one thousand killed and wounded. The fighting grows more desperate each day. The transports are now bringing supplies to within three miles of our right.'"

The group on the Greenwood porch kept silence, then "What from Tennessee?"

"'A cavalry fight at Franklin. Infantry not engaged. A general battle is, however, considered imminent.'"

Molly put her head down in Judith's lap and began to cry. "Oh, I want to see father! Oh, I want to see father! Oh, I miss him so!"

Unity knit very fast. Miss Lucy sat, the paper fallen beside her, her fine, dark eyes on the distant mountains. She saw the old, peaceful, early-century years again, and her brothers and herself, children again, playing in the garden at Fontenoy, playing in the garden here at Greenwood, going into town in the great old coach, watching Mr. Jefferson pass and Mr. Madison. She saw her brilliant girlhood set still in so shining, so peaceful a world! . . . The old White and her ball-gowns, and the roses and serenading. . . . The leisurely progresses, too, from great house to great house, and all in a golden, tranquil world. She saw her beautiful father and mother and a certain lover whom she had had, and her brothers wonderful and gallant. And now the first three were dead, and long dead, and Warwick was with Lee at Culpeper, and Fauquier, yesterday in "the severest cavalry battle yet fought on this continent," and Warwick's son, Edward, fighting in a city besieged! Everywhere kinsmen and friends, fighting! And the gaunt and ruined country, the burning houses and the turned-out fields, the growing hunger, want no longer skulking, but walking all the highroads, care and wounds and sickness, a chill at all hearts and a lessening of the sunlight! "I have lived out of a gold world into an iron one," thought Miss Lucy.

The old Greenwood carriage came round to the door. Judith kissed Molly and rose, Unity with her. It was their day at the hospital. Isham took them into town, Isham thin and sorrowful, driving the old farm-horses, muttering and mumbling of old times and new. The day was hard at the hospital, though not so hard as there had been days. Soldiers from the Wilderness still choked the rooms, and there was sickness, sickness, sickness! — and so little with which to cope with sickness. But it was not so crowded as it had been, nor so desperate. Many had died, and many had grown well enough to go away, and many were convalescent. There were only fifty or so very bad. The two young women, straight and steady, bright and tender, came into a long ward like twin shafts of sunlight.

The ward wanted all the news about Brandy Station it could get, and all the news about Port Hudson and Vicksburg. Cavalry in the ward got into an argument with Artillery, and Infantry had to call the nurses to smooth things down. A man whose arm had been torn from the socket fell to crying softly because there was a piece of shell, he said, between the fingers and he could not get it out.

"'Nerve ends?' — Yes, Doctor, maybe so. . . . Then, don't you reckon the nerve ends in my arm out there in the Wilderness are feeling for my shoulder? Oh, I feel them feeling for it!"

Down the line was a jolly fellow and he sang very loudly —

> "Yankee Doodle had a mind
> To whip the Southern traitors,
> Because they did n't choose to live
> On codfish and potatoes!
> Yankee Doodle, doodle-doo,
> Yankee Doodle dandy —"

Some of the soldiers from the Wilderness, falling wounded in the brush which was set on fire, had been badly burned before their comrades could draw them forth. One of these now, lying wrapped

like a mummy in oil-soaked cotton, was begging pitifully for morphia — and there was no morphia to give.

> "I come from old Manassas with a pocket full of fun;
> I killed forty Yankees with a single-barrelled gun —"

Forenoon, afternoon passed. The nurses dressed and bandaged
wounds, bathed and lifted, gave the scanty dole of medicines,
brought and held the bowls of broth, aired the wards, straightened
the beds, told the news, filled the pipes, read and wrote the home
letters, took from dying lips the home messages, closed the eyes of
the dead, composed the limbs, saw the body carried out to where the
pine coffin waited, turned back with cheer to the ward, dealt the
cards for the convalescent, picked up the fallen checker-piece,
laughed at all jokes, helped sick and weary Life over many a hard
place in the road, saved it many a jolt.

At six o'clock, the two from Greenwood left the hospital. Outside they saw, on the other side of the street, a small crowd gathering
about a bulletin board. They went across as folk always went across
when there was seen to be a bulletin. The crowd was largely composed of country people, old men, women, and boys. It parted before the ladies from Greenwood and the two came close to the board.
A boy, standing on a great stone beneath, alternately mastered,
somewhat slowly, the writing, then, facing around, delivered it in a
high young voice to the crowd.

A farmer, bent and old, touched Judith's sleeve. "Miss Judith
Cary, you read it to us. I could do it spryer than Tom there, but my
eyes are mighty bad."

"I don't mind," said Tom. "They've got so many words that
were n't in the reading-books! You do it, Miss Judith."

Judith stepped upon the stone. The board held an account of the
battle of Brandy Station, later and fuller than that in the morning
paper. She read first — it was always read first — the names of
the killed and wounded. It appeared that this crowd had in them
only a general interest. There were murmurs respectful and pitying,
but no sudden sharp cry from a woman, no groan from a man.

"Further particulars of the fight," read Judith. "The enemy
attacked at daybreak. They had with them artillery with which
they proceeded furiously to shell General Stuart's headquarters.

The cavalry fighting was desperate and the loss on both sides heavy. We had only cavalry and the artillery in action, the enemy having retreated before our infantry arrived. The fight lasted all day and was conducted with extreme gallantry. Many individual acts of heroism occurred both among officers and men. The horse artillery gathered fresh laurels. The spirit of Pelham stays with it. A gunner named Deaderick —

"— A gunner named Deaderick, a strongly built man, held at bay a dozen of the enemy who would have laid hands upon his gun which had been dismounted by a shell striking the wheel. Almost singly he kept the rush back until his comrades could replace the gun, train, and serve it, when the attack was completely repulsed and the gun saved — "

Judith finished reading. The crowd thanked her. She stepped from the great stone and passed with Unity to where the carriage waited. Isham touched the old farm-horses; they passed out of the town into the June country bathed in sunset light.

For a while there was silence, then, "Judith," said Unity, "I am a talkative wretch, I know, but I can be silent as the grave when I want to be! Where is Richard? Is he in the horse artillery?"

"Yes."

"I have never seen you when I did not think you beautiful. But back there, standing on that stone, of a sudden you were most beautiful. It was like a star blazing out, a star with a voice, and something splendid in that, too. Judith, is he that gunner you were reading about?"

"Yes — oh, yes!"

"Well, you don't often cry," said Unity, crying herself. "Cry it out, my dear, cry it out. We have such splendid things nowadays to cry for!"

Judith dried her tears. "No, I don't often cry. . . . Let it rest, Unity, between us, silent, silent — "

That night, at Greenwood, she opened wide the windows of her room, till the moonlight flooded all the floor. She sat in the window seat, in the heart of the silver radiance, her hands clasped upon her knees, her head thrown back against the wood. Before her lay the silver hills; up to her came the breath of the garden lilies. She sat with wide, unseeing eyes; the mind exercising its own vision. It gazed upon the bivouac of the horse artillery; it saw the two days ago battle; and it saw to-morrow's march. It saw the moving guns, and heard the rumbling of them; saw the column of horse and heard the tread, marched side by side with that gunner of the horse artillery. Mists arose and blurred. There was a transition. Judith's mind left the South. It travelled under Northern skies; it sought out and entered Northern prisons. It saw Maury Stafford; saw him walking, walking, a stockaded yard, or standing, standing, before a barred window, looking out, looking up to the stars that shone over Virginia. . . . The prisons, the prisons, North and South, the prisons! Judith fell to shuddering. "O God — O God! Even our enemy — show him mercy!"

Off in the distance a whip-poor-will was calling. The sound was ineffably mournful; the whole night saddened and saddened. The odour of the lilies laid waxen fingers upon the heart. The high, bare sky was worse than a vault hung with clouds. The light wind came like the sigh of an overladen heart. Judith moved, sank forward on the window seat, and wept.

CHAPTER XI

PRISON X

THE stockade enclosed a half-acre of bare earth, trodden hard. The prison was a huge old brick building with a few narrow, grated windows. It had been built to store the inanimate, and now it was crowded with the animate. The inanimate made few demands save those of space and security. The animate might demand, but they did not receive. They had space — after all, each prisoner could move a very little way without jostling another prisoner — and they were kept securely. The gratings were thick, the guards were many, the stockade was high, and there was a Dead Line. As for other requests, for light and air and an approach to sanitation, for a little privacy, for less musty food and more of it, for better water, for utensils and bedding — the inanimate had made no such requests, and the animate requested in vain. What had been good enough for good Northern manufactured goods was good enough for Southern rebels. Everybody knew that Northern prisoners were starving, dying in Southern prisons. "'Exchange, then!' Well, I kind of wish myself that we'd exchange."

There were three floors in the prison, and a number of partitions had been driven across the large, echoing shell. Officers' quarters were the first floor, and officers' quarters were rudely divided into a hot, dark, evil-smelling central hall, and a number of hot, narrow, close, and poorly-lighted rooms in which to sleep and wake. Hall and rooms were hot because it was warm summer-time, and they were so crowded, and there was admitted so little air. In the winter-time they were cold, cold! The prisoners who had been here longest had tried both elements; in the winter-time they pined for summer and in the summer-time they longed for winter. This building was but one of several warehouses converted into places of storage for the animate. There were, in all, in this place, twelve hundred Confederate officers and six thousand Confederate privates.

Twilight was the worst time. Earlier there was all the sunshine that could enter the small windows, and once a day there was exercise in the small sunbaked yard. As soon as it was totally dark a few smoky lamps were lighted and for an hour there was "recreation" in the various central halls. But twilight — twilight was bad! It was the hopeless hour, the hour of home visions, the hour of longing, the hour of nostalgia. It was the hour when men could and did weep in shadowy places. The star that twinkled through the window mocked, and the breeze from the south mocked. The bats that wheeled above the prison yard were Despondency's imps. Melancholy had free entrance; she could and did pass the sentries. Hope deferred was always there. At twilight all hearts sickened.

With the smoky lamps came, on the part of most, — not of all, but of most, — a deliberate taking-up again of life, even of prison life. Heroism reëntered the weary prison. Courage and cheerfulness took the stage, the first a grim and steadfast warrior, the last falsetto enough at times, and then again suddenly, divinely genuine. At times there were brisk gaiety, unfeigned laughter, a quite rollicking joviality. Twilight was over — twilight was over for this time!

Supper was over, too, — soon over! A small cake of meal, more or less musty, a bit of "salt horse," — the meal was not prolonged. It was brought into the hall in a great kettle and sundry pans. The prisoners had each a tin plate, with an ancient knife and fork. There was no table; they sat on benches or old boxes, or tailor fashion on the floor. They had a way of pleasing their fancies with elaborate menus — like the Barmecide in the "Arabian Nights." Only the menus never, never materialized! To-night, in a mess of thirty, a colonel of A. P. Hill's, captured at Fredericksburg, laid out the table. "Mountain mutton, gentlemen, raised in Hampshire! Delicately broiled, served with watercress. No man must take less than two helpings! Brook trout, likewise, speckled beauties, taken this afternoon! There was a pool and a waterfall and some birch trees, and I went in swimming. Light rolls, gentlemen, and wheat muffins, and, I *think*, waffles! Coffee, gentlemen, — don't cheer! — Mocha, with sugar. The urn full and plenty more in the kitchen. Something green, gentlemen, — lettuce, I think, with cucumber and onion sliced thin and a little oil and vinegar. — Don't cheer! This mess has all the early vegetables and all the garden fruit it needs, and is *not* scorbutic! — Gentlemen, a dessert will follow — a little trifling jelly or cream, and I think a dish of raspberries."

The "salt horse" was eaten, the thin cake of old, old meal, the small and watery potato apiece. The mess arose. "For what we have received may one day the enemy be thankful! Amen!"

It was a festal night. They had a prison paper — *The Pen* — issued once a week. Foolscap paper was at a premium as was pen and ink. Therefore there was but one copy. It was read on Monday night by the gathering in division such and such a number. Tuesday night it passed to another division and another social hour. Wednesday night to another, and so on. The privates had their paper, too, and late in the week there were exchanges. This was Monday night and the hall of the editorial staff.

The smoky lamps burned dim in the close and heated air. At times these officers were able to secure tobacco for those who smoked, but more often not. This present week it was not, and the hall missed this disinfectant. There were a few long benches, a dozen stools, some boxes and barrels. Those who could not find seats sat on the floor, or lounged against the darkened walls. They had a table beneath one of the lamps, and a space was kept clear for the performers of the evening. There was to be a debate and other features.

The chairman of the evening arose. "Gentlemen, we will open as usual with Dixie —"

"I wish I was in de land of cotton,
    Old times dar am not forgotten!
        Look away, look away, look away, Dixie Land!
In Dixie Land, whar I was born in,
Early on one frosty morning,
        Look away, look away, look away, Dixie Land!
Den I wish I was in Dixie,
        Hooray, hooray!
In Dixie Land I'll take my stand,
To live an' die in Dixie!
    Away, away, away down South in Dixie;
    Away, away, away down South in Dixie —"

Two hundred men sang it loudly. Bearded, gaunt, unkempt, large-eyed, in unsoldierly rags, they stood and sang Dixie — sang it fiercely, with all their pent power, with all their wild longing. It rolled and echoed through the building; it seemed to beat with

violence at the walls, so that it might get out beneath the stars. It
died at last. The prisoners in Division 3 turned again to the chairman. "Gentlemen, the editors of *The Pen* crave your indulgence.
The latest news by grapevine and underground is just in! The
presses are working overtime in order that presently it may be
served to you hot —"

"The War is over!"

"We are to be exchanged!"

"England has declared —"

"We have met the enemy and he is ours!"

"We have received a consignment of tobacco."

"The rats have cried Hold, enough! A signal victory has been
achieved —"

"No; the bedbugs —"

"The commandant has been called up higher."

"Is — is it an exchange?"

The chairman put that hope out with prompt kindness. "No,
no, Captain! I wish it were. That would be the next best thing to
news of a big victory, wouldn't it! But, see, they approach! Way
for the noble editors! Way for *The Pen* that has — ahem! — swallowed the sword!"

The Junior Editor, having the biggest voice and being used to
commanding Partisan Rangers, was the chosen reader. He stood
forward. "Gentlemen, let me have your attention! — Can't that
lamp be turned up? — Thank you, Colonel!

THE PEN

Light (mental) and Liberty (To the Dead Line)

VOL. I.   No. 20.

PRISON X. JUNE —, 1863

IMPORTANT NEWS

Received by Grapevine, and confirmed by Fresh Fish

"General Lee is thought to be moving northward —"

"*Yaaaih! Yaaaaaihhh! Yaaaaih!*"

"He has certainly left the Rappahannock. Ewell has been observed moving toward the Valley, probably with the intention of falling on Milroy at Winchester —"

"*Yaaaihhhh! Yaaaaaihhh! —*"

"— and crossing the Potomac at Williamsport. Longstreet and A. P. Hill are in motion —"

"*Yaaaih!* Old Pete! *Yaaaih!* A. P. Hill!"

"If General Lee crosses the Potomac, surely all will be well. We trust in God that it's true."

"Amen," said the prisoners. "Amen, amen!"

The reader turned the page.

"Underground and Fresh Fish alike confirm our assurance that Vicksburg is NOT fallen! There is a rumour that provisions are becoming exhausted and that in Vicksburg, too, rats are speared. The Editors of THE PEN heartily wish that we might send a grape-vine to the beleaguered city, 'Nothing is, but only thinking makes it so.' Think of your rat in terms of grace and you will find him good as squirrel."

"The above items exhaust the news of the outer world. THE PEN turns to the world around which runs the Dead Line. Incense first to the Muses! Lieutenant Lamar, ——th Georgia, favours us as follows: —

"Oh, were I a boy in Georgia,
As now I am a man in Hell,
I would haste to the old school-house
With the ringing of the bell!

"Oh, were I a boy in Georgia
As now I am a man in jail,
To go to church on Sunday,
Be sure I would not fail!

"Oh, were I a boy in Georgia,
As now I am a man in chains,
I'd not take the eggs from the bird-nests,
Nor apples from old man Haines!

"Oh, were I a boy in Georgia,
As now I am a man in quod,
I'd be a better son to my mother,
Ere she lay beneath the sod!"

"In another vein Colonel Brown, ——th Kentucky, contributes: —

Air. *Within a mile of Edinboro' Town.*

" 'T was a mile within the Wilderness green,
   In the rosy time of the year;
Artillery boomed and the fight was keen,
   And many men found their bier.
         There Marse Robert, grey and great,
         Struck Joe Hooker, sure as fate!
The Yankee blenched and answering cried, 'No, no, it will not do!
I cannot, cannot, winnot, winnot, munnot lose this battle too!'

"Stonewall had a way of falling from the blue,
   From the blue and on the blue as well!
Their right he crumpled up and many he slew,
   And came on their centre like —!
         Stonewall Jackson, great and grey,
         Fought Joe Hooker on this day!
Yet Hooker, fighting, frowned and cried, 'No, no, it will not do!
I cannot, cannot, winnot, winnot, munnot lose this battle too!'

"Stuart shook his feather and hummed a merry tune,
   Then swung the A. N. V. with might!
He struck Joe Hooker the crown aboon,
   And put the blue army to flight!
         Oh, Jeb Stuart, blithe and gay,
         Beat Joe Hooker night and day!
And Hooker, fleeing, no more frowned and cried, 'No, no, it will not do!
I cannot, cannot, winnot, winnot, munnot lose this battle too!'"

"We pass from the service of the Muses to our editorial of the day. PUBLIC IMPROVEMENTS AND THE CONDITION OF TRADE WITH A GLANCE AT THE PREDICAMENT OF THE UNEMPLOYED."

The really able editorial was read at length. As it had the quality of being applicable as well as dogmatic, as indeed it accurately portrayed the conditions and beliefs of all present, it received full attention and unanimous applause.

The reader bowed his thanks. "Gentlemen, in all our career, we have been actuated by one sole ambition, and that ambition, gentlemen, was to become without any reservation, the Voice of the People! To-night that ambition is realized. We see that we are IT — and we thank you, gentlemen, — we thank you! We will now pass to the Standing Committees and their reports. On Finance; on Sick and Destitute; on State of the Church; on Public Education; on Cleanliness; on the Fine Arts; on Amusements —"

After reports of committees came a page of advertisements.

"A STITCH IN TIME SAVES NINE. — Bring your rips

and rents to Captains Carter and Davenport, Division 10. Entire satisfaction given. Charges moderate.

"INSTRUCTION IN ORATORY, and PARLOUR ACCOM-PLISHMENTS. Reginald De Launay, Division 13. I was once on the stage.

"INSTRUCTION ON THE BANJO. (First get your banjo.) John Paul, Lt. ——th Alabama, Division 24.

"A FIRST-CLASS LAUNDRY. No pains spared, only soap. Patronize us. You will never regret it. Taylor and Nelson, Northwest corner, Division 3, where you see the tub. No gentleman nowadays wears starched linen. One dislikes, too, a glaring white. And nobody likes a world too smooth. Our charges are moderate. We are Old Reliable.

"GUTTA-PERCHA RINGS, Ladies' Bracelets, Watch Chains, Walking-Sticks elaborately carved. Fancy Buttons. Just the things for mementoes of this summer-and-winter resort! Your lady-loves will prize them. Your grandchildren-to-be will treasure them. Call and look them over. Genuine bargains. Washington and Pinckney, Division 30, south side. Upper tier of bunks.

"HAVE YOUR HAIR CUT. It needs it. Barbering of all kinds done with expedition and neatness. We will shave you. We will shampoo you. Our terms are the most reasonable north of Mason and Dixon. Call and see our stock of Arabian perfumes. We are experimenting upon a substitute for soap. Smith and Smith, Division 33.

"COBBLE! COBBLE! COBBLE! Have your sole and uppers parted? Do you need a patch? Come and talk it over. We are amateurs, but we used to watch old Daddy Jim do it. We think we can help you. Our charges are not exorbitant. Porcher and Ravenel, Division 38.

"CIRCULATING LIBRARY. We are happy to inform the public that through the generosity of recent arrivals we have become possessed of another copy of 'Les Miserables,' by Victor Hugo. We have also 'Macaria,' by Miss Evans, Thackeray's 'Vanity Fair,' and Virgil's 'Æneid.' At the closing of the meeting the chairman of the Library Committee will be happy to take names of applicants in order.

"We pass to NOTICE OF DEATHS. We mourn the loss of

Brigadier-General —— ——. This gallant gentleman and soldier passed away yesterday in the prison hospital. A kinsman, detained in this division, was allowed to be with him at the last. General —— asked that the twenty-third psalm be read, and when it was done he lay quiet for a while, then raised himself slightly in his bunk. 'God save the South!' he said, and died. Major ——, ——th South Carolina, is dead. Adjutant ——, ——th Tennessee, is dead. Captain ——, ——th Virginia, is dead. Captain ——, ——th North Carolina, is dead. Lieutenant ——, ——th Virginia Cavalry, is dead. Lieutenant ——, ——th Mississippi, is dead. We hear from the men's side that very many of our comrades in the ranks are dead. So be it! *Dulce et decorum est pro patria mori.*"

There was a moment's pause in the reading. Resumed, *The Pen* took up the Continued Story, Instalment 5.

The Continued Story did not deal with war and war's alarms. The Continued Story was a story of domestic bliss. It was in the quietest vein; true love not too much crossed, marriage bells, home, a child, little details, a table set, flowers, robins singing, talk of a journey. Division 3, leaning forward, listened breathlessly. The instalment closed. "To be continued in our next." A sigh went through the hall.

The hour was almost up. The debate that was scheduled to follow *The Pen* had to be shortened. Even so, it took place, and so interesting was it that various blue guards and officials, drawn by echoes as of Demosthenes, came into the hall and made part of the audience. "WOMAN: HER PLACE IN CREATION. DOES IT EQUAL THAT OF MAN?"

The negative, in this time and place and audience, received scant sympathy. In vain the collegian who had somewhat doubtfully undertaken it, piled Ossa on Pelion, Aristotle on St. Paul, Rousseau on Martin Luther. That woman-famished audience received quotation and argument in stony disapproval. The affirmative soared over Ossa without brushing a pinion. Amid applause from grey and blue alike, the affirmative, somewhere now among the stars, was declared to have won.

The chairman of the evening rose. "Gentlemen, the hour is passed. May you rest well, and have pleasant dreams! To-morrow night the Musical Club will delight us. We extend to the gentlemen

of the North whom I see among us a cordial invitation to honour us
again. Good night — good night!"

Division 3 streamed beneath the smoky lamps out of the close
and dark hall into the dark and close rooms. In each of these were
tiers of bunks, none too wide. Each boasted one grated window
which let in a very little of the summer night. The doors clanged
behind the entering men; outside in the hall and at all exits the
sentries were posted. Within a few minutes the doors were opened
again. "Rounds!" Officer in blue, men in blue, swinging lantern,
vague breath of the outer world — the guardian group went through
each room, examining keenly the tiers of bunks each with its shadowy reclining or sitting inmate, lifting the lantern to peer into corners, shaking the window bars to see that there had been no filing.
Ten minutes, and with or without a gruff "good night!" rounds
were over.

A half hour passed, an hour passed. It was a dark night and
breathless. The stars that might be seen through the window, above
the stockade, showed like white-hot metal points stuck through a
heavy pall. Without the door of a room in which were packed
twenty officers sounded, passing, the tread of the sentry. The sound
died down the hall.

A man stepped lightly and quietly from his bunk. Another left
his as quietly, — another, — another. Those in the upper tier
swung themselves down, noiseless as cats. All twenty were out on the
floor. Whatever of clothing had been laid aside was resumed. Two
men took their places by the door, ear to the heavy panel. Two
watched at the window. All movement was made with the precision
of the drill-yard and in the quietude of the tomb. In the corner, near
the window, was a bunk in which had slept and waked a lieutenant
of nineteen, a light, thin, small-boned youngster. Now four men,
bending over, lifted noiselessly the boards upon which the lieutenant
had lain. Below, stretched smooth, stained and coloured like the
floor, was a bit of tarpaulin, obtained after God knows what skilful
manœuvring! The men turned this back. Beneath gaped a ragged
hole, a yard across, black and deep. Up came a colder air and an
earthy smell.

In this room Maury Stafford was the leader. With a whispered
word he put his hands on the edge of the excavation and swung him-

self down, dropping at last several feet to the floor of the tunnel. One by one the twenty followed, the four from door and window coming last. As best they could, these pulled the boards of the lieutenant's bunk in place over the entrance to that underground, which, with heart-stifling delays and dangers, they had digged. For months they had been digging — a hundred and odd men conspiring together, digging in the night-time, with infinite caution, with strange, inadequate tools, in darkness and silence and danger, a road to Freedom.

From either side of them came a tapping sound, three taps, one tap, four taps, one tap. They made the return signal. "*Trenck,*" said a low voice down the tunnel. "*Latude,*" answered one of the twenty. "All right!" came back the voice; "*Latude,* lead the way."

The men who replaced the boards had given a last backward look to the room and the window through which came the starlight. The slight and thin lieutenant was one of them. "I reckon even at home, in the four-poster in the best room, I'll dream for a while that there's a black, empty coal-mine below me! — *Shh!* — All right, sir."

There was a column moving through the tunnel, the tunnel into which from the several conspiring rooms there were openings, all masked, all concealed and guarded, one by this means, one by that, but alike with the infinite sharpened ingenuity of trapped creatures. The disposal of the earth that was burrowed out — genius had gone to that, genius and a patience incredible. Inch by inch the way had opened. There has been the measuring, too, the calculation of distance. . . . They must dig upward and out at some point beyond the stockade — not too far beyond; they could not afford to dig forever.

The tunnel was finished. To-night they were coming out, coming out somewhere beyond the stockade. There was a rugged gully, they knew, and then at a little distance, the river — the river that, on the other side, laved the Virginian shore. Let them but surprise, overpower whatever picket force might be stationed beyond the stockade, get to the river. . . . Trust them to swim the river!

They crept — a hundred and odd men — through the stifling passage. They could not stand upright. The sweat drenched their bodies, their hands were wet against the walls. The tunnel that they had been digging for ages had never appeared a short one; to-night it seemed to stretch across infinity. At last they reached the end, the upward slope and then the round chamber that they had made beyond — beyond the stockade! The head of the line had a bit of candle, hoarded against this moment. The spurt of the match caused a start throughout the stretched line, the pale flicker of the candle showed drawn faces.

They had two makeshift picks. How the iron had been obtained and the handles fashioned would make a long story. There had been a sifting of the stronger men to the front; now two of these, standing in the round chamber, raised and swung the picks and attacked the tunnel's roof. Earth fell with a hollow sound. The hearts of that company beat in response. They were all bowed in the tunnel; their faces gleamed with sweat; their gleaming hands trembled where they pressed them against the walls. The blows of the picks made music, music that agonized while it charmed. They saw the sky and the open country and the river mirroring the stars. They had not a firearm nor a sword among them, but a few had pocket-knives, and others jagged bits of sheet-iron, billets of wood, even sharpened stones. Now and then the line whispered, but it never spoke aloud. The two at the end of the tunnel gave the picks to another two; the iron swung, the earth fell. To the strained hearing of all it fell ever with a more hollow and thunderous sound. Moreover, the sense of space changed, and time likewise. They knew this very long and dark passage so well; every inch of it was familiar; had they not been digging it since the dawn of time? To-night it was luridly strange. Legions of drums beat in the brain, and there were flashes of colour before the eyes. The line was caught in a strange vein of Becoming, and what would Become no man knew. The hundred and odd hoped for the best, but surely all things were becoming portentous.

The two in the round chamber changed again — Maury Stafford now stood there with another. Rhythmically the picks struck the roof, rhythmically the earth fell. Since Sharpsburg of what had not Maury Stafford thought? The mind had tried to become and remain stoical, the mind had sickened, the mind had recovered; it had known the depths and the middle spaces and the blank wind-swept heights; the depths again, the middle spaces, the heights, and every point between. There had been changes in its structure. In its legions of warring elements some, long dominant, had taken a lower place; others were making good their claims to the thrones. He had been well-nigh a year in prison, and a year in prison counted five of earth. He had seen the minds of others dulled; all things sent to sleep except suffering and useless anger, or suffering and useless despondency. He, too, had known dulness for a time, but it had passed. There came in its place a certain lucidity, a certain hardness, and at the same time a widening. The prison bars held the physical man, but the wings of the inner man had broadened and they beat at vaster walls.

The picks struck, the earth fell. Behind him he heard the breathing of the men. He, too, was dizzy from exertion, from the air of the tunnel. As he worked he was saying over to himself, over and over, old lines that came into his head —

> "This ae night, this ae night,
> Every night and all.
> Fire and sleet and candlelight
> And Christ receive thy soul —"

The officer working with him uttered a low exclamation. "Look!"

Stafford looked, then turned his head. "Be ready, all of you! We're nearly through."

The earth fell, the rift widened. Down into the breathless tunnel, like wine to the exhausted, came a gust of night air. The long queue of waiting men quivered. The hole in the roof widened. . . . The workers were now working very cautiously, very quietly. Even in the dead of the night, even well beyond the stockade, even, as they hoped, in the bottom of the gully running down to the river, there might be wakeful ears. The workers made the least possible noise, the hundred and odd waiting prisoners made none at all. Crouched in silence they breathed the night air and the sweat dried upon them. . . . The hole in the roof became large enough to let a man through. Footholds had already been made along the side of the tunnel. The workers laid down their picks, mounted, and tried their weight upon the edges of the opening. The earth held. "Ready!" breathed Stafford. "McCarthy, you go first."

McCarthy drew himself up and out of the tunnel. "Now, Lamar!" Lamar followed. The queue moved a step forward. The third man had his hands on the edge of the hole. McCarthy's form appeared above, blocking the starlight, McCarthy's face down bent, waxen as the almost burned-out taper which threw against it a little quivering light. McCarthy's whisper came down. "O my God, my God! We turned and dug obliquely. . . . We're still inside the stockade!"

There sounded the discharge of a sentry's piece, followed by a hallooing and the noise of running feet.

CHAPTER XII

THE SIEGE

EIGHT gunboats held the river in front of, above, and below the doomed town. Under the leafy Louisiana shore the blue placed seven mortars. These kept up a steady fire upon the city and the river defences. At intervals the gunboats engaged the lower batteries. There was an abandoned line of works which was seized upon by a cloud of blue sharpshooters. These began to pick off men at the grey guns, and traverses had to be built against them. The grey had in the river batteries thirty-one siege guns, and a few pieces of light artillery. Even of these they had eventually to spare guns for the land defences.

At dawn of the twenty-seventh of May began the engagement in which the Cincinnati was sunk. She had fourteen guns, and she opened furiously upon the upper batteries while four gunboats handled the lower. But the upper batteries sunk her; she went down not far from the shore in water that did not quite cover her decks. Her loss was heavy, from the grey shells and from the grey sharpshooters who picked off her men at the portholes. Night after night blue craft gathered around her, trying to take away the fourteen guns, but night after night the upper batteries drove them away. She stayed there, the Cincinnati, heavy and mournful in the smoke-shrouded river. And day after day, and week after week, the seven mortars and all the gunboats launched their thunders against the water batteries and the town beyond.

Three fourths of a rough circle ran the landward defences. There were exterior ditches, eight and ten feet deep, with provision for the infantry, with embrasures and platforms for artillery. Before them were thrown abatis, palisades, entanglements of picket and telegraph wire. The ground was all ridge and hollow; redan and redoubt and lunette occupied the commanding points, and between them ran the rifle-pits. There was much digging yet to be done, and few men and no great supply of entrenching tools with which to do it.

Night after night fatigue parties were busy. Behind all the salients they made inner lines for time of need; they built traverses against enfilading fires. So fast did the blue sharpshooters pick off officers and men, as they passed from the works to the camps in the rear, that very soon the grey were forced to contrive covered ways. Through the hot nights laboured already wearied men. The five hundred picks and shovels were shared among the troops. Where they gave out, wooden shovels were contrived and bayonets were used as picks. In the night-time the damage of the day must be somehow repaired. The damage of each day was very great.

The centre of the Confederate line, from the Jackson railroad to the Graveyard road, was held by Forney's division. General Martin Luther Smith held from the Graveyard road to the river on the north, and made the left. Carter L. Stevenson's division held from the railroad to the Warrenton road and the river south, and formed the right. Behind Forney lay in reserve Bowen with his Missourians and Waul's Texas Legion. Counting the three thousand and more in hospital, there were twenty-eight thousand men defending Vicksburg. They were all needed. Thrice the number would have found work to do.

Outside the Confederate line ran the Federal line of investment. At the beginning of the siege the two lines were some hundreds of yards apart; as the siege went on the blue drew nearer, nearer. They drew so near at last that, at night, the grey and blue pickets conversed, so near that at places the several ramparts all but touched. Forty-three thousand had Grant at the formal opening of the siege; steadily as it progressed he brought across the river other thousands. By the middle of June he had seventy-five thousand, besides the fleet upon the river. Ninth Army Corps, Thirteenth Army Corps, Fifteenth, Sixteenth, Seventeenth Army Corps, — Grant drew his forces and to spare around the town and its all too meagre defences, its one hundred and two guns and small store of ammunition and its twenty-eight thousand combatants, three thousand of whom were in hospital. Besides the guns of the fleet, there were now two hundred and twenty blue guns in position. They never lacked for ammunition. Seven miles, from the river north of the town to the river south, ran the Confederate lines. Fifteen miles, from Haines's Bluff to Warrenton, enclosing the Confederate, ran the Federal lines.

Grant was strongly posted. He had wide, sheltered hollows in which
to mass his men, and commanding ridge-tops on which to place his
guns. His far-flung position was strong for offence, and equally
strong, in case of an attack from without, for defence. All day and
every day thundered the Federal artillery. All day and every day
the grey lines and the grey town knew the rain of shells. Very early
in the siege the blue prepared to mine.

At Jackson, fifty miles to the east, was Joseph E. Johnston, slowly
gathering troops. At the last and best he had only twenty-four
thousand troops. Between him and the beleaguered place lay an
army of seventy-five thousand men, strongly posted, and strong —
where the grey were weakest — in artillery; with, also, a blue
fleet in the background. At long intervals Pemberton got out a
messenger to him; at long intervals one of his own got into
Vicksburg.

Within all these lines Vicksburg herself crouched and waited.
All her people who might dwelled now in caves. They came out in
the night or during the infrequent silences of the day and returned
to the houses that were not injured. They grew careless about exposure, or rather they grew fatalistic after the manner of courageous,
besieged places. They passed through the streets even when the
shells were raining, or they wandered out toward the lines, or they
sat under some already splintered tree and counted the gunboats
on the dusky river. Courage stayed with them, and even at times
gaiety, though she had a hectic cheek.

On the twenty-second of May the town rocked under the first assault. Four ironclads and a wooden gunboat — thirty-two guns —
opened upon the river batteries. From the land the artillery began
as well, a great force of artillery sending shot and shell against the
Confederate centre and right and into the town beyond. At one
o'clock came the first of three Federal charges, directed against
the line of Stephen D. Lee. The assault was desperate, the repulse
as determined. The grey guns did not spare to-day grape and canister. The grey musketry poured from the trenches volley after volley
in the face of the foe. A blue storming party, Illinois and Ohio and
Missouri, charged a redoubt in which the cannon had made a breach.
They crossed the ditch, they mounted the earthen wall, they fixed
two flags upon the parapet. They hurrahed in triumph. This angle

was uncommanded by any grey work. The flags could be dislodged only by a countercharge and hand-to-hand fighting. Volunteers were called for, and there went a band of Waul's Texans, led by Colonel Pettus of the Twentieth Alabama. The blue artillery opened upon them; there fell a fearful hail. The bullets of the sharpshooters, too, came against them like bees armed each with a mortal sting. The grey rushed on. They dislodged the blue from the fort, then fought them in the ditch below. They used shells like hand grenades, flinging them from the rampart. They took the flags, waved them on high, then sent them back to their colonel, who sent them to Stephen Lee. They beat back the blue storming party. . . . The grey beat back the whole wide, three blue charges, hurled them back upon their lines like torn waves from an iron coast. When dusk came and sullenly the firing ceased, the Federal dead and wounded lay thick, thick, up and down before the Confederate line, by ditch and wall, — perhaps two thousand dead and wounded. In the night-time some were taken away, but very, very many were left. The weather was deadly hot.

Dead and wounded lay there so long that it became frightful. The grey did not love the crying on their front, the gasping voices, the faint, dry, *Water! Water! Water!* — dry and shrill like insects in the grass. The dead became offensive, horrible. The grey sent a flag of truce: General Pemberton's request to General Grant that hostilities be suspended for several hours while the Federal dead were buried and the wounded relieved. It was then the twenty-fifth. Grant, his cigar between his teeth, sitting before his tent out near the Graveyard road, nodded assent. All that afternoon they buried the dead, and removed the yet living. A thunder-shower came down and did something to wash away the stains. In the silence and respite from the shells, Vicksburg left its caves and hurried through trampled gardens back to the homes it loved. Here and there was ruin. The shell might have exploded in the porch, bearing down the white pillars, or in the parlour, shivering the mirrors and the crystal chandeliers, or upon the stair, or in a bedroom. Here and there was wholly ruin. A gaunt framework lifted itself among the roses, or the white magnolias stared at a heap of charred timbers. . . . The truce lasted less than three hours.

There was one cave quite out of town, quite near the lines. It belonged to an old country-house with a fair garden, and it was digged at the time of the bombardment the past summer. Now the house had been burned and the people occupying it had gone into the crowded town. The cave stood empty. It had been made in the side of a tall, vine-draped bank. Dark cedars with heavy and twisted roots overhung it, and on either side there was ivy and honeysuckle. It was a large cave, clean and dry. The family that had moved away had left within it a low bed and a small old dressing-table and other furniture and a little china and tinware. At no great distance trickled and gurgled the spring belonging to the house. One heard it in the night-time, but all day long it was lost in the thunder. Désirée went to it for water only after dark.

The house which had given her refuge had been one of the first demolished. She looked at all the warrens that had been dug in the earth, and then, one rosy evening, she walked out toward the lines. She took the direction of the redan where Edward was stationed, and just on the townward side of the line of sentries she found this ruined house in its ruined garden and the empty cave. The next day in she moved.

Lieutenant Edward Cary got her message, brought him by his commanding officer. "Cary, I was riding by the ruined house, and a very beautiful woman came out of a cave in the hill and said she was your wife, and that she was making her home there, and would you come to Cape Jessamine when you could."

It was two days before he could go to Cape Jessamine. The evening of the truce he went, through the great fresh coolness after the storm. There was yet in the sky a dark blur of cloud with a sweep below it of ragged, crêpe-like filaments, but the lightning and thunder had ceased and the rain was over. Moist fragrance rose from the desolated garden. After all the heat and turmoil there was a silence that seemed divine. Just by the mouth of the cave, half buried in the trailing ivy, Désirée had placed a bench. Here, the first rapture of meeting over, they sat in the evening light, the storm rolling away, an odour coming to them of mignonette.

He gathered her hands in his. "Désirée Gaillard, this is no place for you! They are driving an approach to the redan and are massing guns against it. The shells will fall in this garden. Go back to the town!"

"No; I will not. I like this better."

"The point is that you may be killed."

"No, I will not be. The shells fall, too, in the town. I will be careful."

"Dear heart, I mean it."

"Dear heart, I mean it, too. The danger is not greater than it is in town. Yesterday there a child's arm was torn away."

"Oh —"

"Yes. . . . It is so frightful. And they are burying the dead out there. A soldier told me."

"Yes. . . . How still it seems! And the mignonette . . ."

"It is as still as was the garden at Cape Jessamine. Look how the clouds are drifting by. . . ."

"Désirée, I brought you into the country of Danger. If you had gone to the Fusilier place —"

"I should be dead by now. The country of Danger is a happy country to-night. I fear it no more than you. Indeed, I love it — since you are here. We are not children travelling, you and I. Look at the light trembling up from the west!"

"That night upon the levee. . . . You were the heart of the red light. Now you sit here, heart of the gold light. . . . I love you."

"I love you."

The clouds drifted away, the sun went down clear. The evening star was shining like a silver lamp when the two unlocked their arms, kissed, and rose. All the ruined garden was filled with fireflies, and there stole upward the odour of the mignonette. She went with him to the fallen old brick gateposts. There they embraced and parted. Going down toward the trenches he looked back and saw her standing, the fireflies about her like stars, behind her tall shadowy trees, and, like a hieroglyphic against the sky, the charred rafters of the ruined house.

At dawn the cannonading began anew and lasted all day. Musketry, too, volleyed and rolled. The Federal ammunition never lacked, but the grey were in no position to spend with freedom. Every ridge of the besieging line belched saffron flame, thick smoke, and thunder; every point of vantage sent its stream of minies, horribly singing. On this day the blue began sap after sap. In the night-time the grey sent a detachment from Stevenson's right out upon the river flats, their errand the constructing of an abatis against a possible blue approach that way. A Federal party came against them and there was a bitter skirmish. The gunboats, excitedly waking, thrust a duel upon the river batteries. The night flamed and roared. The grey won out upon the flats and returned with a hundred prisoners. The morning saw the river fight and the sinking of the Cincinnati.

May shook and thundered toward its sulphurous close. The twenty-ninth, thirtieth, and thirty-first were marked by a continuous, frightful bombardment. By now the blue parallels were close, close to every main grey work. They were very close, indeed, to the Third Louisiana Redan. All night the grey engineers and their haggard men dug, dug to repair the daytime breaches, to make inner lines. On the first day of June fire broke out in the town. There threatened a general conflagration, but soldiers and civilians conquered the flames before there was disaster irretrievable. The weather was deadly hot. Fever became epidemic.

There arrived a question of musket caps. Imperatively needed, they must be had. If it were possible for a few daring men to get down the river and across, behind the enemy, to Jackson, General Johnston would send the caps. There were volunteers. Captain Saunders, Lamar Fontaine, a courier named Walker, were the first chosen; later, a noted scout and Lieutenant Edward Cary. At midnight they drifted down the river on logs. The battery under whose shadow they had set out listened for a shout, looked for a leaping flame from some one of the gunboats they must pass. But the gunboats lay silent. There was always driftwood upon the rushing river.

At dawn the mortars on the Louisiana side began to shell the batteries and the town beyond. Later the gunboats took a hand. Six days in succession this bombardment opened with the first light in the east and closed with the latest in the west. Vicksburg lost the last semblance of old times. The bombs ripped houses open as they ripped bodies. The blue began to drive double saps against the principal redans. The grey began to countermine. All the torn, sunbaked line knew that from now on it would stand over volcanoes.

Désirée went into the town and to the hospitals, but when she found there were nurses enough she was glad — though, had there been need, she like all the rest would have worked there until she dropped.

At the door of one of the hospitals she spoke to a surgeon. "There is no yellow fever?"

"No, thank God! Not yet. — I'll strike on wood."

They watched a shell burst in the air above an empty garden. "Well, if they'd only keep that spot for a target! But they won't. . . . When we stopped counting a week ago the hospitals had been struck twenty-one times. It's hard on wounded men to be rewounded. — There's another!"

The shell ploughed a trench across the street, burst against the corner of a brick wall, and brought it down in ruin.

"You can't blame them for getting unnerved, lying there and listening," pursued the surgeon. "Then they don't get well quickly and conditions are unfavourable for amputations and operations. And I've never seen worse wounds than we're getting in this siege. — There's another!"

Désirée went on to a row of caves in a parched hillside. Here were certain of her old friends, and here was a kind of central storeroom from which she with others drew her slender rations. The basket which she had brought she partly filled, then sat upon a stone and asked and answered questions. It was not for long; she was not happy away from Cape Jessamine. They begged her to stay; they represented that a moderate risk was all right, — they ran it here, — but that so near the lines she was in actual danger. She laughed with her beautiful eyes and went her way.

A little farther down the line she paused for a moment beside a young woman in black sitting in the cave mouth, a slate and pencil on her knee and beside her a boy and girl. "You are keeping school, Miss Lily?"

"It isn't exactly school," said Miss Lily, "but one must entertain the children. It is hard on them being penned up like this."

"We're drawing funny pictures," explained the boy. "This is General Grant."

"And this," chimed in the girl, "is General Sherman! Doesn't he look fierce?"

"And this is Yankee Doodle! Look at his feather — all over the slate!"

Miss Lily leaned a little forward, her thin hands clasped about her knees, her luminous dark eyes upon the murky sky. She had a voice of liquid sweetness, all shot with little lights and shadows. "I had such a vivid dream last night. I thought that suddenly all the shells, instead of coming this way, were going that way, and somebody said it would be because General Johnston was coming with a great army and that the enemy's cannon were turned against them. All the sky grew clear red instead of blue, and in it I saw the army coming. It was like the pictures of the Judgment Day. And the flag was in front, and there were clouds and thunders. *And the enemy was swept off the face of the earth.*" She sighed. "And then I woke up, and the shells were coming this way."

"I dreamed, too," said the little girl; "I dreamed about Christmas."

Désirée went back to Cape Jessamine. On the way she walked for a while beside an old negro woman. "Yass, 'm, yass, 'm! De debbil am rainin' fire an' brimstone! En now ef de Lawd 'd only send de manna an' de quails!"

"Are you hungry?" asked Désirée. "You look hungry."

"Well, 'm, dar wuz de chillern. I done hab my ration en dey done hab theirs, but de Lawd Jesus knows growin' chillern need *six* rations! I could n't give 'em six, but I giv 'em mine. — I ben lookin' at de berries in de patch ober dar, but Lawd! de bloom ain't much moh'n fallen!"

Désirée uncovered the basket and shared with her her loaf of bread. The other took it with glistening eyes and profuse thanks. They parted, and Désirée went on to the cave below the cedars in the ruined garden. The day was hot, hot! and the air was thick, and there was always smell of burned powder, and dull, continual noise. But the cave itself was dark and cool. She had drawn the ivy so that it fell like a curtain across the entrance. She drank a cup of water, ate a piece of bread, then lay down upon her pallet. She lay very straight, her hands clasped upon her breast, her dark eyes fixed upon the veil of ivy. The light came in, cool and green like emerald water. The booming of the cannon grew rhythmic like great waves against a cliff. *Edward! Edward!* They beat in her brain — *Edward! Edward!*

She knew that he was gone with the others for the musket caps. Day by day soldiers in numbers passed her garden. She had come to know the faces of many and had made friends with them. Sometimes they asked for water. Sometimes the wounded rested here. An officer, mortally wounded, had been laid upon this pallet and had died here, upheld for the last labouring breath in her arms. The colonel commanding the troops in the redan and trenches at this point stopped occasionally in coming or going. He was a chivalrous, grey-mustached hero who paid her compliments three-piled. It was he who told her of the volunteers for dangerous service, but it was a smoke-grimed, tattered private who brought her a line from Edward, pencilled just at starting. . . . Five days ago.

She lay perfectly still, breathing lightly but deeply. Her mind, like a bird, flew now into this landscape, now into that. Cape Jessamine — Cape Jessamine — and the river rolling over what had been home and life. Her room — the river rolling over her room — the balcony with the yellow rose and the silken dresses in the carved wardrobe. . . . She was in New Orleans. — Mardigras — Rex passing — Louis as Rex — flowers down raining. All the masks — the ball. . . . France — an old house in Southern France with poplars and a still stream. . . . Her eyelids closed. Green water falling, and the cypresses of Cape Jessamine. . . . She turned on her side — *Edward! Edward!*

The great waves continued to break against the cliffs, then arose a deafening crash as of down-ruining land. Désirée sprang to her feet and went and pushed aside the ivy. Thick smoke hung over a salient some distance to the right; she saw men running. Though she had never seen a mine exploded, she knew it for what it was. She watched the thickest of the smoke lift and drift aside, she saw that the flag still waved from the salient and she gathered from the steadiness of the world in general and the rhythmic pursuance of the cannonading that the mine had not been large, or had failed of its full intent. She knew, however, that in the salient there had been moments of destruction and anguish.

Sleep was driven from her eyes. She sat down upon the bench without the door. It was the blazing afternoon. She saw the air upquivering from the baked earth, the ruined wall. The neglected garden looked dead with sultriness. Beyond, in the heat, she saw the camps, tents, huts of dried boughs, small wooden structures. From them to the front ran strange geometric lines that were the covered ways. She saw the sentries, small, metallic-looking figures. Then came trenches, breastworks, redan. Smoke was over them, but here and there it gave and let through the red points of flags, or a vision of soldiers. The horizon all around stood a wall of murk torn by red flashes. That the air rocked with sound was now a matter of course. The ear was accustomed to it, as to the roar of a familiar cataract, or as mechanics and mill-hands might be to the roar of machinery. Distracting sound ceased to be distracting. The attention went where it was needed, as in the silence of the desert. Désirée sat with her hands in her lap, staring into the heat and light. She sat with a certain look of the Sphinx, accepting the spectator's place, since the ages had fixed her there, and yet with a dim and inner query that raised the corners of her lips.

A squad of soldiers came by, paused and asked if they might get water. When they came back from the spring she stopped them with her eyes.

"Did the mine do much harm?"

"No, 'm, mighty little, considering. It hurt a dozen men and gave us some digging and mending to do to-night. Good for us, I reckon! We all are so awful lazy — serving only twenty out of twenty-four hours!"

"Yes," said Désirée. "I've observed how lazy you are. There never were soldiers who did better than you are doing. — Is there any news?"

"They've got their sap rollers within a hundred feet of us. I've got an idea that I'm going to give the captain. If you'd soak wads of cotton in turpentine, and wrap them in pieces of match and fire them from an old large-bore gun into them rollers, you might burn the darned things up!"

"Two of the men who went after caps got in at dawn this morning."

"Two — ?"

"Yes, 'm. Captain Saunders and Walker. They brought two hundred thousand caps between them. They had a lively time getting out, and a livelier getting in."

"The others — ?"

"They have n't been heard from. It was n't an easy job! I reckon if we get two back — and that many caps — it's as good as we could expect."

The day declined. The sun went down like a red cannon ball. The cannonading ceased; the minies ceased. Slowly the smoke drifted away and let the stars be seen. The silence after sound oppressed, oppressed! Désirée sat still upon the bench. The moon rose, round and white, mounted and made the world spectral. At last she stood up. She raised and opened her arms, then closed them on each other and wrung her hands. Then she went out of the night without to that within the cave. The moon came strongly in. When, presently, she lay down upon the pallet, she drew her eyes and forehead out of the pool of silver. *Edward! Edward!*

Between the dead night and the first dawn, an hour before the sharpshooters would begin, she suddenly sat up, then rose to her feet. The moonlight was gone from the floor; there was only the unearthly hush and ebb of the hour. She moved to the entrance, pushed aside the ivy, and stood with held breath. Though she could not see him, she knew when he turned in at the ruined gate. A moment and his voice was in her ears. "Désirée!" — another, and they were clasped in each other's arms. "I got in an hour ago — with the caps. I have till dawn."

Throughout the seventh and eighth of June the firing from the mortars was very heavy and the Federal digging, digging continued. The grey private's device was adopted and a number of sap rollers were set afire and destroyed, exposing the sappers behind and compelling fresh beginnings. On the Jackson road, before Hébert's lines, the blue were using for screen cotton bales piled high upon a flatcar. This shield also was fired by musket balls wrapped in turpentine and tow. Bales and car went up in flames. The grey began new rifle-pits, and in the redans they collected thundering barrels and loaded shells. There was a feeling of impending assault. Now, too, began night sallies — Federal attacks upon the picket lines, Confederate repulses. Sentinel duty, heavy from the first, grew ever more heavy. Men fought during the day, and the same men watched at night. Day and night the trenches must be manned. The lines were long, and by now there were barely eighteen thousand grey effectives. They lived perforce in the trenches; they had no relief from the narrow ditches. The sun of a Southern June blistered and baked; then came torrential rains and soaked all things; then the sun shone again and the heavens became an inverted bowl of brass. On the twelfth of June the troops were put on half-rations; a little later, these, too, were reduced. The water grew low and very impure. There were so many dead bodies — men and animals. Fever appeared in every main work, and in every trench. Men lifted their muskets with shaking hands.

CHAPTER XIII

ACROSS THE POTOMAC

O N the thirteenth of June, Ewell and the Second Corps forded
the Potomac.

> "Come! 'T is the red dawn of the day,
> Maryland!"

sang the men.

> "Come with thy panoplied array,
> Maryland! . . .
> Come, for thy shield is bright and strong,
> Maryland!
> Come, for thy dalliance does thee wrong,
> Maryland! . . ."

From the thirteenth to the twenty-first they bivouacked on and
near the battle-field of Sharpsburg. By now they were used to
revisiting battle-fields. Kernstown — Manassas — many another
stricken field; they knew them once, they knew them twice, they
knew them times again! On the twenty-first, Ewell had orders from
Lee to march northward into Pennsylvania, then eastwardly upon
Harrisburg on the Susquehanna. "Old Dick" broke camp at dawn
of the twenty-second.

South of the Potomac waited Lee with the First and Third Corps.
He waited watching "Fighting Joe Hooker," willing to give him
battle in Virginia if he so elected. On the twentieth he sent a dispatch from Berryville to Richmond, to Mr. Davis.

MR. PRESIDENT: — I have the honour to report, for the information of your Excellency, that General Imboden has destroyed the
bridges on the Baltimore and Ohio Railroad over Evarts's Creek,
near Cumberland; the long bridge across the Chesapeake and Ohio
Canal below Cumberland; the iron bridge across the North Branch
of the Potomac, with the wooden trestle adjoining it; the double-
span bridge across the mouth of Patterson's Creek; the Fink's

patent iron bridge across the mouth of the South Branch of the Potomac, three spans of 133 1-3 feet each, and the wooden bridge over Little Cacapon.

All the depots, water tanks, and engines between the Little Cacapon and the Cumberland are also destroyed, with the block-houses at the mouth of the South Branch and Patterson's Creek.

The Chesapeake and Ohio Canal, about two miles above Old Town, where the embankment is about forty feet high, has been cut, and General Imboden reports that when he left it the entire embankment for about fifty yards had been swept away.

A similar crevasse with like results was also made in the canal about four miles from Old Town.

Lieutenant-Colonel White, of the cavalry, has also cut the Baltimore and Ohio Railroad, east of the Point of Rocks.

General Milroy has abandoned the south side of the Potomac, occupying Harper's Ferry with a picket, and holds the Maryland Heights with about eight thousand men.

General Ewell's corps is north of the Potomac, occupying Sharpsburg, Boonsborough, and Hagerstown. His advance cavalry is at Chambersburg, Pennsylvania.

The First Division of General A. P. Hill's corps will reach this vicinity to-day; the rest follow.

General Longstreet's corps with Stuart's cavalry still occupy the Blue Ridge between the roads leading through Ashby's and Snicker's Gaps, holding in check a large force of the enemy, consisting of cavalry, infantry, and artillery.

The movement of the main body of the enemy is still toward the Potomac, but its real destination is not yet discovered. . . .

If any of the brigades that I have left behind for the protection of Richmond can, in your opinion, be spared, I should like them to be sent to me.

I am, with great respect, your obedient servant,

R. E. LEE, General.

Several days later, Ewell being now so advanced that support for him was absolutely necessary, Longstreet was withdrawn from the edge of the Blue Ridge. With the First Corps he crossed the Potomac at Williamsport. A. P. Hill and the Third followed, crossing at

Shepherdstown. At Hagerstown the two corps united and the resulting column moved northward into Pennsylvania.

Now Jeb Stuart's only fault was that he too dearly loved a raid. He applied to Lee for permission to take three brigades, thread the Bull Run Mountains, attain the enemy's rear, pass between his main body and Washington and so cross into Maryland, joining the army somewhere north of the Potomac. Now Lee's only fault was an occasional too gracious complaisance, a too moderate estimate of his own judgment, a willingness to try for what they were worth the suggestions of subordinates. With entire justice he loved and trusted Stuart and admired his great abilities. He permitted the deflection of the cavalry — only the cavalry must keep him cognizant of every move of the enemy. If Hooker finally crossed the Potomac, he must know it at once, and at once Stuart must fall in upon the right of the grey army of invasion.

Ewell at Sharpsburg broke camp at dawn of the twenty-second. Followed a week of, on the whole, tranquil progress. "Old Dick's" marches were masterly done. Reveille sounded at dawn. An hour later the troops were on the road. Unhurrying and undelayed, they made each day a good march and bivouacked with the setting sun.

How fair seemed the rich Pennsylvania countryside! The Valley of Virginia had worn that aspect before the war. It, too, had had yellow wheat-fields and orchards and turning mill wheels. It, too, had had good brick country-houses and great barns and peaceful towns and roads that were mended when they were worn. It, too, had had fences and walls and care. It had had cattle in lush meadows. "Land of Goshen!" said Ewell's soldiers. "To think we were like this once!"

"Well, we will be again."

"Listen to old Cheerfulness! And yet I reckon he's right, I reckon he's right, I reckon he's right!"

"Of course he's right! I couldn't be low-spirited if I tried. *Hallelujah!*"

The Second Corps did not try. No more did the First nor the Third. The Army of Northern Virginia *was* in good spirits. Behind it lay some weeks of rest and recuperation; behind that the victory of the Wilderness. Worn and inadequate enough as it was, yet this army's equipment was better to-day than it had been. It had the spoils of great battle-fields. Artillery was notably bettered; cavalry was fit and fine; infantry a seasoned veteran who thought of a time without war as of some remote golden age. The Army of Northern Virginia was now organized as it had not been organized before for efficiency. It numbered between sixty and seventy thousand men. It had able major- and lieutenant-generals and a very great commanding general. It was veteran, eager for action, confident, with victories behind it. There was something lifted in the spirit of the men. Behind them, across the Potomac, lay a devastated land, — their land, their home, their mother country! Before them lay a battle, a great battle, the greatest battle yet, perhaps! Win it — win it! and see a great rainbow of promise, glorious and bright, arch itself over the land beyond the river, the land darkened, devastated, and beloved! . . . Before them, as they marched, marched a vision of dead leaders: Shiloh and Albert Sidney Johnston — Port Republic and Ashby — Chancellorsville and Stonewall Jackson — of many dead leaders, and of a many and a many dead comrades. The vision did not hurt; it helped. It did not weaken their hearts; it strengthened them.

The Stonewall Brigade found itself in good heart and upon the road to Greencastle. It was a sunny June day and a sunny June road with oxheart cherry trees at intervals. Corps, divisions, brigades, regiments, companies — one and all had orders, calm and complete, not to plunder. *"The Commanding General,"* ran Lee's general order, *"earnestly exhorts the troops to abstain with most scrupulous care from unnecessary or wanton injury to private property, and he enjoins upon all officers to arrest and bring to summary punishment all who shall in any way offend against the orders on this subject."* To the credit of a poorly clad army, out of a land famished and fordone, be it said that the orders were obeyed. The army was in an enemy's land, a land of plenty, but the noncombatant farming-people of that land suffered but little in purse or property and not at all in person. "I was told," writes a good grey artilleryman, "by the inhabitants that they suffered less from our troops than from their own, and that if compelled to have either they preferred having the 'rebels' camped upon their land. I saw no plundering whatever, except that once or twice I did see branches laden with fruit broken from cherry trees. Of course it goes without saying that the quartermasters, especially of artillery battalions, were confessedly, and of malice aforethought, horse-thieves!"

The Sixty-fifth Virginia admired the Cumberland Valley. "It looks for all the world like the picture of Beulah land in a 'Pilgrim's Progress' I got as a prize for learning the most Bible verses!" — "This landscape makes me want to cry. It looks so — so — so damn peaceful." — "That's so! They don't have to glean no battle-fields. They're busy reaping wheat." — "Cherries! Those cherries are as big as winesaps. I'm going to have cherry pie to-night, —

> "Can she make a cherry pie,
> Billy boy, Billy boy?
> Can she make a cherry pie,
> Charming Billy?"

"Did you hear Early's boys tell about 'Extra Billy' at Winchester?" — "No." — "Well, 't was the artillery going by at a gallop to occupy a work they had just taken, going by the lying-down infantry, and Milroy's other batteries blazing against them from the other hills, and the Yankee sharpshooters just as busy as bees. And the lying-down infantry just cocked its eye up from the earth and said, 'Go it, boys!' But ex-Governor William Smith ain't made like that. He stood up before his regiment just as graceful and easy as if he was going to make a speech, with the blue cotton umbrella over his shoulder, and when that artillery came thundering by, by jingo! he began bowing to every man and some of the horses! He just stood there and beamed and bowed — good old Governor! Everybody knew that he'd just forgotten and thought that he was at a political meeting." — "Probably he did. War's an awful intensifier and a kind of wizard that puts a year in a day, but if a man's been habituated one way for fifty years he'll slip back into it, cannon balls notwithstanding." — "There's a spring-house and a woman churning! *Buttermilk!*" — "Reckon she's got any cherry pies? Reckon she'd sell them to us? Colonel says we've got to pay — pay good Confederate money!"

The Sixty-fifth marched on upon a sunshiny road, beneath blue sky, between crimson-fruited cherry trees. Beyond swelled the green and gold countryside, so peaceful. . . . Butterflies fluttered, honeybees hummed, birds warbled. Dinner was good meat and wheaten bread, taken in cheerful meadows, beneath elms and poplars. Village and farmer people showed themselves not tremendously hostile. Small boys gathered, happy and excited; Dutch farmers, anxiety for their red barns appeased, glowered not overmuch. Women were stiffer and took occasion to hum or sing aloud patriotic Northern songs. Southerners are a polite people, and the women of the Cumberland Valley met with no rudeness. At a cross-roads, the Sixty-fifth passing with jingle and tramp, a Pennsylvania carriage horse, that had never snuffed the battle from afar, took fright at the grey men or the gleam of rifle barrels or the sanguine fluttering colours. Ensued a rearing and plunging, and, from the phaeton behind, a scream. Lieutenant Coffin sprang to the rescue. — The horse stood soothed, though trembling a little still. "Thar now! thar now!" said Billy Maydew at the reins. The twelve-year-old urchin in the driver's seat glued his eyes to the marching Sixty-fifth and gasped with delight. The sprigged muslin and straw bonnet in the embrace of the phaeton made a gallant bid for the austerity of a marble monument.

"You wish to cross the road, madam? Or can you wait until the column has passed?"

"Oh, wait, please, sister! Golly! Look at that blue flag!"

"No, I cannot wait. I wish to cross now. I am going to a funeral."

The last of the Sixty-fifth passed with jingle and tramp. The Fourth was seen looming through the mist. Sergeant Maydew at the horse's head, Lieutenant Coffin beside the phaeton — across the highroad was conducted straw bonnet and sprigged muslin. The two soldiers stood back, Lieutenant Coffin making a courtly bow. It was answered by a stately inclination of the bonnet. The boy reluctantly said, "Get up!" to the horse, and the phaeton slowly climbed a flowery hill.

The lieutenant and the sergeant strode after their regiment. "She was mighty sweet and fine!" volunteered Billy. "I like that dark, soft kind, like pansies. I'll tell you who I think she air like. She air like Miss Miriam Cleave at Three Oaks."

Coffin considered. "I see what you mean. They are a little alike. . . . Three Oaks!"

"I used to think," said Billy, "that I'd be right happy if I could kill you. That was before Port Republic. Then I used to think I'd be right happy when Allan Gold had beat spelling into me and I'd be made sergeant. And after Chancellorsville I thought I'd be right happy if General Jackson got well. But I've thought right along, ever since White Oak Swamp, that I'd be right happy if the Sixty-fifth had back the only colonel I've ever cared much for, and that air Richard Cleave!"

In the afternoon the Sixty-fifth came to the town of Greencastle. It looked a thriving place, and it had shops and stores filled with the most beautiful and tempting goods. Back home, the goods were all gone from the stores, the old stock assimilated and the new never appearing. The shop windows of Greencastle looked like fairyland, a hundred Christmases all in one. "Look-a-there! Look at that ironware!" — "Look at them shirts and suspenders! Coloured handkerchiefs." — "Fancy soap and cologne and toothbrushes!" — "I wish I might send Sally that pink calico and some ribbons, and a hoop." — "Look at that plough — that's something new!" — "Figured velvet waistcoats." — "Lord have mercy! this is the sinfullest town of plutocrats!" — " Try them with Confederate money." — "Sure Old Dick said we might n't take just a little?" — "Oh, me! oh, me! there's a shoe-store and a hat-store and a drug-store." — "Say, Mr. Storekeeper, would you take for that pair of shoes a brand-new fifty-dollar Richmond Virginia bank note with George Washington and a train of cars on it?" — "He won't sell. This gilded town's got so much money it does n't want any more — tired of money." — "Disgusting Vanity Fair kind of a place! Glad the colonel is n't going to halt us!" — *Don't straggle, men !* — "No, sir; we are n't!"

Camp was clean beyond Greencastle — a lovely camp quite removed from Vanity Fair. Apparently the quartermasters had been able to buy. There was coffee for supper, real coffee, real sugar; there were light biscuits and butter and roast lamb. A crystal stream purled through the meadows; upon the hilltops wheat, partly shocked, stood against the rosy sky. The evening was cool and sweet and the camp-fires for a long way, up and down and on either side the road, burned with a steady flame. The men lay upon the earth like dusty acorns shaken from invisible branches. At the foot of the hills the battery and wagon horses cropped the sweet grass.

The good horses! — their ribs did not show as they did on the Virginia side of the Potomac. They were faring well in Pennsylvania. Rank and file, men and horses, guns and wagon train, the Second Corps, Rodes and Jubal Early and "Alleghany" Johnson, and "Dear Dick Ewell" at the head, — the Second Corps was in spirits. To-night it was as buoyant as a cork or a rubber ball. Where there were bands the bands played, played the sprightliest airs in their repertory. Harry Hays's Creoles danced, leaping like fauns in the dying sunset and the firelight, in a trodden space beneath beech trees.

The next morning Rodes and Johnson pursued the road to Chambersburg, but Early's division took the Gettysburg and York road, having orders to cut the Northern Central Railroad running from Baltimore to Harrisburg, and to destroy the bridge across the Susquehanna at Wrightsville and rejoin at Carlisle. Ahead went Gordon's Georgia brigade and White's battalion of cavalry.

The town of Gettysburg, where they made boots and shoes, lay among orchards and gardens at the foot of the South Mountain. It numbered four thousand inhabitants, a large place for those days. It lay between the waters that drain into the Susquehanna and the waters that drain into the Potomac and commanded all the country roads. On the outskirts of this place, a place not marked out on that day from other places on the map, White's cavalry encountered a regiment of militia. The militia did not stand, but fled to either side the macadamized road, through the midsummer fields. A hundred and seventy-five were taken prisoner. On through Gettysburg marched Gordon and the cavalry, the people watching from the windows, and took the pike to York. Behind them came "Old Jube," marching in light order, having sent his trains to Chambersburg, "excepting the ambulances, one medical wagon for a brigade, the regimental ordnance wagons, one wagon with cooking-utensils for each regiment, and fifteen empty wagons to gather supplies with."

It came on to rain. The troops bivouacked somewhat comfortlessly a mile or two out on the York road. Two thousand rations were found in a train of cars. When they had been removed the cars were set afire, and in addition a railroad bridge hard by. These burned with no cheer in the flames seen through a thick veil of chilly rain. "I don't care if I never see Gettysburg again!" said the division.

At dawn rang the bugles. The rain was over, the sun came up, breakfast was good, the country smiled, the division had a light heart. All this day they made a good march, through a pleasant country, leading to York. The cavalry was on ahead toward Hanover Junction, destroying railroad bridges. Gordon and his Georgians acted vanguard for the infantry. Of the main body, Brigadier-General William Smith with the Thirty-first, Forty-ninth, and Fifty-second Virginia headed the column. By reaped wheat and waving corn, by rich woods and murmuring streams, under blue sky and to the song of birds, through a land of plenty and prosperity, the grey column moved pleasantly on to York, and at sunset bivouacked within a mile or two of that place.

Out to Gordon's camp-fire came a deputation—the mayor of York and prominent citizens. Gordon, handsome and gallant, received them with his accustomed courtesy. "Their object," he reports, "being to make a peaceable surrender, and ask for protection to life and property. They returned, I think, with a feeling of assured safety."

The next day was Sunday — a clear midsummer Sunday, the serene air filled with church bells. Gordon's men, occupying York, found well-dressed throngs upon the sidewalks, in the doorways, leaning from the windows. Confederate soldiers had always to hope that the inner man could not be hidden, but shone excellently forth from the bizarrest ragged apparel. Sunburnt, with longish hair, gaunt yet, despite a fortnight with the flesh pots of this Egypt, creature of shred and patches and all covered with the whitish dust of a macadamized road — it needed some insight to read how sweet and sound, on the whole, was the kernel within so weather-beaten a shell. Now Gordon was the Southern gentleman at his best. "Confederate pride, to say nothing of Southern gallantry," reports Gordon, "was subjected to the sorest trial by the consternation produced among the ladies of York. . . . I assured these ladies that the troops behind me, though ill-clad and travel-stained, were good men and brave; that beneath their rough exteriors were hearts as loyal to women as ever beat in the breasts of honourable men; that their own experience and the experience of their mothers, wives, and sisters at home had taught them how painful must be the sight of a hostile army in their town; that under the orders of the Confederate Commander-in-Chief both private property and noncombatants were safe; that the spirit of vengeance and rapine had no place in the bosoms of these dust-covered but knightly men; and I closed by pledging to York the head of any soldier under my command who destroyed private property, disturbed the repose of a single home, or insulted a woman."

Gordon made no tarrying in York, but moved on toward Wrightsville, with orders to burn the long railroad bridge crossing the Susquehanna. A few hours later marched in Early's advance brigade — General ex-Governor William Smith on a fine horse at its head. Now this brigade had a very good band, as bands went in the Confederate service, and this band proposed to enter York playing "Dixie"! Indeed, they had begun the familiar strains when an aide appeared, "General says you 'tooting fellows' are temporarily to lay that air in lavender. When you are in Rome, play what Rome likes, or, in other words, Virginians, take your manners along! He says come up front and play 'Yankee Doodle.'"

York was out of doors for this brigade as it had been for Gordon's. In the sunny mid-afternoon, the column swung into its main street, "Extra Billy" riding at the head, beaming like the sun. Hero of a hundred hustings, he always took his manners with him; and indeed, as they came from his heart, he could not do otherwise. At the head of town he took off his hat, kept it in his hand, and began bowing right and left, always with his hearty, beamy smile. Behind him rode his smiling staff, and behind staff came the band, horns and drums giving "Yankee Doodle."

The citizens of York upon the sidewalks—and they were crowded — developed a tendency to keep pace with the head of the column. It presently arrived that General William Smith, like a magnet, was carrying with him a considerable portion of the population. Before the procession opened the public square, bathed in a happy light. The band, having come to an end of "Yankee Doodle," played "Dixie," then slipped again into the first, then happily blended the two. Staff was laughing, regimental officers broadly smiling, the troops behind in the best of spirits. All poured into the sunny

square, where were more of the inhabitants of York. "Tell 'em to
halt," ordered the ex-Governor, "and tell those tooting fellows to
stop both tunes. These are nice people and I am going to give them
a speech."

He gave it, sitting very firm on his fine horse, to an open-mouthed-
and-eyed crowd, behind him the troops at rest, the whole throng,
invaded and invaders, filling the square and the street. He spoke in
his geniallest fashion, with his mellowest voice and happiest allu-
sions. The warm, yellow, late June sunshine flooded the square,
lighting the curious throng, and that worn, grey, citizen soldiery,
making a splendour of the brass instruments of the band and wrapping General William Smith in a toga of airy gold. "Ladies and
gentlemen (and York has such beautiful ladies)," spoke "Extra
Billy," "as you see, we are back in the Union! May we not hope
that you are glad to see us? I assure you that we are glad to see
you! I wish that we were dressed for visiting, but you'll excuse us,
we know! What we all need on both sides is to mingle more with
each other, so that we shall learn to know and appreciate each
other's good qualities. Now —"

From behind arose a murmur. The aides looked over their shoulders and beheld a pushing to the front on the part of some person or
persons. Whatever it was, cavalry squad trying to pass, aides, or
couriers, general officer, and staff—there was difficulty in attracting
the attention of the grinning, absorbed troops sufficiently to let the
party by.

"Now," continued General William Smith, "we are n't at all the
villains and cut-throats that you 've been seeing in your dreams!
Clothes don't make the man, and we 're better than our outfit.
When this little rumpus is all over and you come visiting us in the
Confederacy of the South (and I hope that the beautiful ladies of
York will come often and come in summer-time, for we want to
have a tournament and crown them all Queens of Love and Beauty)
— when this little border war is over, I say —"

The party from the rear had now got to the front. A thin, stoop-
shouldered man, with a long, thin beard and glittering, small black
eyes, rose in his stirrups, leaned forward, and brought a vehement
hand down upon "Extra Billy's" shoulder. His voice followed —
Jubal A. Early's voice — a fierce sing-song treble. "General Smith,

what the Devil are you about? — stopping the head of this column in this cursed town!"

"Extra Billy's" smile, manly and beaming and fearless, stayed with him. "Why, General, just having a little fun! Good for us all, sir; good for us all!"

Smith's brigade moved on, to be followed by Hoke's and Harry Hays's. Camp was pitched a mile or two out of town, "Old Jube," however, resting with Avery's command in York. "I made," he reports, "requisition upon the authorities for 2000 pairs of shoes, 1000 hats, 1000 pairs of socks, $100,000 in money, and three days' rations of all kinds. Subsequently between 1200 and 1500 pairs of shoes, the hats, socks, and rations were furnished, but only $28,600 in money, which was paid to my quartermaster, the mayor and other authorities protesting their inability to get any more money, as it had all been run off previously, and I was satisfied they made an honest effort to raise the amount called for."

He continues: "A short time before night, I rode out in the direction of Columbia Bridge, to ascertain the result of Gordon's expedition, and had not proceeded far before I saw an immense smoke rising in the direction of the Susquehanna, which I subsequently discovered to proceed from the bridge in question. This bridge was one mile and a quarter in length, the superstructure being of wood on stone pillars, and it included in one structure a railroad bridge, a passway for wagons, and also a tow-path for the canal which here crosses the Susquehanna. The bridge was entirely consumed, and from it the town of Wrightsville caught fire, and several buildings were consumed, but the farther progress of the flames was arrested by the exertions of Gordon's men. . . . On the evening of the twenty-ninth, I received through Captain Elliott Johnston, aide to General Ewell, a copy of a note from General Lee which required me to move back so as to rejoin the rest of the corps on the western side of the South Mountain, and accordingly, at daylight on the morning of the thirtieth, I put my whole command in motion. . . . I encamped about three miles from Heidlersburg, and rode to see General Ewell at that point, and was informed by him that the object was to concentrate the corps at or near Cashtown, and I received directions to move next day at that point. . . . After passing Heidlersburg a short distance, I received a note from General Ewell informing me that General Hill was moving from Cashtown towards Gettysburg, and that General Rodes had turned off at Middletown and was moving toward the same place, and directing me also to move to that point. I therefore continued to move on the road I was then on toward Gettysburg. . . ."

From Greencastle, Rodes and Johnson, Ewell riding at the head of the column, had marched to Chambersburg and thence to Carlisle. They reached the latter place on the twenty-seventh. On this day Robert E. Lee, with Longstreet and A. P. Hill, the First and Third Corps, bivouacked near Chambersburg.

With the grand patience which he habitually exercised, Lee waited for tidings from Stuart. There was room for intense impatience. His cavalry leader, who was to keep him informed of the least move upon the board of the other colour, had failed to do so. Four days in the enemy's country, and no news of Stuart and no news of the blue host south of the Potomac! Was it still south of the Potomac? Surely so, or Stuart's couriers, one after the other, would have come riding in! Surely so, or Stuart himself would be here, falling in on the right as ordered! With entire justice the grey commander loved and trusted the grey cavalry leader. He waited now, in the green Pennsylvania country, with a front of patience, but perhaps with an inner agony. Was Hooker yet in Virginia? Lee sat still in his small tent, his eyes level, his hand resting lightly on the table; then he rose, and said to the adjutant-general that the army would advance, next day, upon Harrisburg.

But that same night, the twenty-eighth, there was a movement at the door of the tent. "Captain ——, from General Longstreet, sir, with the scout, Harrison."

A short, lean, swarthy man in citizen's dress, came forward and saluted.

"You are," said Lee, "the scout General Longstreet sent into Washington?"

"Yes, General. Three weeks ago from Fredericksburg."

"Very well. Give me your report."

"General Longstreet gave me money, sir, and orders to make my way into Washington and to stay there until I had something important to report and could get out. I only managed the last, sir, five days ago. Since then I've been travelling at night and what parts of the day I could without observation. I knew, of course, that the army had crossed or was crossing, and from Washington I struck out toward Frederick. There was talk in Washington that General Hooker would certainly be superseded, and last night I heard that he had resigned and General Meade was in command."

"I have been looking for that. General Hooker was a good fighter, and so is General Meade. But it is of the whereabouts of that army that I want to know."

"I had to hide at Frederick, sir. Three corps were already there. As I left I saw the dust of a fourth."

"*At Frederick!*"

"Yes, sir. I understood from a farmer that they crossed at Edwards's Ferry the twenty-fifth and sixth."

"Have you seen or heard of General Stuart?"

"An ambulance driver told me there was a report that what he called the rebel cavalry had crossed the Potomac and were cutting the Chesapeake and Ohio Canal."

"And the enemy's line of march from Frederick?"

"Toward South Mountain, sir."

"That is all of consequence you have to report?"

"Yes, sir."

"Very well. You have done well, Harrison. Good night!"

The scout and the aide departed. In the tent there was a somewhat heavy silence. Lee drew the map upon the table closer and sat, his forehead upon his hand, studying it. Two candles stood beside him, and the white light showed the beauty of the down-bent head and face. His expression was very quiet, but the adjutant, watching him, ached for the ache that he read there, the ache of a great general who was yet mortal, with a mortal's equipment; of the leader of brave men who were yet mortal with a quiverful of the arrows of mistake and random aim. The hopes of the South hung upon this campaign. All knew it; the adjutant-general knew it; the man bending over the map knew it. . . . Hooker — no, Meade! — was across the Potomac, and advancing. By now he would be somewhere south of Gettysburg. . . . The candles burned clear; Lee sat, very still, his gaze level, his hand upon the map.

Colonel Taylor ventured to speak. "The orders for Harrisburg —"

"Yes, Colonel. We must countermand them. These people are closer than I thought. I wish we had our cavalry. But I make mistakes myself." He rose, moving out of the clear light into the dusk of the tent. "The orders are that all three corps concentrate at Cashtown a little to the west of Gettysburg."

CHAPTER XIV

THE CAVE

ON the thirteenth of June grey countermines were begun from all the main grey works. The men worked continuously upon these, and in the night-time they strengthened the breaches made by the daily fierce cannonade. With the few hundred entrenching tools, with the improvised spades, the bayonet picks, with earth carried in camp-buckets, with all ingenious makeshifts, they burrowed and heaped continuously. But they laboured, now, somewhat weakly. They were so tired. The heat of that Southern land was frightful, and the confinement in the trenches was frightful. The thought began to sicken at those deep troughs in the earth. In the scanty sleep of officers and men they pressed upon the brain; they grew to seem trenches in the brains, troughs filled with dead thoughts, thoughts that still suffered. There was no relief from the trenches, no relief at all, except when a wound came — a bad wound — or fever came — serious fever with delirium — when the wounded or the fevered was borne with some risk from shells and minies to the hospital. Even in the hospital the trenches stayed in the brain. It came that, in the trenches, the tired, tired soldiers looked with something like envy upon the wounded or the fevered as he was borne away. "That fellow's going to get some sleep." — "Stop your nodding, Jimmy! — nodding same as if you were in church!" — "Captain's calling!" — "Go 'way! If you jerk your head back like that you'll break your neck." — "I wouldn't care," said Jimmy, "if it just meant sleeping on and on." — "It wouldn't. You'd be fighting again somewhere else in a jiffy! — O God! these trenches."

Officers and men were dead for sleep. Officers and men had never dreamed of such fatigue. Officers and men handled sword and musket with hands that were hard to keep ennerved and watched the foe with eyes over which the lids would droop. It was growing ghastly at Vicksburg, and the June sun beat down, beat down. In the infrequent times when the river was clear of smoke it lay glittering like diamonds and topazes, paining the weary eye. North and east and south the cloud rarely lifted. A thinner battle cloud overhung the seven-mile Confederate line. The grey could not spend powder as might the blue, nor did they have the blue's great horde of guns. But what with the blue and what with the grey all Vicksburg and its environs dwelled day after day, week after week, in a battle murk. The smoke was always there; the smell, the taste, were always there. The pitiless sun was no less hot for the ashen gauze through which it struck. Shorn of its beams, it rose and moved through the muddy blue, and set like a thick red-gold buckler, from behind which came lances of heat and madness. With the night there came drenching dews and the mist from the river. Heat and cold beat on the same men, cramped forever in the same trenches.

On the tenth day of the siege the eighteen thousand fighting men had been put on half-rations. Later these were greatly reduced. At first five ounces of poor corn or pea flour were issued daily; later the amount fell to three ounces. The mules in the place were slaughtered, but the meat gained in this way fed but a few. After mid-June the cats disappeared from the town. In the spring Vicksburg had had its fair vegetable gardens. Now every eatable root below or stalk or seed above the ground was gone. The small, unripe fruit, peach or quince or fig, the hard green berries, were gathered, stewed, and eaten. All things were eaten that could be eaten, but the men grew large-eyed, and their physical strength flagged. From almost the beginning the water had been bad. The men in the river batteries and the troops upon the right suffered most where all suffered much. The Federal shot and shell had slain, in the first days of the siege, a number of horses and mules. It being the first of the siege and starvation not yet above the horizon, these animals were dragged in the night to the river and thrown in. Now the cisterns were exhausted, the wells were insufficient. They were forced to draw by night the water from the edge of the river, filled with maggots as it was. They dug shallow wells in the hollows and dips of the land and placed sentinels over them to see that the water was not wasted. The water was there for drinking or for the slight cooking that went on; there was never any for washing. Some men forgot the feel of cleanliness; others set their lips and did without. Powder-grime and sweat; drenching rains that lined and floored every trench with miserable mire; fierce, beating suns that made the mire into a dust that stiffened the hair and choked the pores; effluvia, blood, refuse that could not be carted away, that there was not time to bury, — the trenches at Vicksburg and the slight camps behind grew like a bad dream, vague and sickening. Hunger that could not be fed dwelled in Vicksburg, weariness that could not find rest, insufficient sleep, dirt, thirst, wounds, disease. Fever was there hugely, fever and flux, exhaustion, debility, and also hyperexcitement; strange outbreaks of nature and strange sinkings together. Once there was a hint of cholera. Two surgeons stood over the man who had been lifted from the trench and now lay writhing on the earth under a roof of dried pine boughs.

"It looks mighty suspicious," said one in a weary voice, barely rising above a whisper. "That's why I called you. It would be the last stroke."

The other nodded. "You're right there. I've seen it once before, off a ship at Tampa, but I'm not sure that this is it. There's a mock here of everything in the world that's awful, so it may be a mock of that, too."

"I've heard that chloroform is good. One part chloroform, three parts water, two —"

"Yes. There isn't any chloroform."

The man died, but, whatever it had been, that particular disease did not spread. Others did. They spread apace.

A grey mine was started from within the Third Louisiana Redan by sinking a vertical shaft and then digging outward a gallery under the Federal sap. Night and day the grey worked, and night and day worked the blue. The grey worked hungry, the blue worked fed. The grey worked heavy-lidded, with long, long shifts. The blue worked, rested and refreshed, with short shifts. The blue had every modern appliance for their work, the grey had not. The grey worked with desperation upon their inclined gallery; the blue drove steadily and apace toward the salient of the redan.

Now and then there were assaults where the enemy thought his cannon or his mines had made a practicable breach. These were driven back, and then the great guns belched flame and thundered.

The grey guns answered where answers were most strongly indicated; never had they had ammunition to spend on mere pleasure of
defiance. Now here, now there, along the lines, leaping from place
to place like lightning, musketry flamed and crackled. Always the
blue minies kept up their singing, and always the many and deadly
sharpshooters watched to pick off men and officers. The gunboats
and the mortars from the Louisiana shore helped with a lavish hand
the land guns. Day chiefly saw the bombardments, but there were
nights when the region shook; when the bombs, exploding, reddened
the sky; when, copper-hued, saffron-tinged, the clouds rolled over
the place; when there was shriek and thunder, light and murk, glare
and horror of the great city of Dis.

Désirée could not rest within the cave or on the bench among the
ivy sprays. Hard-by was now a field hospital, and now each morning she left the ruined garden, mounted a little rise of ground, descended it, and found herself under a shed-like structure amid
ghastly sights and sounds of suffering. Here she ministered as best
she might. Like other Southern women she was familiar with plantation accidents. She knelt and helped with capable hands, preferring to be there and occupied than to sit in the torn garden and hear
upon the wind the sobbing and crying of this place. At night, lying
upon her pallet, she sometimes stopped her ears against it. Sight
horrified the brain, but hearing twisted the heartstrings. She never
fancied that she distinguished Edward's voice; if he were hurt he
would not cry aloud. But she trembled to hear the others crying,
and though she loved life she would have died for them if she could
have thereby stopped the crying.

Now and again she went into the town. It was a place now of
thin-faced heroism, large-eyed endurance, seldom-speaking women,
patient children. Hunger was in the town as well as at the lines, hunger and fever, hunger and fever! Mourning was there, too; not loud
but deep. There were so many widows, so many orphans. There
were sisters with a brother's death upon their hearts; there were be-
trothed girls who now would never marry. All were brave, with a
dumb heroism. The past told. Aryan emigrants, women of the dark
Teutonic forest, Pictish women, women of a Roman strain, Angle
and Dane and Celt and Saxon, Gaul and Iberian and Hebrew, —
yes, and women of Africa, — the wide past of famished sieges, of

back to the wall, of utter sacrifice, came again to the town of Vicksburg upon the Mississippi River.

Désirée returned to Cape Jessamine. The ruined garden was ruined now, indeed, torn by shot and shell, sunbaked, withered, dead. Post, beam, and rafter of the burned house no longer stood like a hieroglyphic against the sky. An exploding shell had wrecked the last support and all had fallen. Désirée, passing close, one day, saw a snake among the warped timbers. The trees had lost all greenness. They, too, suffered deadly injury from the shells. The flowers were all withered. They could not bloom in that heavy and sulphurous air. The bed of mignonette grew yellow and thin and wan. It lost its odour. The birds were gone long ago. One neither heard the buzz of bees nor saw a butterfly. It was as though a wizard's wand were waving away life and loveliness.

Désirée kept her beauty, but it grew beauty of the inner outward, beauty of a myriad complexities, subtleties, intensities. Memory was there and forecasting, and everything heightened. She had her Leonardo look; she went from hour to hour, not unsmiling, but the smile was remote from mirth and near to thought. Her physical being was clean, poised, and strong. She fared as scantily as all the others, but she did not perceptibly weaken. Or if the body weakened, she drew deep upon the innermost reserve and braced nerve and muscle with her will. The field hospital thought her tireless.

As she left the garden one day, a mine was sprung under the nearest salient and a breach made through which a blue wave at once undertook to pour. The grey meeting it, there followed three minutes of shock and roar, when the blue went back. It was an ugly breach, and while the grey cannon thundered it must be quickly mended. All the men possible fell to digging, while sand bags were brought and great bolsters of earth wrapped in old tenting. "Hurry!" said the captains. "Dig fast!"

Désirée went nearer and nearer. A man with a spade, making some headway with a hillock of earth, which, as he loosened, another scraped into a sack, fell dead, the brain pierced by a sharpshooter's bullet. The man with the sack made a "*Tchk!*" with his tongue, then turned to shout for another digger. His eyes fell on Désirée.

"What are you doing here, ma'am? This ain't no place for a woman."

Désirée bent and took the spade from the dead man's grasp. "I am strong," she said, "and I like to dig. Hold the sack open." She worked for an hour, until the breach was fully mended. At the last her fellow worker and she struck the dirt from their hands, and, straightening themselves, looked at each other. "You do fine," he said. "I reckon you must have had some digging to do once."

"Yes, I had," she answered. "For a long time and much of it. I am coming again."

The next day there was a bombardment that shook earth and sky. When, in the late afternoon, it was over, the air rested thick as on the slopes of a volcano in action, dusk and thick and heavy with the sullen odour of strife. Through the false twilight, Désirée, now at the cave, saw looming figures, litter-bearers. She knew they would come in at the ruined gate, and they came. She met them by the fallen house. "I am not badly hurt," said Edward's voice. "Don't think it! And how blessed to have Cape Jessamine to come to —"

The time wore on toward late June. The month of roses, here, was a month of red flowers of death. Outward from the Third Louisiana Redan dug feverishly the grey miners driving a gallery beneath the Federal sap. Outward from the blue lines dug fast and far the blue sappers, making for the Third Louisiana Redan that crowned a narrow ridge. Within the redan, seeing the explosion approach, the grey built a second parapet some yards behind the first. On the twenty-fifth the explosion came. The salient was wrecked, six men who were digging a shaft were buried alive. Through the thick smoke and infernal din was pushed a blue charge, hurrahing. The grey were ready at the second parapet. The Sixth Missouri, held by Forney in reserve, poured into the injured works. "*Yaaaaih!*" they yelled; "*Yaaaaih! Yaaaaihhhh!*" and checked the blue with a deadly volley. Their colonel — Colonel Erwin — mounted the shattered parapet. He waved his sword. "Charge, men, charge!" A minie killed him, but his men poured over the parapet. There was fierce hand-to-hand fighting. Dark came, the blue holding ditch and slope of the outer, now ruined parapet, the grey masters of the inner works.

In the middle of the night the two Confederate mines beyond the stockade redan were exploded, filling up the Federal sap and parallels and destroying their sap rollers. There was also this night a transfer of guns, a Dahlgren gun being added to the battery facing the enemy's works on the Jackson road, and a ten-inch mortar mounted on the Warrenton road. Off and on, throughout this night, arose a fierce rattle of musketry, came an abortive blue attempt to storm the grey line. Half the grey men watched; the other half slept upon its arms.

Life in the town grew tense and vibrant. Also something high and clear came into it and a certain *insouciance*. The caves gave parties. There was no room to dance and there was nothing to eat; but parties the slight gatherings were called. In the hospitals the wounded ceased to blench at the crashing shells. The surgeons and nursing women went lightly between the pallets, nor turned their heads because a roof was struck. The large-eyed children played quietly in the cave mouths, or gathered about some woman who told them of Cinderella and Beauty and the Beast. The negro mammies crooned the babies to sleep. Officers and men passed through the streets, exhibiting a certain wan jauntiness. Commissariat and quartermasters said pleasant things about the squirrel's store with which they must feed an army, and the powder-horn and pouch of shot from which they must keep it in ammunition. The non-combatant citizens did their share toward keeping up the general spirits. Songs appeared, and there was a general and curious readiness to laugh. A Vicksburg newspaper faced with a thoughtful brow the giving-out of paper and a consequent suspension of issue. It did not want to suspend. It viewed a forlorn little wallpaper shop, and it went across and purchased the dusty stock. The next morning it came out with a backing of noble arabesque, of morning glories on trellises, of green and gold leaves and cabbage roses.

Down at Cape Jessamine undeniably there was happiness. Edward Cary's wound was not grave. It disabled, kept him lying, thin and pale, on the pallet which for light and air Désirée had dragged near to the cave entrance. But there was no fever. His superb, clean manhood told. The two of them kept bodily poise, and with it the mental. They were happy; a strange, personal happiness in the midst of menace and the gathering public woe. It was not selfishness; they would have laid aside bliss itself like a gold mantle and gone down to lazar rags and the cold and dark forever if they could thereby have rescued their world. That could not be; they were here on a raft together in the midst of the ocean; they could only serve themselves and each other. They had had few days and hours together. The lover's passion was yet upon them; each to the other was plainly aureoled. He lay with the veil of ivy drawn back so that he might see the battle cloud. She tended him, she prepared their scanty food, she brought water at nightfall from the little spring. Sometimes she left him to go help awhile in the field hospital. But he was as badly hurt as many there; with a clear conscience she might choose to tend this wounded soldier. She did so choose.

The hot days went by beneath the bowl of brass that was the sky. The murk came up to the cave, the steady thunder shook the ivy sprays. Désirée sat upon the earth beside the pallet. Sometimes they talked together, low-voiced; sometimes, in long silent spaces, they looked each on the aureoled other. He was most beautiful to her, and she to him. A faint splendour dwelled in the cave and over this part of the withered garden, a strange, transforming, golden light. They smelled the honeysuckle, they smelled the mignonette. They thought they heard the singing of the birds.

On the twenty-sixth the mortars upon the Louisiana side began again to throw huge shells into the town, while the gunboats opened a rapid and heavy firing upon the lower batteries. This continued. On the twenty-eighth the grey exploded a mine before the lunette on the Baldwin's Ferry road, where the Federal sap was within six yards of the ditch. At point after point now, the blue line held that near the grey. At places the respective parapets were fearfully close. There was fighting with hand grenades, there was tossing of fire-balls against the sap rollers behind which worked the blue miners.

Night attacks grew frequent; all the weakened grey soldiers lay on their arms; no one, day or night, could leave the trenches. The wounded, the fevered, the hunger-weakened, the sleepless — Vicksburg's defenders grew half wraith, half scarecrow.

In the dead night of the twenty-ninth, after five hours of a sultry and sullen stillness, every blue cannon appeared to open. From the Louisiana shore, from the river, from the land, north, east, and south, came the blast.

Désirée parted the mat of ivy and watched with Edward from the mouth of the cave.

"The twenty-ninth!" he said. "It is, I think, the beginning of the end. I doubt if we can hold out another week."

She sat on the earth beside him, her head against the pillow. Lip and ear must be near together; at any distance the blast carried the voice away. "The beginning of the end. . . . You think General Johnston will not come?"

"How can he? I saw the force that he had. It is not possible. He is right in refusing to play the dare-devil or to sacrifice for naught. He should have been listened to in the beginning."

"And we cannot cut our way out?"

"Evacuate? How many could march ten miles? No. Troy's down — Troy's down!"

"Richmond is Troy."

". . . That is true. Then this is one of the small Asian towns."

Without the ivy sprays there was a red and awful light. They saw the world as by calcium. The stars were put out, but the flashes burnished the piled battle clouds. Bronze and copper and red gleamed the turreted fierce clouds. Below were now sharply shown, now hidden, the Vicksburg lines, the heaped, earthen front. Redan and redoubt and lunette and the long ragged rifle-pits between, — now they showed and now the smoke drove between.

"It repeats and repeats," said Edward. "Life's a labyrinth, and the clue broke at the beginning."

"Love is the clue."

"Love like ours? There must be many kinds of love."

"Yes. But love in all its degrees. From love of thought to love of the snake that I saw again to-day. Love in all its degrees casting out hate in all its degrees. Love that lives and lets live. Love that is wise."

"Is it always wise?"

"It can be made so. All other clues will break like packthread."

The light grew intenser. Houses in the town had been set afire. Air and earth shook, all the heavy, buried strings vibrated. Sound rolled against the ear like combers of a sea, deep, terrific, with a ground swell, with sudden, wild accesses as when world navies are wrecked. The smell of powder smoke gathered, familiar, familiar,

familiar! Marching feet were heard, going down to the lines — the City Guard probably, called to come and help.

"Packthread," said Edward. "All this to break like packthread and go out like flaming tow. . . . Love and Thought the sole weavers of relations. Love and Thought the related and the relation. . . ."

The rapid and heavy cannonading stopped with the amber dawn. The Federal sappers were again under the Third Louisiana Redan. They worked behind a timber-and-wire screen against which in vain the grey threw hand grenades and fire balls. Lockett, the chief engineer, had a barrel, filled with a hundred and twenty-five pounds of powder and carrying a time fuse of fifteen seconds, rolled over the parapet toward the blue shelter. The explosion sent the timber screen in a thousand fragments into the air; behind it there came a shouting and running. All this day there was heavy firing from the river.

The morning of July first all division commanders received from General Pemberton a confidential note. It stated succinctly that apparently the siege of Vicksburg could not be raised and that supplies were exhausted. There remained an attempt at evacuation. The note asked for reports as to the condition of the troops and their ability to make the marches and endure the fatigues necessary to a successful issue. The major-generals put the note before the brigadiers, and the brigadiers before the colonels. There was but one answer. The *morale* of the men was good — yes! and again yes! But for the rest, for their physical condition, so hungry, so tired, so staggering from weakness . . .

This was in the morning. At one in the afternoon of this first of July the enemy exploded their great mine under the Third Louisiana Redan. The fuse was lit, the fuse burned, the spark reached fifteen hundred pounds of powder. There was an awful, a rending explosion. Earth, defences, guns, men and men and men were blown high into the air. The Sixth Missouri suffered here. There was made a crater twenty feet deep and fifty across. The Third Louisiana Redan was no more.

All day the second, a part of the day the third, the blue land batteries, the blue gunboats, the blue mortars bombarded Vicksburg. On the Fourth of July the place surrendered.

CHAPTER XV

GETTYSBURG

THE sun of the first day of July rose serene into an azure sky where a few white clouds were floating. The light summer mist was dissipated; a morning wind, freshly sweet, rippled the corn and murmured in the green and lusty trees. The sunshine gilded Little Round Top and Big Round Top, gilded Culp's Hill and Cemetery Hill, gilded Oak Hill and Seminary Ridge. It flashed from the cupola of the Pennsylvania College. McPherson's Woods caught it on its topmost branches, and the trees of Peach Orchard. It trembled between the leaves, and flecked with golden petals Menchey's Spring and Spangler's Spring. It lay in sleepy lengths on the Emmitsburg road. It struck the boulders of the Devil's Den; it made indescribably light and fine the shocked wheat in a wheat-field that drove into the green like a triangular golden wedge. Full in the centre of the rich landscape it made a shining mark, a golden bull's-eye, of the small town of Gettysburg.

It should have been all peace, that rich Pennsylvania landscape — a Dutch peace — a Quaker peace. Market wains and country folk should have moved upon the roads, and a boy, squirrel-hunting, should have been the most murderous thing in the Devil's Den. Corn-blades should have glistened, not bayonets; for the fluttering flags the farmers' wives should have been bleaching linen on the grass; for marching feet there should have risen the sound of the scythe in the wheat; for the groan of gun wheels upon the roads the robin's song and the bobwhite's call.

The sun mounted. He was well above the tree-tops when the first shot was fired — Heth's brigade of A. P. Hill's corps encountering Buford's cavalry.

The sun went down the first day red behind the hills. He visited the islands of the Pacific, Nippon, and the Kingdom of Flowers, and India and Iran. He crowned Caucasus with gold, and showered largess over Europe. He reddened the waves of the Atlantic. He touched with his spear lighthouses and coast towns and the inland green land. He came up over torn orchard and trampled wheatfield; he came up over the Round Tops and Culp's Hill and Cemetery Hill. But no one, this second day, stopped to watch his rising. The battle smoke hid him from the living upon the slopes and in all the fields.

The sun travelled from east to west, but no man on the shield of which Gettysburg was the centre saw him go down that second day. A thick smoke, like the wings of countless ravens, kept out the parting gleams. He went his way over the plains of the West and the Pacific and the Asian lands. He came over Europe and the Atlantic and made, on the third morning, bright pearl of the lighthouses, the surf, and the shore. The ripe July country welcomed him. But around Gettysburg his rising was not seen. The smoke had not dispersed. He rode on high, but all that third day he was seen far away and dim as through crêpe. All day he shone serene on other lands, but above this region he hung small and dim and remote like a tarnished, antique shield. Sometimes the drift of ravens' wings hid him quite. But an incense mounted to him, a dark smell and a dark vapour.

The birds were gone from the trees, the cattle from the fields, the children from the lanes and the brookside. All left on the first day. There was a hollow between Round Top and Devil's Den, and into this the anxious farmers had driven and penned a herd of cattle. On the sunny, calm afternoon when they had done this, they could not conceive that any battle would affect this hollow. Here the oxen, the cows, would be safe from chance bullet and from forager. But the farmers did not guess the might of that battle.

The stream of shells was directed against Round Top, but a number, black and heavy, rained into the hollow. A great, milk-white ox was the first wounded. He lay with his side ripped open, a ghastly sight. Then a cow with calf was mangled, then a young steer had both fore legs broken. Bellowing, the maddened herd rushed here and there, attacking the rough sides of the hollow. Death and panic were upon the slopes as well as at the bottom of the basin. A bursting shell killed and wounded a dozen at once. The air grew thick and black, and filled with the cry of the cattle.

A courier, returning to his general after delivering an order, had his horse shot beneath him. Disentangling himself, he went on, on foot, through a wood. He was intolerably thirsty — and lo, a spring! It was small and round and clear like a mirror, and as he knelt he saw his own face and thought, "She would n't know me." The minies were so continuously singing that he had ceased to heed them. He drank, then saw that he was reddening the water. He did not know when he had been wounded, but now, as he tried to rise, he grew so faint and cold that he knew that Death had met him. . . . There was moss and fern and a nodding white flower. It was n't a bad place in which to die. In a pocket within his grey jacket he had a daguerreotype — a young and smiling face and form. His fingers were so nerveless now that it was hard to get the little velvet case out, and when it was out it proved to be shattered, it and the picture within. The smiling face and form were all marred, unrecognizable. So small a thing, perhaps! — but it made the bitterness of this soldier's death. The splintered case in his hands, he died as goes to sleep a child who has been unjustly punished. His body sank deep among the fern, his chest heaved, he shook his head faintly, and then it dropped upon the moss, between the stems of the nodding white flower.

A long Confederate line left a hillside and crossed an open space of corn-field and orchard. Double-quick it moved, under its banners, under the shells shrieking above. The guns changed range, and an iron flail struck the line. It wavered, wavered. A Federal line leaped a stone wall, and swept forward, under its banners, hurrahing. Midway of the wide open there was stretched beneath the murky sky a narrow web — woof of grey, warp of blue. The strip held while the heart beat a minute or more, then it parted. The blue edge went backward over the plain; the grey edge, after a moment, rushed after. "Yaaaiihhh! Yaaaiiihhhh!" it shouted, — and its red war-flag glowed like fire. The grey commander-in-chief watched from a hillside, a steady light in his eyes. Over against him on another hill, Meade, the blue general, likewise watched. To the south, across the distant Potomac, lay the vast, beleaguered, Southern fortress. Its gate had opened; out had poured a vast sally party, a third of its bravest and best, and at the head the leader most trusted, most idolized. Out had rushed the Army of Northern Virginia. It had crossed the moat of the Potomac; it was here, on the beleaguer's ground.

Earth and heaven were shaking with the clangour of two shields. The sky was whirring and dim, but there might be imagined, suspended there, a huge balance — here the besiegers, here the fortress's best and bravest. Which would this day, or these days, tip the beam? Much hung upon that — all might be said to hang upon that. The waves on the plain rolled forward, rolled back, rolled forward. When the sun went down the first day the fortress's battle-flag was in the ascendant.

A great red barn was the headquarters of "Dear Dick Ewell." He rode with Gordon and others at a gallop down a smoky road between stone fences. "Wish Old Jackson was here!" he said. "Wish Marse Robert had Old Jackson! This is the watershed, General Gordon — yes, sir! this is the watershed of the war! If it does n't still go right to-day — It seems to me that wall there 's got a suspicious look —"

The wall in question promptly justified the suspicion. There came from behind it a volley that emptied grey saddles.

Gordon heard the thud of the minie as it struck "Old Dick." "Are you hurt, sir? Are you hurt?"

"No, no, General! I'm not hurt. But if that ball had struck you, sir, we'd have had the trouble of carrying you off the field. I'm a whole lot better fixed than you for a fight! It don't hurt a mite to be shot in a wooden leg."

Three grey soldiers lay behind a shock of wheat. They were young men, old schoolmates. This wheat-shock marked the farthest point attained in a desperate charge made by their regiment against a larger force. It was one of those charges in which everybody sees that if a miracle happens it will be all right, and that if it does n't happen — It was one of those charges in which first an officer stands out, waving his sword, then a man or two follow him, then three or four more, then all waver back, only to start forth again, then others join, then the officer cries aloud, then, with a roar, the line springs forward and rushes over the field, in the cannon's mouth. Such had been the procedure in this charge. The miracle had not happened. After a period of mere din as of ocean waves the three found themselves behind this heap of tarnished gold. When, gasping, they looked round, all their fellows had gone back; they saw them a distant torn line, still holding the flag. Then a rack of smoke came between, hiding flag and all. The three seemed alone in the world. The wheat-ears made a low inner sound like reeds in quiet marshes. The smoke lifted just enough to let a muddy sunlight touch an acre of the dead.

"We've got," said one of the young men, "to get out of here. They'll be countercharging in a minute."

"O God! let them charge."

"Harry, are you afraid —"

"Yes; I'm afraid — sick and afraid. O God, O God!"

The oldest of the three, moving his head very cautiously, looked round the wheat-shock. "The Army of the Potomac's coming." He rose to his knees, facing the other way. "It's two hundred yards to the regiment. Well, we always won the races at the old Academy. I'll start, Tom, and then you follow, and then you, Harry, you come straight along!"

He rose to his feet, took the posture of a runner, drew a deep breath and started. Two yards from the shock a cannon ball sheared the head from the body. The body fell, jutting blood. The head bounded back within the shadow of the wheat-shock. Tom was already standing, bent like a bow. A curious sound came from his lips, he glanced aside, then ran. He ran as swiftly as an Indian, swiftly and well. The minie did not find him until he was halfway across the field. Then it did, and he threw up his arms and fell. Harry, on his hands and knees, turned from side to side an old, old face, bloodless and twisted. He heard the Army of the Potomac coming, and in front lay the corpses. He tried to get to his feet, but his joints were water, and there was a crowd of black atoms before his eyes. A sickness, a clamminess, a despair — and all in eternities. . . . Then the sound swelled, and it drove him as the cry of the hounds drives the hare. He ran, panting, but the charge now swallowed up the wheat-shock and came thundering on. In front was only the dead, piled at the foot of the wall of smoke. He still clutched his gun, and now with a shrill cry, he stopped, turned, and stood at bay. He had hurt a hunter in the leg, before the blue muskets clubbed him down.

A regiment, after advancing a skirmish line, moved over broken and boulder-strewn ground to occupy a yet defended position. In front moved the colonel, half turned toward his men, encouraging them in a rich and hearty voice. "Come on, men! Come on! Come on! You are all good harvesters, and the grain is ripe, the grain is ripe! Come on, every mother's son of you! Run, now! just as though there were home and children up there! Come on! Come on!"

The regiment reached a line of flat boulders. There was a large, flat one like an altar slab, that the colonel must spring upon and cross. Upon it, outstretched, face upward, in a pool of blood, lay a young figure, a lieutenant of skirmishers, killed a quarter of an hour ago. "Come on! Come on!" shouted the colonel, his face turned to his men. "Victory! To-night we'll write home about the victory!"

His foot felt for the top edge of the boulder. He sprang upon it, and faced with suddenness the young dead. The oncoming line saw him stand as if frozen, then with a stiff jerk up went the sword again. "Come on! Come on!" he cried, and plunging from the boulder continued to mount the desired slope. His men, close behind him, also encountered the dead on the altar slab. "Good God! It's Lieutenant — It's his son!" But in front the colonel's changed voice continued its crying, "Come on! Come on! Come on!"

A stone wall, held by the grey, leaped fire, rattled and smoked. It did this at short intervals for a long while, a brigade of the enemy choosing to charge at like intervals. The grey's question was a question of ammunition. So long as the ammunition held out, so would they and the wall. They sent out foragers for cartridges. Four men, having secured a quantity from an impatiently sympathetic reserve, heaped them in a blanket, made a large bundle, and slung it midway of a musket. One man took the butt, another the muzzle, and as they had to reckon with sharpshooters going back, the remaining two marched in front. All double-quicked where the exposure was not extreme, and ran where it was. The echoing goal grew larger — as did also a clump of elms at right angles with the wall. Vanguard cocked its eye. "Buzzards in those trees, boys — blue buzzards!"

Vanguard pitched forward as he spoke. The three ran on. Ten yards, and the man who had been second and was now first, was picked off. The two ran on, the cartridges between them. "We're goners!" said the one, and the other nodded as he ran.

There was a grey battery somewhere in the smoke, and now by chance or intention it flung into the air a shell that shrieked its way straight to the clump of elms, and exploded in the round of leaf and branch. The sharpshooters were stilled. "Moses and the prophets!" said the runners. "That's a last year's bird's nest!"

Altogether the foragers brought in ammunition enough to serve the grey wall's immediate purpose. It cracked and flamed for another while, and then the blue brigade ceased its charges and went elsewhere. It went thinned — oh, thinned! — in numbers. The grey waited a little for the smoke to lift, and then it mounted the wall. "And the ground before us," says a survivor, "was the most heavenly blue!"

A battalion of artillery, thundering across a corner of the field, went into position upon a little hilltop. Facing it was Cemetery Hill and a tall and wide-arched gateway. This gateway, now clearly seen, now withdrawn behind a world of grey smoke, now showing a half arch, an angle, a span of the crest, exercised a fascination. The gunners, waiting for the word, watched it. "Gate of Death, don't it look? — Gate of Death." — "Wonder what's beyond?" — "Yankees." — "But they ain't dead — they're alive and kicking!" — "Now it's hidden — Gate of Death." — "This battle's going to lay over Sharpsburg. Over Gaines's Mill — over Malvern Hill — over Fredericksburg — over Second Manassas — over —" "The Gate's hidden — there's a battery over there going to open —" "One? there's two, there's three —" "*Cannoneers, to your pieces!*"

A shell dug into the earth and exploded. There was a heavy rain of dark earth. It pattered against all the pieces. It showered men and horses, and for a minute made a thick twilight of the air. "Whew! the Earth's taking a hand! Anybody hurt?" — "*Howitzer, load!*"

"Gate of Death's clear."

An artillery lieutenant, — Robert Stiles, — acting as volunteer aide to Gordon, was to make his way across the battle-field with information for Edward Johnson. The ground was strewn with the dead, the air was a shrieking torrent of shot and shell. The aide and his horse thought only of the thing in hand — getting across that field, getting across with the order. The aide bent to the horse's neck; the horse laid himself to the ground and raced like a wild horse before a prairie fire. The aide thought of nothing; he was going to get the order there; for the rest his mind seemed as useless as

a mirror with a curtain before it. Afterwards, however, when he had
time to look he found in the mirror pictures enough. Among them
was a picture of a battalion — Latimer's battalion. "Never, before
or after, did I see fifteen or twenty guns in such a condition of wreck
and destruction as this battalion was! It had been hurled backward, as it were by the very weight and impact of metal, from the
position it had occupied on the crest of a little ridge, into a saucer-
shaped depression behind it; and such a scene as it presented! — guns
dismounted and disabled, carriages splintered and crushed, ammunition chests exploded, limbers upset, wounded horses plunging and
kicking, dashing out the brains of men tangled in the harness; while
cannoneers with pistols were crawling round through the wreck
shooting the struggling horses to save the lives of the wounded
men."

Hood and his Texans and Law's Alabamians were trying to take
Little Round Top. They drove out the line of sharpshooters behind
the stone wall girdling the height. Back went the blue, up the steeps,
up to their second line, behind a long ledge of rock. Up and after
went the grey. The tall boulders split the advance like the teeth of a
comb; no alignment could be kept. The rocks formed defiles where
only two or three could go abreast. The way was steep and horrible,
and from above rained the bullets. Up went the grey, reinforced now
by troops from McLaws's division; up they went and took the second
line. Back and up went the blue to the bald and rocky crest, to their
third line, a stronghold, indeed, and strongly held. Up and on came
the grey, but it was as though the sky were raining lead. The grey
fell like leaves in November when the winds howl around Round
Top. Oh, the boulders! The blood on the boulders, making them
slippery! Oh, the torn limbs of trees, falling so fast! The eyes
smarted in the smoke; the voice choked in the throat. All men were
hoarse with shouting.

Darkness and light went in flashes, but the battle odour stayed, and
the unutterable volume of sound. All the dogs of war were baying.
The muscles strained, the foot mounted. Forward and up went the
battle-flag, red ground and blue cross. Now the boulders were foes,
and now they were shields. Men knelt behind them and fired upward. Officers laid aside their swords, took the muskets from the
dead, knelt and fired. But the crest of Round Top darted lightnings

— lightnings and bolts of leaden death. Death rained from Round Top, and the drops beat down the grey. Hood was badly hurt in the arm. Pender fell mortally wounded. Anderson was wounded. Semmes fell mortally wounded. Barksdale received here his death-wound. Amid the howl of the storm, in the leaden air, in scorching, in blood and pain and tumult and shouting, the small, unheeded disk of the sun touched the western rim of the earth.

A wounded man lay all night in Devil's Den. There were other wounded there, but the great boulders hid them from one another. This man lay in a rocky angle, upon the overhanging lip of the place. Below him, smoke clung like a cerement to the far-flung earth. For a time smoke was about him, thick in his nostrils. For a time it hid the sky. But now all firing was stayed, the night was wheeling on, and the smoke lifted. Below, vague in the night-time, were seen flickering lights — torches, he knew, ambulances, litter-bearers, lifting, serving one in a hundred. They were far away, scattered over the stricken field. They would not come up here to Devil's Den. He knew they would not come, and he watched them as the ship-wrecked watch the sail upon the horizon that has not seen their signal, and that will not see it. He, shipwrecked here, had waved no cloth, but, idle as it was, he had tried to shout. His voice had fallen like a broken-winged bird. Now he lay, in a pool of his own blood, not greatly in pain, but dying. Presently he grew light-headed, though not so much so but that he knew that he was light-headed, and could from time to time reason with his condition. He was a reading man, and something of a thinker, and now his mind in its wanderings struck into all manner of by-paths.

For a time he thought that the field below was the field of Waterloo. He remembered seeing, while it was yet light, a farmhouse, a distant cluster of buildings with a frightened air. "La Belle Alliance," he thought, "or Hougomont — which? — These Belgians planted a lot of wheat, and now there are red poppies all through it. — Where is Ney and his cavalry? — No, Stuart and his cavalry —" His mind righted for a moment. "This is a long battle, and a long night. Come, Death! Come, Death!" The shadowy line of boulders became a line of Deaths, tall, draped figures bearing scythes. Three Deaths, then a giant hour-glass, then three Deaths, then the hour-glass. He stared, fascinated. "Which scythe? The one that starts out of line — now if I can keep them still in line — just so long will I live!" He stared for a while, till the Deaths became boulders again and his fingers fell to playing with the thickening blood on the ground beside him. A meteor pierced the night — a white fire-ball thrown from the ramparts of the sky. He seemed to be rushing with it, rushing, rushing, rushing,— a rushing river. There was a heavy sound. As his head sank back he saw again the line of Deaths, and the one that left the line.

Below, through the night, the wind that blew over the wheat-fields and the meadows, the orchards and the woods, was a moaning wind. It was a wind with a human voice.

Dawn came, but the guns smeared her translucence with black. The sun rose, but the ravens' wings hid him. Dull red and sickly copper was this day, hidden and smothered by dark wreaths. Many things happened in it, variation and change that cast a tendril toward the future.

Day drove on; sultry and loud and smoky. A squad of soldiers in a fence corner, waiting for the order forward, exchanged opinions. "Three days. We're going to fight forever — and ever — and ever." — "You may be. I ain't. I'm going to fight through to where there's peace —" "'Peace!' How do you spell it?" — "'They cry Peace! Peace! and there is no Peace!'" — "D'ye reckon if one of us took a bucket and went over to that spring there, he'd be shot?" — "Of course he would! Besides, where's the bucket?" — "I've got a canteen." — "I've got a cup —" "Say, Sergeant, can we go?" — "No. You'll be killed." — "I'd just as soon be killed as to perish of thirst! Besides, a shell'll come plump-ing down directly and kill us anyhow." —"Talk of something pleas-ant." — "Jim's caught a grasshopper! Poor little hoppergrass, you ought n't to be out here in this wide and wicked world! Let him go, Jim." — "How many killed and wounded do you reckon there are?" — "Thirty thousand of us, and sixty thousand of them." — "I wish that smoke would lift so's we could see something!" — "*Look out! Look out! Get out of this!*"

Two men crawled away from the crater made by the shell. A heavy tussock of grass in their path stopped them. One rose to his knees, the other, who was wounded, took the posture of the dying Gaul in the Capitoline. "Who are you?" said the one. — "I am

Jim Dudley. Who are you?" — "I — I did n't know you, Jim. I'm Randolph. — Well, we're all that's left."

The dead horses lay upon this field one and two and three days in the furnace heat. They were fearful to see and there came from them a fetid odour. But the scream of the wounded horses was worse than the sight of the dead. There were many wounded horses. They lay in wood and field, in country lane and orchard. No man tended them, and they knew not what it was all about. To and fro and from side to side of the vast, cloud-wreathed Mars's Shield galloped the riderless horses.

At one of the clock all the guns, blue and grey, opened in a cannonade that shook the leaves of distant trees. A smoke as of Vesuvius or Ætna, sulphurous, pungent, clothed the region of battle. The air reverberated and the hills trembled. The roar was like the roar of the greatest cataract of a larger world, like the voice of a storm sent by the King of all the Genii. Amid its deep utterance the shout even of many men could not be heard.

Out from the ranks of the fortress's defenders rushed a grey, world-famous charge. It was a division charging — three brigades *en échelon*, — five thousand men, led by a man with long auburn locks. Down a hill, across a rolling open, up an opposite slope, — half a mile in all, perhaps, — lay their road. Mars and Bellona may be figured in the air above it. It was a spectacle, that charge, fit to draw the fierce eyes and warm the gloomy souls of all the warrior deities. Woden may have watched and the Aztec god. The blue artillery crowned that opposite slope, and other slopes. The blue artillery swung every muzzle; it spat death upon the five thousand. The five thousand went steadily, grey and cool and clear, the vivid flag above them. A light was on their bayonets — the three lines of bayonets — the three brigades, Garnett and Kemper and Armistead. A light was in the eyes of the men; they saw the fortress above the battle clouds; they saw their homes, and the watchers upon the ramparts. They went steadily, to the eyes of history in a curious, unearthly light, the light of a turn in human affairs, the light of catastrophe, the light of an ending and a beginning.

When they came into the open between the two heights, the massed blue infantry turned every rifle against them. There poured a leaden rain of death. Here, too, the three lines met an enfilading fire from the batteries on Round Top. Death howled and threw himself against the five thousand; in the air above might be heard the Valkyries calling. There were not now five thousand, there were not now four thousand. There was a clump of trees seen like spectres through the smoke. It rose from the slope which was the grey goal, from the slope peopled by Federal batteries, with a great Federal infantry support at hand. Toward this slope, up this slope, went Pickett's charge.

Garnett fell dead. Kemper and Trimble were desperately wounded. Save Pickett himself, all mounted officers were down. The men fell — the men fell; Death swung a fearful scythe. There were not now four thousand, there were not now three thousand. And still the vivid flag went on; and still, high, thrilling, clear and dauntless, rose from Pickett's charge the "rebel yell."

There was a stone wall to cross. Armistead, his hat upon the point of his waved sword, leaped upon the coping. A bullet pierced his breast; he fell, was captured, and the next day died. By now, by now the charge was whittled thin! Oh, thick as the leaves of Vallombrosa, the fortress's dearest and best lay upon that slope beneath the ravens' wings! On went the thin, fierce ranks, on and over the wall, on and up, into the midst of the enemy's guns. The two flags strained toward each other; the hands of the grey were upon the guns of the blue; there came a wild mêlée. . . . There were not two thousand now, and the guns were yet roaring, and the blue infantry gathered from all sides. . . .

"The smoke," says one Luther Hopkins, a grey soldier who was at Gettysburg, "the smoke rose higher and higher and spread wider and wider, hiding the sun, and then, gently dropping back, hid from human eyes the dreadful tragedy. But the battle went on and on, and the roar of the guns continued. After a while, when the sun was sinking to rest, there was a hush. The noise died away. The winds came creeping back from the west, and gently lifting the coverlet of smoke, revealed a strange sight. The fields were all carpeted, a beautiful carpet, a costly carpet, more costly than Axminster or velvet. The figures were horses and men all matted and woven together with skeins of scarlet thread."

CHAPTER XVI

BACK HOME

IF he who ruleth his spirit is greater than he that taketh a city, Robert E. Lee was a general doubly great. The gallantry of the three days' fighting at Gettysburg he left like a golden light, like a laurel wreath, with his men. The responsibility for Gettysburg, its strategy and its tactics, he laid with quietness upon his own shoulders and kept it there. In the last hour of the third day, after the last great charge, after Pickett's charge, when the remnant that was left was streaming back, he rode into the midst of that thin grey current. He sat Traveller, in the red light, in the murk and sorrow of the lost battle, and called upon the men to reform. Pickett came by, his sword out, his long auburn hair dank with sweat. "Get your men together, General," said Lee. "They did nobly. It is all my fault."

If the boyishness in Jeb Stuart, his dear love of dancing meteors, had swept him in the past weeks too far from his proper base, he was now fully and to the end by his general's side. He kept his gaiety, his *panache*, but he put on the full man. He was the Stuart of Chancellorsville, throwing a steady dart, swinging a great shield. Longstreet, the "old war horse"; A. P. Hill, red-shirted, a noble fighter; "Dear Dick Ewell" — each rose, elastic, from the disastrous field and played the man. That slow retreat from Gettysburg to the Potomac, through a hostile country, with a victorious, larger army hovering, willing to strike if only it could find the unguarded place, was masterly planned, masterly done. The Army of Northern Virginia retired grudgingly, with backward turnings, foot planted and spear brandished. It had with it pain and agony, for it carried its wounded; it had with it appalling knowledge that Vicksburg was fallen, that the battle behind them, hard-fought for three days, was lost, that the campaign was lost, that across the river the South was mourning, mourning, that at last all were at the death-grapple. It knew it all, but it went steadily, with lips that could yet manage a smile. For all its freight of wounded, for all the mourning of its banners, it went ably; a long, masterly retreat, with effective stands and threatenings. But how the wounded suffered, only the wounded knew.

The rain came down as it usually did after the prolonged cannonadings of these great battles. It came down in sullen torrents, unfriendly, cold, deepening the deep reaction after the fever of the fight. It fell in showers from a sky leaden all the day, inky all the night. At twilight on the fourth, A. P. Hill and the Third Corps swung in silence out upon the Fountain Dale and Monterey road. They marched away in the rain and darkness. All night Longstreet and the First stayed in position at the Peach Orchard. But the foe did not attack, and at dawn Longstreet and the First followed A. P. Hill. When the dawn broke, grey and wet, Ewell and the Second Corps alone were there by Seminary Ridge. Again the blue — they also gathering their wounded, they also mourning their dead — made no movement to attack. Ewell and the Second followed the First.

The rain came down, the rain came down — rain and wind and low-hanging clouds. Forty thousand men marched in a silence which, now and then, it was felt, must be broken. Men broke it, with song that had somehow a sob in it, with laughter more strained than jovial. Then came down the silence again, leaden with the leaden rain. But march in silence, or march in mirth, the Army of Northern Virginia marched with its *morale* unbroken. *Tramp, tramp!* through the shifting sheets of rain, through the wind that bent the tree-tops. . . . With Hood's division marched four thousand and more of Federal prisoners. With these, too, the silence was heavy.

But there was not silence when it came to the fearful train of the wounded. Fifteen miles, along the Chambersburg Pike, stretched the train of the wounded and of ordnance and supply wagons, with its escort of cavalry and a score of guns. The convoy was in the charge of Imboden, and he was doing the best he could with those long leagues of hideous woe. The road was rough; the night dark, with wind and rain. "Woe!" cried the wind. "Woe, woe! Pain and woe!"

Ambulances, carts, wagons, crowded with the wounded, went

joltingly, under orders to use all speed. Cavalry rode before, cavalry guarded the rear, but few were the actual guards in among or alongside the wagons. Vanguard and rear guard needed every unhurt man. For miles there were, in sum, only the wounded, the jaded wagon horses, the wagon drivers with drawn faces. Orders were for no pausing, no halts. If a wagon became disabled, draw it out of the road and leave it! There must be rapid travelling through the night. Even so, if the blue were alert, the blue might strike the train before day. Rapid motion and no halting — "On!" beneath the blackness, in the teeth of wind and rain. "Woe!" cried the wind. "Woe, woe! Pain and woe!"

The wagons were springless. In many there was no straw. Numbers of the wounded lay upon bare boards, placed there, in some cases, hours even before the convoy could start. Many had had no food for long hours, no water. Their rough clothing, stiff with dried blood, abraded and inflamed their wounds. The surgeons had done what bandaging was possible, but many a ghastly hurt went unbound, unlooked to. With others the bandages slipped, or were torn aside by pain-maddened hands. There was blood upon the bed of all the wagons, blood and human refuse. Upon the boards lay men with their eyes gone, with their jaws shot through and crushed, with their arms, their legs mangled, with their thighs pierced, their bowels pierced, with tormenting stomach wounds, with a foot gone, a hand gone. There were men with fever and a horrible thirst, and men who shook in a death chill. There were men who were dead. And on them all poured the rain, for the canvas wagon covers, flapping in the wind, could not keep it out. And the road, cut by countless wheels and now washed into ridge and hollow, would have been rough for well folk, in cushioned vehicles. "On! On! No halting for any one! — Good God, man! Don't I know they are suffering? Don't I *hear* them? Do you reckon I *like* to hear them? But if I'm going to save General Lee's trains I've *got* to get on! *Get on, there!*" "Woe!" cried the wind. "Woe, woe! pain and woe."

"Oh, Jesus Christ, have mercy upon me!"

"Just let me die, O God! just let me die!"

"If there's anybody at all outside, won't they stop this wagon? If there's anybody driving, won't you stop this wagon? Please! You don't know how it hurts — Please! . . . Ah! — *Aaahh! — Aaahh!*"

"Curse you! — Curse war! — Curse living and dying! Curse God! Ah! — *Ahhh! — Aaahhh!*"

"For God's sake! just lift us out and let us die lying still, on the roadside. . . . O God! O God!"

"O God! O God!"

"I am dying! I am dying! . . . Mary, Mary, Mary! Lift me up!"

"We are dying! We are dying!"

"O Jesus of Nazareth —"

"During this one night," says Imboden, "I realized more of the horrors of war than I had in all the two preceding years."

The Second Corps, marching by the Fairfield road, marched in rain and wind and weariness. Ewell, wooden-legged now, irascible, heroic, sighing for "Old Jackson," handling his corps as "Old Jackson" would have approved, rode in front. Jubal Early, strange compound but admirable fighter, — Jubal Early guarded the rear with the brigades of Hoke and Smith and Gordon and Harry Hays. Between were Rodes's division — Iverson and Daniels, Dole, Ramseur and O'Neal — and "Alleghany" Johnson's division — Steuart and Jones and Nicholls and the Stonewall Brigade. With each division heavily moved upon the road its artillery — Charlottesville Artillery, Staunton Artillery, Louisiana Guard Artillery, Courtney Artillery, King William Artillery, Orange Artillery, Morris Artillery, Jeff Davis Artillery, Chesapeake Artillery, Alleghany Artillery, First Maryland Battery, Lee Battery, Powhatan Artillery, Salem Artillery, Rockbridge Artillery, Third Richmond Howitzers, Second Richmond Howitzers, Amherst Artillery, Fluvanna Artillery, Milledge's Georgia Battery.

The Stonewall Brigade bent its head and took the blast. The rain streamed from the slanted forest of rifle barrels; the wind blew out the officer's capes; the colours had to be furled against it. All the colours were smoke-darkened, shot-riddled. The Stonewall was a veteran brigade. It had an idea that it had been engaged in war since the rains first came upon the earth. Walker, its general, a good and gallant man, plodded at its head, his hat brim streaming wet, his horse's breath making a little cloud. *Tramp! tramp!* behind him marched the Stonewall — a long, swinging gait, a "foot cavalry" gait.

The Sixty-fifth Virginia, Colonel Erskine, covered the way with a mountain stride. It was nearing now the pass of the South Mountain, and its road lay uphill. It had done good service at Gettysburg, and it had its wounded in that anguished column over on the Chambersburg Pike. It had left its dead upon the field. Now, climbing the long hills, colours slanted forward, keen, bronzed faces slanted forward, man and beast streaming rain and all battling with the gusty wind, the Sixty-fifth missed its dead, missed its wounded, knew that the army had suffered defeat, knew that the high hopes of this campaign lay in ashes, knew that these days formed a crisis in the war, knew that all the sky had darkened over the South, knew that before it lay grim struggle and a doubtful end. The units of the Sixty-fifth knew many things that in the old piping time of peace they had never thought to know.

The grain in the fields was all broken down, the woods clashed their branches, through flawed sheets of dull silver the distant mountain crests were just divined. The wind howled like a banshee, and for all that it was July the air was cold. The Sixty-fifth thought of other marches. Before McDowell — Elk Run Valley — that was bad. Elk Run Valley was bad. Before Mechanicsville — coming down from Beaver Dam Station — that was bad. Bath to Romney — that was worst. . . . We've had plenty of bad marches — plenty of marches — plenty of heroic marches. We are used to marching — used to marching . . . Marching and fighting — marching and fighting. . . .

Tall and lean and tanned, the Thunder Run men opposed the wind from the mountains. Allan Gold and Sergeant Billy Maydew exchanged observations.

"I would n't be tired," said Billy, "going up Thunder Run Mountain. I air not tired anyhow."

"No, there's no help in being tired. . . . I hope that Tom and Sairy are dry and warm —"

"I don't mind wet," said Billy, " and I don't mind cold, and I can tighten my belt when I'm hungry, but the thing that air hard for me to stand air going without sleep. I tell my will to hold hard and I put tobacco in my eyes, but sleep sure air a hard thing for me to go without. I could sleep now — I could sleep — I could sleep . . . Yes; I hope all Thunder Run air dry and warm — Mr. Cole and Mrs.

Cole and Mother and Christianna and Violetta and Rosalinda and
the children and Grandpap and the dawgs and Steve Dagg — No;
I kinder hope Steve air wet and whimpering. . . . Thunder Run's
a long way off. I could go to sleep — and sleep — and sleep . . ."
"I'm not sleepy," said Allan. "But I wish I had a pitcher of
milk —"

The Sixty-fifth determined to try singing.

> "O my Lawd, whar you gwine?
> Keep in de middle ob de road!
> Gwine de way dat Moses trod,
> Keep in de middle ob de road —"

> "The butcher had a little dog,
> And Bingo was his name.
> BB–i–n–g–o–go! B–i–n–g–o–go!
> And Bingo was his name —"

Toward four o'clock, as the head of the column neared Fairfield,
came from the rear a burst of firing — musketry, then artillery.
There was a halt, then the main body resumed the march. Early,
in the rear, deployed Gordon's brigade and fought back the long skirmish line of the pursuing blue. Throughout the remainder of the
afternoon there was fitful firing — sound, water-logged like all else,
rising dully from the rear. Down came the night, dark as a bat's
wing. The Second Corps bivouacked a mile from Fairfield, and,
waking now and then in the wet and windy night, heard the rear
guard repelling half-hearted attacks.

Reveille echoed among the hills. The Second rose beneath a still
streaming sky. The Stonewall, camped on a hillside, sought for
wood for its fires and found but little, and that too wet to burn. It
was fortunate, perhaps, that there was so little to cook. The Sixty-
fifth squatted around a dozen pin-points of light and did its best
with the scrapings of its commissary. "Well, boys, the flesh pots of
Egypt have given us the go-by! D'ye remember that breakfast at
Greencastle? Oohh! Wasn't it good?" . . . "Hold your hat over
the fire or it'll go out!" . . . "I wish we had some coffee . . ."
"Listen at Gordon, way back there, popping away at Yanks! —
Did you hear about his men burning fence rails? No? — well,
't was out beyond York. 'Men!' says Marse Robert's General
Order, 'don't tech a thing!' 'All right, Marse Robert!' says we, as

you can testify. Gordon's as chivalrous as Young Lochinvar, or 'A Chieftain to the Highlands Bound,' or Bayard, or any of them fellows. So he piles on an order, too. 'Don't touch a thing! especially not the fences. Gather your wood where Nature has flung it!' Well, those Georgia boys had to camp that night where Nature had n't flung any wood — neither Cedar of Lebanon nor darned pawpaw bush! Just a nice bare field with rail fences — our kind of fences. Nice, old, dry, seasoned rails. Come along Gordon, riding magnificently. 'General, the most wood around here is musket stocks, and of course we ain't going to burn them! Can't we take just a *few* rails?' 'Boys,' says Gordon, being like a young and handsome father to his men. 'Boys, you can take the top rail. That will leave the fences high enough for the farmer's purposes. Now, mind me! don't lay your hand on anything but the top rail!' And off he goes, looking like a picture — leaf of Round Table, or what not. Whereupon company by company marched up and each took in turn the top rail."

"Must have been an all-fired lasting top rail —"

"— And they had supper and went to bed cheered and comforted. And by and by, in the morning, just after reveille, comes Gordon, fresh as a daisy. And he looks at the boundaries of that field, and he colours up. 'Men,' he says in a kind of grieved anger, 'you have disobeyed orders!' Whereupon those innocents rose up and assured him that not a man had touched anything but a top rail!"

Fall in! Fall in! Column Forward!

It rained, and rained. You saw the column as through smoke, winding toward the pass of the South Mountain. From the rear came fitfully the sound of musketry. But there was no determined pursuit. Early kept the rear; Stuart, off in the rain and mist, lionbold, and, throughout the long retreat to the fortress, greatly sagacious, guarded the flanks. A. P. Hill and Longstreet were now beyond the mountains, swinging southward by the Ringgold road. With the First and the Third rode Lee, grey on grey Traveller, in the grey rain, his face turned homeward, turned toward the fortress of the South, vast, mournful, thenceforth trebly endangered. It was the sixth of July. A year ago had been the Seven Days.

Back on the road of the wounded there was trouble. Imboden, having crossed the mountain, determined upon a short cut by a country road to Greencastle. On through the small town rode the vanguard, the Eighteenth Virginia Cavalry. Behind, as rapidly as might be, came the immense and painful train. On the outskirts of the place a band of civilians attacked a weakly guarded portion of the column. They had axes, and with these they hewed in two the wagon yokes or cut the spokes from the wheels. The wagon beds dropped heavily upon the earth. *"Ahh!"* groaned the wounded. *"Ahhh! Aaaahh!"*

Back in wrath came a detachment of the Eighteenth, scattering or capturing the wielders of axes. The long train passed Greencastle. Before it lay the road to Williamsport, the road to the Potomac. The rain was streaming, the wind howling, and now the Federal cavalry made its appearance. All the rest of the day the train was subjected to small sudden attacks, descents now on this section, now on that. The grey escort, cavalry and artillery, beat them off like stinging bees; the grey wagoners plied their long whips, the exhausted horses strained forward yet again, under the wagon wheel was felt again the ridge and hollow of the storm-washed road. "Woe!" cried the wind. "Woe, woe! Pain and woe!"

There came a report that blue troops held Williamsport, but when late in a stormy afternoon the head of Imboden's column came to this place, so known by now, frontier, with only the moat of the river between the foe's territory and the fortress's territory, — when the advance rode into town, there were found only peaceful Marylanders. The grey convoy occupied Williamsport. At last the torturing wagons stopped, at last the moaning hurt were lifted out, at last the surgeons could help, at last the dead were parted from the living. Imboden requisitioned all the kitchens of the place. There arose a semblance of warmth, a pale ghost of cheer. Here and there sounded even a weak laugh.

"Say, Doctor! after hell, purgatory seems kind of good to us! That was hell back there on the road — hell if ever there was hell . . . *Ouch!* . . . *Ooooghh! Doctor!*"

"Doctor, do you reckon I'll live to get across? I want to see my wife — I want to see her so badly. — There's a boy, too, and I've never seen him —"

"How air we going to get across? Air there boats?"

"Who's keeping the Yankees away? Jeb Stuart? That's good. . . .

Oh, Doctor, you ain't going to cut it off? Please, Doctor, please, sir, don't! No, it won't mortify — I'm just as sure of that! Please just put it in splints. It ain't so badly hurt — it ain't hurting me hardly any. . . . Doctor, Doctor! for God's sake! — Why, I could n't walk any more! — why, I'd have to leave the army! . . . Doctor, please don't — please don't cut it off, sir. . . ."

The rain came down, the rain came down, a drenching, sullen storm. Wide, yellow, and swollen rolled the Potomac before Williamsport. Imboden procured several flatboats, and proceeded to the ferrying across of those of the more slightly wounded who thought that once in Virginia they might somehow get to Winchester. In the midst of this work came news of the approach of a large force of Federal cavalry and artillery — Buford and Kilpatrick's divisions hurrying down from Frederick.

Imboden posted every gun with him on the heights between the town and the river. Hart, Eshleman, McClanahan — all faced the eighteen rifled guns with which presently the blue opened. A sharp artillery battle followed, each side firing with rapidity and some effect. Imboden had his cavalry and in addition seven hundred wagoners organized into companies and headed by commissaries, quartermasters, and several wounded officers. These wagoners did mightily. This fight was called afterwards "The Wagoners' Battle." Five blue cavalry regiments were thrown forward. The Eighteenth Virginia Cavalry and the Sixty-second Virginia Mounted Infantry met them with clangour in the rain-filled air. McNeill's Partisan Rangers came to the aid of the wagoners down by the river. Eshleman's eight Napoleons of the Washington Artillery, Hart's and McClanahan's and Moore's batteries poured shot and shell from the heights. Through the dusk came at a gallop a courier from Fitzhugh Lee. "Hold out, General Imboden! We're close at hand!" From the direction of the Hagerstown road broke a clap of war thunder, rolling among the hills. "Horse Artillery! Horse Artillery!" yelled Imboden's lines, the Eighteenth, the Sixty-second, the Partisan Rangers, and the Wagoners. *Yaaaihh! Yaaaaihh! Yaaaaaaihh! Forward! Charge!*

July the seventh broke wet and stormy. The First and Third Corps were now at Hagerstown. Ewell and the Second nearer South Mountain, yet watchfully regarding the defiles through which might pour the pursuit. But Meade had hesitated, hesitated. It was only on the afternoon of the fifth that a move southward was begun in earnest. The Sixth Corps, on the same road with Ewell, struck now and again at the grey rear guard, but the rest of the great blue army hung uncertain. Only on the seventh did it pour southward, through the country between the Monocacy and the Antietam. In the dusk of this day Lee met Stuart and ordered an attack at dawn. Time must be gained while a bridge was built across the swollen river.

All day the eighth the heavy air carried draggingly the sound of cannon. So drowned with rain were the fields and meadows that manœuvring there was manœuvring in quagmires. The horsemen of both sides must keep to the roads, deep in mire as were these. Dismounted, they fought with carbines in all the sopping ways, while from every slight rise the metal duellists barked at one another. At last the Fifth Confederate Brigade drove the Federal left, and the running fight and the long wet day closed with one gleam of light in the west.

On July the ninth the Army of Northern Virginia occupied a ten-mile line from the Potomac at Mercersville to the Hagerstown and Williamsport road. A. P. Hill held the centre, Longstreet the right, Ewell the left, stretching toward Hagerstown. Forty thousand infantry and artillery stood ready. Stuart with eight thousand horsemen drew off to the north, watching like a falcon, ready for the pounce. The rain ceased to fall. A pale sunshine bathed the country, and in it gleamed the steel of the Army of Northern Virginia. The banners grew vivid.

All day Lee waited in line of battle, but Meade was yet hesitant. The tenth dawned, and Stuart sent word that the Army of the Potomac was advancing through the defiles of South Mountain. All this day the grey dug trenches and heaped breastworks. The sun shone, ill was forgotten; hope sprang, nourished by steadfastness. There were slight cavalry encounters. The night of the tenth was a warm and starry one. The grey slept and rose refreshed. Ewell and the Second now left Hagerstown. Each corps commanded one of the three roads glimmering eastward, and Stuart patrolled all the valley of the Antietam. Lee had laid his pontoon bridge across to Falling Waters. All night long there passed into Virginia the wounded and a great portion of the trains.

July twelfth was a day of cloud and mist. Still the grey waited; still Meade, with his sixty-five thousand infantry and artillery, his ten thousand cavalry, hung irresolute. Kelly at Hancock had eight thousand men. He could be trusted to flank the grey. And in the rear of the grey was the river, turbid, wide, deep, so swollen as hardly to be fordable. Halleck telegraphed Meade from Washington peremptory orders to attack. But the twelfth passed with only slight encounters between reconnoitring parties.

On the thirteenth down came the rain again, a thick, cold, shifting veil of wet. Again Meade stayed in his tents. The Army of the Potomac understood that on the morrow it would attack. In the mean time reinforcements were at hand.

That night, in the rainy dusk, Stuart drew a cordon between the opposed forces. Behind the screen of horsemen, behind the impenetrable, rainy night, the Army of Northern Virginia prepared to re-cross the Potomac. Beneath the renewed rains the river was steadily rising; it was go now, or abide the onset of the sixty-five thousand along the Antietam and on the Sharpsburg Pike, with Kelly's eight thousand marching from Hancock, and other troops on the road from Chambersburg. Down came the rain and the night was Egyptian black.

The artillery and the balance of the trains must cross by the pontoon bridge. Bonfires were built on the northern and the southern bank, but all the wood was wet, and the flickering light proved deceitful as any darkness. The rolling smoke mounted and overhung the landings like genii from Arabian bottles. With sullen noise the guns crossed, hour after hour of sullen noise. The wagons with the wounded crossed. A heavy wagon, in which the badly hurt were laid thick, missed its way, and, with its horses, went blindly over the side into the rushing water, where all were drowned. After the guns and the wagons came the men of Longstreet's corps. Dawn found the First not yet over-passed, while the Third waited on the pebbly stretch between the water and the hills. In the mean time Ewell and the Second had undertaken the ford.

That which, a month before, had been a pleasant summer river, — clear, wide, and tranquil, not deep, and well known by now to the Second Corps, — was to-night a monster of the dark, a mill-race of the Titans. The heaped wood set afire on either bank lit the water but a few yards outward. Between the several glares was darkness shot with rain, shaken by wind. And always the bonfires showed thronging men, a broad moving ribbon running upwards and back from the water's edge, and between these two throngs a void and blackness. It was like a vision of the final river — a great illustration out of "Pilgrim's Progress." Company by company went down into the river; company by company slowly mounted on the farther side, coming up from the water into strange light, beneath tall shadowy trees. The water was up to the armpits. It was cold and rushing water. The men tied their cartridge boxes around their necks; they held their muskets above their heads; now and again a short man was carried across upon the shoulders of a tall and strong man. Sergeant Billy Maydew carried Lieutenant Coffin across thus.

The Sixty-fifth kept its cartridges dry, held its muskets high. It had crossed into Maryland with song and joke and laughter, stepping easily through water to the mid-thigh, clear water, sparkling in the sun. It returned into Virginia through a high and stormy water, beneath a midnight sky. The sky of its fortunes, too, was dark. There was no singing to-night; each man, breasting the flood, needed all his wits merely to cross. The red light beat upon the Sixty-fifth going down from the Maryland shore, rank after rank, entering the water in a column of three. Rank by rank, the darkness swallowed it up, officers and men, colonel, lieutenant-colonel, captains, lieutenants, the chaplain, the surgeons, the noncommissioned officers, all the men, Thunder Run men, men from the mountainous Upper Valley counties, — all the Sixty-fifth, rank by rank dipped out of the light into the darkness. The darkness swallowed the regiment, then the darkness gave it again to the light on the Virginia shore. Up to the gate of the fortress, through the red flare of torches, came the Sixty-fifth. A man with a great rich, deep voice, broke into song in the night-time, in the wind and rain, as he came up beneath the sycamores. He sang "Dixie," and the Sixty-fifth sang it with him.

All night, endlessly across the river, out of light into darkness, then into light again, came the slowly unwinding ribbon of the regiments. All night the Second Corps was crossing by the ford as all night the First was crossing by the unstable bridge of boats. In the grey morning there crossed A. P. Hill and the Third. The last brigade was Lane's North Carolinians. It made the passage, and then Stuart drew his thousands steadily to the waterside. Meade's advance, Kilpatrick and Buford, saw from the hill-tops the river dark with swimming horsemen.

CHAPTER XVII

BREAD CAST ON WATER

PRISON X had a catechism which it taught all the newly arrived.
Question. Where are we?
Answer. In the North.
Q. Do we find the North interesting?
Ans. We do not.
Q. Where is the country of our preference?
Ans. South of the Potomac.
Q. Do we find this prison pleasing?
Ans. We do not.
Q. Have we an object in life?
Ans. We have.
Q. What is it?
Ans. To get out.
Q. Again?
Ans. To get out.
Q. Again?
Ans. To get out — and stay out.
Q. Both are difficult?
Ans. Both are difficult.
Q. Have all apparent ways been tried?
Ans. All apparent ways have been tried.
Q. Uprisings, tunnels, sawing window bars, bribing guards, taking a corpse's place, etc., have all been tried?
Ans. They have all been tried.
Q. And they have failed?
Ans. They have failed.
Q. What is to be done?
Ans. I do not know.
Q. Have you an object in life?
Ans. I have an object in life.
Q. What is it?

Ans. To get out — and stay out.

Q. To get South?

Ans. To get South.

Maury Stafford was not a newcomer, but the substance of this catechism was graved in his mind and daily life and actions. He had passed the stage of violently beating against the bars, and had passed the stage of melancholia, and the stage of listlessly sitting in what fleck of sunshine might be found in winter, or hand's breadth of shade in summer. He had settled into the steady stage, the second wind. He knew well enough that, though it might last the longest, this stage, too, would expire. When it did, it might not come again. He had seen it expire in others and it had not come again. He had seen the dead moon of hope that followed, the mere continuance of breathing in a life of shards and weeds. He had seen the brain grow sick in the hands of the will; he had seen the wrists of the will broken across. . . . He meant to make the steady stage last, last, last! — outlast his last day in Prison X.

The August day was hot — almost the hottest, said the papers, on record. Prison X was careful now not to have too many prisoners at once in the prison yard. But to-day the heat seemed to breed humanity; at any rate, there came an order that a fair number of rebels at once might go out into the air. In the officers' yard as many as fifty were permitted to gather at a time. The small, sunbaked, sordid place looked west. At this hour of the morning it was in the prison's shadow, and cooler than it would be later in the day.

Some of the grey prisoners walked up and down, up and down; others sat alone, or in twos and threes, in the shadow of the wall. There was talk, but not loud talking. There was no briskness in the yard, no crisp bubbling of word and action. Languor reigned, and all the desirable lay without the walls. One tree-top showed above them, just the bushy head of an airy, mocking giant.

At ten, the yard being filled, there came in through the gate, where were double guards, three or four officers in blue and a Catholic priest. The yard knew the inspecting officers, and bestirred itself to only a perfunctory recognition — perfunctory, not listless; it being a point of honour not to look listless or broken in presence of the opposing colour. One of these blue officers the yard liked very well, a bluff and manly fellow, with a frown for the very many things he could not alter and a helping hand with the few that he could. The grey made a subtle difference to show here in their greeting.

For the priest — they had never seen him before; and as novelty in prison is thrice novelty, the various groups welcomed with an interested gaze the stout-built, rusty-black figure with a strong face, rosy and likable. "Holy Virgin!" said the priest. "If the South is any warmer than this, sure ye'll be afther thanking the Saints and us for bringing you North! Are there any sons of the Church in sound of my voice?"

There was one — a lieutenant in the last stages of consumption. He sat in the sun with a red spot in each cheek and eyes bright as a bird's. The well-liked blue officer brought the priest to this boy. He was but nineteen, and evidently had not a month to live. "Good morning, Lieutenant!" said the officer. "Father Tierney's a cordial in himself! And if, being a Catholic, you'd like —"

"Were he twenty times a Ribil," said Father Tierney, *sotto voce*, "he's a sick human crathure and a dying man."

"Then I'll leave you with him for a little," said the officer, and walked away.

"Peace go with you!" said Father Tierney. "My poor son, if you've done any harm in the flesh, the Lord having taken away the flesh will take away that, too. — You are not one of those who —" Father Tierney spoke for thirty seconds in a lowered voice.

"No," said the lieutenant, "I used to try, but I gave it up when I saw that I was going to get out anyhow. But a lot of us are still trying — There's one over there that's trying, I'm certain. He's been awful good to me. If he could — if you could now —"

"The man standing in the shadow of the wall?"

The man standing in the shadow of the wall was only a stride or two away. The blue officers had their backs turned; the grey prisoners were listlessly minding their own business; guards and sentries had their eyes on their superiors. The sun blazed down, the green tree-top just nodded.

"Good morning, my son," said Father Tierney.

"Good morning, Father."

Father Tierney took off his hat and with it fanned his rosy, open face. "Holy Virgin! 'T is warmer here in the District than it is in Maryland — Maryland being my home, my son."

"Which half of Maryland, Father?"

"The 'Maryland, my Maryland' half, my son."

"That," said Stafford, "is the half that I like best. It is the nearest to Virginia."

"What," said Father Tierney, "if ye had a wishing-cap, would ye wish for?"

"Gold and a blue suit, Father."

"A uniform, ye mane?"

"No. A hospital steward's suit. Blue linen. I've got it worked out."

"My son," said Father Tierney, in a brisk, full voice, "ye've a look of mortal fever! The Saints know it does n't become us to boast! But I was born with a bit of a medical faculty sticking sthraight out and looking grave. — Let me lay my finger on your pulse."

Stafford's palm closed upon something hard and round and yellow. His eyes met the priest's eyes.

"It's a weary number of soul miles ye'll have been travelling, my friend," thought the priest. "There's something in you that's been lightning branded, but it's putting out green shoots again."

The blue officer was seen approaching. Father Tierney turned with heartiness to meet him. "That poor lad yonder, Captain, he's not long for this sinful world! If you've no objection I'd like to come again — That's thrue! That's thrue enough! 'Who'd mercy have must mercy show.' — Captain, darlint, it's hot enough to melt rock! Between the time I left Ireland and came to America, and that's twinty years ago, I went a pilgrimage to Italy. Having seen Rome I wint to Venice. There's a big palace there where the Doges lived, and up under the palace roof with just a bit of lead like a coffin lid between you and the core of the blessed sun in heaven — there's the prisons they call *piombi*. — Now you usually think of cold when you think of prisons, but I gather that heat's more maddening —"

Prison X was as capricious as any other despot. The next day was as hot a day, but only so many might go into the air at once. Many, waiting their turn in the black, stifling hall, got no other gleam than that afforded by the grudged opening and the swift closing of the outer door. The next day again the heat held and the despot's ill humour held. At long intervals the door opened, but before a score had passed, it closed with a grating sound.

The fourth morning Stafford found himself again in the sun and shadow of this yard. The earth was harder-baked, the blue sky more fiercely metallic, the bushy head of the one tree seen over the wall more decisively mocking. With it all there was a dizziness in the air. He knew that he had been buoyed by the second wind. As he came out from the gloom into the glare a doubt wound like a snake into his brain. He feared the wind — that it would not last — it was so very sickening out here.

He took the shade of the wall, pressed his shoulder against the bricks and closed his eyes. For a minute or more the spirit sank, then the will put its lips to some deep reservoir and drank. Stafford opened his eyes and stood from the wall. Second wind or third wind, it held steady.

The consumptive lieutenant was not in the yard. He had had a hemorrhage and was now in the hospital watching Death come a stride a day. The yard held a fair number of men, listless in the heat, walking slowly, standing, or seated, with hands about the knees and bowed heads, on the parched, untidy ground. The guards at the small gate, a gate which opened on another yard, not free to prisoners, with beyond it the true, heavy gate — the guards suffered with the heat, held their rifles languidly. The moments went on, a line of winged creatures now with broken wings, creeping, not flying, an ant-line of slow moments, each with its burden of lassitude, ennui, enfeebled hope. The one tree-top was all green and gold and shining fair and heavenly cool, but it was set in Paradise, and from Paradise, like Abraham, it only looked across the gulf, a gulf in which it acquiesced. And so it was a mocking tree, more fiend than angel. . . .

The figures of the sentries at the gate grew energized; they tautened, stood at salute. Into the yard came on inspection a group of officers, among them the one whom the prisoners held to be human. With them came Father Tierney.

"The top of the morning to ye, children!" said Father Tierney. "Sure it's a red cock feather the morning's wearing!" He came nearer. "Where's the lieutenant that was coughing himself away, poor deluded lad!"

He looked about him, then came over to the wall, a big, rusty-black figure, standing so close that he made another wall for shadow. His eyes and Stafford's met.

"The lieutenant, poor lad!" demanded Father Tierney, his strong, rich voice rolling through the yard, "it's the hospital he's in?"

"Yes," said Stafford. "He had a bad hemorrhage and they took him yesterday."

"Tell me," said Father Tierney, "a bit about him, and I'll write it to his parents. Parents — especially mothers — have the same kind of heartbreak on both sides of the line."

The officers passed on. The thirty-odd grey prisoners walked or sat or stood as before. Stafford was a little in shadow, and the priest's bulky form, squared before him, cut off the more crowded part of the enclosure.

Father Tierney, discoursing of parents, dropped his voice with suddenness. "It's the smallest possible bundle. You're sure you can hide it under your coat?"

"Yes —"

"And his father's a ribil fighting with Johnston — and his mother in Kentucky — Holy Powers!" said Father Tierney, "the heat in this place's fearful and I once had sunsthroke — *Quick!* — It's giddy enough — *Have you got it?* — I'm feeling this minute!" He straightened himself, wandered to a neighbouring stone, and, sitting down, called to the nearest guard who came up. "Is there a cup of water handy, my son? I had a sunsthroke once and this yard's Gehenna to-day, no less!"

Two days later, just at sunset, a hospital steward passed through the hall of the officers' side of Prison X, nodded to the sentries at the door, crossed the yard, was let pass the small gate, crossed the court beyond, pretty well occupied as it was with blue soldiers, and approached the heavy, final gate. An official of some description was ahead of him, and he had for a moment to wait. The gate opened, the man in front passed through; there came a moment's vision of a green tree against a rosy sky — the tree whose head showed above the prison wall. The hospital steward stepped forward. He had the word — it had been bought with a gold-piece of considerable denomination. He gave it; the gate creaked open, he passed out.

The sunset looked a fabulous glory; the one tree had the sublimity of the pathless forest.

At dark he found the priest's lodging and, waiting for him, a suit of civilian clothes. He proposed to get to the river that night, swim it, and find dawn and the Virginian shore. "Whist!" said Father Tierney. "You'll be afther attacking a fretful porcupine! Put out your hand, and you'll touch a pathrol. They're thicker on the river bank than blue flies. No, no! you thravel by road till you're twenty-five miles from here. You'll come to a hamlet called —— and there you'll find a carpenter shop and a negro named Taylor. He's a faithful freedman and well thought of by the powers that be. You stop and ask for a drink of water, and thin you say in a whisper across the gourd, 'Benedict Tierney and a boat across.' You'll get it. — It's risky by the road, thrue enough, but divil a bit of risk would there be if you wint shtraight down to the river! The hedgehog would shoot as many quills at you as was necessary."

"Whether I get clear away or not, you have put me under an obligation, Father, which —"

"Whist, my son, I'm Southern, I tell ye! Drink your wine, and God be good to the whole of us!"

The night was still and starry, dry and warm. Stafford walked in company yet of the second wind. Bliss, bliss, bliss, to be out of Prison X! He went like a child, wary as a man, but like a child in mere whiteness of thought and sensuousness of being. The stars — he looked up at them as a boy might look his first night out of doors. Bright they were and far away, and the flesh crept toward them with a pleasure in the movement and a sadness for the distance. The slumberous masses of the trees, the dim distinction of the horizon, the sound of hidden water, the flicker of fireflies, the odour of the fields, the dust of the glimmering road — all had keenness, sonority, freshness of first encounters. For a long time he was not conscious of fatigue. Even when he knew at last that he was piteously tired, night and the world kept their vividness.

Between two and three o'clock some slight traffic began upon the road. A farm-gate opened to let out a great empty wagon and a half-grown boy with a whip over his shoulder. The horses turned their heads westward. Stafford, rising from a rock-pile, asked a lift, and the boy gave it. All rattled westward over the macadam

road. The boy talked of the battle of last month — the great battle
in Pennsylvania.

"Did n't we give them hell — oh, did n't we give them hell ? They
saw we killed twenty thousand!"

"Twenty thousand. . . . It is not, after all, strange that we de-
duced a hell. . . . How fresh the morning smells!"

Horses, wagon, and boy were but going from one farm to another.
Two miles farther on Stafford thanked the youngster and left this
convoy. Light was gathering in the east. He was now met or overtaken and passed by a fair number of conveyances. In some there
were soldiers; others held clusters of loudly talking or laughing men.
A company of troopers passed, giants in the half-light. He concluded
that he must be near an encampment, and as he walked he debated
the propriety of turning from the road and making his way through
woods or behind the screen of hills. Men on horseback, in passing,
spoke to him. At last, as the cocks were crowing, he did turn from
the road. The lane in which he found himself wound narrowly
between dew-heavy berry-bushes and an arch of locust trees.
Branch and twig and leaf of these made a wonderful fretted arch
through which to view the carnation morning sky. Ripe berries
hung upon the bushes. Stafford was hungry and he gathered these
and ate. A bird began to sing, sweet, sweet! Holding by the stem of
a young persimmon he planted his foot in the moist earth of the
bank, and climbed upward to where the berries grew thickest. Briar
and elder and young locust closed around him. Above the bird sang
piercingly, and behind it showed the purple sky. The dewy coolness
was divine. His head was swimming a little with fatigue and hunger,
but he was light-hearted, with a curious, untroubled sense of identity
with the purple sky, the locust tree, the singing bird, even with the
spray of berries his hand was closing on.

The bird stopped singing and flew away. A horse neighed, the
lane filled with the sound of feet. Stafford saw between the bushes
the blue moving forms. He crouched amid the dimness of elder
and blackberry, not knowing if he were well hidden, but hoping for
the best. The company, pickets relieved and moving toward an encampment, had well-nigh passed when one keen-eyed man observed
some slight movement, some overbending of the wayside growth.
With his rifle barrel he parted the green curtain.

This encampment was an outstretched finger of the encampment of a great force preparing to cross the Potomac. It appeared, too, that there had been recently an outcry as to grey spies. Stafford proffered his story — a Marylander who had been to the city and was quietly proceeding home. He had turned into the lane thinking it a short cut — the berries had tempted him, being hungry — he had simply stood where he had climbed, waiting until he could plunge into the lane again; — behold the whole affair!

He might have won through, but in the guardhouse where he was searched they found a small, worn wallet whose contents damned him. Standing among the berry-bushes, his hand had gone to this with the thought that he had best throw it away before danger swooped — and then he had refrained, and immediately it was too late. The sergeant looked it through, shook his head, and called a lieutenant. The lieutenant took the papers in a bronzed hand, ran them over, and read a letter dated two years back, written from Greenwood in Virginia and signed Judith Cary. He folded it and returned it to the wallet which he kept.

"Of course you know," he said in an agreeable voice, "that this is your death-warrant. I wonder at you for such monumental carelessness! Or, perhaps, it was n't carelessness."

"No," said Stafford, "it was n't carelessness. But I am not a spy. Yesterday I escaped from Prison X."

"Tell that," said the lieutenant, "to the marines. Sergeant, we move before noon, and jobs of this sort must be put behind us! There's a drumhead court sitting now. Bring him across."

The tree was an oak with one great bough stretching like a warped beam across a cart track. Stafford divined it when he and the blue squad were yet three hundred yards away. It topped a slight rise and it thrust that arm out so starkly against the sky. He knew it for what it was. The world and the freshness of the world were as vividly with him as during any hour of the preceding vivid twelve. Every sense was vigorously functioning; the whole range of perception was lit; length and breadth and depth, he felt an intimacy of knowledge, a sure interpenetration. He saw wholly every little dogwood tree, every stalk of the long grass by the roadside; the cadence of the earth was his, and the taste of existence was in his mouth. He had a steady sense of the deep that was flowing into the mould of life and then out of the mould of life. He felt eternal. The tree and that stark limb bred in him no fear.

A party of cavalry came up behind the foot soldiers.

"Where are you going?" asked the officer at the head.

"To hang a spy," answered the lieutenant. "On the tree yonder."

"Yes?" said the officer. "Not the pleasantest of work, but at times necessary. — It's a lovely morning."

"Isn't it? The heat's broken at last."

The troopers continued to ride alongside, and so all mounted the little rise and came together upon the round of dry sward beneath the tree. A curt order or two left the blue soldiers drawn up at one side of this ring, and the prisoner with the provost guard in the centre, beneath the tree. Stafford glanced down at the rope that was now about his neck. It lay curled there like a tawny serpent, visible, real, real as the bough up to which, too, he glanced — real, and yet profoundly of no tremendous importance. He had a curious fleeting impression as of a fourth dimension, as of the bough above arching a portal, on the other side of which lay utter security. Upon the way thither he had been perfectly silent, and he felt no inclination now toward speech or any demonstration. He stood and waited, and he was not conscious of either quickening or retarding in Time's quiet footfall.

The cavalry officer, in the course of a checkered existence, had witnessed a plenty of military executions — so many, in fact, that Pity and Horror had long since shrugged their shoulders and gone off to sleep. They had left a certain professional curiosity; a degree of connoisseurship in how men met death. He now pushed his horse through the scrub to the edge of the ring. The action brought him within twenty feet of the small group in the centre, and, upon the blue soldiers standing back a little, face to face with the bareheaded prisoner. The officer looked, then swung himself from the saddle, and, with spurs and sabre jingling, strode into the trodden ground. "A moment, Lieutenant, if you please! I have somewhere seen your prisoner — though where —"

He came closer. Stafford, worn to emaciation, dressed in rough civilian clothes, with the rope about his bared neck, returned his gaze. Memory stepped between them with a hand to each. The air darkened, grew filled with thunder, jagged lightning, and whistling rain, the parched earth was quagmire, the dusty trees Virginia cedars with twisted roots, wet, murmuring in a harsh wind. There was heard the rattle of Stonewall Jackson's musketry, and, above the thunder, Pelham's guns.

"Ox Hill!" exclaimed Marchmont with an oath.

Stafford's eyelids just quivered. "Ox Hill," he repeated.

Suddenly, with the thunder of Pelham's guns, the bough above was no longer the arch of a portal. It was an oak bough with the end of a rope thrown across it. Life streamed back upon him. The clarity, the silver calm, the crystal quality went from things. He staggered slightly, and the blood drummed in his ears.

Marchmont was speaking rapidly to the lieutenant and the provost officer. "How do you know that he is a spy? Said he was an escaped prisoner — escaped from Prison X? Could n't you wait to find out? Believe it? Yes, I believe it. He's a Southern officer — he did me the best of turns once — day when I thought I was a prisoner myself — day of Chantilly. — Yes. Colonel Francis Marchmont. Marchmont Invincibles. Remand him, eh? — until we telegraph to the Commandant at X. No use treating him as a spy if he is n't a spy, eh? Remember once in Italy when that game was nearly played on myself. — You will wait, Lieutenant, until I send an orderly back with a note to your general? Know him well — think I can arrange matters. — Thanks! Here, Roberts!"

Roberts galloped off. The group beneath the tree, the soldiers drawn up at one side, the troopers and their colonel stayed as they were, waiting. The bright sands ran on, the breeze in the oak whispered like a dryad, the bees buzzed, there came an odour of the pine. Stafford's hand and lip were yet stained with the berries. He stood, the tawny cirque about his neck, waiting with the rest.

Roberts returned. He bore a folded piece of writing which he delivered to Marchmont. The latter read, then showed it to the lieutenant, who spoke to the sergeant of the provost guard. Two not unkindly hands loosened the circle of rope and lifted it clear from the prisoner. Marchmont came across with outstretched hand.

"Major Stafford, I thought I could manage it! As soon as the matter is verified from X — I shall see if I cannot personally arrange an exchange. I am pretty sure that I can do that, too."

His teeth gleamed beneath his yellow mustache. "I have n't at the moment a flask such as you raised me from the dead with! — Jove! the fine steel rain and the guns with the thunder, and Caliph pressed hard, and it was *peine forte et dure* —"

"It was a travelled road," said Stafford; "presently some one else would have come by and released you. But this is not a travelled road and I was very near to death." He looked at his berry-stained hands. "I don't think I cared in the least about death itself. It seemed, standing here, a perfectly unreal pasteboard arch, a piece of stage furniture. But I have a piece of work to do on this side of it . . . and so, on the whole, I am glad you came by." He laughed a little. "That has a mighty ungracious sound, has it not? I should thank you more heartily — and I do!"

A month from this day he stood upon Virginia earth, duly exchanged. He had been put across at Williamsport. Marchmont had pressed upon him a loan of money and a horse. For a week he had been, in effect, Marchmont's guest. A strange liking had developed between the two. . . . But now he was alone, and in Virginia, — Virginia that he had left more than a year ago when the army crossed into Maryland and there followed the battle of Sharpsburg. He was alone, riding through a wood slowly, his hands relaxed upon the saddlebow, lost in thought.

About him was the silence of the warm September wood. It was a wood of small pines, scarred and torn, as were now all the woods of this land by the heavy hand and heel of a giant war. That was a general war, but to each man, too, his own war. Stafford's had been a long war, long and sultry, stabbed with fierce lightnings. He had scars enough within, stains of a rough and passionate weather, marks of a lava flow. But to-day, riding through the September wood, he felt that the war was over. He was drawing still from that deeper stratum of being, from the colder, purer well. His mind had changed, and without any inner heroics he was prepared to act upon that change. He had never been weak of will.

In Winchester, when he entered it at sunset, he found a small grey command, and on the pillared porch of the hotel and in the bare general room various officers who came and went or sat at the table writing. Stafford, taking his place also at this long and heavy board and asking for pen and ink, fell into talk, while he waited, with an infantry captain sitting opposite. Where was General Lee and the main army?

"Along the Rapidan, watching Meade on the other side. Where have you been," said the captain, "that you did n't know that?"

"I have been in prison. — On the Rapidan."

"Yes. But Longstreet, with Hood and McLaws, has been ordered to Tennessee to support Bragg. There 'll be a great battle down there."

"Then there's inactivity at the moment with us?"

"Yes. Marse Robert 's just resting his men and watching Meade. Nobody exactly knows what the next move will be."

A negro boy brought the writing-materials for which Stafford had asked. He left the captain's conversation and fell to writing. He wrote three letters. One was to General Lee, whom he knew personally, one to the general commanding his own brigade, and one to Warwick Cary. When he came to the envelope for the last-named letter he glanced across to the captain, also writing. "The Golden Brigade, General Cary — Warwick Cary? Do you know if it is with Longstreet or by the Rapidan?"

"By the Rapidan, I think. But Warwick Cary was killed at Gettysburg."

Stafford drew in his breath. "I had not heard that! I am sorry, sorry. . . . I begin to think how little I have heard. I have been in Prison X since Sharpsburg. . . . General Cary killed!"

"Yes. At the head of his men in a great charge. But the brigade is by the Rapidan."

"It was not the brigade I was thinking of," said the other.

He sat for a moment with his hand shading his eyes, then he slowly tore into pieces the letter to Warwick Cary. The remaining two letters he saw placed in the mail-bag for army headquarters. The next morning early he rode out of Winchester, out upon the Valley Pike. Before him lay Kernstown; beyond Kernstown stretched beneath the September mist the long, great war-road with its thronging memories. He touched his horse and for several days travelled southward through the blackened Valley of Virginia.

CHAPTER XVIII

THREE OAKS

THE countryside lay warm and mellow in the early autumn air. The mountains hung like clouds; the vales cherished the amber light. The maple leaves were turning; out on the edge of climbing fields the sumach was growing scarlet, the gum trees red as blood. The sunlight was as fine as old Canary. *Caw! Caw!* went the crows, wheeling above the unplanted fields.

The Three Oaks' carriage, Tullius driving, climbed the heavy fields, where, nowadays, the roads were never mended. This region, the head of the great main Valley, was a high, withdrawn one. From it men enough had gone to war, but as yet it had not itself become a field for contending armies. No cannon here had roused the echoes of the Blue Ridge, no smoke of musketry drifted through the forest glades. News of the war came by boat up the James, or from the lower towns, — Lexington, Staunton, Charlottesville, — in the old, red, high-swung stages, or brought by occasional horsemen, in saddle-bags filled with newspapers. The outward change in the countryside was to be laid to the door, not of violent commission but of omission — omission less spectacular, but no less assured of results. The roads, as has been said, were untended, fallen into holes, difficult to travel. A scrub of sassafras, of trailing berryvines, of mullein, was drawing with slender fingers many a field back into the wild. The fences were broken, gaps here and gaps there, trailed over by reddening vines. When the road passed a farmhouse the fences there were a ghastly, speckled, greyish white; innocent of whitewash for now going on three years. The horseblocks showed the same neglect; the spring-houses, too, and the outbuildings and negro cabins. The frame farmhouses looked as dolefully. The brick houses kept more an air of old times, but about these and their gardens there dwelled, too, a melancholy shabbiness. Everywhere was a strange feeling of a desert, of people gone away or sunken in dreams, of stopped clock-hands, of lowered life, of life holding itself very still, yet of a life that knew heavy and painful heart-beats. There were not many cattle in the fields; you rarely saw a strong, mettled horse; those left were old and work-worn and thin. There seemed not so many of anything; the barnyards lacked feathered people, the duck-ponds did not flower in white and gold as of yore, the broods of turkeys were farther between, even the flower gardens seemed lessened in colour, the blooms farther apart. At long intervals the Three Oaks' carriage met or overtook slow travellers on the road. Chiefly they were women. In the same way the fields and gardens, the dooryards and doorsteps of the houses presented to view women and children.

Miriam remarked upon this. "Just women and babies and old Father Timé. I have n't seen a young man to-day. I have n't seen a boy — not one over fifteen. All gone. . . . And maybe the cannon balls to-day are playing among them as they played with Will."

"Miriam," said her mother, "be as strong as Will! How shall you be merry with him when you do meet if you go on through life like this?"

"I don't see that you have any right to say that to me," said Miriam. "I do everything just the same. And it seems to me that I can hear myself laughing all the day. Certainly I don't cry. I never was a cry-baby."

"I had rather you cried," answered Margaret Cleave.

"Well, I'm not going to cry. . . . Look at that calf in the meadow yonder — little brown thing with a mark on the forehead! Does n't it look lonely — usually there are two of them playing together. Here comes an old man with a bucket."

It was an old negro with a great wooden bucket filled with quinces. He put up a beseeching hand and Tullius stopped the horses. "Dey's moughty fine quinces, mistis. Don' yo' want ter buy 'em? Dey dries fust-rate."

"They're dry already," said Miriam. "They're withered and small."

"Yass 'm. Dar ain' anything dishyer war ain't shrivelled. But I sho does need ter sell 'em, mistis."

"I can't pay much for them," said Margaret. "Money's very scarce, uncle. It's withered, too."

"Yass 'm, dats so! I ain't er-gwiner ax much, mistis. I jes' erbleeged ter sell 'em, kase de cabin's bare. Ef ten dollars 'll suit you — "

Mrs. Cleave drew from her purse two Confederate notes. The seller of quinces emptied his freight into the bottom of the roomy equipage. He went on down the road, slow swinging his empty bucket, and the Three Oaks' carriage mounted the last long hill. It was going to the county-seat to do some shopping. The sunshine lay in dead gold, upon the road and the fields on either hand. There was hardly wind enough to lift the down from the open milkweed pods. The mountains were wrapped in haze.

"War-shrunk quinces!" said Miriam. "Do you remember the Thunder Run woman with blackberries to sell a month ago? She said the same thing. I said the berries were small and she said, 'Yass, ma'am. The war's done stunt them.'"

"I wonder where the army is to-day!"

"You're thinking of Richard. You're always thinking of Richard."

"Miriam, do you not think of Richard? Do you not love Richard?"

"Of course I love Richard. But you're thinking of him all the time! Will's only got me to think of him."

"Miriam!"

Miriam began to shudder. Dry-eyed, a carnation spot in each cheek, she sat staring at the dusty roadside, her slight figure shaking. Her mother leaned across and gathered her into her arms. "O child, child! O third of my children! The one dead, and another perhaps dying or dead, at this moment, and in trouble, with a hidden name — and you, my littlest one, tearing with your hands at your own heart and at mine! And the country. . . . All our men and women, the warring and the warred upon. . . . And the world that wheels so blindly — all, all upon one's heart! It is a deal to think on, in the dead of night — "

"I don't mean to be hard and wicked," said Miriam. "I don't know what is the matter with me. I am mad, I think. I remember that night after the Botetourt Resolutions you said that war was a Cup of Trembling. I did n't believe you then. — I don't believe we're going to find a sheet of letter-paper in town, or shoes or flannel either."

There were three stores in town and the Three Oaks' carriage stopped before each. A blast had passed over the country stores as over the country fields, a sweeping away of what was needed for the armies and a steady depletion of what was left. For three years no new stock had come to the stores, no important-looking boxes and barrels over which the storekeeper beamed, hatchet in hand, around which gathered the expectant small fry. All the gay calicoes were gone, all the bright harness and cutlery. China had departed from the shelves, and all linen and straw bonnets and bright wool. The glass showcases, once the marvel and delight of childish eyes, were barren of ribbons and "fancy soap," of cologne, pictured handkerchief boxes, wonderful buttons, tortoise-shell combs, and what-not. The candies were all gone from the glass jars, the "kisses" and peppermint stick. There were no loaves of sugar in their blue paper. There was little of anything, very little, indeed, — and the merchant could not say as of old, "Just out, madam! — but my new stock is on the way."

They found at last a quire or two of dusty foolscap, paid thirty dollars for it, and thought the price reasonable. Shoes were not to be discovered — "any more than the North Pole!" said the small old man who waited upon them. "Yes, Mrs. Cleave; it's going to be an awful thing, this winter!" They bought a few yards of flannel, and paid twenty dollars the yard; a few coarse handkerchiefs, and paid three dollars apiece for them; a pound of tea, and paid for it twenty-five dollars. When at last Tullius tucked their purchases into corners of the carriage, they had expended five hundred dollars in bright, clean, handsome Confederate notes.

There were other shoppers in a small way in the stores, and, it being a fine morning, people were on the streets. It was the day of the month that was, by rights, court-day. The court-house was opened, and an ancient clerk attended, but there was no court. Out of habit, the few men left in town' gathered in the court-house yard or upon the portico between the pillars. Out of habit, too, the few men left in the countryside were in town to-day, their horses fastened at the old racks. Moreover, in this, as in other counties, there was always a sprinkling of wounded sons, men home from the hospital, waiting for strength to go back to the front; now and then, too, though more rarely, an officer or private home on furlough. The little town, in the clutch of adversity as were all little towns through the great range of the South, was not in the main a dolorous or dejected place. The fine, clear, September air this morning carried laughter. And everywhere nowadays there bloomed like a purple flower a sense of the heroic. The stage was not due for hours yet, and so there was no crowd about the post-office where the last bulletin, read and re-read and read again, was yet posted upon a board beside the door.

The ladies from Three Oaks exchanged greetings with many an old friend and country neighbour. Margaret Cleave was honoured by all, loved by many, and her wistful, dark, flower-like daughter had her friends also. Everybody remembered Will, everybody knew Richard. It used to be "Have you heard from Captain Cleave?" — "Have you heard from Major Cleave?" — "Have you heard from Colonel Cleave?" — Now it was different. Most people hereabouts believed in Richard Cleave, but they, somewhat mistakenly, did not speak of him to his mother. There was always a silence through which throbbed a query. Margaret Cleave, quiet, natural, unafraid, and unconstrained, never told where was Richard, never spoke of him in the present, but equally never avoided reference to him in the past. It was understood that, wherever he was, he was in health and "not unhappy." His old friends and neighbours asked no more. In the general anxiety, the largeness of all reference, too great curiosity, or morbid interest in whatever strangeness of ill fortune came to individual folk, had little place.

The two moved with naturalness among their fellows, going to and fro on various errands. When all were accomplished they went for dinner to a fair pillared house of old friends on the outskirts of town. Dinner was the simplest of meals and all were women who sat at table. They talked of the last-received letters, the latest papers, the news of recent movements, battles, defeats, victories, hardships, triumphs, — Averell's raid in western Virginia, the cavalry fighting near the White Sulphur, the night attack on Fort Sumter, the fighting in Arkansas, the expected great battle in Tennessee. The one-course dinner over, they sat for an hour in the cool, deep parlour, where they took up baskets and fell to carding lint while they talked — now of prices and makeshift, how to contrive shoes, clothing, warmth, food, medicines, what-not, and how to continue to send supplies to the men in the army. Then, while they carded lint, Miriam was asked to read aloud. She did so, taking the first book that offered from the table. It was "Lalla Rookh," and she read from it with a curious, ungirlish brilliancy and finish. When she put the book down she was asked if she would not sing.

"Not if you do not wish to," said her mother.

Miriam got up at once. "I do wish to."

Her mother, following her to the piano sat down and laid her fingers on the keys.

"Sing," said some one, "'Love launched a Fairy Boat.'"

> "Love launched a fairy boat
> On a bright and shining river,
> And said, 'My bark shall float
> O'er these sunny waves forever.
> The gentlest gales shall fill the sails
> That bear me onward cheerily,
> And through Time's glass the sand shall pass
> From morn till evening merrily,
> From morn till evening merrily . . .'
> Love launched a fairy boat —"

Margaret rose quickly. The others with exclamations gathered around as the mother laid the slight figure on the sofa.

"She is frightfully unwell," said Margaret. "Will — Richard — the strain of this war that should never have been!" She loosened the girl's dress at the throat, bathed her temples. "There, my dear, there, my dear —"

Miriam sat up. "What is the matter? The world got all black. . . . Let us go home, mother."

They only waited for the stage to come in. From the carriage, drawn up near the post-office, they watched it rumble up, within its depths a hurt soldier or two and the usual party of refugeeing women and children. The jaded horses stopped before the post-office; the driver climbed down with the mail-bag, all the town came hurrying. A man standing on a box, beneath the bulletin board, began to read in a loud voice from an unfolded paper: "Cavalry encounters along the Rapidan — General Lee in Richmond conferring with the President — Longstreet's corps taking train at Louisa Court-House. Destination presumably Tennessee. — *Cumberland Gap. Tennessee. September ninth. To-day General Frazer, surrounded and cut off by superior force of enemy, surrendered with two thousand men —*"

The Three Oaks' carriage went heavily homeward, up and over the long hills. A light from the west was on the Blue Ridge, the sky clear, the winds laid. At last they saw the home hill, and the three giant oaks.

For a long time Miriam kept awake, lying in her narrow bed, her head on her mother's breast, but at last her eyes closed. Presently she was asleep, breathing quietly. Margaret, for the child's more easy lying, slipped her arm from beneath her, then waited until, with a little sigh, she settled more deeply among the pillows, then rose, waited another moment, and stepped lightly from the room. The hall window showed a sky yet red from the sunset. Across was the room that since boyhood had been Richard's. The mother entered it, closed the door, and moving to an old, leather-covered couch, lay upon it face downward.

Outside the dusk closed in; the stars peered through the branches of the poplar without the window. Margaret rose, stood for a moment looking at the sword slung above the mantel, then quit the room, and going downstairs, ate her slender supper while Mahalah discoursed of a ghost the negroes had seen the night before.

It had been a frightful ghost — "Er ha'nt ez tall ez dat ar cedar ob Lebanon, an er part grey an' er part white an' er part black! An' it had n't no mo' *touch* to hit den de air has, an' whar de eyes was was lak two candles what de wind's blowin', and it kept er-cryin' lak somebody in de mountains — *wooh!* — *wooh!* — *wooh!* — No,'m, Miss Margaret! hit wa'n't 'magination. What we gwine 'magine for, when ever'body could see hit wif their own two eyes?"

Mahalah cleared the table, closed the shutters, and carried the lamp into the wide hall, where she set it on a leaf-table beside her mistress's workbasket. Then, still muttering of the "ha'nt," she threw her apron over her head, and departed for the quarter. Margaret mounted the stair and stood listening at Miriam's half-open door. The girl was sleeping quietly, and the mother, turning, came down again to the hall, and took her low chair beside the table and the basket of lint she was carding. The night was mild and soft, the front door standing open, the scent of the autumn flowers perceptible.

Margaret Cleave, sitting carding lint, the lamplight upon her brown hair, her slender hands, the grave beauty of her face, — Mar-

garet Cleave thought of many things. In the midst of her thinking
she heard a step upon the gravel before the house. A man mounted
the porch steps and came into the light from the open door. He had
raised his hand to the knocker when he saw the mistress of the house
sitting in the lamplight by the table.

Margaret rose and came forward. She saw that it was a soldier,
an officer.

"Good evening," she said; then as she came closer, — "One moment! . . . Major Stafford!"

With a gesture for silence she took up the lamp and led the way
into the parlour. "My daughter is not well and has fallen asleep.
But we can talk here without disturbing her."

"I came," said Stafford, "hoping to find Colonel Cleave. I have
ridden from Lexington to-day. He is not here?"

"No."

The two faced each other, her eyes large, enquiring, quietly hostile. Stafford, moving with steadiness upon that changed level, met
her gaze with a gaze she could not read. She turned slightly, sank
into a great chair, and motioned him to one opposite. He continued
to stand, his hand touching the table. There was a bowl of roses on
the table, and soft lights and shadows filled the room.

"Mrs. Cleave, will you tell me where I may find him?"

"No. You must understand that I cannot do that. . . . We heard
that you were in prison."

"I have been in prison since Sharpsburg. Latterly I found a
friend and four days ago I was exchanged. I have come straight to
Three Oaks."

"Yes? Why?"

Stafford walked the length of the room and stood a moment at a
window, looking out into the night. He had fought his fight; it was
all over and done with. Those last weeks in prison he had known
where the victory would fall, and that first night out his mind had
parted as finally as was possible with one vast country of his past, a
dark country of strain and longing, fierce attraction, fierce repulsion.
On the starlit road from Prison X, in the quietude of the earth,
victory profound and ultimate had come, soft as down. Before he
gathered the berries in the by-road, before the soldiers took him,
before Marchmont came, he had touched the larger country.

He came back to the table where Margaret sat, a rose in her hand, her eyes upon its petals.

"I came to Three Oaks," he said, "to make retribution."

"Retribution!"

Stafford faced her. "Mrs. Cleave, what do you know — what has he told you — of White Oak Swamp?"

Margaret laid the rose from her hand. "I know that somewhere there was treachery. I know that my son was guiltless of that charge. I know little more except that — except that, either you, also, were strangely misled, involved in that dreadful web of error — or that — or that you swore falsely."

"I swore falsely."

There was a silence. She sat looking at him with parted lips. He kept the quietness with which from his entrance he had moved and spoken, but as he stood there there grew a strange feeling in his face, and suddenly he raised his hand and covered his eyes. The clock in the hall ticked, ticked. Far out in the night a whip-poor-will was calling. The walls of the room seemed to expand. There came a sense of armies, of camp-fires stretching endlessly, of movements here and there beneath the canopy of night, of a bugle's distant shrilling, of the wheels of cannon, of a dim, high-borne flag.

At last it grew intolerable. Margaret broke it with a thrilling voice. "And you come here to tell this to *me*?"

"I came," said Stafford, "to tell it to Richard Cleave. I have written it to General Lee and my brigade commanders — and to others. By now it is in their hands."

The silence fell again, while the mother's heart and brain dealt with the action and its consequences. At last she put her hands before her face.

"I am joyful," she said, and her voice was thrillingly so, "but I am sorrowful too —" and her voice veiled and darkened. "Unhappy man that you are —!"

"If you will believe me," said Stafford, "I am not unhappy. It was not, I think, until I ceased to be unhappy that I could see clearly either the way that I had travelled or the way that I am to travel. I will not speak of what is past, nor of remorse for what is past. I am not sure that what I feel is remorse. I have seen the ocean when, lashed by something in itself or out of itself, it wrecked and ruined, and I have seen the ocean when it carried every bark in safety. It was the same ocean, and what is the use of words? But I will take now the blame and double blame of White Oak Swamp. I wished to say this to him, face to face —"

"He took another name, and rejoined before Second Manassas. He joined Pelham's Battery, of the horse artillery. He called himself Philip Deaderick."

"*Deaderick!* The rain and Pelham's guns . . . I remember."

"He is to-night wherever his battery is. Somewhere on the Rapidan. He would not let — what happened — ruin his life. He went back to the army that he loved. He has done his duty there. Moreover, no friend that knew him believed him guilty. Moreover, the woman that he loves has kept the steadiest faith — not less steady than mine, who am his mother. . . . I will tell you this because it should be told you."

"Yes," he said, "it should be told me. I have loved Judith Cary. But I want her happiness now. I wrote to her last night. I could n't do it before."

The clock ticked, ticked. The whip-poor-will cried. *Whip-poor-will! whip-poor-will!* Margaret sat very still, her elbow on the table, her hand shading her eyes.

The quiet held a moment longer in the Three Oaks' parlour, then he broke it. "I have said all, I think, that needed to be said. It does not seem to me to be a case for words. You understand that the machinery has been set in motion, and that the weight will be lifted and laid where it belongs. I shall try when I reach the army to see Colonel Cleave. You will understand that I wish to do that, and why I wish it. Had he been here to-night I should have said to him little more, I think, than I have said to you. I should have said that the old, unneeded hatred had died from within me, and that I asked his forgiveness."

He took his hat from the chair beside him. "I'll ride to town and sleep there to-night. In the morning I'll turn toward the Rapidan —"

Margaret rose. "It is late. You have been riding all day. You are tired and thin and pale — you have been in prison." Suddenly as she looked at him the tears came. "Oh, the world, the world that it is! Oh, the divided heart of it, the twisted soul, the bitter and the sweet and the dark and the light —" She dashed the tears away and came over to him with her hand held out. "See! it is all over now. It is far to town, and late. Stay at Three Oaks to-night. — Tullius shall put your horse up, and I will call Mahalah to see to your room —"

CHAPTER XIX

THE COLONEL OF THE SIXTY-FIFTH

THROUGH the cool October sunlight three grey regiments and a battery of horse artillery were marching upon a road that led from the Rapidan to the Rappahannock. They were coming up from Orange Court-House and their destination was the main army now encamped below Kelly's Ford.

The air was like wine and the troops were in spirits. There were huge jokes, laughter, singing, and when at noon the column halted in a coloured wood for dinner, the men frisked among the trees like young lambs or very fauns of Pan. They were ragged, and they did n't have much for dinner, but gaiety was in their gift and a quite superb "make the best of it." They were filled with quips and cranks; they guffawed with laughter. They lay upon the earth, hands beneath their heads, one knee crossed above the other, and sang to the red oak leaves on the topmost branch.

> "I dreamed a dream the other night,
> When everything was still; —
> I dreamed I saw Susannah
> Come running down the hill. . . .

> "O Susannah, don't you weep,
> Nor mourn too long for me —
> I 'se gwine to Alabama,
> With my banjo on my knee!"

> "Old Grimes is dead, that good old man,
> Whom we shall see no more —"

The Sixty-fifth Virginia's spirits flew in feathers. The Sixty-fifth was, for this period of the war and on the Southern side, a full regiment. It carried nearly five hundred muskets. It was practically half as large as it had been on the day of First Manassas. It had passed through three years of deadly war, but as a regiment it possessed skill as well as courage, and — with one exception — it had had fair luck. And then it had gathered recruits. It was a good regiment to belong to — a steady, fine regiment.

Officers' mess spread its table on the golden, fallen leaves of a hickory beside a sliding, ice-cool rivulet. The four hundred and odd men were scattered, in perhaps fifty messes, through the grove. The smoke of their fires rose straight and blue. The metal of the stacked muskets reflected a thousand little saffron flames. The leaves drifted down. The day was ineffably sweet, cool, and fragrant. *Caw! caw!* went the crows in a neighbouring field.

The Sixty-fifth believed in friendship. It believed in cousins. It believed in the tie of the County. The river, winding between willow and sycamore from croft to croft, — the chain of little valleys, the end of one touching the beginning of another, — the linked hills, each with its homestead, — the mountains with their mountain cabins, — all was so much framework in and over and about which flowed the mutual life. In its consciousness hill called to hill and stream to stream — Thunder Run to other runs and creeks — other mountains to Thunder Run Mountain. The Sixty-fifth experienced a profound unity — a unity bred of many things. Physical contiguity played its part, a common range of ideas, a general standard of conduct, a shared way of seeing, hearing, tasting. Upon all was the stamp of community in effort, community in danger, community in event. It was not to the erection of separateness that brothers, cousins, friends, acquaintances, even in a minor degree enemies, shared heat and cold, the burning sun or the midnight, stumbling darkness of the road, storm and fatigue and waking through the night, hunger, thirst, marchings and battles and the sight of battle-fields, that their hearts together failed, shrivelled, darkened, or expanded, rose and shouted. So deeply alike now was their environment and the face of their days that their own faces were grown strangely alike. Sometimes the members of the Sixty-fifth differed in opinion, sometimes they squabbled, sometimes they waxed sarcastic, sometimes they remarked that the world was too small for such or such a comrade and themselves. Then came the battle — and when in the morning light they saw such or such an one, it was "Hello, Jim — or Jack — or Tom! I'm right down glad you weren't killed! Fuss at you sometimes, but I'd have missed you, all the same!"

The Sixty-fifth sat cross-legged in the coloured wood near Rappahannock, and ate its diminutive corn-pone and diminutive rasher of bacon. No Confederate soldier ever felt drowsily heavy after dinner. Where there was so little to digest, the process accomplished itself in the turn of a hand. There was little, too, to smoke, now — worse luck! But there was always — except in the very worst straits — there was always something out of which might be gotten a certain whimsical amusement.

The Sixty-fifth had had an easy march, and was going to have another one. The Sixty-fifth knew this country like a book, having fought over most steps of it. It had a pleasant feeling of familiarity with this very wood and the shining stretch of road narrowing toward a dark wood and the Rappahannock. The Sixty-fifth had every confidence in Marse Robert, commanding all; in Old Dick, commanding the Second Corps, in Alleghany Johnson, commanding the division; in Walker, commanding the Stonewall; in Colonel Erskine, commanding the Sixty-fifth. Its confidence in the Sixty-fifth itself was considerable. Dinner done, it fell, lying beneath the trees, now to jokes and now to easy speculation.

"What is Marse Robert moving us for?"

"Meade's walking again. Stalking up and down north side of Rappahannock. Same as Burnside last year. Marse Robert's bringing us and the ——th and ——th, over from Orange, to lay the ghost. — Oh, and I forgot the horse artillery!"

"Horse artillery's all right, down there by that sumach patch, eating parched corn. . . . This is what you might call golden weather. Listen to the crows. *Caw! caw! caw!* Just like old Botetourt."

"If I were Allan Gold, I'd let that shoe alone. He can't mend it."

"Whose shoe is it? Allan's?"

"No. It's Lieutenant Coffin's. He's had a pale blue letter, and it said that the young lady was visiting in Fredericksburg — and ain't we on the road to Fredericksburg?"

"I see — I see!"

"And of course lieutenant would like to have a whole shoe. You'd like it yourself under the circumstances. Allan's mighty handy, and he told him he thought he could do it —"

"If I had a knife — Allan! Here's a scrap of good leather. Catch! — Ain't no pale blue letter in mine. Wish there was."

Sergeant Billy Maydew, at the head of a small reconnoitring

party, appeared and reported to the colonel. "We went to the river, sir, and two miles up and two miles down. As far as could be seen, things air all quiet. We thought we saw a smoke across the river — back agin' the sky. We met a foraging party — cavalry. It said General Lee was at Kelly's Ford, and that it was understood the enemy meant to cross. That air all I have to report, sir."

The column took again the road. Of the three regiments, the Sixty-fifth came last. Behind it rumbled a small wagon train, and in rear of these the battery from the horse artillery. The battery was an acquisition of the morning. It had come out of the yellow and red woods in the direction of Culpeper, and had proceeded to "keep company." The Sixty-fifth liked the artillery very well, and now it fraternized as jovially as discipline would allow. "An old battery of Pelham's ? Pelham was a fighter! Saw him at Second Manassas with his arm up, commanding! Looked like one of those people in the old mythology book. — Glad to see you, old battery of Pelham's!"

The afternoon was a wonderful clear one of high lights and blue shadows, of crisply moving air. All vision was distinct, all sound sonorous. Even touch and taste and smell had a strange vigour. And, by way of consequence, all faculties were energized. Past and present and future came all together in the hands, in one wonderful spice apple. And then, just as life was most worth living, the column, the road bending, clashed against a considerable Federal force, that, crossing the Rappahannock at Beverly's Ford, had come down the river through the wonderful afternoon.

The Sixty-fifth fought from behind a brown swale of earth with a rail fence atop. The rails were all draped with travellers' joy; together they made a flimsy screen through which sang the bullets. *Zipp! zziipp! zzzip!* went the minies, thick as locusts in Egypt. The two other regiments ahead were fighting, too; the wagons were scattered, the horses stampeded, the negro teamsters ashen with panic. The battery of horse artillery drove in thunder to the front, the guns leaping, the drivers shouting, the horses red-nostrilled, wide-eyed. Down sprang the gunners, into action roared the pieces; there was a bass now to answer the minies' snarling treble. But the blue had guns, too, more guns than the grey. They came pounding into the fight.

The Sixty-fifth fought with desperation. It saw Annihilation, and it strove against it through every fibre. The men fired kneeling. The flame had scarcely leapt ere the hand felt for the cartridge, the teeth tore at the paper, the musket flamed again. The metal scorched all fingers; powder grime and sweat marred every face. The men's lips moved rapidly, uttering a low monotone, or, after biting the cartridge, they closed and made a straight line in each powder-darkened countenance. A shell tore away a length of the fence, killing or maiming a dozen. Through the smoke was seen the foe, gathering for a charge. The charge came and was repelled, but with loss. Two captains were down, a lieutenant, many men. A gun, back on a hillside, was splitting the fence into kindling wood. The grey battery — the old battery of Pelham's — silenced this gun, but others came. They bellowed from three different points. The grey battery began itself to suffer. Doggedly it poured its fire, but a gun was disabled, a caisson exploded, horses and men dead or frightfully hurt. The two forward regiments had a better position or met a less massed and determined attack. They had come upon a hornet's nest, truly, but their fire at least kept the hornets at bay. But the Sixty-fifth was in the thick of it, and like to be overpowered. It had to get away from where it was in the cross-fire of the batteries — that was clear. Erskine dragged it back to a field covered with golden sedge. Out of the sheet of gold sprang small dark pines, and above the roar and the smoke was the transparent evening sky. Panting, devastated, powder-blackened, bleeding, the Sixty-fifth felt for its cartridges, bit them, loaded, fired on a dark blue wedge coming out of a wood. The wedge expanded, formed a line, came on with hurrahs. At the same instant a monster cylindrical shell, whooping like a demon, hurled itself against the grey battery. A second gun was put out of the fight. The sky went in flashes of red, the air in toppling crashes as of buildings in earthquake. When the smoke cleared, the blue had gone back again, but dead or dying in the sedge were many grey men. Colonel Erskine, slight, fiery, stood out, his hand pressing his arm from which blood was streaming. "Sixty-fifth Virginia! You've got as splendid a record as is in this army! You can't run. There isn't anywhere to run to. — White flag? No — o! You don't raise a white flag while I command! — Put your back to the wall and continue your record!"

"All right, sir," said the Sixty-fifth. "All right — Oh, the colonel! — oh, the colonel —"

The colonel fell, pierced through the brain. A captain took his place, but the captains, too, were falling. . . .

Billy Maydew and Allan Gold saw each other through a rift in the smoke. They were close together.

"Billy," said Allan, "I wish you were out of this."

"I reckon it's the end," said Billy, loading. "You look all kind of shining and bright, Allan. — Don't you reckon Heaven'll be something like Thunder Run ?"

"Yes, I do. Sairy and Tom, and the flowers and Christianna —"

"And all the boys," said Billy, "and the colonel — Here air the darn Yanks again —"

A short-range engagement changed into hand-to-hand fighting. Already the aiding battery had suffered horribly. Now with a shout the blue pushed against it, seizing and silencing one of the two remaining guns. The grey infantry thrust back by the same onset, the grey artillerymen beaten from the guns, were now as one — four hundred grey men, perhaps, in a death clutch with twice their number. Down the road broke out a wilder noise of fighting — it would seem, somehow, that there was an access of forces. . . . The blue, immediate swarm was somehow pushed back. Another was seen detaching itself. The ranking officer was now a captain. He hurried along the front of the torn and panting line. "Don't let's fail, men! — Don't let's fail! Everybody at home — everybody at home knows we could n't — Give them as good as we take! Here they come! — Now — now! —"

There was, however, a wavering. The thing was hopeless and the Sixty-fifth was deadly tired. With the fall of Erskine the trumpets had ceased to call. The Sixty-fifth looked at the loud and wide approach of the enemy, and then it looked sideways. Its lips worked, its eyelids twitched. The field of sedge expanded to a limitless plain, heaped all with the dead and dying. The air no longer went in waves of red; the air was sinking to a greenish pallor, with a sickness trembling through it. Here was the swarm of the enemy. . . . The Sixty-fifth knew in its heart that there was some uncertainty as to whether it would continue to stand. The day was dead somehow, the heart beating slow and hard. . . .

The blue overpassed the ruined, almost obliterated line of the rail fence, came on over the sedge. "Don't let's fail, men!" cried the captain. "Don't let's fail! We've never done it — Stand your ground!" — A minie ball entered his side. A man caught him, eased him down upon the earth. "Stand it out, men! stand it out!" he gasped.

"*Sixty-fifth Virginia! Front! Fix bayonets! Forward! Charge!*"

The Sixty-fifth Virginia obeyed. It wheeled, it fixed bayonets, it charged. It charged with a shout. As by magic, even to itself, its aspect changed. It was as though a full regiment, determined, clothed in the habit of victory, vowed to and protected by War himself, sprang across the sedge, struck against, broke and drove the blue. All the pallor went out of the atmosphere, all the faintness out of life. Every hue came strong, every line came clear, life was buoyant as a rubber ball.

And now at last, as the blue fell back, as there came a shouting from down the road, as a mounted aide appeared, — "Hold your own! Hold your own! Stuart's coming — horse and guns! Hold your own!" — as the smoke cleared, in the shaft of light that the westering sun sent across the field, the Sixty-fifth recognized why it had charged. In its ranks were men who had come in during the past year as recruits, or who had been transferred from other regiments. To these the Sixty-fifth apparently had charged, changing rout into victory, because a gunner from the disabled battery — the old battery of Pelham's — had sprung forward, faced for an instant the Sixty-fifth, then with a waved arm and a great magnetic voice had ordered the charge and led it. But most of the men of the Sixty-fifth were men of the old Sixty-fifth. Now, in the face of another and violent rush of the foe, the Sixty-fifth burst into a shout. "*Richard Cleave!*" it shouted; "*Richard Cleave!*"

Twenty-four hours later, a great red sun going down behind the pines, Cleave found himself summoned to the tent of the Commander of the Army. He went, still in the guise of Philip Deaderick. Lee sat at a table. Standing behind him were several officers, among them Fauquier Cary, now General Cary. Beyond these was another shadowy group.

Lee acknowledged the gunner's salute. "You have been known as Philip Deaderick, gunner in ——'s battery?"

"Yes, sir."

"But you are Richard Cleave, colonel of the Sixty-fifth?"

"I am Richard Cleave, sir. I was colonel of the Sixty-fifth."

Lee moved his head. The tent was filled with shadows. A negro servant, bringing a lamp, set it on the table. In at the tent flap came the multitudinous hushed sound of the gathering night. "Major Stafford!" said Lee.

Stafford came out of the dusk and stood before the table. There were five feet of earth between him and Cleave. The latter drew a quickened breath and held high his head.

"When," asked Lee, watching him, "when did you last see the officer whom I have just called?"

"Sir, I saw him at Chantilly, in the dusk and the rain —"

"You knew that he was taken at Sharpsburg?"

"Yes."

"He has been in prison ever since — until the other day when he broke prison. He has been, I think, in another and worse prison — the prison of untruth. Now he breaks that prison, too. — Major Stafford, you will repeat to Colonel Cleave what you have written in these letters" — he touched them where they lay upon the table — "and what you have to-day told to me."

Stafford's controlled, slow speech ceased its vibration in the tent. It had lasted several minutes, and it had been addressed to a man who, after the first few words, stood with lowered eyes. It was a detailed explanation of what had occurred at White Oak Swamp in '62, and it was given with a certain determined calm, with literalness, and with an absence of any beating of the breast. When it was ended there was a defined pause, then through the tent, from the great general at the table to the aide standing by the door, there ran a sound like a sigh. The man most deeply concerned stood straight and quiet. He stood as though lost in a brown study, like one who has attention only for the inward procession of events.

Lee spoke. "As quickly as possible there shall be a public reversal of the first decision." He paused, then rested his grave eyes upon Stafford. "As for you," he said, "you will consider yourself under arrest, pending the judgment of the court which I shall appoint.

You have done a great wrong. It is well that at last, with your own eyes, you see it for what it is." He withdrew his gaze, rose, and going over to Cleave, took his hand. "You have gone through bitter waters," he said. "Well, it is over! and we welcome back among us a brave man and a gallant gentleman! Forget the past in thought for the future! The Sixty-fifth Virginia is yours again, Colonel Cleave. Indeed, I think that after yesterday we could not get it to belong to any one else!"

"Colonel Erskine, sir, —"

From the shadow hard-by came Fauquier Cary's moved voice. "Erskine would have rejoiced with the rest of us, Richard. He never believed —"

"Come, General Cary," said Lee, "and you, too, gentlemen, — come and give your hands to Colonel Cleave. Then we will say good night."

The little ceremony was over, the kindly words were spoken. One by one the officers saluted and left the tent, Fauquier Cary tarrying in obedience to a sign from Lee. When all were gone, the General spoke to Cleave whom he had been watching. "You would like a word alone with —" His eyes indicated Stafford.

"Yes, General, if I may —"

"I am going across for a moment to General Stuart's. I will leave you here until I return."

He moved toward the tent opening. "Richard," said Cary, — "Richard, I have no words —" He dropped his kinsman's hands; then, in following Lee, passed within a few feet of Stafford. He made a gesture of indignation and grief, then went by with closed lips and eyelids that drooped. Stafford felt the scorn like a breath from hot iron.

The tent was empty now save for the two. "We cannot stop here," said Cleave. "I must go farther. Why have you changed? Or are we still wearing masks?"

"If there is any mask I do not know it," said the other. "What is change, and why do we change? We have not found that out. But there is a fact somewhere, and I have — changed. I will answer what you will not ask. I love her, yes! — love her so well now that I would have her happy. I have written to her, and in my letter I said farewell. She will show it to you if you wish."

"I do not wish —"

"No," said Stafford. "I believe that you do not. Richard Cleave, I have not somehow much feeling left in me, but . . . You remember the evening of Chantilly, when I came to Pelham's guns? In the darkness I felt you threatening me."

"Yes."

"Well, I did all that you knew of me, and I was all, I suppose, that you thought me. . . . There is never any real replacement, any real atonement. To my mind there is something childish in all our glib asking for forgiveness. I do not know that I ask you for your forgiveness. I wish you to know, however, that the old inexcusable hatred is dead in my soul. If ever the time arrives when you shall say to yourself 'I forgive him' —"

"I could say it for myself. I could not say it — not yet — *for the regiment.*"

Stafford flung out his hand. "I, no more than you, foresaw that ambush beyond the swamp! I meant to procure what should seem your disobedience to General Jackson's orders. I saw nothing else, thought of nothing else —"

"If you had seen it —"

The silence held a moment; then said the other painfully, "Yes. You are perhaps right. In what a gulf and hollow man's being is rooted! . . . I will not ask again for what I see would be difficult for any man to give — Here is General Lee."

Cleave slept that night in the tent of Fauquier Cary. When, in the dusk of the morning, reveille sounding clearly through the woods by Rappahannock, he rose, and presently came out into the autumn world, an orderly met him. "There's a negro and a horse here, sir, asking for you. He says he comes from your county."

From under the misty trees, out upon the misty road before the tent, came Tullius and Dundee. "Yaas, Marse Dick," said Tullius. "Miss Margaret, she done sont us. She say she know all erbout hit, en' that Three Oaks is er happy place!"

CHAPTER XX

CHICKAMAUGA

IT is said to be easy to defend a mountainous country," said General Braxton Bragg, commanding the Army of Tennessee, "but mountains hide your foe from you, while they are full of gaps through which he can pounce upon you at any time. A mountain is like the wall of a house full of rat-holes. Who can tell what lies hidden behind that wall?"

The wall was the Cumberland Range. The several general officers, riding with General Bragg, uttered a murmur, whether of agreement or disagreement was not apparent.

General D. H. Hill, lately sent from Virginia to the support of the forces in Tennessee, made a sound too gruff for agreement. He fell back a pace or two and drew up beside General Cleburne. "You *can* know mountainous country, you know," he said. "It's a matter of learning, like everything else."

"True enough," agreed the other. "But there's precious few of mankind with any talent for learning!"

The group sitting their horses in the scrub oak, in the September sunshine, gazed in a momentary silence upon Pigeon Mountain and Missionary Ridge and the towering Lookout Mountain. Bragg, brave, able in his own way, but melancholy, depressed, ill in body and mind, at war with himself and all his subordinates, sat staring. Below him lay the slender valley of the Chickamauga. Clear, sinuous, the little stream ran between overbending shrubs and trees. A vague purple mist hung over the valley and the tree-clad slopes beyond. The knot of horsemen fell silent, there in the oak scrub, looking at the folds of the Cumberland Range. Past them on the Lafayette road marched endlessly the Army of Tennessee. Tanned and gaunt, ragged and cheerful, moving out from Chattanooga, but moving out, there was assurance, to give fight, by went the grey, patient, hardy legions, corps of Hill, Polk, Buckner, and Walker, divisions of Cheatham, Cleburne, Breckinridge, Liddell, Hindman,

Bushrod Johnson, Preston, and Stewart. Colours, mounted officers, grey foot soldiers and grey foot soldiers and grey foot soldiers, the rumbling guns, old, courageous battalions, on they went, endlessly. The dust rose and clothed them; the purple mountains made a dreamy background. The party, sitting their horses on the scrub-covered low hill, looked again westward.

Bragg spoke to one of his corps commanders, Leonidas Polk, bishop and general. "Chickamauga! This was Cherokee country, was n't it?"

"Yes, General. Cherokee Georgia. Chief Ross had his house near here. 'Chickamauga' means *River of Death*. For ages they must have gone up and down, over these ridges and through these vales, hunting and warring, camping and breaking camp —"

"Killing and being killed. We've only changed the colour, not the actuality. McLemore's Cove! The scouts think that Rosecrans is going to push a column across Missionary Ridge and occupy McLemore's Cove. I think they are mistaken. They are often mistaken."

"General Forrest —"

"He is near Ringgold, I suppose. General Forrest does not keep me properly informed as to where he is —"

Cleburne came in with his rich Irish voice. "Well, that would make quite a shower of notes, would n't it, sir?"

"I have never had the pleasure of meeting General Forrest," said D. H. Hill. "He must be a remarkable man."

"He is a military genius of the first order," said Cleburne.

Bragg continued to gaze upon the Chickamauga. "The three gaps in Pigeon Mountain are Bluebird and Dug and Catlett's. We will of course hold these, and if Crittenden or Thomas is really in McLemore's Cove, I will dispatch a force against them. General Longstreet's arrival cannot now be long delayed."

Longstreet, travelling from Louisa Court-House in Virginia by Petersburg, Wilmington, Augusta, and Atlanta, because Burnside held the shorter Knoxville route, had in all nine hundred miles to traverse, and to serve him and his corps but one single-track, war-worn grey railroad of dejected behaviour. Lone and lorn as was the railroad, it rose to the emergency and deserved the cheers with which, after long days of companionship, Longstreet's troops finally quitted the rails. On the sixteenth the regiments of Hood began to arrive at Dalton. On this day also Rosecrans, a tenacious, able general, completed the drawing of his lines — eleven miles, northeast to southwest — from Lee and Gordon's Mills on the east bank of Chickamauga to Stevens's Gap in Lookout Mountain.

On the eighteenth, General Bragg, at Lafayette, issued the following order: —

"1. Bushrod Johnson's column, on crossing at or near Reed's Bridge will turn to the left by the most practical route, and sweep up the Chickamauga toward Lee and Gordon's Mills.

"2. Walker, crossing at Alexander's Bridge, will unite in this move, and push vigorously on the enemy's flank and rear in the same direction.

"3. Buckner, crossing at Tedford's Ford, will join in the movement to the left, and press the enemy up the stream from Polk's front at Lee and Gordon's.

"4. Polk will press his forces to the front of Lee and Gordon's Mills, and if met by too much resistance to cross, will bear to the right and cross at Dalton's Ford or at Tedford's, as may be necessary, and join the attack wherever the enemy may be.

"5. Hill will cover our left flank from an advance of the enemy from the cove, and by pressing the cavalry on his front, ascertain if the enemy is reinforcing at Lee and Gordon's Mills, in which event he will attack them in flank.

"6. Wheeler's cavalry will hold the gaps in Pigeon Mountain, and cover our rear and left and bring up stragglers.

"7. All teams, etc., not with the troops should go toward Ringgold and Dalton beyond Taylor's Ridge. All cooking should be done at the trains. Rations when cooked will be forwarded to the troops.

"8. The above movements will be executed with the utmost promptness, vigour, and persistence."

"That's an excellent order," said D. H. Hill. "The only fault to be found with it is that it's excellent-too-late. Some days ago was the proper date. Then we could have dealt with them piecemeal; now they're fifty thousand men behind breastworks."

The aide wagged his head. "Even so, we can beat them, General."
D. H. Hill looked at him a little sardonically. "Of course, of course,
we can beat them ! But have you noticed how many men we lose
in beating them ? And have you any idea how we are to continue to
get men? It takes time to grow oaks and men. What the South
needs is some Cadmus to break the teeth out of skulls, sow them,
and raise overnight a crop of armed men! There are plenty of skulls,
God knows! We are seeing in our day a curious phenomenon. Armies
are growing younger. We are galloping toward the cradle. The V.
M. I. Cadets will be out presently, and then the nine- and ten-
year-olds. Of course the women might come on afterwards, though,
to tell the truth," said Hill, "they've been in the field from the first."

"Here's General Forrest."

Forrest rode up. "General Hill, ain't it ? Good morning, sir.
I am going to fight my men dismounted. This is going to be an
infantry battle."

"I have heard, General," said Hill, "that you have never lost
a fight. How do you manage it ? "

"I git there first with the most men."

"You don't hold then with throwing in troops piecemeal ? "

"No," said Forrest, with a kind of violence. "You kin play the
banjo all right with one finger after another, but in war I clutch with
the whole hand!"

He rode on, a strange figure, an uneducated countryman, behind
him no military training or influence, no West Point; a man of
violences and magnanimities, a big, smoky personality, here dark,
here clearly, broadly lighted. "He was born a soldier as men are
born poets." "Forrest!" said General Joseph E. Johnston long afterwards. "Had Forrest had the advantage of a military education
and training, he would have been the great central figure of the war!"

The sun of the eighteenth of September sank behind the mountains. A cool night wind sprang up, sighing through the bronzing
wood and rippling the surface of the Chickamauga. Three brigades
of Hood's division, marching rapidly from Dalton, had come upon
the field; with them Hood himself, with his splendid personal reputa-
tion, his blue eyes and yellow hair and headlong courage. He had
now his three brigades and three of Bushrod Johnson's. That church-
man militant, Leonidas Polk, held the centre at Lee and Gordon's

Mills, and D. H. Hill the left. Joseph Wheeler and his cavalry watched the left flank, Forrest and his cavalry the right.

The country was rough, the roads few and poor, the fords of the Chickamauga in the same category. Dusk of the eighteenth found Hood and Walker across the stream, but other divisions with the fords yet to make. At dawn of the nineteenth, the Army of the Cumberland began to put itself into position. In the faint light the outposts of the blue caught sight of Buckner's division fording the Chickamauga at Tedford's. In the mist and dimness they thought they saw only a small detached grey force. Three brigades of Brannan's division were at once put forward. In the first pink light Buckner's advanced brigade clashed with Croxton's. With a burst of sound like an explosion in the dim wood began the battle of Chickamauga — one of the worst in history, twice bloodier than Wagram, than Marengo, than Austerlitz, higher in its two days' fallen than Sharpsburg, a terrible, piteous fight.

Forrest, on the right, was immediately engaged. "We've stirred up a yaller-jacket's nest," he said, and sent to General Polk a request for Armstrong's division of his own corps. The centre needing cavalry, too, there was returned only Dibbrell's brigade. Dibbrell's men were dismounted, and together with John Pegram's division — also, in this battle, acting foot soldiers — began a bloody, continued struggle. The point of the blue wedge had been four infantry brigades and one of cavalry, but now the thickness was disclosed, and it fairly proved to be Rosecrans in position. While the grey had moved up the Chickamauga, that able blue strategist, under the cover of night, had moved down the opposite bank. The grey crossed — and found their right enveloped! The Fourteenth Army Corps, George H. Thomas commanding, was here, and later there were reinforcements from the Twenty-first, Crittenden's corps. The storm, beginning with no great fury, promptly swelled until it attained the terrific. Forrest sent again for infantry support. None came, the centre having its own anxieties. "If you want to git a thing done, do it yourself," quoth Forrest, and rode up to John Pegram. "We've got to have more fighters and I'm going to fetch them. Hold your ground, General Pegram, I don't care what happens!"

"All right, sir. Neither do I," said Pegram, and held it, with the loss of one fourth of his command. The pall of smoke settled, heavily, heavily! The dismounted troops fought here in the open, here behind piled brushwood and fallen logs, while the few grey batteries spoke from every little point of vantage. From the woods in front leaped the volleys of the blue, came whistling the horrible shells. The brushwood was set afire, the cavalrymen moving from place to place. They fought like Forrest's men. Rifle barrels grew too hot to touch; all lips were blackened with cartridge powder. There was a certain calmness in the face of storm, *sotto voce* remarks, now and then a chuckling laugh. The finger of Death was forever pointing, but by now the men were used to Death's attitudinizing. They took no great account of the habitual gesture. When he came to sweep with his whole arm, then of course you had to get out of his way! The hot day mounted and the clangour of the right mounted. Back came Forrest, riding hard, at his heels the infantry brigades of Wilson and Walthall. A line of battle was formed; Wilson and Walthall, Dibbrell and Pegram and Nathan Bedford Forrest advancing with a yell, coming to close range, pouring volley after volley into the dense, blue ranks. The dense, blue ranks answered; Death howled through the vale of Chickamauga. Wilson's men took a battery, hard fought to the last. The grey brigade of Ector came up and formed on Wilson's right. Fiercely attacked, Ector sent an aide to Forrest. "General Forrest, General Ector is hard pressed and is uneasy as to his right flank." Forrest nodded his head, his eyes on a Federal battery spouting flame. "Tell General Ector not to bother about his right flank! I'll take care of it." The aide went back, to find Wilson's brigade, on Ector's left, in extremity. Ector sent him again, and he found Forrest now in action, directing, urging his men forward with a voice like a bull of Bashan's and with a great, warlike appearance. "General Forrest, General Ector says that his left flank is now in danger!" Forrest turned, stamped his foot, and shouted, "Tell General Ector that, by God! I am here, and I will take care of his left flank and of his right flank!"

On went the grey charge, infantry and dismounted cavalry. *Yaaaaih! Yaaaaihh! Yaaaaiiihhhh!* it yelled and tossed its colours. Back it pressed the blue, back, back! The first line went back, the second line went back . . . and then was seen through rifts in the smoke the great third line, breastworks in front.

George Thomas was a fighter, too, and he flung forward Brannan and Baird and Reynolds, with Palmer and Van Cleve of Crittenden's corps. Out of the smoky wood the blue burst with thunder, flanking Wilson and opening a furious enfilading fire. It grew terrible, a withering blast before which none could stand. Wilson was forced back, the whole grey line was forced back. Forrest's guns were always clean to the front. They must be gotten back — but so many of the horses were dead or dying, and so many of the artillerymen. Those left put strength to the pieces, got them off, got them back through the brush in ways that could afterwards hardly be remembered. There was a piece entirely endangered — all the horses down and most of the men. Forrest shouted to four of his mounted escort. Cavalry dropped into the places of battery horses and drivers. In a twinkling they were harnessed — off went cavalry with the gun through the echoing wood, the smoke wreaths, and the shouting. The grey went back not far: the blue but regained their first position. It was high noon. Then entered the fight the divisions of Liddell and Cheatham.

Liddell had two thousand men. Bursting through the undergrowth they came into hot touch with Baird's re-forming lines. They broke the brigades of King and Scribner; they took two batteries; yelling, they pursued their victory. The smoke lifted. The two thousand were in the concave of a blue sickle, their line overlapped, right and left — Brannan's men now and R. W. Johnson, of McCook's corps. Liddell, wheeling to the right, beat from that deadly hollow a justifiable retreat.

Cheatham came over a low hill with five brigades. It was a veteran division, predestined to grim fighting. Down on the Alexander Bridge road he formed his line, then, as Walker's commands were pressed back, as the hurrahing blue columns swept forward, he entered the battle with the precision of a stone from David's sling. The blue wavered, broke! In rushed Cheatham's thousands, driving the foe, fiercely driving him. The foe withdrew behind his breastworks, and from that shelter turned against the grey a concentrated fire of musketry and artillery. The grey stood and answered with fury. The ground was all covered with felled trees, piles of brushwood, timber shaken down like jackstraws. No alignment could be kept; the men fired in groups or as single marksmen. As such they strove to advance, as such they were mowed down. The blue began to hurrah. Palmer of Crittenden's corps came swinging in with a flanking movement. But Palmer's hurrahing lines were checked, as had been Brannan's and Johnson's. In through the woods, now all afire, came A. P. Stewart's division of Buckner's corps. Alabama and Tennessee, three thousand muskets, it struck Palmer's line and forced it aside. Van Cleve came to help, but Van Cleve gave way, too, pressed by the grey across the vast, smoke-filled stage to the ridge crowned by earthworks that like a drop-scene closed the back. The roar of battle filled all space; officers could not be heard, nor, in the universal smoke, could waved sword or hat be seen. Off to the right, Forrest's bugles were ringing. Now and then drums were beaten, but this noise seemed no louder than woodpeckers tapping, lost in the crash of the volleys. Alabama and Tennessee pressed on. It was half past two o'clock.

Hood had three brigades of his own division and three of Bushrod Johnson's, and now, from the Lee and Gordon's Mills road, Hood, unleashed at last, entered the battle. Into it, yelling and firing, double-quicked his tall grey lines. He came with the force of a catapult. *Yaaaih! Yaaaiiiihhh!* yelled Tennessee, North Carolina, Arkansas, and Texas. They struck the Chattanooga road and drove the blue along it, toward the westering sun. Up at a double swung the fresh blue troops of Negley and Wood, Davis and Sheridan. In the descending day they pushed the grey again to the eastward of the contested road.

At sunset in came Patrick Cleburne, general beloved, marching with his division over wildly obstructed roads from Hill on the extreme right. But it was late and the dark and smoky day was closing down. Night came, filled with the smell and taste of burned powder and of the wood smoke from all the forest afire. The firing became desultory, died away, save for now and then a sound of skirmishers. The two armies, Army of Tennessee, Army of Cumberland, rested.

They rested from strife, but not from preparation for strife. The two giants, the blue and the grey, were weary enough, but between Chickamauga and the slopes of Missionary Ridge they did small sleeping that Saturday night, the nineteenth of September, 1863.

All night rang the axes. "Log-works," said the grey giant. "At dawn, I am going to storm log-works." Fifty-seven thousand strong was the blue giant and the grey about the same. "To-morrow's fight," said both, "is going to lay over to-day's." "Where," said, in addition, the grey — "where is General Longstreet?"

The soldiers who might sleep, slept on their arms, under a sulphurous canopy. All the forest hereabouts was thick with brushwood and summer-parched. It burned in a hundred places. The details, gathering the wounded, carried torches. It was lurid enough, all the far-flung field. There were very many wounded, many dead. Blue and grey alike heard the groaning of their fallen. *Ahh! ahhh!* groaned the forest. And the word that was always heard, as soon as the guns were silent, was heard now, steady as cicadas in a grove. *Water! Water! Water! Water! Water!* There was a moon, but not plainly seen because of the gauze that was over the earth. A chill and restless night it was, filled with comings and goings, and movements of large bodies of troops.

Just before midnight Longstreet appeared in person. The weary grey railroad had brought him, in the afternoon, to Catoosa platform, near Ringgold. With two aides he took horse at once and pushed out toward the field of action. But the woods were thick and the roads an unmarked tangle. He came at last upon the field and met General Bragg at midnight. Behind him, yet upon the road, were three brigades of Hood's division and Kershaw's and Humphrey's, of McLaws's.

There was a council of war. It was understood, it was in the air, that the past day had been but a prelude. Now Bragg announced to his officers a change of plan. The Army of Tennessee was divided into two wings. The right was composed of Walker's and Hill's corps, Cheatham's division, and the cavalry of Forrest. Leonidas Polk commanded here. The left was formed by Hood's and Buckner's corps, the division of Hindman, and Joe Wheeler's cavalry, and Longstreet commanded this wing.

"And the plan of attack?"

"As it was to-day. Successive pushes from right to left. The attack to begin at daylight."

But daylight was not far away, and the movements to be made were many. The sun was above the tree-tops when Breckinridge advanced upon the Chattanooga road and opened the battle of the twentieth. "Sunday," said the men. "Going to church — going to church — going to a little mountain church! Going to be singing — Minie singing. Going to be preaching — big gun preaching. We've got what the General calls a *ponshon* for Sunday service. . . . Lot of dead people in this wood. Have n't you ever noticed how much worse a half-burned cabin looks than one burned right down? That one over there — it looks as if home was still a-lingering around. Go 'way! it does! You boys have n't got no imagination. — No imagination — no imagination — No shoes and pretty nearly no breakfast. . . . I wish this here dust was imagination —

"The sun shines bright in the old Kentucky home;
    'T is summer, the darkies are gay,
The corn-top's ripe and the meadow's in the bloom,
    While the birds make music all the day."

"Birds all fly away from battle-fields" — "Not when there are nestlings! Saw a tree set on fire by hot shot from Yankee gunboat on the Tennessee. Marched by it when it was jest a pillar of flame, and, by gum! there was a mocking-bird dead on her nest, with her wings spread out over the little birds. All of them dead. . . . It made you wonder. And, by gum! the captain, when he saw it — the captain saluted!"

"The young folks roll on the little cabin floor,
    All merry, all happy and bright;
By 'n' by hard times comes a-knocking at the door,
    Then, my old Kentucky home, good night!"

"Whew! That's a pretty line of breastworks over there before Helm's brigade! Reckon that's what Billy Yank was building all night long! — Helm's going forward —" *Kentuckians! Charge bayonets! Double-quick!*

Helm was killed, heroically leading his brigade. The colonel of the Second Kentucky was killed, the colonel of the Ninth badly wounded. The Ninth lost a third of its number. "I went into the fight," says the colonel of the Second, "with thirty officers and two hundred and seventy-two men, and came out with ten officers and one hundred and forty-six men. Both officers and men behaved gallantly." The colonel of the Fourth was badly wounded; the Sixth had its losses; the Forty-first Alabama went in with something over three hundred men, and lost in killed twenty-seven, in wounded, one hundred and twenty. Three captains of the Second were killed at the foot of the works, and the colour-sergeant, Robert Anderson, having planted the flag a-top, died with his hands about the staff. Adams's Louisiana brigade came to the help of Helm. Adams, severely wounded, was taken prisoner. The combat raged, bitter and bloody. There was a long, long line of well-erected breastworks, with a shorter line at right angles. The divisions of Thomas fought grimly, heroically; the brigades of Breckinridge went to the assault as heroically. Nowadays no Confederate brigade, no Confederate regiment, had full complement of muskets. They were skeleton organizations, gaunt as their units, but declining to merge because each would keep its old, heroic name. Spare as they were, they threw themselves, yelling, against the log-works. Breckinridge was tall and straight and filled with fiery courage. Vice-President, on a time, of the United States, now grey general on the chessboard, he showed here, as there, a brilliant, commanding personality. His men, proud of him, fought with his own high ardour. The withering blast came against them; they shouted and tossed it back. Now there came also against the breastworks the division of Cleburne.

Patrick Romayne Cleburne, — thirty-six years old, but with greying hair above his steel-grey eyes, Irishman of the county of Cork, one time soldier in the English army, then lawyer in the city of Helena and the State of Arkansas, then private in the Confederate army, then captain, then colonel, then brigadier, and now major-general, — Patrick Cleburne commanded a division that, also, had its personality. The division's heart and his heart beat in unison. "He was not only a commander, but a comrade fighting with his men." Arkansas, Tennessee, Texas, Alabama, Mississippi, and the Irish regiment adored Cleburne, and Cleburne returned their love. "To my noble division," he wrote to a lady, "and not to myself, belong the praises for the deeds of gallantry you mention." Cleburne's division had its own flags, and on each was worked a device of "crossed cannon inverted," and the name of the battle-fields over which it had been carried. "Prior to the battle of Shiloh," says General Hardee, "a blue battle-flag had been adopted by me for this division, and when the Confederate battle-flag became the national colours, Cleburne's division, at its urgent request, was allowed to retain its own bullet-ridden battle-flags. . . . Friends and foes soon learned to watch the course of the blue flag that marked where Cleburne was in the battle. Where this division defended, no odds broke its lines where it attacked, no numbers resisted its onslaught — save only once — and there is the grave of Cleburne and his heroic division." Now at Chickamauga, Cleburne and forty-four hundred bayonets swung into battle to the support of Breckinridge. Before Cleburne, also, at short range, were breastworks, and now from these there burst a tempest of grape and canister, with an undersong of musketry. It was a fire that mowed like a scythe. Wood's brigade had to cross an old field bordering the Chattanooga road, an old field marked by a burning house. Crossing, there burst against it, from hidden batteries to right and left, a blast as from a furnace seven times heated. Five hundred men fell here, killed and wounded. On the left Lucius Polk's brigade came against breastworks cresting a hill covered with scrub oak. Blue and grey engaged with fury. Down poured the blast from the ridge, canister and grape and musketry. Lucius Polk's men lay down behind the crest of a lower ridge, and kept up the fight, losing in no great time three hundred and fifty officers and men. Deshler's brigade moved forward. A shell came shrieking, struck Deshler in the breast, and killed him. Cleburne shook his head. "Too much loss of good life!" — and withdrawing the division four hundred yards, took up a strong defensive position.

Breckinridge and Cleburne, there was loss of life enough. What was gained was this: Thomas called for reinforcements, and Rosecrans, to strengthen his left, began to weaken his right. To the aid of Baird and Johnson, Palmer and Reynolds behind the breastworks, came first a brigade of Negley's division, then regiments from Palmer's reserve, and then from the left troops of McCook and Sheridan.

The divisions of Gist and Liddell, Walker's corps, moved to the aid of Breckinridge, Gist throwing himself with fury against the works before which Helm had fallen. It was eleven o'clock. Bragg ordered in Stewart's division. The three brigades — Clayton, Brown, and Bate — charged under a deadly fire, "the most terrible fire it has ever been my fortune to witness." Brown's men, exposed to an enfilade, broke, but Clayton and Bate rushed on past the clearing, past the burning house, past the Chattanooga road. They drove the blue within entrenchments, they took a battery and many prisoners. Thomas sent again to Rosecrans, and Rosecrans further weakened his right. His adjutant forwarded an order to McCook. The left must be supported at all hazards, "even if the right is drawn wholly to the present left." After Van Cleve had been sent, and Sheridan and Negley, there came yet another message that the left was heavily pressed. The aide bringing it stated that Brannan was out of line and Reynolds's right exposed. Rosecrans sent an order to Wood, commanding a division —

"*The general commanding directs that you close up on Reynolds as fast as possible and support him.*"

It was the fatal, the pivotal order. Wood moved — and left a great opening in the blue line of battle. Toward the filling of this gap there moved with precision two brigades of Sheridan's. But some one else moved first, with a masterful change of plan, made with the swiftness of that glint of Opportunity's eye.

Longstreet had made a column of attack, three lines, eight brigades. Long, grey, magnificent, these moved forward, steady as steel, eyes just narrowed in the face of the hurricane of shot and shell. "Old Pete," "the old war horse," rode with them, massively directing. The smoke was drifting, drifting over the field of Chickamauga, over the River of Death and the slopes of Missionary Ridge. Underfoot was dust and charred herbage and the dead and the wounded. On the right the roar of the fight never ceased — Forrest, Breckinridge, Cleburne, Walker, Stewart, and George Thomas behind his breastworks.

Longstreet with his eight brigades, swinging toward the right, saw, through a rift in the smoke, the movement of Wood and the gap which now, suddenly, was made between the Federal right and left. A kind of slow light came into Longstreet's face. "*By the right flank, wheel! — Double-quick! — Forward! Charge!*"

Hood was leading. His line struck like a thunderbolt the foe in reverse, struck McCook's unprepared brigades. There sprang and swelled an uproar that overcrowed all the din to the right. McCook broke, the grey drove on. They yelled. · *Yaaaih! Yaaaihh! Yaaaaihh!* yelled the grey. Hood rose in his stirrups and shouted an order to Bushrod Johnson. "Go ahead, and keep ahead of everything!" A minie ball shattered his thigh. He sank from his horse; Law took command; on swept the great charge. Brigades of Manigault and Deas, McNair, Gregg, Johnson, Law, Humphrey, Benning, with Patton Anderson, of Hindman's division, they burst from the forest into open fields running through smoky sunshine backward and upward to ridges crowned by Federal batteries. All these broke into thunder, loud and fast, but the blue infantry, surprised, broken, streamed across the fields in disorder. Behind them came the vehement charge, long, triumphant, furious, with blare and dust and smoke and thunder, with slanted colours, with neighing chargers, with burning eyes and lifted voices. All the *élan* of the South was here. Brigade by brigade, Longstreet burst from the forest. Yelling, this charge drove the blue from their breastworks, took the house that was their headquarters, took twenty-seven pieces of artillery, and more than a thousand prisoners, laid hand upon hospitals and ordnance trains, slew and wounded and bore the blue back, back! McCook suffered heavily, oh, heavily! "I have never," says D. H. Hill, — "I have never seen the Federal dead lie so thickly on the ground save in front of the sunken wall at Fredericksburg."

There was a line of heights behind the Vidito house, beyond the Crawfish Spring road. Thomas seized these, and here the blue rallied and turned for a yet more desperate struggle. It came. Hindman and Bushrod Johnson proposed to take those heights by assault. They took them, but at a cost, at a cost, at a cost! When they won to the Vidito house, the women of the family left whatever hiding-place from the shells they had contrived, and ran, careless of the whistling death in the air, out before the house. They laughed, they wept, they welcomed. "God bless you! God bless you! It's going to be a victory! It's going to be a victory! God bless you!" The grey, storming on, waved hat and cheered. "It's going to be a victory! It's going to be a victory! God bless you!"

Up on the sides of the ridge it came to hand-to-hand fighting, a dreadful, prolonged struggle, men clubbing men with muskets, men piercing men's breasts with bayonets, men's faces scorched, so near were they to the iron, flaming muzzles! Over all roared the guns, settled the smoke; underfoot the earth grew blood-soaked. Inch by inch the grey fought their way; inch by inch the blue gave back, driven up the long slope to the very crest of the ridge. The sun was low in the heavens.

On Horseshoe Ridge the fight grew fell. And now came to the aid of the right wing, came in long, resistless combers, the brigades of Hill. They came through the woods afire, over the clearings sown with dead and wounded, up the slope of Horseshoe. Once more the summit flamed and thundered — then the blue summit turned grey. Over the crest, down the northern slope of the ridge swept the united wings, right wing and left wing. They made a thresher's fan; before it the blue fell away, passed from the slope into deep hollows of the approaching night. Right wing and left wing shouted; they shouted until Lookout Mountain, dark against the sunset sky, might have heard their shouting.

On the field of Chickamauga, by the River of Death, thirty thousand men lay dead or wounded, or were prisoners or missing. If there were Indian spirits in these woods they might have said in council that September night: "How fierce and fell and bloody-minded is this white man who wars where once we warred! Look at the long files of his ghost, rising like mist from Chickamauga, passing like thin smoke across the moon!"

CHAPTER XXI

MISSIONARY RIDGE

ALL day the twenty-first the shattered blue army lay in position at Rossville, five miles away. But Bragg, his army likewise shattered and exhausted, his ammunition failing, did not attack. At night Rosecrans withdrew to Chattanooga, entrenching himself there. On the twenty-second, Bragg followed, and took up position on Missionary Ridge and along the lower slopes of Lookout. The blue base of supplies was at Stevenson, in Alabama, forty miles away. Cut the road to this place and Rosecrans might be compelled to evacuate Chattanooga.

Bragg sent Law's brigade to hold the Jasper road. Wheeler, too, in a raid, wrought mischief to the blue. To the latter the possession of the Tennessee River and the building of a bridge became of supreme importance. Down the stream Rosecrans sent fifteen hundred men and a flotilla of pontoons, while a land force marched to guard them. Before the grey could gather to the attack the bridge was built. A day or two later came to the aid of the blue "Fighting Joe" Hooker and two corps of the Army of the Potomac. On the twenty-second of October, Grant arrived in Chattanooga and superseded Rosecrans.

There occurred the night battle of Wauhatchie, — four brigades of Hood's attacking Geary's division of the Twelfth Corps, — a short, hard fight, where each side lost five hundred men and nothing gained. But now to the South to lose five hundred men was to lose five hundred drops of heart's blood, impossible of replacement. Men now in the South were worth their weight in gold.

There came to the grey camps news that Sherman, with a considerable force, was on the road from Memphis. Hooker, with the Eleventh and Twelfth Corps, was here. Grant was here. From the Knoxville side Burnside threatened. Action became imperative.

Bragg acted, but not, perhaps, with wisdom. On the fourth of November, Longstreet's corps and Wheeler's cavalry found themselves under orders for Knoxville. Longstreet remonstrated, but orders were orders. Grey First Corps, grey cavalry marched away, marched away. The weakened force before Chattanooga looked dubious, shook its head. Later, Bragg detached two other brigades from the thin grey lines and sent them after Longstreet on the Knoxville campaign. Burnside was to be fought there, and here were only Hooker, Grant, and Sherman!

Ten thousand infantry and artillery, five thousand horse, marched away. The loss at Chickamauga had been perhaps sixteen thousand. What remained of the Army of Tennessee had to hold an eight-mile line. It was a convex; right and left in hollow ground, the centre on the flank of Lookout Mountain and the crest of Missionary Ridge. On the twenty-second, Grant began under cover certain operations.

In this region the weather is mild, even on the twenty-fourth of November. A crimson yet burned in the oak leaves, and the air, though mist-laden, was not cold. Grey cliffs form a palisade on Lookout Mountain. Above is the scarped mountain-top, below, long wooded slopes sinking steeply to the levels through which bends and bends again the Tennessee. One grey brigade — Walthall's Mississippi brigade — was stationed on this shoulder of Lookout; below it steep woods, above it the cliffs, with creepers here and there yet scarlet-fingered. The day was tranquil, quiet, pearly grey, with fog upon the mountain-head. From early morning the fog everywhere had been very dense, so dense that men could not be distinguished at a hundred yards. It was known that affairs were on the point of moving. Walthall and his Mississippians were alert enough — and yet the day and the woods and the whole far-flung earth were so dreamy-calm, so misty-still, that any battle seemed impossible of quick approach. There was the odour of wet earth and rotting leaves, there was the dreamy, multitudinous forest stir, there was the vague drifting mist — the soul was lulled as in a steady boat. Walthall's men rested on the earth, by quiet little camp-fires. Their arms were at hand, but it seemed not a day of fighting. The day was like a grey nun. The men grew dreamy, too. They drawled their words. "This air a fine view, when it's right clear," they said. "Yes. This air a fine view. But when the Lord laid out the Tennessee River he surely took the serpent for a pattern! He surely did. Never see such a river for head and tail meeting — and I've seen a lot of rivers since Dan Tucker rang the court-house bell, and we all stood around and heard Secession proclaimed. Yes, sir. I've seen a lot of rivers, — big rivers and little rivers and middle-sized rivers, — but I never see a river twisted like the Lord's twisted the Tennessee!" — "I wish," said a comrade, "that the Lord'd come along and put his finger and thumb together and flip away those danged batteries over there on Moccasin Point — jest flip them away same as you'd flip a pig-nut. Kind of funny looking over there to-day anyhow! Ef I had a glass —"

"Captain's got a glass. He's looking —"

"So much fog you can't see nothing. There's batteries on the Ridge beyond Lookout Creek, too —"

"I kin usually feel it in my bones when we're going to have a fight. Don't feel nothing to-day, but just kind of studious-like. The world's so awful quiet."

"Cleburne's men are away off there at Chickamauga Creek —"

"Most of the enemy's tents are gone," said the captain, "and they have removed their pontoon bridges. When this fog lifts —"

Walthall came by, talking to his adjutant. "As far as you can tell for the fog they are moving rapidly on the left. General Stevenson showed me an order from General Bragg. Stevenson has the whole defence on this side of Chattanooga Creek."

"Do you think they will attack to-day?"

"Who can tell? If this miserable fog would lift —"

Crack! crack! crack! crack! out of the woods to the westward rang the muskets of the picket line. Instantaneously, from the batteries on Moccasin [Point, from the batteries on the ridge over the creek, sprang a leap of light that tore the fog. Followed thunder, and the ploughing of shells into the earth of Lookout. The grey brigade sprang to arms. In tumbled the pickets. "Yankees above us —"

"Above —!"

The Lookout cliffs were tall and grey. They crowned the mountain with an effect from below of robber castles. The November woods were so sere and leafless that in clear weather, looking up the long slopes, you would see with distinctness wall and bastion. To-day there was fog, fog torn by the crowding yellow flashes of many rifles. The flashes came from the base of the cliffs. They came from blue troops, troops that had crept from the west, around the shoulder of Lookout, along the base of the cliffs — troops that were many, troops of Hooker's that had come up from the valley of Lookout Creek, stealing up the mountain in silence and security, in the heavy fog. Now they hurrahed and sprang down from among the cliffs. Many and ready, they dropped as from the clouds; they took the grey brigade in reverse. And with instantaneous thunder the batteries opened all along the front.

The blue — Geary's division — came over the shoulder of the mountain in three lines. From time to time in the past weeks the grey had constructed rude works of stones and felled wood. Now the men fought from one to another of these; withdrawn from one base to a second, from a second to a third, they fought from facet to facet of Lookout. The ground was intolerably rough, with boulder and fallen timber and snares of leafless vines. Now the grey were upon a slope where the casemented batteries of Moccasin Point had full play. There was an old rifle-pit dug downward and across. It gave the men passing over this shoulder a certain vague and ineffective shelter. Walthall's men, forced from Lookout, came to Craven's house, and here, in hollow ground, made a stand and sent for reinforcements. Pettus's brigade appearing at last, the fight was renewed. It waged hotly for a while, but the odds were great. The November day spread its mists around. Mississippi and Alabama fought well on Lookout; but there was somehow a sinking at the heart, a dreary knowledge that Grant had perhaps a hundred thousand men and the Army of Tennessee a third of that number; that General Bragg was a good man, but not a soldier like Lee or Jackson or Johnston; that Longstreet should never have been detached; that there was a coldness in this thickening fog; that the guns on Moccasin Point were as venomous as its name; and that War was a nightmare oftener than one would think. Two months had passed since Chickamauga. That was a great battle, that was a great, glorious, terrible, hot-blooded, crashing battle, with the woods ringing and the blue breaking before you! This was not that. Two months of sickness, two months of hard picketing, two months of small rations and difficult to get, two months of dissatisfaction with the commanding general and his plan of campaign, of constant criticism, of soreness, of alternation between the fractious and the listless, two months of fretting and waiting in an unhealthy season, in an unhealthy situation, — the Army of Tennessee was in a conceiving mood that differed palpably from the mood of Chickamauga! It was ready for bogies, ready for — what? It did not know. At dusk the command that had been posted on Lookout, pressed backward and down throughout the foggy day, halted at the foot of the mountain, on the road leading outward and across a half-mile of valley to Missionary Ridge. Here in darkness and discontent it waited until midnight, when, under orders from Cheatham, it sank farther down to McFarland's Spring. At dawn it was marched across the lowland to Missionary Ridge, and was put into position on that solemn wave of earth. It found here the other commands forming the Confederate centre.

Patrick Cleburne, ordered with his division after Longstreet on the Knoxville expedition, received at Chickamauga Station a telegram from the general commanding. "We are heavily engaged. Move up rapidly to these headquarters."

Cleburne moved. That night, the night of the twenty-third, he spent immediately behind Missionary Ridge. With the first light he began to construct defences. It was known now that in great force Grant had crossed the Tennessee, both above and below Chickamauga. It was known that the great blue army, Grant with Sherman and Hooker, had burst from Chattanooga like a stream in freshet; the dark blue waves were seen wherever the fog parted. They coloured all the lowland; they lifted themselves toward the heights. Already the waves had taken Lookout; already they were lapping against the foot of Missionary. Cleburne held the hollow ground on the right of Missionary, near the tunnel of the East Tennessee and Georgia Railroad. His orders were to hold this right at all hazards. Cleburne obeyed. There was a detached ridge which he wished to gain before the blue, now rapidly advancing, should gain it. He sent Smith's Texas brigade, but the blue had greatly the start. When the Texans reached the foot of the ridge, they were fired upon from the top. Smith, turned by his right flank, climbed Missionary Ridge and took position upon its crest.

Below, in the hollow ground stretching toward the Chickamauga, Cleburne disposed the remainder of his troops. Hardee, experienced, able, stanch, came and approved. They burned a bridge across the Chickamauga. Dark was now at hand. The fog was disappearing, but the flames from the burning bridge had a curious, blurred, yellow, heatless effect. An aide came up with news.

"They've overrun Lookout, sir. Our men there have come over to Missionary."

"What loss?"

"I don't know, sir. Some one said they came like driftwood. I know that there's a flood gaining on us."

"Where there's a flood," said Cleburne, "thank the Saints, there's usually an Ark! Set the axes to work, Major. We're going to run a breastwork along here."

There was that night an eclipse of the moon. The men who were making the breastwork stopped their work when the blackness began to steal across. They watched it with a curious look upon their lifted faces. "That thar moon," said a man, — "that thar moon is the Confederacy, and that thar thing that's stealing across it — that thar thing's the End!"

"That ain't the kind of talk —"

"Yes, it is the kind of talk! When you've come to the End, I want to know it. I ain't a-going to stop building breastworks and I ain't a-going to stop biting cartridges, but I want to know it. I want to be able to point my finger and say, 'Thar's the End.'"

The black moved farther upon the silver shield. All the soldiers rested on their axes and looked upon it. "When the Confederacy ends I want to end, too, — right then and thar and hand in hand! But the Confederacy ain't going to end. I reckon we've given it enough blood to keep it going!"

But the first speaker remained a pessimist. "What we give our blood to is the earth and the sea. We don't give no blood to the Confederacy. The Confederacy ain't gaining blood; she's losing blood — drop by drop out of every vein. She lost a deal at Chickamauga and she's going to lose a deal —"

"The black is three quarters over. God! ain't it eerie?"

"The man that says the Confederacy is going to end is a damned coward and traitor! That thing up there ain't nothing but a passing shadow —"

Cleburne came by. "Too dark to dig, boys? Never mind! There'll be light enough by and by."

The black veil drew across, then slowly passed. Cold and bright the moon looked down. Cleburne's men built their breastwork, then, straightening themselves, wiped with the back of their hands the sweat from their brows. Their work had made them warm, but now was felt the mortal chill of the hour before dawn. The woods began to sigh. They made a mysterious, trembling sound beneath the concave of the sky. The sky paled; on the east above the leafless trees came a wash of purple, desolate and withdrawn. The November day broke slowly. There was a mist. It rose from the streams, it hung upon bush and tree, it hid enemy from enemy, it almost hid friend from friend.

With the light came skirmishing, and at sunrise the batteries opened from the ridge the blue had seized. At ten o'clock there arrived the Federal advance upon this front. It came through the light mist, in two long lines of battle. Its bands were playing. Davis's division, three divisions of Sherman's, Eleventh Corps of the Army of the Potomac, Sherman commanding all. There was a hill near the tunnel, and Cleburne held this and the woodland rolling from the right. He had guns in position above the tunnel gaping like a black mouth in the hillside, gaping at the hurrahing rush of Sherman's men.

All day on this right the conflict howled. Hardee and Hardee's corps were cool and stanch; Cleburne was a trusted man, hilt and blade. Sherman launched his thunderbolts, blue charge after blue charge; "General Pat" flung them back. The sky was dark with the leaden rain; the November woods rang; Tunnel Hill, Swett's and Key's batteries, flamed through the murk; Texas and Arkansas, Georgia and Tennessee, grappled with Indiana, Illinois, Iowa, Ohio. All day, to and fro, in the leafless woods, under the chill sky, over a rugged ground, they swung and swayed. Now the blue seemed uppermost, and now the grey, but at last the grey charged with bayonets. After this the blue rested, a sullen sea, held back by Tunnel Hill and all the grey-hued slopes around. The afternoon was well advanced, the smoke-draped woods dim enough. Cleburne's men smiled, nodding their heads. "That old eclipse wa'n't nothing! This Confederacy's immortal — Yes, she is! She's got a wreath of immortelles. — I'm going to ask General Pat if she has n't! You artillerymen did first-rate, and we infantry did first-rate, and if the cavalry had n't been sent away I reckon they'd have done as well as it lies in cavalry to do. — Now, if the centre and the left —"

A courier came over stock and stone, pushing a foam-flecked horse — "General Cleburne! — Order from General Hardee —"

Cleburne read: "*General: Send at once all possible troops to support centre. It's much in danger.*"

Cleburne took Cummings and Maney and with them set face to Missionary Ridge. A little way through the darkening wood and a gasping aide met him — "From General Hardee, sir! They've pierced our centre. They're on the Ridge — they've overflowed Missionary Ridge. We're all cut to pieces there — demoralized. — General Hardee says, form a line so as to meet attack. Do the best you can for the safety of the right wing —"

Missionary Ridge rose two hundred feet. It rose steeply, with a narrow plateau a-top. It was seamed with gullies, shaggy with woods. In places, however, the wood had been cleared, leaving the stumps of trees, gaunt, with sere, slippery grass between. At the foot of the Ridge were grey works, and now, within the last twenty-four hours, the grey had built other works along the crest. For lack of entrenching-tools and of time, they were slight enough — a shallow ditch, a slight breastwork, dark against a pallid sky. Here, at the top of Missionary, and there at the foot, were gathered the Confederate centre, together with the troops driven yesterday from Lookout. Missionary Ridge was like a crag, rising from a blue, determined sea.

Officers looked at the lines. "What do you think of it?"

"Bad."

"Even here at the top we don't command all approaches."

"No. Those ravines are natural covered ways. They can come close and our guns never harm them."

"Do you understand this order?"

"No. I don't —"

"'Brigades to divide. One half to defend the foot of Missionary, one half to remain on crest. If the enemy attacks in force, fire once' — that is, the force at the foot fire once — 'and retire to the works above —' H'mmm!"

This day was not the humid, languid, foggy day of yesterday. It was cool and still, but the sun was out. The Confederate centre, high on Missionary, saw to-day its foe.

The foe was massing, massing, on level and rolling ground below. In the amber air it could be plainly seen. It was in two vast lines of battle, with large reserves in the background, and hovering skirmishers before. The grey, watching, estimated its front, from wing to wing, as two and a half miles. Being formed, it advanced a mile and stood. Now it could be seen with extreme plainness, a blue sea just below. It had, as always, many bands and much music. These made the air throb. At intervals, like blossoms in a giant's garden, swayed the flags. The crest of Missionary watched.

"They're the boys for an imposing advance!"

"How many d' ye suppose they've got?"

"Don't know. Don't know about Ulysses. Xerxes had a million."

"Hope they're all there. Hope they are n't trying any flank and rear foolishness."

"Hope not, but I would n't swear to it! I've got a distrust of Grant — though it may not be well founded, as the storekeeper said when the clerk and the till were found on the same train."

"Wish there was water up here on Sinai! My mouth's awful dry."

A man spat. "It's curious how many this morning I've heard say their mouth was awful dry and they felt a little dizzy —"

"It's the altitude."

"Six hundred feet? No. It's something else. I don't know just what it is —"

Voices died. There fell a quiet as before a thunderstorm, an oppressive quiet. Missionary Ridge, its brows faintly drawn and raised, looked forth upon the sea. The sea stood broodingly quiet, without music now, the coloured blossoms still upon their stems. It held and held, the quietude.

Far off a dozen cannon boomed — Sherman's sullen last attack upon Cleburne. The grey ridge, the blue sea, bent heads to one side, listening. The far-off iron voices ceased to speak. Silence fell again. Up on Missionary a lieutenant drew his hand across his forehead. When it fell again to the sword hilt the palm was wet with sweat, the back was wet. The lieutenant was conscious of a slight nausea. There was a drumming, too, in his ears. He took himself to task. "This will never do," he said; "this will never do —" Suddenly he thought, "The men are looking at me" — and stood up very straight, smiling stiffly.

Off on the horizon three cannon spoke, one after the other, with the effect of a signal. The sound died into silence — there followed a moment of held breath — the storm broke.

All the great blue guns — and they were many — opened upon the grey centre. There burst a howling, a shrieking, a whistling of artillery. The sky grew suddenly dark. From Missionary the grey answered, but it was a far lesser storm that they could launch. So much the lesser storm it was that it may be said that Missionary early saw its fate, towering, resistless, close. The sea lifted itself, moving forward like a spring tide while the cannon shook the firmament. It moved so close that the face of it was seen, it moved so close that the eyes of it were seen. It came like the tide that drags under the rocks.

Then was shown the fatalness of that order. All the grey troops at the foot of Missionary fired with precision, one point-blank volley in the face of the sea. *If they advance in force, fire once and fall back — If they advance in force, fire once and fall back.*

Only officers, and not all the officers, knew that the order was of hours' standing. As for the men, they only saw that after one volley they were in retreat. The lines above only saw that after one volley the lines below were in retreat. Over Missionary ran something like the creeping of flesh at midnight when the nightmare is felt in the room. The grey troops of the lower line began to climb. Before them rose the scarped earth, boulder-strewn, seamed and scarred, here with standing wood, here with crops of tree-stumps like dark mushrooms. Behind them was the dark blue shouting sea, and all the air was mere battle-smoke and thunder. The artillery echoed frightfully. It was as though the mountains of the region were convoluted walls of a vast shell. The vibrations were flung from one wall to another; they never passed out of that wildly disturbed, hollow chamber. So loud were the cracks of sound, so steady the humming, that orders, right or wrong, that encouraging shouts of officers, were not well heard. In the tormenting roar, with the knowledge of the lost left, in ignorance of Cleburne's dogged stand on the right, with a conception, like a darting spark in the brain, of the isolation of Missionary, of fewness of numbers, of a lack here of leadership, with a feeling of impotence, with a feeling of dread, the grey lower lines began to climb Missionary to the upper lines. At first they went steadily, in fair order. . . . The surges of sound and light filled the universe. A sudden message rocked through every brain. *They 're coming after us, over the breastworks!* Instantaneously the waves of light passed into waves of darkness. With a shriek as of a million minies came panic Fear.

On the slopes of Missionary there was now no order. It was *sauve qui peut.* The blue tide overswept the breastworks and came on, and the grey fled before it.

In this war it had come to the grey, as it had come to the blue, to retreat, to retreat hastily and in confusion, to retreat disordered. The grey, as the blue, had some acquaintance with Panic, had occasionally met her in the road. But to-day Panic meant not to stop at a bowing acquaintance. She aimed at a closer union and she attained her end. Each man there felt her bony clutch upon his throat and her arms like a Nessus shirt about his body. . . .

Up — up — up! and the dark tree-stumps got always in the way. Men stumbled and fell; rose and went blindly on again — save those whom the black hail from the guns had cut down forever. These lay stark or writhing among the stumps. Their pale fellows went by them, gasping, fleet-footed. Up — up — up!

The troops upon the crest, white-faced, tight-lipped, at last received the lower line, staggering figures rising through the murk. Officers were here, officers were there, hoarse-voiced, beseeching. There came at the top a wraithlike order out of chaos; there was achieved a skeleton formation. But many of the men had rushed below the Ridge, stumbling down into the protecting forest, their hands to their heads. Others fell upon the earth and vomited. Many were wounded, and now, memory returning where they lay sunk together on the level ground, they began to cry out. All were as ghastly pale as bronze could turn, from all streamed the sweat. When they staggered into line, as many, Panic to the contrary, did stagger, their hands shook like leaves in storm. For minutes they could not duly handle their pieces. To the line a-top of Missionary, the line looking down upon the mounting tide, they were as an infectious disease. It was horrible to see Terror and the effect of Terror; it was horrible to feel finger-tips brushing the throat.

In the mean time the tide mounted. It had no orders to mount.

It was expected, when the lower line was taken, that it would wait for some next indicated move. But always the higher grey line was raining fire upon it, the grey batteries were spouting death. It became manifest that the road of safety was up Missionary. On its top grew the nettle Danger from which only might be plucked the flower Safety. The blue kept on because that was the best thing and only thing to do. Moreover, they soon found that the gullies and miniature ridges of Missionary afforded protection. The whole vast wave divided into six parties of attack, and so came up the face of Missionary.

"Who," asked Grant from the eminence where he stood, — "who ordered those men up the hill ?"

He spoke curtly, anger in his voice. "Some one will suffer for it," he said, "if it turns out badly."

But, for the blue, it did not turn out badly. . . .

When the thunder and shouting was all over, when the short desperate mêlée was ended, when the guns were silenced and taken, when the blue wave had triumphed on the height of Missionary, and the grey had fallen backward and down, when the pursuit was checked, when the broken grey army rested in the November forest, when the day closed sombrely with one red gleam in the west, three soldiers, having scraped together dead leaves and twigs and lit a fire, nodded at one another across the blaze.

"Did n't I tell you," said one, "that that thar moon was the Confederacy and that that thar thing stealing across it was the End ?"

"And did n't I tell you," said the second, "that thar don't nothing end ? Ef a thing has been, it Is."

"Well, I reckon you 'll allow," spoke the third, "that we 've had an awful defeat this day ?"

"A lot of wise men," said the second, "have lived on this here earth, but the man that 's wise enough to tell what 's defeat and what is n't has n't yet appeared. However, I 'll allow that it looks like defeat."

"Would n't you call it defeat if every army of us surrendered, and they took down the Stars and Bars from over the Capitol at Richmond ?"

"Well, that depends," said the second. "Got any tobacco ?"

That same night Bragg crossed the Chickamauga, burning the bridges behind him. The Army of Tennessee fell back to Ringgold, then to Dalton. While at this place, Bragg, at his own request, was relieved from command. The Army of Tennessee came into the hands of Joseph E. Johnston.

CHAPTER XXII

DALTON

O N the twelfth of March, 1864, Ulysses S. Grant was placed in command of all the Federal armies, and on the twenty-sixth joined the army in Virginia. He says: —

"When I assumed command of all the armies, the situation was about this: the Mississippi was guarded from St. Louis to its mouth; the line of the Arkansas was held, thus giving us all the Northwest north of that river. A few points in Louisiana, not remote from the river, were held by the Federal troops, as was also the mouth of the Rio Grande. East of the Mississippi we held substantially all north of the Memphis and Charleston railroad as far east as Chattanooga, thence along the line of the Tennessee and Holston Rivers, taking in nearly all of the State of Tennessee. West Virginia was in our hands, and also that part of old Virginia north of the Rapidan and east of the Blue Ridge. On the seacoast we had Fort Monroe and Norfolk, in Virginia; Plymouth, Washington, and New Berne, in North Carolina; Beaufort, Folly and Morris Islands, Hilton Head and Port Royal, in South Carolina, and Fort Pulaski, in Georgia; Fernandina, St. Augustine, Key West, and Pensacola, in Florida. The remainder of the Southern territory, an empire in extent, was still in the hands of the enemy.

"Sherman, who had succeeded me in the command of the Military Division of the Mississippi, commanded all the troops in the territory west of the Alleghanies and north of Natchez, with a large movable force about Chattanooga. . . . In the East, the opposing forces stood in substantially the same relations toward each other as three years before or when the war began; they were both between the Federal and Confederate capitals. . . . My general plan now was to concentrate all the force possible against the Confederate armies in the field. There were but two such . . . east of the Mississippi River and facing north; the Army of Northern Virginia, General Robert E. Lee commanding, was on the south bank of the Rapidan, confronting the Army of the Potomac; the second, under General Joseph E. Johnston, was at Dalton, Georgia, opposed to Sherman, who was still at Chattanooga. Besides these main armies the Confederates had to guard the Shenandoah Valley — a great storehouse to feed their armies from — and their line of communications from Richmond to Tennessee. Forrest, a brave and intrepid cavalry general, was in the West with a large force, making a larger command necessary to hold what we had gained in Middle and West Tennessee. . . . I arranged for a simultaneous movement, all along the line."

"On the historic fourth day of May, 1864," says General William T. Sherman, "the Confederate army at my front lay at Dalton, Georgia, composed, according to the best authority, of about forty-five thousand men, commanded by Joseph E. Johnston, who was equal in all the elements of generalship to Lee, and who was under instructions from the war powers in Richmond to assume the offensive northward as far as Nashville. But he soon discovered that he would have to conduct a defensive campaign. Coincident with the movement of the Army of the Potomac, as announced by telegraph, I advanced from our base at Chattanooga with the Army of the Ohio, 13,559 men; the Army of the Cumberland, 60,773; and the Army of the Tennessee, 24,465 — grand total, 98,797 men and 254 guns."

Johnston took command at Dalton in December and spent the winter bringing back efficiency to the shaken Army of Tennessee. In his account of the following campaign, he says: "An active campaign of six months, half of it in the rugged region between Chattanooga and Dalton, had so much reduced the condition of the horses of the cavalry and artillery, as well as of the mules of the wagon-trains, that most of them were unfit for active service. . . . In the course of an inspection, and as soon as practicable, I found the condition of the army much less satisfactory than it had appeared to the President on the twenty-third of December. There was a great deficiency of blankets; and it was painful to see the number of bare feet in every regiment. . . . There was a deficiency in the infantry, of six thousand small arms. . . . The time of winter was employed mainly in improving the discipline and instruction of the troops and in attention to their comfort. Before the end of April more than five thousand absentees had been brought back to their regiments. Military operations were confined generally to skirmishing between little scouting parties of cavalry of our army with pickets of the other. . . . The effective strength of the Army of Tennessee, as shown by the return of May first, 1864, was 37,652 infantry, 2812 artillery, and 2392 cavalry. . . . On the fifth, the Confederate troops were formed to receive the enemy. . . . My own operations, then and subsequently, were determined by the relative forces of the armies, and a higher estimate of the Northern soldiers than our Southern editors and politicians, or even the Administration, seemed to entertain. This opinion had been formed in much service with them against Indians, and four or five battles in Mexico — such actions, at least, as were then called battles. Observation of almost twenty years of service of this sort had impressed on my mind the belief that the soldiers of the Regular Army of the United States were equal in fighting qualities to any that had been found in the wars of Great Britain and France. General Sherman's troops, with whom we were contending, had received a longer training in war than any of those with whom I had served in former times. It was not to be supposed that such troops, under a sagacious and resolute leader, and covered by entrenchments, were to be beaten by greatly inferior numbers. I therefore thought it our policy to stand on the defensive, to spare the blood of our soldiers by fighting under cover habitually, and to attack only when bad position or division of the enemy's forces might give us advantages counterbalancing that of superior numbers. So we held every position occupied until our communications were strongly threatened; then fell back only far enough to secure them, watching for opportunities to attack, keeping near enough to the Federal army to assure the Confederate Administration that Sherman could not send reinforcements to Grant, and hoping to reduce the odds against us by partial engagements." And later, of the situation in July before Atlanta: "The troops themselves, who had been seventy-four days in the immediate presence of the enemy, labouring and fighting daily, enduring toil and encountering danger with equal cheerfulness, more confident and high-spirited even than when the Federal army presented itself before them at Dalton, and though I say it, full of devotion to him who had commanded them, and belief of ultimate success in the campaign, were then inferior to none who ever served the Confederacy or fought on this continent."

And again, toward the elucidation of this campaign, General Sherman speaks: "I had no purpose to attack Johnston's position at Dalton in front, but marched from Chattanooga to feign at his front and to make a lodgment in Resaca, eighteen miles to his rear, on his line of communication and supply. This movement was partly but not wholly successful; but it compelled Johnston to let go at Dalton and fight us at Resaca, where, May thirteenth to sixteenth, our loss was 2747 and his 2800. I fought offensively and he defensively, aided by earth parapets. He fell back to Calhoun, Adairsville, and Cassville. . . . I resolved to push on toward Atlanta by way of Dallas. Johnston quickly detected this, and forced me to fight him, May twenty-fifth to twenty-eighth, at New Hope Church, four miles north of Dallas. . . . The country was almost in a state of nature — with few or no roads, nothing that an European could understand. . . . He fell back to his position at Marietta, with Brush Mountain on his right, Kenesaw his centre, and Lost Mountain his left. His line of ten miles was too long for his numbers, and he soon let go his flanks and concentrated on Kenesaw. We closed down in battle array, repaired the railroad up to our very camps, and then prepared for the contest. Not a day, not an hour, not a minute, was there a cessation of fire. Our skirmishers were in absolute contact, the lines of battle and the batteries but little in rear of the skirmishers, and thus matters continued until June twenty-seventh, when I ordered a general assault . . . but we failed, losing 3000 men to the Confederate loss of 630. Still the result was that within three days Johnston abandoned the strongest possible position and was in full retreat for the Chattahoochee River. We were on his heels; skirmished with his rear at Smyrna Church on the fourth day of July, and saw him fairly across the Chattahoochee on the tenth, covered and protected by the best line of field entrenchments I have ever seen, prepared long in advance. No officer or soldier who ever served under me will question the generalship of Joseph E. Johnston. . . . We had advanced into the enemy's country one hundred and twenty miles, with a single-track railroad, which had to bring clothing, food, ammunition, everything requisite for 100,000 men and 23,000 animals. The city of Atlanta, the gate city opening the interior of the important State of Georgia, was in sight; its protecting army was shaken but not defeated, and onward we had to go. . . . We feigned to the right, but crossed the Chattahoochee by the left, and soon confronted our enemy behind his first line of entrenchments at Peach Tree Creek, prepared in advance for this very occasion. At this critical moment the Confederate Government rendered us most valuable service. Being dissatisfied with the Fabian policy of General Johnston, it relieved him and General Hood was substituted to command the Confederate army. Hood was known to us to be a 'fighter.' . . . The character of a leader is a large factor in the game of war, and I confess I was pleased at this change."

But in the early Georgian spring, pale emeralds and the purple mist of the Judas tree, July and that change were far away. The Army of Tennessee, encamped in and around Dalton, only knew that "Old Joe" was day by day putting iron in its veins and shoes upon its feet; that the commissariat was steadily improving; that the men's cheeks were filling out; that the horses were growing less woe-begone; that camp was cheerful and clean, that officers were affable, chaplains fatherly, and surgeons benevolent ; that the bands had suddenly plucked up heart; that the drills, though long, were not too long; that if the *morale* of the Army of Tennessee had been shaken at Missionary Ridge, it had now returned, and that it felt like cheering and did cheer "Old Joe" whenever he appeared. Men who had been wounded and were now well; men who had been on furlough, men who had somehow been just "missing," came in steadily. Small detachments of troops appeared, also, arriving from Canton, Mississippi, and from northern Alabama. The Army of Tennessee grew to feel whole again — whole, bronzed, lean, determined, and hopeful.

From northern Alabama came in March the ——th Virginia. For the ——th Virginia there had been the siege of Vicksburg and the surrender; then the long slow weeks at Enterprise, where the Vicksburg men were reorganized; then service with Loring in northern Mississippi; then duty in Alabama. Now in the soft spring weather it came to Dalton and the Army of Tennessee.

The village was filled with soldiers. The surrounding valley was filled with soldiers. From the valley, rude hills, only partially cleared, ran back to unbroken woods. There was Crow Valley and Sugar Valley, Rocky Face Mountain, Buzzard Roost and Mill Creek Gap, and many another pioneer-named locality. And in all directions there were camps of soldiers. Sometimes these boasted tents, but oftenest they showed clusters or streets of rude, ingenious huts, brown structures of bark and bough, above, between, and behind them foliage and bloom of the immemorial forest. Officers had log cabins, very neatly kept, with curls of blue smoke coming out of the mud chimneys. Headquarters was in the village, a white house with double porch, before it headquarters flag, and always a trim coming and going. At intervals the weary and worn engines, fed by wood, rarely repaired, brought over an unmended road a train of dilapidated cars and in them forage, munitions, handfuls of troops. But in the increasing confidence at Dalton, in the general invigoration and building-up, the tonic air, the running of the sap, the smiling of the world, even the East Tennessee, Virginia, and Georgia, and the Western and Atlantic, roadbed and rolling-stock and force of men, took on, as it were, an air of lively instead of grim determination. Outside of the town was the parade ground. Drill and music, music and drill, and once or twice a great review! Here came Johnston himself, erect, military, grey-mustached, with a quiet exterior and an affectionate heart, able and proud. With him rode his staff. Staff more than worshipped Johnston; it loved him. Here, too, came the lieutenant- and major-generals — Hardee, one of the best — and Hood the "fighter," well-liked by the President — Patrick Cleburne and Cheatham and Stewart and Carter Stevenson and Walker, and many another good leader and true. Here the artillery, reorganized, was put through manœuvres, and Joe Wheeler's cavalry trotted across, and in the morning light the bugles blew. It was a lovely Southern spring, with soft airs, with dogwood stars and flame-coloured azalea, with the fragrance of the grape and the yellow jessamine, with the song of many a bright bird, building in the wood. The Army of Tennessee, strong at Chickamauga, fallen ill at Missionary Ridge, convalescent through the winter, was now in health again.

There was a small house, half hidden behind two huge syringa bushes. It had a bit of lawn no bigger than a handkerchief, and the bridal wreath and columbines and white phlox that bordered it made the handkerchief a lace one. Here lived Miss Sophia and Miss Amanda, gentlewomen who had seen better days, and here "boarded," while the army was at Dalton, Désirée Cary.

Miss Sophia designed and carried out wonderful bouquets of wax flowers. Miss Amanda was famed for her bead bags and for the marvellous fineness of her embroidery. Miss Sophia was a master-hand at watermelon rind "sweetmeats," carving them into a hundred pretty shapes. Miss Amanda was as accomplished in "icing" cakes. Sweetmeats and wedding and Christmas cakes, embroidery, and an occasional order of wax flowers had for years "helped them along." Long visits, too, after the lavish, boundless Southern fashion, to kinsfolk in South Georgia had done much; — but now there was war, and the kinsfolk were poor themselves, and nowhere in the wide world was there a market for wax flowers, and there was no sugar for the sweetmeats, and no frosted cakes, and life was of the whole stuff without embroidery! War frightfully snatched their occupation away. As long as they could visit, they visited, and they valiantly carded lint and knit socks and packed and sent away supplies and helped to devise substitutes for coffee and tea and recipes for Confederate dishes. But kinsmen had died on the field of battle, and kinswomen had grown poorer and poorer. One had made her way to Virginia where her boy was in hospital, and another had gone to Savannah, and another's house had been burned. Miss Sophia and Miss Amanda had retired up-country to this extremely small house which they owned. Beside it and its furniture they apparently owned nothing else. Even the stout, sleepy negro woman in the kitchen was a loan from the last visited plantation. Désirée, applying for board, was manna in the wilderness. They took her — with faintly flushed cheeks and many apologies for charging at all — for fifty dollars a week, Confederate money. She had a bare white room with a sloping roof and a climbing rose. There was a porch to the house, all bowered in with clematis and honeysuckle. Miss Sophia and Miss Amanda rarely sat on the porch; they sat in the parlour, where there were the wax flowers and a wonderful sampler and an old piano, and, on either side the fireplace, a pink conch shell. So Désirée had the porch and the springtime out of doors.

Captain Edward Cary's beautiful wife made friends quickly.

Officers and men, the ——th Virginia had now for months rested her
bound slave. It was not long before that portion of the Army of
Tennessee that had occasion from day to day to pass the house
began to look with eagerness for the smiling eyes and lips of
Désirée Gaillard. Sometimes she was out in the sunshine, gravely
pondering the lace border of the handkerchief. Army of Tennessee
lifted hat or cap; she smiled and nodded; Army of Tennessee went
on through brighter sunshine. She was presently the friend of all.
After a while Johnston himself, when he rode that way, would stop
and talk; Hardee and Cleburne and others often sat beneath the
purple clematis and, sword on knees, talked of this or that. They
sent her little offerings — small packets of coffee or of sugar, once
a gift of wine, gifts which she promptly turned over to the hospital.
If they had nothing else, they brought her, when they rode in from
inspection of the scattered camps, wild flowers and branches of
blossoming trees.

Edward came to her when it was possible. The ——th Virginia
was encamped among the hills. Often at dusk he found her at the
gate, her eyes upon the last soft bloom of the day. Or, if she knew
that he was coming, she walked out upon the road toward the hills.
The road was a place of constant travel. Endlessly it unrolled a
pageant of the times. War's varied movement was here, the multi-
plicity of it all; and also the unity as of the sound of the sea, or
the waving of grass on a prairie. Troops, incoming or outgoing,—
infantry, artillery, cavalry,—were to be found upon it. The commissariat went up and down with white-covered wagons. Foragers
appeared, coming in to camp with heterogeneous matters. Ordnance
wagons, heavy and huge, went by with a leaden sound. Mules and
negroes abounded — laughter, adjuration, scraps of song. Then
came engineers, layers-out of defences and the clay-plastered workers upon them. Country people passed — an old carryall filled
with children — a woman in a long riding-skirt and calico sunbonnet riding a white horse, gaunt as death's own — sickly looking
men afoot — small boys, greybeards, old, old negroes hobbling with
a stick — then, rumbling in or out, a battery, the four guns very
bright, the horses knowing what they drew, breathing, for all their
steadiness, a faint cloud of brimstone and sulphur, the spare artillerymen alongside or seated on caissons — then perhaps cavalry,

man and horse cut in one like a chesspiece — then a general officer with his staff — couriers, infantry, more foragers, a chaplain bound for some service under the trees, guard details, ambulances, more artillery, more cavalry, commissariat, "Grand Rounds," more infantry. . . . Désirée loved the road and walked upon it when she liked. She grew a known figure, standing aside beneath a flowering tree to let the guns go by, or the heavy wagons; moving, slender and fine, upon the trampled verge of the road, ready with a friendly nod, a smile, a word — a beautiful woman walking as safely upon a military road as in a hedged garden. The road loved to see her; she was like a glowing rose in a land of metal and ore. And when a mile from town, perhaps, she met her husband, when, turning, she came with him back through the sunset light, when they moved together, of a height, happy, it was as though beings of another race trod the road. There needed no herald to say, "These are gods!"

But much of the time Désirée was alone. She asked for work at the hospital and was given it, and here she spent several hours of each day. There were no wounded now at Dalton, only the ill, and these in the wisely cared-for, steadily built-up army, lessened always in number. Suffering there was, however, now as always; moanings and tossings, delirium, ennui, pain to be assuaged, crises to be met, eyes to be closed, convalescence to be tended. In Dalton as elsewhere the Confederate women nursed with tenderness the Confederate ill. Désirée did her part, coming like something cordial, something golden, into the whitewashed ward. When her hours were over, back she came to the house behind the syringas, bathed and dressed, and ate with Miss Sophia and Miss Amanda a Confederate dinner. Then for an hour they sewed and knitted and scraped lint; then, when the afternoon had lengthened, she took the palmetto hat she had braided and went out of the lace handkerchief yard to the road and walked upon it.

Miss Sophia and Miss Amanda had attacks of remonstrance. "Dear Mrs. Cary, I don't think you should! A young woman and — pardon us if we seem too personal — and beautiful! It's not, of course, that you would suffer the least insult — but it is not customary for a lady to walk for pleasure on a public road where all kinds of serious things are going on —"

Désirée laughed. "Not if they are interesting things? Dear Miss Sophia, I stopped at the post-office and brought you a letter."

Miss Sophia put out her hand for the letter, but she held to her text a moment longer. "I do not think that Captain Cary should allow it," she said.

The letter was from Richmond, from the cousin who had gone to nurse her son. Miss Sophia read it aloud.

MY DEAR SOPHIA: —

I am here and George is better — thank God for all His mercies! The wound in the leg was a bad one and gangrene set in, necessitating amputation, and then came this pneumonia. He will live, though, and I shall bring my son home and keep him while I live! The city is so crowded, it is frightful. We in Georgia do not yet know the horrors of this war. I could hardly find a place to lay my head, but now a billiard-room in a hotel has been divided off into little rooms, each no bigger than a stall in my stable, and I have one of these. I go for my meals to a house two streets away, and I pay for shelter and food twenty-five dollars a day. Flour here is two hundred and fifty dollars a barrel. Butter is twelve dollars a pound. We live on cornbread, with now and then a little bacon or rice. Yesterday I bought two oranges for George. They were eight dollars apiece. Oh, Sophia, it's like having George a little boy again! Two days ago there was a dreadful excitement. I heard the cannon and the alarm bell. George was a little light-headed and he would have it that there was a great battle, and that the boys were calling, and he must get up! At last I got him quiet, and when he was asleep and I went to supper I was told that it was a Yankee raid, led by an officer named Dahlgren, who was killed. The reserves had been called out and there was great excitement. We have since heard fearful reports of the object of the raid. The President and his Cabinet were to be killed, the prisoners freed and set to sacking the city which was then to have been burned. Oh, my dear Sophia, what a world we live in! I was in Richmond on my wedding journey. I feel dazed when I think of now and then. Then it was all bright-hued and gay; now it is all dark-hued, with the strangest restlessness! I never saw so many women in black. You always hear military sounds, and the people, for one reason or another, are out of doors in great numbers.

The church bells have been taken down to be melted into cannon. The poverty, the suffering, the crowding are frightful. But I do not believe there is another such people for bearing things! George is a great favourite in the ward. They say he has been so patient and funny. My dear Sophia, I always think of you with your plum-colour silk bag and your spools of embroidery thread! I wish I had those spools of thread. Yesterday I had to do some mending, and I went out and bought one spool for five dollars. — George is waking up! I will write again. If he only gets well, Sophia, — he and the country!

Your affectionate cousin,

Miss Sophia folded the letter. "Dear George! I am glad enough that he will get better. He was a sad tease! He used to say the strangest things. I remember one day he said that behind Amanda embroidering he always saw a million shut-in women sticking cambric needles into the eyes of the future. And he said that I had done the whole world in wax, and he wondered how it would be if we ever got before a good hot fire. — He was n't lacking in sense either, only it never had a chance to come out, Maria spoiling him so, and darkeys and dogs always at his heels. — No, dear Mrs. Cary, you 're a young woman, and — you 'll pardon me, I know! — a beautiful one, and I don't think Captain Cary ought to allow it!"

March went, April went, May came. On the first of May, Désirée, walking on the road, thought she observed something unusual in the air. Presently there passed cavalry, a great deal of cavalry. She leaned against a wayside tree and watched. Presently there rode an officer whom she knew.

He lifted his hat, then pushed his horse upon the dusty turf beneath the tree. "We 're ordered out toward the Oostenaula! Sherman 's in motion. The volcano is about to become active."

"Is it going to overflow Dalton?"

"Well, it would seem so! Though sometimes there 's a new crater. We 'll see what we 'll see. Anyhow, Cary 'll be sending you to the rear."

"I 'll fall back when the army falls back."

Edward came that night and plead with her. She could go to

Kingston on the cars and thence to Rome to the westward, out of the region of danger —

"Edward," she said, "have n't I been a good campaigner?"

"The best —"

"Then, when you can do a thing well, why do something else poorly? This is the way I am going to live, and when you wed me you wed my way of life."

"If harm came to you, Désirée —"

"And I might say, 'If harm came to you, Edward,' — I know that harm may come to you, but — I don't say it, and you must not say it either. With you is my home, my Cape Jessamine, and I am not going to leave it."

"With you is *my* home, my Cape Jessamine — and all the gods know I love you here —"

"I am not going to Rome. Let us walk a little, in the moonlight."

The next day came in from Savannah Mercer's brigade of fourteen hundred. On the third the scouts reported a great force of the enemy at Ringgold. On this day, too, the cavalry pickets were driven in along the Cleveland road. On the fifth the great blue host formed in line of battle near Tunnel Hill. Over against them were drawn the grey. The fifth and the sixth were days of skirmishing, of reconnoissance, of putting forth fingers and drawing them back. In the first light of the seventh, under a wonderful sunrise sky, the blue army began a general advance.

CHAPTER XXIII

THE ROAD TO RESACA

For seven days Rocky Face Mountain echoed the rattling fire. Milk Mountain behind also threw it back, and Horn Mountain behind Milk. Crow Valley saw hard fighting, and Mill Creek Gap and Trail Gap. Alabama troops were posted above the last two and on the top of the Chattoogata Ridge. Here they laid in line huge stones, ready for the throwing down when the pass below should darken with the blue. They made also slight breastworks and rifle-pits. At Dug Gap were stationed two regiments of Arkansas and a brigade of Kentucky cavalry. On the eighth, Hooker attacked these in force. Kentucky fought dismounted; Kentucky and Arkansas together did mightily. Johnston sent to Hardee to dispatch aid to this point. Up to Dug Gap came Patrick Cleburne with Lowrey's and Granbury's brigades. Cleburne came at a double-quick, through the intense heat, up the rough mountain-side. The woods rang with fighting until the dark came down. Then Geary rested in the valley below and Cleburne on the heights above, and the stars shone on both. Stewart's and Stevenson's divisions held Rocky Face Mountain. Old Rocky Face saw tense fighting, stubborn as its own make-up. Skirmish upon skirmish occupied the hours. Here, too, were breastworks and rifle-pits, and the blue advanced against them, and the blue went back again, and came again, and went back again. All the time the batteries kept up a galling, raking fire. Pettus's Alabama brigade was at the top of the mountain, at the signal station. Brown and Reynolds and Cumming were lower down, toward the valley. And on the floor of the valley, here visible in square or roughly circular clearings, here hidden by the thick woods, was a host of the enemy. Morning, noon, and afternoon went on the skirmishing. On the ninth occurred a determined assault upon Pettus's line. There was a bloody, protracted struggle, and while the mountain flamed and thundered, the blue sharpshooters paid deadly attention to the brigades below of Cumming and Reynolds. The

Alabamians on Rocky Face repelled the assault; down, down it sank to the floor of the valley. After an interval a line of battle appeared before Cumming. The Georgian threw forward skirmishers. There was a battalion of artillery — Major John William Johnston's battalion. Cherokee Artillery, Stephens's Light Artillery, Tennessee Battery, all came into action. The major commanding — once the captain of the Botetourt Artillery, of the "homesick battery" of Chickasaw Bayou and Port Gibson — placed his guns with skill and saw them served well and double well. Together with Cumming's skirmishers the battalion checked the blue advance along this line.

Hour after hour, day after day, continued the skirmishing to the west of Dalton. Now and again, among the slighter notes, struck the full chord of a more or less heavy engagement. But there came no general and far-flung battle. There was loss of life, but not great loss, and all the attacks were repelled. Joseph E. Johnston watched with his steady face.

On the afternoon of the ninth came the first indication that the blue, behind the long cover of the mountains, were moving southward toward Snake Creek Gap, halfway between Dalton and Resaca. Hood with three divisions was at once ordered upon the road to Resaca, where was already Cantey's brigade, come in the day before. Observing the grey movement, the blue advance by Snake Creek drew back for the moment. The air around Dalton continued smoky, the rifles to ring. The blue made a night attack, thoroughly repulsed by Bates's division. On the eleventh arrived at Resaca from Mississippi Leonidas Polk with Loring's division. On this day Cantey sent a courier to General Johnston. Sherman's was certainly a turning movement, a steady blue flood rolling south by Snake Creek Pass, between Milk and Horn Mountains.

Before break of day on the twelfth, Johnston sent Wheeler with two thousand cavalry, supported by Hindman, to the northern end of Rocky Face to reconnoitre in force. Was the whole Federal army moving toward Resaca, or not? Rounding Rocky Face, Wheeler clashed with Stoneman's cavalry. After a sharp engagement, the blue fell back down the western side of Rocky Face. Retiring, they set fire to a great number of their wagons. The smoke arose, thick and dark, but the grey reconnoissance, piercing it, saw enough to assure it that Sherman intended no pitched battle at Dalton. The whole vast blue army was moving southward behind the screen of Rocky Face and the Chattoogata Ridge, south and east upon Resaca and the grey line of communications. Wheeler returned at dusk and reported.

Night fell. The Army of Tennessee, after days of fighting, nights of alarms, lay now, in its various positions, in a world that seemed suddenly, strangely silent. The army, that was by now a philosopher, welcomed the moment with its quiet. It threw itself upon the warm earth and slept with the determination of the dead. Ten o'clock, eleven o'clock, twelve o'clock, one o'clock! A bugle blew — another at a distance — another. Drums began to beat. The Army of Tennessee rose to its feet. *Marching orders! The road to Resaca? All right!*

Grey infantry, grey artillery, grey wagon-train, grey cavalry rear guard, grey stanch generals, grey stanch men, the Army of Tennessee took the starlight road to Resaca, where were already Hood with the three divisions, Cantey's brigade, and Polk with the division of Loring. The night rolled away, the morning wind blew fresh, the streamers of the dawn flared high above the Georgia woods. The Army of Tennessee moved with a light and swinging step. Of this campaign a week had marked itself off, like a bead, half dark, half bright, on a rosary string. At Dalton, Atlanta lay a hundred and twenty miles to the southward. When the army came to Resaca, Atlanta was eighteen miles the nearer.

Back in Dalton, in the house behind the syringas, there was protest. Miss Sophia protested with a waxen dignity, Miss Amanda with tears in her eyes. Both were so moved that they came out of the parlour upon the clematis porch where Désirée was supervising the cording of a small hair-trunk. "Follow the Army!" cried Miss Sophia, and "Follow the Army!" echoed Miss Amanda. "Oh, dear Mrs. Cary, are you sure that it's *wise* —"

"It's the wisdom of Solomon," said Désirée, on her knees. "Of the Song of Solomon. — Now, uncle, that's done! Can you carry it out to the wagon, or shall I help you?"

The ancient darkey lifted it. "No, 'm. I kin tote it." He went down the path toward the gate and an ancient, springless wagon.

Désirée rose. Miss Amanda's tears overflowed, and Miss Sophia was so agitated that she leaned against the doorpost, and her thin old hand trembled where it touched her linsey skirt. "You've been as good as gold to me," said Désirée. "I've loved this little house. I'm going to think of it often. Dear Miss Sophia, dear Miss Amanda, good-bye!"

"Oh, it's not wise," cried Miss Sophia; "I feel that it's not wise!"

"If you'd just quietly wait," said Miss Amanda, "until the army comes back through Dalton."

But Désirée thought that that would be too long. She smiled and broke some purple clematis from the porch to take with her, and then the two ladies went with her to the gate, and she kissed them both, and they said "God bless you!" and she mounted the wagon; and from the place where the road turned southward looked back and waved her hand. The lace handkerchief yard and the syringa bushes and the shingled roof above them sank out of her life.

"I'se gwine tek de duht road," said the negro. "Less ob fool soldiers projeckin' erlong dat one!"

The horse was worn and old, the wagon the same. Out of Dalton, over trampled fields, then between wooded hills, went, slowly enough, the wagon, the hair-trunk, Désirée, and the negro. "Don' yo' fret, mistis! I'se gwine git yo' dar befo' de battle. I'se gwine git yo' dar befo' midnight ennyhow!"

"What is your name?"

"Nebuchadnezzar, mistis."

"And the horse?"

"Dat ar horse name Julius Cæsar. He good horse ef he had ernough ter eat."

The day was warm, the sky a deep blue, all neighbouring vegetation covered with a tawny felt of dust. Trampling feet and trampling feet of horses and men, wagon wheels and wagon wheels and wagon wheels, had gone over that road. It was a trough of dust, and when the wind blew it up, a sandstorm would not have been more blinding. It seemed clear now of troops — all were withdrawn into the haze to the southward. As for the enemy, he must be moving on the other side of the low mountains, unless, indeed, he were already in force at Resaca — and the grey were going into battle — and the grey were going into battle.

"Julius Cæsar goes pretty slow," said Désirée.

There was little débris in the road or by the wayside, no wrecked, left-behind wagons, little or no discarded accoutrement, few broken-down or dying horses, very few ill or wounded men, or mere footsore stragglers. Johnston's movements were as clear-cut as so many cameos. He left no filings behind; he did not believe in blurred edges. He might place an army here to-day, and the morrow might find it a knight's move or a bishop's or a rook's or a queen's away; but always it went cleanly, bag and baggage, clean-lined, self-contained, with intention and poise. If his army was in retreat, the road behind him hardly bore witness to the fact.

Horse and wagon crept on toward Resaca. Morning wore to afternoon, very warm, very — "Nebuchadnezzar, what do you make of that dust before us? I make smoke as well as dust. And now I make firing! Listen!"

"Reckon better tuhn back —"

"No, no! Go on! When it is necessary to stop, we will stop until they let us by. It's rear guard fighting probably —"

The cloud mounted. A few hundred yards and a bullet came and sheared away a leafy twig from the oak under which they were passing. It fell upon Désirée's lap. A few yards farther, a second struck the dusty road in front of the horse. The confused sound down the road swelled into tumult.

"Gawd-er-moughty!" said Nebuchadnezzar. "Mus' git out ob dis! Dey're projeckin' dishyer way!"

"Drive into the bank!" ordered Désirée. "No! there where it is wider! Don't be afraid! Look how steady Julius Cæsar stands!"

"Yass, 'm. Think I'll git out en hol' him. — Lawd hab mercy, heah dey come!"

They came like a storm of the desert, two colours, one driving, one giving back, but in so great a cloud of road dust and carbine smoke, and in so rapid motion that which was which and whose were the shouts of triumph was not easy to tell. The horses' hoofs made a thunder; all grew large, enveloped the earth, brought din and suffocation, roared by and were gone. There was a sense that the victorious colour was grey — but all was gone like a blast of the genii. The wagon had been nearly overturned. Some one had ridden violently against it — then there had sounded a shout, "'Ware! A woman!" and the wild course, pursued and pursuers, ever so slightly swerved. Désirée, thrown to her knees, laid hold of the wagon edge and waited, but not with closed eyes. A colour was in her cheek; she looked in this torrent as she had looked upon the levee, above the Mississippi in anger. The torrent passed, the rage of noise sank, the choking, blinding dust began to settle. Nebuchadnezzar came from the lee side of Julius Cæsar. He was ashen, whether with dust or with fear.

"Whoever in dey born days see de like ob dat? Christian folk actin' de debbil lak dat! Hit er-gwine ter bring er jedgment! Yo' ain' huht, mistis?"

"No," said Désirée. "I felt as though something were bearing down upon me out of 'Paradise Lost.'"

"What dat blood on yo' ahm?"

Désirée looked. "A bullet must have grazed it. I never felt it. It does n't hurt much now."

They did not get to Resaca that night. Julius Cæsar was too tired, the road too heavy, and one of Wheeler's outposts, stopping the wagon, insisted that it was not safe for it to go farther in the darkness. With the first fireflies they turned aside to a "cracker's" cabin in a fold of the hills and asked for hospitality. A tall, lean, elderly woman and her tall, lean daughters gave them rude shelter and rude fare. In the morning the wagon and Julius Cæsar and Nebuchadnezzar and Désirée went on again toward Resaca.

To-day they overtook more limping soldiers than had been the case on yesterday. The wagon gave "lifts" to several and would have given more but that Julius Cæsar was so evidently a weary and worn foot soldier himself. They came upon a bank topped by a pine tree, and under it, his arm overhanging the road, was stretched a soldier overtaken by a fever. His face was flushed and burning hot, his eyes bright and wild. "Point Coupée Artillery!" he said; "Point Coupée Artillery!" over and over again. Désirée made Nebuchadnezzar draw rein. She got out of the wagon, climbed the bank, and knelt beside the man. "Point Coupée Artillery!" he said. "Water! Point Coupée Artillery. Water!" There was no spring anywhere near. She had had a bottle of water, but had given it all to two soldiers a mile back. Together she and Nebuchadnezzar got the artilleryman into the wagon, where he lay with his head against her knee. "Point Coupée!" she said. "Louisiana!" and her hand lay cool and soft upon the burning forehead. They carried him two miles, until they came to the house of a widow, who took the fevered man in and gave him water and a bed, and could be trusted, Désirée saw, to nurse him. Going on for a mile, they came up with a boy with a badly cut foot and a man with a bandaged head and his trouser leg rolled up to the thigh, bandaged, too, with a bloody cloth. Both were white-lipped with the heat and weariness, and Désirée and Nebuchadnezzar and Julius Cæsar took them on upon the road. Désirée said that she was tired of riding and walked beside the wagon, and when they came to a hill, Nebuchadnezzar, too, got down and walked. The two honest stragglers, though worse for the wear, were cheerful souls and inclined to talk. "Near Resaca? Yes, ma'am; right near now. It's mighty good of you to give us a lift! Old Joe certainly can't begin the battle till Robin and me get there!"

Robin put in his oar. "Man on horseback came riding along awhile ago and turned off toward the Connesauga, an' he said that Loring met the Yanks yesterday as they were streaming out of Snake Creek Gap, and held them in check for three hours until Hardee and Hood came up and formed, and that then things stopped and were holding their breath on that line when he left —"

"Old Blizzard's a good one! Never'll forget him at Fort Pemberton! 'Give them blizzards, men!' says he. 'Give them blizzards!'"

"My husband was at Fort Pemberton. Were you at Vicksburg?"

"Vicksburg! Should think I was at Vicksburg! Were you, ma'am?"

"Yes. In a cave down by the ——th Redan."

"I was down by the river, back of the Lower Batteries. Vicksburg! We thought that nothing could ever happen any more after Vicksburg! But things just went on happening —"

"Firing ahead of us," said the boy.

It rose and fell in the distance to the left of the road. A turn and they came upon pickets. Followed a parley. "You two want to join your regiment, and the lady wants to get to Resaca? Resaca isn't a big place, ma'am, and the fighting's going to be all around it and maybe through it. Hadn't you better —"

"No, I had n't. My husband is Captain Cary of the ——th Virginia. I know, sir, that you are going most courteously to let me pass."

When Désirée Gaillard said "most courteously," when she smiled and looked straight and steady with her dark eyes, it was fatal. Nothing short of positive orders to the contrary would have kept those grey pickets from letting her pass. The wagon went on, and, having pierced a skirmish line lying down waiting, came, in the dusty forenoon, to Stevenson's division, drawn up in two lines across and on either side of the Dalton and Resaca road.

An officer stopped the advance. "There's going to be fighting here in five minutes! You should n't have been let to pass the pickets. You can't go on and you can't go back. They've got their batteries planted and they're coming out of the wood yonder. — There's the first shell!" He looked around him. "Madam, I'll agree that there are n't many safe places in the Confederacy, but I wish that you were in one of them! You two men report to the sergeant there! Uncle, you drive that cart behind the hill yonder — the one next to the one with the guns on it. When you're there, madam, you'd better lie close to the earth, behind one of those boulders. As soon as we've silenced their fire and the road's clear, you can go on. — Not at all! Not at all! But it is extremely unwise for a lady to be here!"

The eastern side of the hill offered fair shelter. Nebuchadnezzar took the old horse from the wagon and fastened him to a small pine. Désirée sat down in the long cool grass beside a grey boulder. Before her stretched rugged ground, and far and wide she saw grey troops, ready for battle. Johnston had wasted no moment at Resaca. With skill and certitude he flung down his battle line, horseshoe-shaped, Hardee holding the centre, Polk on the left bent down to the Oostenaula, Hood on the right resting on the Connesauga. Earthworks sprang into being, salients for artillery — hardy and ready and in high spirits the Army of Tennessee faced the foe. Throughout the morning there had been general skirmishing, and now a fierce attack was in progress against Hindman's division of Hood's corps. It spread and involved Stevenson. The latter had the brigades of Cumming and Brown in his front line, in his second those of Pettus and Reynolds. All the ground here was rough and tangled, rock-strewn, overlaid with briars and a growth of small bushy pines. The men had made some kind of breastworks with rotted logs and the rails from a demolished fence. What especially annoyed were the blue sharpshooters. There was a ridge in the possession of these, from which they kept up a perpetual enfilading fire, addressed with especial vigour against Cumming's line and against Johnston's battalion ranged upon a long hillside by Cumming.

From the foot of her small adjoining hill, Désirée could see these pieces plainly. Elbow on knee, chin in hand, she sat and watched. Six guns were in action; the others, expectant, waiting their time. The horses were withdrawn below the hill. Here, indifferent, long trained, they stood and cropped the grass in the face of thunder and gathering smoke. The caissons were in line behind the pieces, and from them powder and grape and canister travelled to the fighting guns. They were fighting hard. From each metal bore sprang yellow-red flowers of death. The hill shook and became wreathed with smoke. Through it she saw the gun detachments, rhythmically moving, and other figures, officers and men, passing rapidly to and fro. Shouted orders came to her, then the thunder of the guns covered all other sound. The antagonist was a blue battery on a shoulder of the ridge and blue infantry somewhere in the thick wood below. This battery's range was poor; most of the shells fell short of the grey hill. But the sharpshooters on the nearer spur were another guess matter. Out of the tops of thick and tall pine trees came death in the shape of pellets of lead — came with frequency, came with a horrible accuracy.

Désirée shuddered as she looked.

"Oh," she cried. "Oh, to be God just one minute!"

She found Nebuchadnezzar beside her. "Gawd ain' mixed up wif dis. Hit's de Debbil. — Dar's ernother one struck! See him spinnin' 'roun'. . . . Hit meks me sick."

The battalion commander — twenty-five years old, brown-eyed, warm-hearted, sincere, magnetic, loved by his men — rode rapidly, in the rolling smoke, across the hilltop, from the guns engaged to those that waited. "Forward into battery! On Captain Van den Corput's left."

He turned and rode back to the thundering battery. The smoke parted and he and his grey horse were plainly seen. A minie ball came from the wood and pierced his thigh. "This morning," says General Stevenson's report, "was wounded the brave Major J. W. Johnston." The smoke of battle rolled over the hill and the battalion of artillery, and over the Dalton and Resaca road, and over Stevenson's division.

Later, there was a great movement forward. Wheeler, ordered to discover the position and formation of the blue left, brought Johnston information which resulted in an order to Hood to make a half-change of front and drive the enemy westward. Hood, with the divisions of Stewart and Stevenson and supported by Walker, swept with his wild energy to the task. Stevenson in advance had the hottest fighting, but all fought superbly. At sunset the enemy's extreme left was forced from its position.

From the top of a railroad cut near the Dalton road, Johnston gave an aide an order for Hood. "Prepare to continue movement at daybreak. Let the troops understand that fighting will be renewed." Off galloped the aide and sought through the gathering dusk for General Hood, but missed his road, and after some searching came back to the railroad cut to find General Hood now with General Johnston. Hood was speaking: "The men are in wild spirits! I am, too, sir, if we are going to fight to a finish!"

Two or three prisoners were brought to the cut. Questioned, two refused to answer; a third stated that he belonged to Whittaker's brigade, Stanley's division, Fourth Army Corps; that the blue line of battle ran northeast and southwest, and that the blue army looked for victory. Wheeler rode up, received orders, and in the fading light drew his cavalry out along the railroad. Night was now at hand. Johnston and those with him turned their horses and rode rapidly from the right toward the left, back to headquarters, established in a small house behind Selden's battery. Here they found General Hardee. "All well with us, sir! They tried to storm Cleburne's position, but signally failed!"

"Nothing from the left?"

"There has been firing. Here comes news now, I think."

Up came an aide, breathless, his horse bleeding. "General Johnston — from General Polk, sir!"

"Yes, yes —"

" They attacked in force, sir, driving in our troops and seizing a hill which commands the Oostenaula bridges. They at once brought cannon up. General Polk is about to move to retake the hill."

" The Oostenaula bridge! . . . The guns now!"

The heavy firing rose and sank, rose again, then finally died in the now full night. The ridge commanding the bridge to the south, held by Dodge and Logan of McPherson's corps, was not retaken. Tidings that it was not came to the group by Selden's battery. And on the heels of this came another breathless messenger. " General — from General Martin! He reports that the enemy have thrown pontoons across the Oostenaula near Calhoun. They crossed two divisions this afternoon."

Silence for a moment, then Johnston spoke crisply. "Very well! If he crosses, I cross. General Hood, the order for the advance at daybreak is revoked." He spoke to an aide. "Get the staff together! — General Walker, you will at once take the road to Calhoun with your division. Is Colonel Prestman here? — Colonel, the engineers are to lay to-night a pontoon bridge across the Oostenaula, a mile above the old bridges. General Hardee — What is it, General Hood ?"

"Not to attack in the morning! General Johnston, do you not think —"

"I do occasionally, sir. At present I think that General Sherman ardently desires to place himself in our rear."

"We rolled them back this afternoon! And if at dawn we accomplish even more —"

"Yes, sir, 'if.' You 'rolled back,' very gallantly, part of the Fourth Army Corps."

"But, sir, —"

"Circumstances, sir, alter cases. It was General Sherman's intention to place a huge army astride the railroad here at Resaca. That intention was defeated. He proposes now to cross the Oostenaula and cut our lines at Calhoun. It is that movement that demands our attention."

"I only know, sir, that it is expected at Richmond that we take the offensive."

"Yes, sir. Many things are expected at Richmond. — You have your order, General. Now, General Hardee —"

An hour or two later, the commander of the Army of Tennessee returned with Hardee from the left toward which they had ridden. The two were friends as well as superior and subordinate. Johnston had great warmth of nature; he was good lover, good hater. Now he rode quietly, weary, but steadily thinking. The light of the house behind Selden's battery appeared, a yellow point in the thickened air. "How far that little candle . . . Hardee! I've had ten wounds in battle, but before this summer ends I'm going to have a worse wound than any!"

"I don't know what you mean, General," said Hardee.

"Don't you?" said Johnston. "Well, well! perhaps I shan't be wounded. The stars are over us all. — Here is the house."

As the two dismounted, an aide came forward. "There is some one waiting here, General, to speak to you. A lady— Mrs. Cary—"

Désirée came into the light from the open door. "Mrs. Cary!" exclaimed Hardee. "How in the world —"

Johnston took her hand in his. It was cold, and the light showed her face. "My dear, what is it —"

"General," said Désirée, "I left Dalton yesterday, and to-day I got by the lines, and this afternoon into Resaca. And awhile ago, when the fighting had stopped, I found where was ——'s brigade and the ——th Virginia. And I went there, to headquarters, to find out if my husband was unhurt. His regiment was in the attack on the enemy's left. It was in the advance and it lost heavily. When night came and the troops were withdrawn, they took back with them all their wounded they could gather. But the ——th was well ahead, and the enemy was reinforced and threatening in its front. When it was ordered back it had to leave its hurt. They are there yet — they are there now. My husband is among the missing. . . . They were very kind, the colonel and General ——. They would not let me pass, but they asked for volunteers to go. Some brave men volunteered and went. They brought back a number of the wounded — but they did not bring back my husband. They said they sought everywhere and called as loudly as they dared. They said that if he were living — But I can seek better than they and I am not afraid to call aloud. General —— said that he would not let me go, and I said that I would bring an order from you that should make him let me go. I have come for it, General."

"The enemy is very close to that front. They will fire at any sound."

"I shall go silently. Do I not want to bring him safely?"

"You would have to have men with you."

"Three of those men said they would go again. But I said no. An old negro brought me in his wagon from Dalton. He is old but strong, and he is willing, and we can manage together."

"If I let you go —"

"I shall love you forever. If you let me go you will do wisely and rightly —"

"It is not a time," said Johnston, "to measure by small standards or weigh with little weights. You may go."

A host of stars looked down on the wooded hills and narrow vales. There was a space of about an acre where, long ago, trees had been girdled and felled. The trunks of some still lay upon the earth, bare of bark, gleaming grey-white, like great bones of an elder age. Elsewhere there were mere stumps, serried rows of them, with a growth of mullein and blackberry between. There were stones, too, half-buried boulders, and in a corner of the field, pressing close to a rail fence, a thicket of sumach.

Edward Cary lay in this angle. He had fallen at dusk, leading his men in the final charge. It was twilight; the grey wave went on, shouting. He saw and heard another coming, and to avoid trampling he dragged himself aside into this sumach thicket by the fence. He had a bullet through his shoulder, and he was losing blood beside from a deep wound above the knee. It was this bleeding that brought the roaring in his ears and at last the swoon. He had bandaged it as well as he could, but a bone in his hand was shattered and he could not do it well. He thought, "I shall bleed to death." After a while life and the content of life went to a very great distance — very far off and small like a sandbar in a distant ocean. Time, too, became a thin, remote, and intermittent stream. Once, he had no idea when, he thought that there were voices and movement on the sandbar. He wet his lips and thought that he spoke aloud, but probably it was only in thought. All things vanished for a while, and when he next paid attention the sandbar was very quiet and farther off than ever. The wind was blowing in the sumach on the sandbar, and a star was shining over it. . . . No! it was the light of

a lantern. There were hands about his wound, and the sound of
tearing cloth, and the feel of a bandage drawn tightly with a bit of
forked stick for a tourniquet, and then water with a dash of brandy
at his lips — and then an arm beneath his head and a face down
bent. "Désirée Gaillard," he breathed.

CHAPTER XXIV

THE GUNS

MORNING broke with a heavy mist over Oostenaula and Connesauga, over Rocky Face and Snake Creek Gap, over the village of Resaca, over the Western and Atlantic Railroad, over the grey army and the blue army. A keen, continual skirmishing began with the light. It extended along the whole front, but with especial sharpness upon Hardee's line. Some blue cannon opened here, and for a time it seemed that at any moment the main bodies, blue and grey, might crash through the fog into a general and furious battle. Stevenson's division, moving forward, reoccupied the position gained the evening before. Wrapped in the mist, wet with the morning dew, the men fell to work upon log and rail and stump defences. Hindman's line was next to Stevenson's, and a blue battery, well placed, was sending against Hindman, engaged in thrusting back a blue assault, a stream of grape and canister. Stevenson, ordered to help out Hindman, sent Max Van den Corput's battery of Johnston's battalion to a point eighty yards in front of his own line — a ragged hill, rising abruptly from the field, with a wide and deep ravine beyond. In dust and thunder the battery came to this place; the guns were run into position, the guns were served, steady, swift, and well. "But," says Stevenson, "the battery had hardly gotten into position when the enemy hotly engaged my skirmishers, driving them in, and pushing on to the assault with great impetuosity. So quickly was all this done that it was impossible to remove the artillery before the enemy had effected a lodgment in the ravine in front of it, thus placing it in such a position that, while the enemy was entirely unable to remove it, we were equally so, without driving off the enemy massed in the ravine beyond it, which would have been attended with great loss of life. The assaults of the enemy were in heavy force and made with the utmost impetuosity, but were met with a cool, steady fire which each time mowed down their ranks and drove them back, leaving the ground thickly covered in places with their dead. . . ."

Along Hardee's line the white puffs of cannon smoke showed all day through. In the early afternoon came a courier with a note from Walker, now at Calhoun. "No movement of the enemy observed. Think report of passage of Oostenaula unfounded." Johnston read, then dispatched an order to Hood. "Prepare to attack enemy's left as indicated yesterday evening. Three brigades of Polk's and Hardee's will support." But later, as Hood was preparing to move forward, there came a more breathless messenger yet from Walker. "The first report was true, General! They crossed at Lay's Ferry. Two divisions are over, and others on the way." Johnston listened with an impassive face, then sent at once and countermanded Hood's order. Stewart's division only was not checked in time. It attacked, and was roughly handled before it could be recalled.

Lieutenant T. B. Mackall, aide-de-camp to General Mackall, chief of staff, kept a journal of the operations, during these days, of the Army of Tennessee. May fifteenth, 1864, he writes: —

" . . . 7 A.M. General Johnston has been on hill where Selden's battery is posted since firing began; is just going to ride to the right, leaving General Mackall here. Skirmishing and artillery still going on. 10 A.M. General Johnston returned to Selden's battery an hour ago. Answer sent to cipher of the President received yesterday: ' *Sherman cannot reinforce Grant without my knowledge, and will not as we are skirmishing along our entire line. We are in presence of whole force of enemy assembled from North Alabama and Tennessee.*' Ferguson's brigade of cavalry, also Brigadier-General Jackson have reached Rome. Wheeler has just gone to upper pontoon bridge, which will not be ready for crossing for fifteen minutes. It is in long range of the six-gun battery put up last night on the hill which they captured. 11 A.M. Very heavy musketry and artillery firing going on, apparently on Hindman's line. Just before it became so rapid General Johnston rode up the Dalton road, apparently on account of some news brought by Hampton from Hardee. About 11.15 battery on our extreme right opened. Firing slackened on Hindman's front. Battery on hill on our left enfilades our trenches; riflemen annoying to our gunners. 12 M. General Johnston has come back to Selden's battery. The firing on extreme right three quarters of an hour ago caused by enemy's crossing

Connesauga in rear of Hood, capturing Hood's hospital. A brigade of our cavalry after them, supported by a brigade of Stewart's. Captain Porter, who went with General Johnston, came back. Says last reports represent our troops driving enemy's cavalry. 1.30 P.M. Heavy musketry and artillery on Hindman's front; began about fifteen minutes ago. Lieutenant Wigfall has just come up to say enemy are making a very determined attack on Hindman. General Johnston preparing to mount to ride to Hood's. Firing continuous. 3.30 P.M. Few minutes after writing above rode off to General Hood's with General Mackall, who accompanied General Johnston. Found Hood where Dalton dirt road and railroad are near each other and where we now are. Hindman, a few minutes after we arrived, repulsed the enemy, who came up in some places to his breastworks. Our reserves not used. Orders given for Stewart to take enemy in flank; for wagons which were sent back to be brought up to Resaca. Stevenson and Hindman to take up movement of Stewart. Featherston brought from Polk's line, also Maney and —— from Cheatham. These supports came up in very short time. Stevenson, however, sent word that enemy in three lines were preparing to attack Stewart's centre. 3.40 P.M. (In rear of Stewart's line near railroad) Stewart directed to receive attack and pursue. But slight skirmishing now; enemy not making attack. 9.30 P.M. At house behind Selden's battery (headquarters at night). Orders given to withdraw from this place; arrangements made and trains moving. This afternoon, about 4.30 P.M., Stewart, in obedience to orders to attack if his position was not assaulted, advanced; soon his line was broken by a terrible fire of Hooker's corps, who were ready to attack. I had been sent to accompany Major Ratchford to General Featherston (held in reserve) to order him in the General's name to take position in support of Stewart, near Green's house.

"*Monday, May 16.* On Calhoun and Adairsville road, two miles south of Calhoun. While in field in rear of Stewart's line and near railroad last night, about dark, corps and division commanders assembled and instructions given to effect withdrawal of army to south bank of Oostenaula. Enemy had crossed force to south bank of river at Dobbin's Ferry; reported two divisions. Walker was facing them, immediately in our front. He was entrenched, his line extending from Oostenaula River to Tilton on Connesauga. . . . In two hours after Stewart's repulse, Cheatham, Hindman, Cleburne, etc., were assembled around the camp-fires. Hardee had been there all evening. Routes and times fixed; cars to be sent for the wounded; wagons and ambulances and most of artillery to cross pontoons above; troops and artillery on Polk's line on railroad and small trestle bridge; an hour occupied in giving orders, etc., and all dispersed, going to their headquarters. We rode in; wagons not brought over. After writing dispatches . . . lay down (sleeping on porch of house in rear of Selden's battery); waked by noise — firing, confusion, etc.; saddle and mount. General Loring comes up; all ride to roadside at foot of Selden's battery, passing through Hindman's column, going to railroad bridge. Cheatham's pass from his line over small trestle bridge below. Night cloudy. Firing of musketry and small arms on Hood's line, which was rapid and continuous on first waking, decreased. These troops (Cheatham's and Hood's) did not seem at all alarmed, rather noisy and in very good humour. Enemy's line on river remarkably quiet. . . . Near Calhoun, 5.30 P.M. Order given to send wagons back one mile and a half south of Adairsville. 6.30 P.M. Our wagons parking; saddling.

"*Tuesday, May 17.* We reached Adairsville just before day, a little ahead of troops. Cultivated, rolling country from Resaca to Adairsville."

Edward Cary lay, not in the hospital that was raided, but in a house in the village. It was a fairly large house, and upstairs and down it was filled with the wounded. The surgeons and the village women had their hands full. He lay quite conscious, much weakened, but going to recover. There were a number of pallets in this upper hall where he had been placed. Officers and men occupied them, some much hurt, others more slightly. A surgeon with a woman to help went from bed to bed. The more frightful cases were downstairs, and from that region there came again and again a wailing cry from flesh and blood and bone under probe and saw. Out of doors the sun shone hot, and in at the open, unshaded windows came a dull sound of firing. The flies were bad. Two girls with palm-leaf fans, moving from pallet to pallet, struggled with them as best they might, but in the blood and glare and heat they settled again. The wounded moved their heads from side to side, fought them away with their hands. Désirée came up the stairs and into the hall. She had hanging at her waist a pair of scissors, and in her arms a bolt of something dusty-white. Unrolled at the stairhead, and cut swiftly into lengths, it proved to be mosquito netting. "I found it in a little store here. They did n't know they had it."

The hot, bright morning went on. Outside the firing swelled and sank and swelled again. Sometimes it sounded far away, sometimes as though it were in the street below. The less injured, the reasonably comfortable, listened with feverish interest. "On the right again! — Stevenson and Stewart have had the brunt. — No! that's centre now. — Cleburne, I think. He's a good one! Who's passing through the street below? Old Joe? Give him a cheer, whoever's got a voice!"

The morning wore on to hot noon. The village women had furnished kettlefuls of broth that stony necessity made very thin. Such as it was, it tasted good to the wounded who could eat and drink. For those who turned moaningly away their comrades had the divinest pity. "Poor fellow! he's badly off! I reckon he's going to die — Do you remember, at Baker's Creek, how he fought that gun all alone?"

Hot noon wore into sultry afternoon. The sun went behind a smooth pall of greyish cloud. His going did not lessen the heat; there was no air, a kind of breathless oppression. In the midst of it, and during what seemed a three-quarter circle of firing, north, east, and west, surgeons and orderlies appeared in the upper hall. "We've got to move you folk! Yankees marching on Calhoun and so's the Army of Tennessee. Six miles by rail and the wagons are ready to take you to the station. Cheer up, now! the whole Western Atlantic's reserved for us!"

The crowded wagons drew off, each in a dust-cloud. They jolted, the straw was thin in the bottom. The wounded tried to set their teeth, but many failed and there were groans enough. The surgeon, riding at the end of the wagon, kept up a low, practised, cheerful talk, and some of the less hurt helped as best they might the others. Désirée, because her eyes were so appealing, because she expected to go and said as much, was given place upon the bed of one of the larger wagons. She sat, curled up upon the straw, Edward's head upon her lap, her bent knee and the softness of her skirt easing, too, the position of a grizzled lieutenant with a bullet through his cheek. The line of wagons jolted through the dust to the station, where was the weary, rusty engine, and the weary, dingy cars. Six miles over that roadbed with green wood for fuel, with stalling and hesitations and pauses for examination, meant a ride of an hour.

From some of the cars all the seats had been removed; others had seats at one end, while two thirds of the flooring was bare. The badly hurt were laid in rows upon the planks; those less injured were given the seats, two, sometimes three, to a bench; others with bandaged arms and heads must stand. Every box-on-wheels was crowded, noisy, hot, of necessity dirty, of necessity evil-smelling. The cars and their burden made the best of it; there was much suffering but no whining. The engine wheezed and puffed, the wheels moved, the train rolled southward out of Resaca. The more lively of the passengers, who were by windows, talked for the benefit of the others. "Troops moving on both roads — everybody getting in column — quiet and orderly — Old Joe fashion! Still firing on the fringe of things — regular battle-cloud over on our right! — Going to cross the river! Pretty river and pretty name for it. — Rivers and mountains — I've learned more geography in this war!"

The train creaked and wavered across the Oostenaula. At the station some one had given a wounded officer a newspaper procured from headquarters — a three-days' old issue of a Milledgeville paper. The officer had both eyes bandaged across, and the man beside him could not read aloud because his wound was in the throat. A third, sitting on the floor, propped against the side of the car, tried, but after he had read the headline he said that the letters all ran together. The headline had said "GREAT BATTLE IN VIRGINIA" and the car — that part of it which was at all at ease enough to listen — wanted to hear. Désirée, standing beside Edward, took the paper and read aloud. Her voice was sweet and deep and clear as a bell.

"*From Richmond. There has been a great battle in the Wilderness —*"

"The Wilderness! Like Chancellorsville —"

"*General Grant crossed on the fourth to the south side of Rapidan. We met them on the fifth. The battle raged all day with varying success, but when darkness fell the honours remained with us —*"

"Hip — hip — hooray!"

"At dawn the attack was renewed, and this day saw also a bloody struggle. General Longstreet, we regret to report was severely wounded—" "Old Pete! How he struck at Chickamauga!" *"At sunset Gordon of Ewell's attacked the enemy's right flank with such fury that he drove him for a mile, capturing his entrenchments and a great number of prisoners. Darkness closed the battle. Our loss very heavy, the enemy's much greater. As we go to press we learn that on the eighth Grant began to move toward Spottsylvania Court-House."* "The eighth! A week ago! Is that all it says?"

"There is nothing more from Virginia. But here is a letter from Ripley, Mississippi. Forrest has been through that place, the enemy after him —"

"Read that!"

On creaked the slow train, past the windows unrolled the Georgia countryside, and where one saw a road one saw grey troops, grey infantry, grey artillery, grey wagon-trains, all moving with the train of the wounded, moving deeper into Georgia, moving toward Atlanta. They moved nor fast nor slow, and if it was an army in retreat it did not look the rôle. On went the train, in the heat, with the wounded. No sun tormented, but the pall of the clouds held in the heat. There had been two buckets of water to each car, but the water gave out before they had been fifteen minutes from Resaca.

Hardee's corps, reaching Calhoun, moved by Johnston's orders out upon the Rome road to where was met the Snake Creek Gap road to Adairsville, upon which road the enemy was advancing. Here Hardee deployed, formed a line, and held the blue in check while the remainder of the grey came up. Joe Wheeler, in the rear, retarded all advance from Resaca itself. The blue passage of the Oostenaula met, too, with certain delays. Sherman, moving from Dalton behind Rocky Face to cut the grey lines at Resaca, found the Army of Tennessee there before him. Moving now behind Oostenaula to come upon the rear of the grey at Calhoun, he found himself, as at Resaca, again face to face.

Back in front of Resaca, under the darkening sky, upon the mound in front of Stevenson's line, above the ravine which had filled with a blue host, stood yet the four guns which had been cut off early in the day. "I covered the disputed battery with my fire," says Stevenson, "in such a manner that it was utterly impossible for the enemy to remove it, and I knew that I could retake it at any time, but thought it could be done with less loss of life at night, and therefore postponed my attack. When ordered to retire I represented the state of things to the general commanding, who decided to abandon the guns." And says Hood: "During the attack on General Stevenson a four-gun battery was in position thirty paces in front of his line, the gunners being driven from it and the battery left in dispute. The army withdrew that night, and the guns, without caissons or limber-boxes, were abandoned to the enemy, the loss of life it would have cost to withdraw them being considered worth more than the guns."

These four pieces constituted the only material lost or abandoned during the seventy days. Now they stood there in a row with their grey friends and comrades gone, with the blue rear guard not yet come to take them; stood there in a solitude after throngs, in a silence after sound. The sky was iron grey, the grass was trampled, the dead lay upon the slope. The guns were all alone. Their metal was cold, their lips no longer red; they stood like four sentinels frozen in death. They stood high, against the wide and livid heaven. The cloudy day declined; the night came dark and close, and into its vastness the guns sank and disappeared like the guns of an injured ship at sea.

CHAPTER XXV

THE WILDERNESS

I T might have been guessed from the first," said Cleave. "Only, fortunately or unfortunately, mankind never makes such guesses. Given, with all our talk to the contrary, North and South, a common stock, with common qualities, common intensities of purpose; then given the division of the whole into two parts, two thirds of the mass on that side of the line, one third on this; then, in addition, push to the larger side manufacturing towns and the control of the sea — and it ought not to have taken an eagle's vision to see on which side the dice would fall."

Allan pondered it. "There have been times from the beginning — from First Manassas on — when we lacked little of winning. A very little more several times and they would have cried, Peace!"

"That is true. It was n't impossible, impossible as it looked. It only was n't at all probable."

"And it is less probable now?"

"It is not at all probable now."

The two moved on in silence, Cleave riding Dundee, Allan walking beside him. They were in one of the glades of the Wilderness, the Sixty-fifth bivouacking at hand, Cleave going to brigade headquarters and the scout joining him from some by-path. It was sunset, and a pink light touched the Wilderness. "We have come to a definite turn," said Cleave, "or rather, we came to it at Gettysburg, — Gettysburg and Vicksburg." He looked about him. "A year ago, we were in this Wilderness. I had a cloud upon me that I did not know would ever be lifted — a cloud upon me and a sore heart." He lifted his hat and rode bareheaded. "But the light upon this Wilderness was more rosy then than now."

Night fell. Far and wide rolled the Wilderness. An odour rose from the dwarf pine and oak and sweet gum and cedar, from the earth and its carpet of the leaves of old years, from the dogwood, the pink azalea, and the purple judas-tree, from rotting logs and orange and red fungi, from small marshy bottoms where the frogs were croaking, from the dry, out-worn "poison fields," from dust and from mould, — a subtle odour, new as to-day, old as sandal-wood cut in the East ten thousand years ago. Far and wide stretched the Wilderness. Its ravines were not deep, its hills were not high, but it had a vastness as of the desert, where, neither, are the ravines deep nor the hills high. The stars rimmed it, and a low whispering wind went from cedar covert to sweet-gum copse, from pine to oak, from dogwood to judas-tree. It lifted the dust from the narrow, trampled, hidden roads and powdered with it the wayside growth. It murmured past the Tabernacle Church, and the burned house of Chancellorsville, and Dowdall's Tavern and the old Wilderness Tavern, by Catherine Furnace and along the old Turnpike and the Plank Road. It bore with it the usual sounds of the Wilderness by night and it bore also, this May as last May, the hum of great armies, not roused yet, not furiously battling, but murmurous — a dreamy, not unrestful sound adding itself to the region's natural voice.

A group of officers, sitting by the embers of a camp-fire, listened to the two voices, and watched the pale light along the northern horizon. "It's like the lights of a distant city over there."

"A hundred and forty thousand men make a city. . . . Not so distant either."

"Grant! I never met him in the old Mexican days, — nor afterwards. He went pretty far down. But I have met a man or two who knew him, and they liked him — a bulldog, reticent, tenacious kind of person —"

"Very good soldierly qualities — especially when backed by one hundred and forty thousand men with promise of all reinforcements needed! — Heigho!"

"He had a kind of rough chivalry, also, — consideration, simplicity. Sincere, too —" He stirred the embers with his scabbard point. "Well! we've got a job before us now."

"We've won, once before, in this place."

"The fourth of May! Last fourth of May it was Stonewall Jackson — lying over there by Dowdall's Tavern — with just a week to live. Stuart —"

"It's come to a question of figures. If they can keep on doubling us in number, if they can add and add reinforcements and we cannot, if they have made up their minds to stand all the killing necessary, then, with a determined general, it is not impossible that after years of trying they may get between us and Richmond."

"They may eventually. I don't think they will do it this campaign."

"No. I reckon not —"

The group fell silent, looking out upon the waves of wooded land and the light on the horizon. "I was through here," said one at last, "ten years ago. I was riding with a farmer — a young man — and I remember that I said it was like a region that had gone to sleep in its cradle and never waked up, and he said that that was what was the matter with it — that nothing ever happened here! I wonder —"

"Don't wonder. What's the use?"

"It's a strange world!"

"Strange! That's the thing about the universe I think of most at night — how *queer* it is!"

"Unity! That's what they teach — all the philosophers! And yet a unity that tears its own flesh —"

"Sometimes unity does that very thing. I've seen a man do it."

"Yes, when he was distraught!"

"That's what I say. You can nearly go mad at night, thinking how mad we all are!"

"Don't think. At least not now. You can't afford it."

"I agree with Cary. There's a time to think and a time not to think. The less the soldier thinks the better."

"Think!" said Fauquier Cary. "No one ever thinks in war. The soldier looks at his enemy, and then he looks at his murdering piece, and then instinctively he discovers the best position — or what seems to him the best position — from which to fire it. And then he reloads, and he looks again at the enemy, and instinct does the job for him once more — and so on, *ad infinitum*. But he never *thinks*." He rose and stood, warming his one hand. "If he did that, you know, there'd be no war!"

"And would that be a good thing?"

"It depends," said Cary, "on what you call a good thing. — Listen! Jeb Stuart and his cavalry, moving on the old Turnpike —"

The grey soldiers, too, had their camp-fires. The light of these flared, to the eyes of the blue, on the southern horizon. Here likewise was the effect of the lights of a city — a smaller city, a city of sixty thousand. But when you were actually back of the pickets, in the camps, it was not like a city. It was only dusky lights here and there in the midst of shadows, only camp-fires in the Wilderness. The grey men scattered around them, resting after rapid marching, were in an eve-of-battle mood. Eve-of-battle mood meant tenseness, sudden jocularity, sudden silences, a kind of added affectionateness between brothers and intimates, often masked by brusqueness, a surreptitious consideration, a curious, involuntary "in honour preferring one another." Even among the still at this hour very busy people, the generals cogitating orders, the aides and couriers standing waiting or setting out with their messages, the ordnance train people, the movers of guns from one point to another, the ambulance folk, the drivers of belated wagons, the cavalry patrols, eve-of-battle feeling was apparent. But it was most in force in the resting army. Eve-of-battle mood had many ingredients. Among them was to be found in the cup of many the ingredient of fear. Men hid it, but it was there. It fell on the heart at intervals, fell like a cold finger tap, like the icy drop of water falling at intervals, hour after hour, on the brow of the tortured in an old dungeon. When the battle was here it would disappear; always the amount of it lessened in constant ratio to the approach of the firing. The first volley — except in the case of the coward — dissipated it quite. With some the drop was heavier and more insistent than with others, but there were few, indeed, who had not at some time felt that cold and penetrating touch. It was only a thing of intervals; it came and went, and between its comings one was gay enough. There had long ago ceased the fear of what it could do to one. It was not pleasant — neither was sea-sickness — but the voyage would be made. The Army of Northern Virginia knew that it was going to fight. The world knows that it fought as have fought few armies.

A company lying upon the earth in a field of cedars began to sing.

"We're tenting to-night on the old camp-ground!
Give us a song to cheer —"

"That's too mournful!" said a neighbouring company. "Tell the Louisianians to sing the 'Marseillaise.'"

> "Many are the hearts that are weary to-night!
> Wishing for the war to cease;
> Many are the hearts that are looking for the right,
> To see the dawn of peace.

> "Tenting to-night, tenting to-night,
> Tenting on the old camp-ground. . . ."

As always, eve-of-battle, there was going on a certain redding up. Those who had haversacks plunged deep within them, gathered certain trifles together and tied them into a small bundle with a pencilled direction. Diaries were brought up very neatly and carefully to date. Entries closed with "Battle to-morrow!" or with "This time to-morrow night much will have happened"; or sometimes with such things as "Made up my quarrel with Wilson to-day"; or "Returned the book I borrowed from Selden"; or "Read a psalm and a chapter to-day"; or "Wrote home." Eve-of-battle saw many letters written. There was a habit, too, of destroying letters received and garnered. Here and there a man sat upon a log and tore into little bits old, treasured sheets. The flecks lay like snow upon the earth of the Wilderness.

> "We're tired of war on the old camp-ground
> Many are dead and gone. . . .

> "We're tenting to-night on the old camp-ground, . . .
> Tenting to-night, tenting to-night,
> Tenting to-night on the old camp-ground."

All the spirit of this army was graver than it had been a year ago, than it had been six months ago. During the past winter a strong religious fervour had swept it. This evening, in the Wilderness, in many a command there was prayer and singing of hymns. Swaths of earth, black copses of cedar and gum, divided one congregation from another. One was singing while another prayed; the hymns were different, but the wide night had room for all — for the hymns and for "Tenting to-night," and for the "Marseillaise" which now Hays's Louisianians were singing. All blended into something piteous, something old and touching, and of a dim nobility. The pickets out in the deep night listened.

"Just as I am, without one plea
Save that thy blood was shed for me,
And that Thou bid'st me come to thee,
O Lamb of God, I come, I come!"

A soldier, standing picket and hearing the singing behind a dusky wave of earth, had his doubts. "If we really come to him — if the Yankees over there really came to him — if we both came, why, — *there would n't be any battle to-morrow.* . . . Seeing that he said, 'Love your enemy' — which if everybody did presently there'd be no enemy — no more than an icicle in the sun." He sighed and shifted his musket. "They think they mean what they're singing, but they don't —"

Relieved, he sought his mess and the corner of leaves and boughs in which they meant to sleep. Before lying down he spoke to the man next him. "John, I've got a letter and a little bit of package here that I want you to keep. I am going to be killed to-morrow."

"No, you ain't!"

"Yes, I am. I am positively certain of it. I am going to be killed about noon."

"You've just got one of those darned presentiments, and half the time they don't come to nothing!"

"This one will. You take the letter and the little bit of package. I am going to be killed to-morrow, about noon." And he was killed.

Night grew old. The flare of the cities sank away; tattoo beat, then, after a little, taps. The Wilderness lay awake. She communed with her own heart. But the men whom she harboured slept. Night passed, the stars paled, pure and cool and fresh came on the dawn — wild roses in the east, in a field of forget-me-not blue. Shrill and sweet, near and remote, a thousand bugles blew reveille in the Wilderness.

Ewell and A. P. Hill moved westward, deeper into the Wilderness. Longstreet, marching from the south side of the James, was not yet up, though known to be approaching. About breakfast time an artillery officer came upon a small fire, and bending over it, stiffly, being wooden-legged, General Ewell, a first-rate cook and proud of it. He insisted on giving the other a cup of coffee.

"Is there any objection, sir," said the officer, after drinking, "to our knowing what are orders?"

"No, sir, — none at all, — just the orders I like! To go right down the Plank Road and strike the enemy wherever I find him!"

He found him, in the person of the Fifth Corps, near Locust Grove, at the noon hour. The battle of the Wilderness began, — a vast infantry battle, fought in thick woods, woods so thick that in those coverts of dwarf pine and oak artillery could not be used, so thick that an officer could not see his whole line, so thick that the approach of troops was often known only by the noise of their movement through the scrub, or, as night came down, by the light from the mouths of the muskets. This was the battle of the first day, and it was long and sanguinary and indecisive. Corps of Ewell and Hill — corps of Hancock and Warren and Sedgwick fought it. Ewell gained and held an advantage, but Wilcox and Heth of Hill's had a desperate, exhausting struggle with Hancock's men. Poague's battalion of artillery strove to help, but artillery in the Wilderness could do little. Six divisions charged Heth and Wilcox. They held their own, but they barely held it. When darkness fell and the thunders were stilled there came a promise that during the night they should be relieved. Resting upon it, they built a rude breastwork, and then, worn out, dropped upon the earth and slept.

Lee sent a courier on a swift horse to meet Longstreet and order a night march. At one o'clock of a starlit night the latter took the road, and at daylight of the sixth he came to Parker's Store, on the edge of the Wilderness, three miles behind Hill's line of battle, and as he came he heard the roar of battle upon this front.

Hancock fell in the grey light on Heth and Wilcox. The Wilderness echoed the musketry and the shouting. It was a furious onslaught, for a time a furious answer — and then Wilcox's line, exhausted, decimated, broke and rolled in confusion down the Orange Plank Road. When the men reached Poague's artillery they made a wavering stand. The guns, crashing into battle, did what they might to help. But Hancock's shouting lines came on. A furious musketry fire burst in the face of the guns, a leaden rain hard pelting from just across the road, the drops falling thick and fast among the guns and the gunners and a company of mounted officers behind. The grey infantry, exposed to volley after volley, broke again; all the place became a troubled grey sea, cross-waves and confusion.

Lee rode out from the group of officers. "Rally, men, rally!" he cried. "General Longstreet is coming!"

"*O Marse Robert! O Marse Robert!*"

The boisterous rain came and came again from the coverts of the Wilderness. Hancock's men shouted loudly. They saw the grey overthrow. "Hurrah! Hurrah! Hurrah!" they shouted.

Lee rose in his stirrups. "Rally, Army of Northern Virginia! —"

"*Longstreet! Longstreet!*"

Double-column and double-time, Longstreet came down the Plank Road. Deploying, Kershaw came into line under fire to the right. Deploying, Field swung across on the left. "Charge, Kershaw!" ordered Longstreet. Kershaw charged, and flung back the shouting blue advance; Field, on the left, advancing at a run, swept past the smoking guns and Lee, sitting Traveller. Gregg's Texans were in front. "General Lee! General Lee!" they shouted. Lee lifted his hat, and then he spurred grey Traveller and kept beside the Texans.

"He's going in with them!" exclaimed an aide. "He mustn't do that!"

Gregg turned his head. "General Lee, you mustn't go with us! We can't allow that, sir!"

Now the men saw, too. "Do you mean — No, no! that won't do! *General Lee to the rear!*"

"But, men —"

There rose a cry. "We won't go on unless you go back! *General Lee to the rear!*"

A man took hold of Traveller's bridle and turned him.

On dashed the Texans — eight hundred of them. They went now through open field, now through pines. They struck Webb's brigade of Hancock's corps. Blue and grey, there sprang a roar of musketry. Four hundred of the eight hundred fell, lay dead or wounded; then with a loud and long cry there swept to the aid of Gregg, Benning's Texans, Georgia, and Alabama. Law and Benning and Gregg pushed back the blue.

For hours it was the tug of war. Blue and grey they swayed and swung and the Wilderness howled with the conflict. Smoke mounted. The firing waxed until sound was no more discrete but continuous. Although it was not night the Wilderness grew dark. And beneath the solid roof of smoke and sound men lay gasping on mother earth, dyeing the grass with their blood, plucking with their fingers at strengthless stems, putting out their tongues where there was no moisture, biting the dust. In the sick brain, to and fro, went the words "*This is the end,*" and "*Why? O God, why?*"

The blue left rested south of the Plank Road. With four brigades under Mahone, Longstreet began a turning movement. It succeeded. Mahone struck the blue, flank and rear, while Longstreet hurled other troops against their front. The blue line crumpled up, surged in confusion back upon the Brock Road. The noise grew heavier, the Wilderness darker.

And then occurred one of those things called coincidences. One year ago a very great general had been given death in the Wilderness by a mistaken volley from his own men. Now on this day in the Wilderness a general, not so great, but able, and necessary that day to the grey fortunes, rode with a brigade which he was about to place in line, through the wood alongside the Plank Road. The wood was thick and the road wound. Longstreet, with him Generals Jenkins and Kershaw, pressed forward through the oak scrub, torn and veiled with smoke, and now in many places afire. All the air was now so thick, it was hard in that wild place to tell friend from foe. As had done Lane's North Carolinians last year, so this year did Mahone's men. They saw or felt the approach of a column, whose colour they could not see; some command parallel with the moving troops chanced just then to deliver fire; Mahone's men thought that the shots came from the approaching body, hardly outlined as it was in the murk. They answered with a volley. Jenkins was killed, and Longstreet severely wounded.

"What are you doing? What are you doing?" shouted Kershaw; and at last grey understood that it was grey.

Says the artillery officer, Robert Stiles, who has been quoted before: "I observed an excited gathering some distance back of the lines, and, pressing toward it, I heard that General Longstreet had just been shot down and was being put into an ambulance. I could not learn anything definite as to the character of his wound, but only that it was serious — some said that he was dead. When the ambulance moved off, I followed it for a little way. . . . The members of his staff surrounded the vehicle, some riding in front, some on one side and some on the other, and some behind. One, I remember, stood upon the rear step of the ambulance, seeming to desire to be as near him as possible. I never on any occasion during the four years of the war saw a group of officers and gentlemen more deeply distressed. They were literally bowed down with grief. All of them were in tears. One, by whose side I rode for some distance, was himself severely hurt, but he made no allusion to his wound, and I do not believe that he felt it. . . . I rode up to the ambulance and looked in. They had taken off Longstreet's hat and coat and boots. The blood had paled out of his face, and its somewhat gross aspect was gone. I noticed how white and dome-like his great forehead looked and, with scarcely less reverent admiration, how spotless white his socks, and his fine gauze undervest, save where the black red gore from his breast and shoulder had stained it. . . . His eyelids frayed apart till I could see a delicate line of blue between them, and then he very quietly moved his unwounded arm, and with his thumb and two fingers carefully lifted the saturated undershirt from his chest, holding it up a moment, and heaved a deep sigh."

The grey attack, disorganized by Longstreet's fall, hung in the wind, until Lee came up and led it on. But time had been lost, and though much was done, it was not that which might have been done. The blue were behind long lines of log breastworks on the Brock Road. Again and again the grey beat against these. At times they took this work or that, but could not hold it. Along the front of one command the breastwork caught fire. The blue fought to put it out, but could not; flame and smoke made a barrier alike to grey or blue. On the Plank Road, Burnside fell upon Law's Alabamians and a Florida brigade, but Heth came up and with Alabama and Florida thrust back Burnside. At sunset, though the sun could not be seen in the Wilderness, Ewell flung Gordon with Pegram and Hays against the Federal right. The assault was well planned and determined to desperation. The blue right was driven as had been the blue left in the morning. The sun sank, black night came, and the battle closed. There lay in the Wilderness perhaps two thousand dead in grey and five thousand wounded. There lay in the Wilderness more than two thousand dead in blue and twelve thousand wounded. There were three thousand in blue captured or missing. There were fifteen hundred grey prisoners.

Night was not so black in all parts of the Wilderness. In parts it was fearfully red. The Wilderness was afire. Pine and oak scrub and the dry leaves beneath and the sedge in open places, — they flared like tow. They flared where the battle had been fought; they flared where were the wounded. Here and there in the Wilderness arose a horrible crying. Volunteers and volunteers, blue and grey, companies of volunteers, plunged into the smoke, among the red tongues. They did what the fire would let them do. They brought out many and many and many. But an unknown number of hundreds were burned to death.

All day the seventh they skirmished. The night of the seventh the blue, weary of the Wilderness, moved with swiftness southeast toward Spottsylvania Court-House. "Get so between him and Richmond," said Grant, as at Dalton Sherman was saying, "Get so between him and Atlanta." But as Johnston moved on inner lines and with more swiftness than Sherman, so Lee moved on inner lines and with more swiftness than Grant. Flexible as a Toledo blade was the grey army. With the noise of the blue column on the Brock Road sprang almost simultaneously the sound of the grey column moving cross-country and then by the Shady Grove Road. Grant, bent on "swinging past" Lee, came to Spottsylvania in the bright morning light of the eighth of May, to find Jeb Stuart drawn across the Brock Road; behind him the First Corps.

CHAPTER XXVI

THE BLOODY ANGLE

ROUGHLY speaking, the Confederate position in the three days' battle of Spottsylvania — country of Alexander Spottswood, sometime periwigged Governor of the Colony of Virginia — was a great reversed V, the apex turned northward, the base laved by the river Po, the First Corps holding the western face, the Second Corps the eastern, the Third Corps at first in reserve, but afterwards sufficiently involved, Lee himself at Spottsylvania Court-House, just within the eastern line. The country was a rough one of oak and pine, though not so densely wooded as the Wilderness, the weather upon the ninth and tenth dazzlingly hot and dusty, the eleventh and twelfth days of fog and streaming rain. It was a strong position.

On May eighth, the two antagonists entrenched themselves, made their dispositions and placed their batteries. On May ninth, there was much skirmishing, heavy enough at times to be called an engagement. On this day, on the blue side, there was killed General Sedgwick. From the beginning of the campaign, Jeb Stuart had most seriously interfered with the blue host. On the eighth, Grant ordered Sheridan to strike out independently for Richmond and so draw Stuart away from the field of Spottsylvania. At sunrise on the ninth, Sheridan and ten thousand horsemen took the Telegraph Road that stretched from Fredericksburg to Richmond. At sundown they came to Beaver Dam Station and the Virginia Central Railroad. Here they captured a trainload of wounded and prisoners on the way from Spottsylvania to Richmond. Here they released three hundred and seventy Federal captives, and here they set fire to all trains and buildings and tore up the railroad track and made birds' nests of the telegraph wires. And here they heard Stuart on their heels. On the tenth, they crossed the South Anna at Ground Squirrel Bridge, not without skirmishing. At night Stuart's shells rained into their camps. On the eleventh, one blue brigade had an encounter with Munford at Ashland while the main force swept on to Glen Allen. Here they met Stuart's strong skirmish line, and, driving it in at last, came to Yellow Tavern, six miles from Richmond.

Back in Spottsylvania, all day the tenth of May there was fighting, fighting by the river Po, between Heth's division and troops of Hancock, artillery work and skirmishing along all lines; in the afternoon a great blue assault, desperately repelled. The Federal loss this day was four thousand, the Confederate, two thousand.

The eleventh saw a lull, a still and oppressive pause in things. The blue made a reconnoissance, much interfered with by grey sharpshooters, but a reconnoissance big with results. What had been cloudy knowledge became clear; there sprang into intense light a thing that might be done. That night the Federal Second and Ninth Corps slept on their arms in a sheltering wood a thousand yards and more from the salient that marked the grey centre, from the narrow part of the V, held by Edward Johnson's division of Ewell's corps.

All day the eleventh the grey had strengthened breastworks and made inner lines. There was a fine, slow rain, and the mist of it, added to the smoke from the burning forest and the clouds from the cannon mouth, made a dull, obscuring atmosphere. In the afternoon came with positiveness the statement of a reconnoitring party. A blue column, in motion southward, had been observed to cross the Po. At the same time arrived a message from Early. "Certainly some movement of the enemy to the left." Now another flank movement of Grant's, another attempt to "swing past," another effort to get between the Army of Northern Virginia and Richmond was so probable, so entirely on the cards, that Lee accepted the report as correct and prepared to act accordingly. He prepared to move during the night that supple, mobile army of his, and in speed and silence again to lay it across Grant's road. Among other orders he sent one to his artillery chiefs. All guns on the left and centre that might be "difficult of access" were to be withdrawn at nightfall. So, later, they would be ready to come swiftly and noiselessly into column. Having received the order, Ewell's chief of artillery removed all guns from the high and broken ground at the point of the V. Toward midnight Lee received assurance that the blue movement across the Po had been but a reconnoissance. Mahone and

Wilcox, whom he had sent toward Shady Grove, were recalled, and the Army of Northern Virginia prepared to meet on this ground the Army of the Potomac. Certain orders were countermanded, certain others given. But through some negligence or other the order to restore to their original position the guns "difficult of access" did not that night reach the proper officers. When the first pallid light came into the sky the guns were away from the salient, the point of the V. And a thousand yards in the forest lay, on their arms, waiting for the dawn, the Second and Ninth Army Corps.

The salient — for hundreds of yards it thrust itself out toward the blue, like a finger pointing from a clenched hand. And the finger nail was the Bloody Angle.

Billy Maydew, rising from the wet earth at four o'clock, found that the rain was coming down and the world was wrapped in fog. "Thunder Run Mountain can't see Peaks of Otter this morning!" he said. He stood up, tall and lean and twenty-one, and stretched himself. "Hope grandpap and the dawgs air setting comfortable by the fire!"

Certainly the Stonewall Brigade, Johnson's division, Ewell's corps, was not warm and comfortable. Felled wet trees did as well for breastwork and traverse and abatis as dry, but they were not so good for camp-fires. The fires this streaming break-of-day were a farce. The ground behind the breastworks was rough and now very muddy, and the great number of stumps of trees had a dismal look. Where a fire was kindled the smoke refused to rise, but clung dark, thick, and suffocating. The air struck shiveringly cold, and the woods north and east and west of the sharp salient were as invisible as a fog-mantled coast. Billy, standing high in the angle's narrowest part, had a curious feeling. He had never been on a ship or he might have thought, "I am driving fast into something behind that fog." As it was, he shook off the slight dizziness and looked about him — at the thronged deck where everybody was trying to get breakfast, at the long trenches, each side of the salient and rounding the point, at the log and earth breastworks and the short traverses, at the abatis of felled trees, branches outward, much like the swirl of waves to either side the ship's prow. He looked at the parapets where the guns had been, and then, brigade headquarters' fire being near, he listened to an aide from the division commander. "General

Johnson says, sir, that he has sent again for the guns, sent for the third time. They're coming, but the road is frightfully heavy. He says the moment they are here, get them into position and trained. In the mean time keep the sharpest kind of lookout."

Billy had not thought much of it before, but now it came over him. "We air in a darned defenceless position out here."

He went back to where his mess was struggling with a fire not big enough to toast hard-tack. He had hardly joined them when a drum beat and an order rang the length and breadth of the salient. *Fall in!*

He was down in one of the trenches, the Sixty-fifth with him, right and left. Turning his head, he saw Cleave stand a moment looking at the platforms where the batteries had been and now were not, then walk along the trenches and speak to the men. Lieutenant Coffin he saw, too, slight, pale, romantic-looking, and troubled at the moment because he had unwittingly stepped into a mud-hole which had mired him above the knee. He had a bit of scrap iron and with it was scraping the mud away, steadying himself, shoulder against a tree.

Billy smiled. "Ain't he a funny mixture? Hates a speck of mud 'most as much as he hates a greyback! Funny when I think of how I used to hate *him!*" He looked along the line and at the companies in reserve and at the clusters of officers, with here or there a solitary figure, and at the regiments of the Stonewall Brigade, and the other brigades of Johnson's division, and then out through a crack between two logs, to the picket line beyond the abatis and to the misty wood. "I don't know that I hate anybody now," said Billy aloud.

"Don't you?" asked the man next him. "I wouldn't be a namby-pamby like that! I couldn't get along without hating, any more than I could without tansy in the spring-time!"

"Oh, thar air times," said Billy equably, "when I think I hate the Yanks."

"Think! Don't you know?"

Billy was counting the cartridges in his cartridge-box. "Why," he said when he had finished, "sometimes of course I hate them like p'ison oak. But then thar air other times when I consider that — according to their newspapers — they hate me like p'ison oak, too. Now I do a power of wrong things, I know, but I air not p'ison oak.

And so, according to what Allan calls 'logic,' maybe they air not p'ison oak either. Thar was a man in the Wilderness. The fire in the scrub was coming enough to feel the devil in it — closer and closer. And his spine was hurt and he could n't move, and he had his shoulder against a log, one end of which was blazing. He was sitting there all lit up by that light, and he had his musket butt up and was trying to beat out his brains. Me and Jim Watts got him out, and he was from Boston and a young man like me, and I liked him just as well as ever I liked any man. He put his arms around my neck and he hugged me and cried, and I hugged him, too, and I reckon I cried, too. And Jim and me got him out through the scrub afire. He wa'n't no p'ison oak, no more'n I were."

"Well, what 're you fighting for?"

"I am fighting," said Billy, "for the right to secede."

Out in the fog a picket fired. Another and another followed. There arose a sputter of musketry, then a sound of voices and of running feet, heavy on the sodden earth. In a moment there was commotion, up and down, within the salient. In fell the pickets — anyhow — over the breastworks. "They're coming! they're coming! All of them! It looked like —!"

They came, Barlow's division in two lines of two brigades each "closed in mass," Birney's division, Mott's division, Gibbon behind. Barlow came over an open space, Birney through a wood of stunted pines and by a marsh. Together they wrapped with fire the extended finger that was the salient. There rose a grey shouting, "The guns! the guns! Hasten the guns!" The guns were coming — Page's and Cutshaw's — the guns were hastening, coming in two lines, twenty-two guns, through the tangled, sopping wood — horses and drivers and cannoneers straining every nerve. The ground was frightful beneath foot and wheel. Two guns got up in time to fire three rounds into the looming blue. Then the storm broke, and the angle became the spot on earth where, it is estimated, in all the history of the earth the musketry fire was the heaviest. It became the "Bloody Angle."

Billy fired, bit a cartridge, loaded, fired, loaded, fired, loaded, fired, and all over and over again, then, later, used his bayonet, then clubbed his musket and struck with it, lifted, struck, lifted, struck. Each distinct action carried with it a more or less distinct thought. "This is going to be hell here, presently," thought the first cartridge. "No guns and every other Yank in creation coming jumping!" "*Thunder Run!*" thought the second; "*Thunder Run, Thunder Run, Thunder Run!*" Thought the third, "I killed that man with the twisted face." Thought the fourth, "I forgot to give Dave back his tin cup." The fifth cartridge had an irrelevant vision of the school-house and the water-bucket on the bench by the door. The sixth thought, "That man won't go home either!" Down the line went the word, *Bayonets!* and he fixed his bayonet, the gun-bore burning his fingers as he did so. The breastwork here was log and earth. Now other bayonets appeared over it, and behind the bayonets blue caps. "I have heard many a fuss," said the first bayonet thrust, "but never a fuss like this!" "Blood, blood!" said the second. "I am the bloody Past! Just as strong and young as ever I was! More blood!"

The trenches grew slippery with blood. It mixed with the rain and ran in red streamlets. The bayonet point felt first the folds of cloth, then it touched and broke the skin, then it parted the tissues, then it grated against bone, or, passing on, rending muscle and gristle, protruded, a crimson point. Withdrawn, it sought another body, sought it fast, and found it. Those men who had room to fire kept on firing, the blue into breast and face of the grey, the grey into breast and face of the blue. Flame scorched the flesh of each. Pistols were used as well as muskets. Where there was not room to fire, or time to load, where one could not well thrust with the bayonet, the stock of gun or pistol was used as a club. Where weapons had been wrested away men clutched with bare hands one anothers' throats. And all this went on, not among a dozen or even fifty infuriated beings, but among thousands. Over all was the smoke, through which, as through a leaky roof, poured the rain.

The blue came over the breastwork, down the slippery side, into the trenches. Their feet pressed dead bodies or slipped in the bloody mire. The grey seemed to lift them bodily and throw them back upon the other side. Then across the parapet broke out again the storm of musketry. There were four thousand defending the salient, there were thrice as many pressing to the attack. From the rear Ewell was throwing forward brigades, but they could not come in time. The twenty-two guns were now here, but only two were unlimbered, when the blue finally overran the Bloody Angle.

They poured into the salient, they took three thousand grey prisoners, amongst them Johnson himself and General Steuart; they took twenty of Page and Cutshaw's twenty-two guns. They swept on, hurrahing, to the second line across the salient, and here they met the troops of Hill and Early. Gordon and Rodes, brigades of Lane and Ramseur and Perrin, brigades of Mississippi and South Carolina, artillery from any quarter that could be brought to bear, all crashed against the rushing blue. All day it lasted, the battle of the broken centre, with movements of diversion elsewhere; an attack, violently repulsed, upon Anderson of Longstreet's; and Early's victory over Burnside. But it was over and around the salient that man's rage waxed hottest. So dense in the rain-laden air was the smoke, both from the artillery and the enormous volume of musketry, that although they were neighbours, indeed, neither side now clearly saw its target. Each side fired at edges and gleams of humanity. Now a work was captured and held, perhaps for five, perhaps for twenty minutes. Then it was retaken. Now it was the Stars and Stripes that waved above it, and now it was the Stars and Bars. The abatis became a trap to take the living and hold the dead. It and all the standing trees were riddled by bullets, split into broomstraw. Trees of considerable diameter, bit in twain by the leaden teeth, crashed down upon the commands beneath. The artillery, roaring into the battle from every feasible point, raked the ground with canister, bringing down the living and dreadfully mangling the already fallen. The face of the earth was kneaded into a paste with blood and water. The blood seemed to have gotten upon the flags. And always from the rear was handed on the ammunition. . . . The Sixty-fifth was among the uncaptured. Billy had become an automaton.

Night closed the conflict. The blue had gained the capture of three fourths of a division, but little since or beside. When total darkness came down there lay upon the field of Spottsylvania sixteen thousand Federal dead and wounded. The grey loss was not so great, but it was great enough. And never now with the grey could any loss be afforded. With the grey the blood that was lost was arterial blood.

At dawn Lee still held the great V, save only the extreme point, the narrow Bloody Angle. This was covered and possessed by the blue, and at the dawn details came to gather the wounded and bury the dead. The dead lay thronged. The blue buried their own, and then they came and looked upon the trenches on the grey side of the breastworks, and the grey dead lay there so thick that it was ghastly. They lay in blood stiffened with earth, and their pale faces looked upwards, and their cold hands still clutched their muskets. A ray from the rising sun struck upon them. "With much labour," says a Federal eye-witness, "a detail of Union soldiers buried these dead by simply turning the captured breastworks upon them."

Back somewhere near the river Po, in the width of the V, a mounted officer met a mounted comrade. The latter was shining wet, he and his horse, from a swollen ford. Each drew rein.

"Have you anything to eat?" said the one from across the Po. "I am dizzy, I am so famished."

"I've got a little brown sugar. Here —"

He poured it into the hollow of the other's hand, who ate it eagerly. "Has anything," asked the first, "been heard from Richmond way — from Stuart?"

The other let fall his hand, sticky with the sugar. He looked at his fellow with sombre eyes. "Where have you been," he said, "not to have heard? — Stuart is dead."

CHAPTER XXVII

RICHMOND

"From lightning and tempest; from plague, pestilence and famine; from battle and murder, and from sudden death,
"Good Lord, deliver us."

B Y most the words were sobbed out. May the eighth, and the Wilderness vast in the minds of all, and fresh battle impending, now at Spottsylvania! It was a congregation of men and women, dusky in raiment, bereaved, torn by anxieties, sick with alternating hope and fear. Only on one's bed at night, or here in church, could the overladen heart speak without shame or acknowledgment of weakness. Outside, one must be brave again. The overladen heart expressed itself not loudly but very truly. The kneeling women looked crushed and immobile in that position. Over them was flung a veil of black, and a hand, potent from the beginning of ages, seemed yet more heavily to press downward their bowed heads. The men knelt more stiffly, but they, too, rested their foreheads on their clasped hands, and the tears came from between their closed lids.

On rolled the service, through to the benediction. Richmond in Saint Paul's came out of church into the flower-perfumed sunlight. Here, men and women, they took up life again, and took it up with courage. And as the proper face of courage is a smiling one, so with these. Laughter, even, was heard in Richmond — Richmond scarred and battle-worn; Richmond, where was disease and crowding and wounds and starvation; Richmond ringed with earthworks; Richmond the city contended for; Richmond between her foes, Army of the Potomac threatening from the Wilderness, Army of the James, lesser but formidable, threatening from the river gate; Richmond, where the alarm bell was always ringing, ringing! Two days ago it had pealed the news that Butler, bringing up a fleet from Fortress Monroe, had made a landing at Bermuda Hundred. Thirty-nine ships there were in all — thirty-eight, when a gunboat, running upon a torpedo, was blown into fragments. They landed thirty-six thousand troops and overran the narrow ground between the Appomattox and the James. Petersburg was threatened, and from that side Richmond. The bell told it all with an iron tongue. Pickett was at Petersburg, reinforced by Hagood's brigade, and troops were coming from the Carolinas — some troops, how many no one knew save that they could not be many. Yesterday again the thrilling, rapid, iron tongue had spoken. The enemy had seized and was wrecking the Petersburg railroad. . . . So many words had come forward in this war, had their day, or short or long, and gone out of men's mouths! Now the word "Petersburg" came forward, it being its turn. The alarm bell called out the militia and the City Battalion and the clerks from the various departments. They were all ready if the blue cannon came nearer.

Storm and oppression were in the air — and yet the town on its seven hills was fair, with May flowers and the fresh green of many trees in which sang the mating birds. The past winter and early spring there had existed, leaping like a sudden flame, dying to a greying ember, and then leaping again, a strange gaiety. It had seized but a certain number in the heavy-hearted city, but these it had seized. Youth was youth, and must sing some manner of song and play a little no matter what the storm. There were bizarre "starvation parties," charades, concerts, dances, amateur theatricals, an historic presentation of "The Rivals." It was all natural enough; it had its place in the symphony of 1864. But now it was over. The soldiers had gone back to the front, the campaign had begun, and no one could really sing, watching the wounded come in.

Judith and Unity Cary walked up Grace Street together. They were not wearing black; Warwick Cary had never liked it. Moreover, in this year of the war a black gown and bonnet and veil would cost a fearful amount, and there were known to be women and children starving. The day was bright and warm, with drifts of perfume. An officer of the President's staff lifted his cap, then walked beside them.

"Is n't it a lovely day? — If I were a king with a hundred palaces, I should have around each one a brick wall with wistaria over it!"

"No, dark red roses —"

"I should n't have a wall at all — unless it were one with a number of gates — and only one palace! A reasonable palace, with an unreasonable number of white roses —"

A lieutenant-colonel, aged twenty-six, with an arm in a sling, and a patch over one eye, here joined them. "Good morning! Is n't it a lovely day! I was just thinking it was n't half so lovely a day as the days are at Greenwood, and lo and behold! just then it became just as lovely! — What do you think! It's confirmed that Beauregard is on his way from North Carolina —"

"Good!"

"'Beau canon, Beauregard! Beau soldat, Beauregard!
Beau sabreur! beau frappeur! Beauregard! Beauregard!'

Now I've shocked that old lady crossing the street! Harry, tell her it was a Russian hymn!"

They walked on beneath the bright trees. "The —— wedding has been postponed," said Unity. "They thought there was time, but two days before the day they had set, he had to go. It will be as soon as he comes back."

"By George! but I was at a wedding out in Hanover!" said the lieutenant-colonel. "The bride was dressed in homespun, with a wreath of apple blossoms. The bridesmaids were in black, just taken as they were from all the neighbouring families. The groom had lost his arm and a piece of shell at Mine Run had cut away an ear, just as neat! The best man was a lame civilian who had somehow inherited and held fast a beautiful black broadcloth suit, — very tight pantaloons and a sprigged velvet waistcoat! He had acted, he told me, as best man at thirty weddings in the last year 'because he had the clothes.' The wedding guests had come in what they had and it was a wonderful display. The bride had six brothers and a father marching on the Wilderness, and the groom was just out of hospital. There were three wounded cousins in the house, and in the stable a favourite war-horse being doctored for a sabre cut. Most of the servants had left, but there was a fiddler still on the place, and we danced till midnight. There was a Confederate bride-cake, and a lot of things made with dried apples and sorghum. By George, it was fine!"

"The bell!"

The iron voice rang through the city. Faces came to the open windows, questioning voices arose, men passed, walking rapidly, the aide and the lieutenant-colonel said good-bye in haste and went with the rest. The loud ringing ceased; it had not lasted long enough to mark anything very terrible. Judith and Unity waited by a honeysuckle-draped gate until the clamour had ceased, and then until there came reassurance from a passer-by. "Nothing alarming! A slight engagement at Drewry's Bluff, and a feint this way!"

The kinsman's house where Judith had stayed before sheltered now the two sisters. Judith was here because, during the weeks of inaction preceding the opening of the campaign, Cleave could now and again come to Richmond for a day. Unity was here because of sheer need of change, so weary long had been the winter at Greenwood. Change was change, even if both plays were tragedies. Now they went into the house that, like all houses in Richmond, was filled with people. Of the three sons, one had died in prison and the others were with Lee. The house was murmurous with the voices of women and quite elderly men, across which bubbled the clear notes of children. So much of the great State was overrun now by the foe, so many homes were burned, so much subsistence was destroyed, so impossible was it to stay in the old home region, that always, everywhere, occurred a movement of refugees. There was a tendency for the streams to set toward Richmond; unwise but natural. Almost every quarter was now threatened; one went into peaceful fields to-day, and to-morrow one must move again. Richmond! Richmond was surely safe, Richmond would surely never fall. . . . There was a restless straining, too, toward the heart of things. So the refugees came to Richmond and, with the troops coming and going, and Government and the departments and the inmates of the great hospitals and the inmates of the mournful prisons, crowded the city.

Judith and Unity had together the small, high-up, white room behind the tulip tree that had been Judith's before and during and after the Seven Days. Now they climbed to it, laid away their things, and prepared for the three o'clock dinner. Judith sat in the window-seat, her hands about her knee, her head thrown back against the white wood, her eyes on the shimmering distance seen between the boughs.

"Once this window faced as it should," she said; "I could watch the camp-fires each night — and I watched — I watched. But now I wish it were a northwest window."

Unity, at the mirror, coiled her bright, brown hair. "By the time it was cut you might need another."

"That is true," said Judith. "The sky reddens all round, and one needs a room all windows."

They went downstairs. As they approached the cool dining-room, with its portraits and silver and old blue china, a very sweet voice floated out. "He said, 'Exactly, madam! You take your money to market in the market-basket, and you bring home what you buy in your pocketbook!'"

The next day and the next they spent in part at a hospital, in part breathlessly waiting with the waiting city for news, news, news! — news from Spottsylvania, where the great fighting was in progress; news from south of the river, where Butler, most hated of all foes, was entrenched, where there was fighting at Port Walthall; news, on the tenth, of Sheridan's approach, of much burning and destroying, news that Stuart was countering Sheridan. "Oh, it is all right, then!" said many; but yet by day and by night there was tenseness of apprehension.

All the town was hot and breathless. The alarm bell rang, the dust whirled through the streets. The night of the tenth, Judith and Unity were wakened by a drum beating. A minute later a voice spoke outside their door. "Sheridan is within a few miles of Richmond. He is moving on us with eight thousand horse. Your cousin says you had better get up and dress."

All of the household except the sleeping children gathered on the porch that overhung the pavement. It was two o'clock. The drum was still beating and now there came by soldiers. *We're going out the Brook Turnpike*, said the drum. *Out the Brook Turnpike. Meet them! We're going to meet them!* Three or four regiments passed. The drum turned a corner and the sound died, going northward. The streets were filled with people as though it were day. They went up and down quietly enough; without panic, but seized by a profound restlessness. Toward four o'clock a man came riding up the street on horseback, stopping every hundred yards or so to say in a loud, manly voice, "The President has heard from General Stuart. With Fitzhugh Lee and Hampton and Munford, General

Stuart has taken position between us and a large cavalry force under Sheridan. There has been a fight at Ashland in which we were victors. General Stuart is now approaching Yellow Tavern. The President says, 'Good people, go to bed, Richmond's got a great shield before it!'"

The eleventh dawned. Richmond now heard the cannon again, from the north and from the south. Judith and Unity heard them from the hospital windows. There was a delirious soldier whom they had to hold in bed because he thought that it was his battery fighting against odds, and Pegram was calling him. "Yes, Major! I'm coming! Yes, Major! I've got the powder. I'm coming!" By ten o'clock ran through the excited ward the tidings that they were fighting, fighting in Spottsylvania, "Fighting like hell." The sound of cannon came from the south side. "Butler over there — New Orleans Butler! ——! —— ——! When's Beauregard coming?"

"General Beauregard has come. He is at Petersburg."

"Miss What's-your-name, why don't you warm your hands? That ain't any way to touch poor sick soldiers with them icicles like that! — O Lord, O Lord! Why'd I ever come here?"

"Them cannon's getting louder all the time. Louder'n', louder'n', louder —"

"Shoo! They can't cross the river. Where's Jeb Stuart? What's he doing?"

"He's fighting hard, six miles out, at Yellow Tavern. Uptown you can hear the firing!"

A young man struggled up in bed, first coughing, then breathing with a loud, whistling sound. The doctor glanced his way, then ·d at a nurse. "It's come. I'll give him something so he can go easily. Let him lean against you. Tell the men to try to be quiet."

Out at Yellow Tavern, six miles north of Richmond, Sheridan was formed in line of battle. Over against him was Stuart, his men dismounted. The blue delivered a great volley, advanced, volleyed again, advanced, shouting. The grey returned their fire. James Stuart, sitting his horse just behind his battle-line, swung his hat, lifted his voice that was the voice of a magician, "Steady, men, steady! Give a good day's account of yourself! Steady! Steady!"

The firing became fiercer and closer. There was a keening sound in the air. Stuart's voice suddenly dropped; he swayed in his saddle.

A mounted courier pressed toward him. "Go," he said; "go tell General Lee and Dr. Fontaine to come here." The courier spurred away and the men around Stuart lifted him from his horse, and, mourning, bore him to the rear.

That evening they brought him into the city and laid him in the house of his brother-in-law. His wife was sent for, but she was miles away, in the troubled, overrun countryside, and though she fared toward him in haste and anguish, she spoke to him no more alive. Friends were around him — his mourning officers, all the mourning city. The President came and stood beside the bed, and tried to thank him. "You have saved Richmond, General. You have always been a bulwark to us . . ." He asked for a hymn that he liked — "I would not live alway." He had lived but thirty-one years. He asked often for his wife. "Is she come?" . . . "Is she come?" She could not come in time. The evening of the twelfth he died, quite peacefully, and those who looked on his dead face said that the sunshine abided.

They buried Jeb Stuart in Hollywood, buried him with no pageantry of martial or of civil woe. One year ago there had been in Richmond for Stonewall Jackson such pageantry. To-day

"We could not pause, while yet the noontide air
Shook with the cannonade's incessant pealing . . .

"One weary year ago, when came a lull,
With victory in the conflict's stormy closes,
When the glad spring, all flushed and beautiful,
First mocked us with her roses —

"With dirge and bell and minute gun we paid
Some few poor rites, an inexpressive token,
Of a great people's pain, to Jackson's shade,
In agony unspoken.

"No wailing trumpet and no tolling bell,
No cannon, save the battle's boom receding,
When Stuart to the grave we bore, might tell,
With hearts all crushed and bleeding . . ."

But the people thronged to Hollywood, above the rushing river. Hollow and hill, ivy-mantled oaks and grass purpled with violets, the place was a good one in which to lay down the outworn form that had done service and was loved. Flowers grew there with a wild luxuriance. To-day they were brought beside from all gardens—

> "We well remembered how he loved to dash,
> Into the fight, festooned from summer's bowers.
> How like a fountain's spray, his sabre flash,
> Leaped from a mass of flowers —"

To-day flowers lined the open grave; they covered the coffin and the flag.

Back in the hospital a man with three wounds wailed all night. " I had a brother and he was living up North and so he thought that-er-way. And he wrote that he held by the Nation just as hard as I held by the State. And so he up and joined the Army of the Potomac and came down here. And in the Wilderness the other day — and in the Wilderness the other day — oh, in the Wilderness the other day — I was sharpshooting! I was up in a tree, close to the bark, like a 'pecker. There was a gully below with a stream running down it, and on the other side of the gully was an oak with a man in it, close to the bark like a 'pecker. And we were Yank and Johnny Reb, and so every time one of us showed as much as the tip of a 'pecker's wing, the other one fired. We fired and fired. And at last he wasn't so cautious, and I got him. And first his musket fell, down and down, for he was up high. And then the body came and it hit every bough as it came. And something in me gave a word of command. It said 'Go and look.' I got down out of the oak, for I was in an oak tree, too, and I went down one side of the gully and up the other. And he was lying all doubled up. And I got another word of command, ' Turn him over.' And I did, and he was my brother. . . . And I'm tired of war."

CHAPTER XXVIII

COLD HARBOUR

THESE were the moves of the following two weeks. Six days, from the day of the Bloody Angle to the eighteenth of May, the two armies stayed as they were, save for slight, shifting, wary movements, as of two opposed Indians in the brush. On the eighteenth, the blue attacked — again the salient. Ewell, with thirty guns, broke and scattered the assault. On the nineteenth, the "sidling" process recommenced. On this day Ewell came into contact with the Federal left, and in the engagement that ensued both sides lost heavily. The night of the twentieth, the Army of the Potomac, Hancock leading, started for the North Anna. The morning of the twenty-first, the Army of Northern Virginia struck, by the Telegraph Road, for the same stream. It had the inner line, and it got there first. At noon the twenty-second it began to cross the river. That night Lee and his men rested on the southern bank. Morning of the twenty-third showed on the opposite shore the head of the blue column.

The blue crossed at Jericho Ford, and by the Chesterfield Bridge, not without conflict and trouble. It won over, but over in two distinctly separated wings, and that which separated them was Robert Edward Lee and the Army of Northern Virginia. Here was now another V, the point now upon the river, unassailable, the sides entrenched, the blue army split in twain. Followed two days of unavailing attempts to find a way to crush the V. Then, on the night of the twenty-sixth, the blue, having fairly effectively hidden its intention, "sidled" again. The Army of the Potomac left the North Anna, taking the road for the Pamunkey which it crossed at Hanover. The V at once became a column and followed.

The two antagonists were now approaching old and famed war grounds. On the twenty-eighth, grey cavalry and blue cavalry — Sheridan against Fitz Lee and Wade Hampton — crashed together at Hawes's Shop. That night Army of the Potomac, Army of Northern Virginia, watched each the other's camp-fires on the banks of the Totopotomoy. In the morning Grant started for the Chickahominy, but when he reached Cold Harbour it was to find Lee between him and the river.

Two days the two foes rested. There had been giant marching through giant heat, constant watching, much fighting. The country that was difficult in the days of McClellan was not less so in the days of Grant. Marsh and swamp and thicket and hidden roads, and now all desolate from years of war. . . . The first of June passed, the second of June passed, with skirmishes and engagements that once the country would have stood a-tiptoe to hear of. Now they were nothing. The third of June the battle of Cold Harbour crashed into history. . . .

The dawn came up, crowned with pale violets, majestical and still. Upon the old woods, the old marshes, hung a mist, cool and silvery. There came a sweet cry of birds in the grey tree-tops. Lee's long grey lines, concave to the foe, stretched from Alexander's Bridge on the Chickahominy to the upper Totopotomoy. On the low earthworks hung the gossamers, dewy bright. Grant held the Sydnor's Sawmill, Bethesda Church, and Old Cold Harbour line, roughly paralleling the other. But he was north of Lee; Lee was again between him and Richmond — Richmond so near now, so very near! Richmond was there before him — no room now for "swinging past," and the lion was there, too, in the path.

Grant attacked in column. Deep and narrow-fronted, he thrust against the grey earthworks like a giant mill-race rather than a wide ocean, like one solid catapult rather than a mailed fist at every door. Twenty deep, the Second and Sixth Corps poured into the depression that was the grey centre. Second and Sixth came on with a shout, and the grey answered with a shout and with every musket and cannon. Following the Second and Sixth the Eighteenth, phalanxed, dashed itself against a salient held by Kershaw. . . . The battle of Cold Harbour was the briefest, the direst! Death swung a scythe against the three corps. They were in the gulf of the grey, and Fate came upon them from three sides. In effect, it was all over in a very few minutes. . . . The shattered three corps fell back to what cover they could find. Here they fired ineffectively from this shelter and from that. Before them, between them and the Army of Northern Virginia, stretched the plain of their dead and dying, and both lay upon it like leaves in autumn. Orders came that the three corps should again attack. The more advanced commands obeyed by opening fire from behind what shelter they had found or could contrive, but there was no other movement. Put out a hand and the wind began to whistle and the air over that plain to grow dark with lead! Grant sent a third order. *Corps of Hancock, Smith, and Wright to advance to the charge along the whole line.* Corps commanders repeated the order to division commanders; division commanders repeated it to the brigadiers, but that was all. The three corps stood still. Statements, differing as to wording but tallying in meaning, travelled from grade to grade, back to Headquarters. "It is totally impossible, and the men know it. They are not to be blamed."

By noon even Grant, who rarely knew when he was beaten, knew that he was beaten here. The firing sank away. "The dead and dying lay in front of the Confederate lines in triangles, of which the apexes were the bravest men who came nearest to the breastworks under the withering, deadly fire." Dead and wounded and missing, ten thousand men in blue felt the full force of that hour. Stubborn to the end, it was two days before Grant would send a flag of truce and ask permission to bury his dead and gather the wounded who had not raved themselves to death. "Cold Harbour!" he said, much later in his life; "Cold Harbour is, I think, the only battle I ever fought that I would not fight over again under the circumstances!"

"In the opinion of a majority of its survivors," comments a Federal general, "the battle of Cold Harbour never should have been fought. It was the dreary, dismal, bloody, ineffective close of the Lieutenant-General's first campaign with the Army of the Potomac, and corresponded in all its essential features with what had preceded it. The wide and winding path through the tangled Wilderness and the pines of Spottsylvania, which that army had cut from the Rapidan to the Chickahominy, had been strewn with the bodies of thousands of brave men, the majority of them wearing the Union blue."

The Campaign of the Thirty Days was ended. Fifty-four thousand men was the loss of the blue; something over half that number the loss of the grey. Eighty thousand men lay dead, or writhing in war-hospitals, or sat bowed in war-prisons. From the Atlantic to the Far West the current of human being in these States was troubled. There grew a sickness of feeling. The sun seemed to warm less strongly and the moon to shine less calmly. As always in war, the best and bravest from the first were taking flight; many and many of the good and brave were left, but they began to be conscious of a loneliness. *"All, all are gone — the old, familiar faces!"* And over the land sounded the mourning of homes — the mourning of the mothers and daughters of men. In the South life sank a minor third. The chords resounded still, but the wrists that struck were growing weak. *Largo . . . Largo.*

For a week Army of Northern Virginia, Army of the Potomac, stood opposed on the old lines. They entrenched and entrenched, working by night; they made much and deadly use of sharpshooters, they engaged in artillery duels, in alarums and excursions. On both sides life in the trenches was very frightful. They were so crowded, and the sharpshooters would not let you sleep. The water was bad, and little of it, and on the grey side, at least, there was hunger. The sun in heaven burned like a fiery furnace. Far and wide, through the tangled country, lay the unburied bodies of men and horses. Sickness appeared, — malaria, dysentery. Hour after hour, day after day, you lay in the quivering heat, in the unshaded trench. Put out arm or head — some sharpshooter's finger pulled a trigger.

In these days there began in the Valley of Virginia a movement of vandalism under Hunter who had succeeded Sigel. On the fifth of June, Lee sent thither Breckinridge with a small force. On the twelfth, with his calm, reasoned audacity, acting under the shadow of Grant's continually reinforced army, he detached Jubal Early, sent him with Stonewall Jackson's old Second Corps, by way of Charlottesville to the old hunting-grounds of the Second Corps, to the Valley of Virginia.

The night of the twelfth of June, Grant lifted his tents and pushed to the eastward away from Richmond, then to the south, to Wilcox Landing below Malvern Hill, on the James. Here, where the river was seven hundred yards in width, fifty feet in depth, he built a very great bridge of boats, and here the Army of the Potomac crossed to the south side of the James. Grant turned his face toward Petersburg, twenty miles from Richmond.

The forces of the North were now where McClellan had wished to place them, using the great waterway of the Chesapeake and the James, something more than two years ago. They were in a position to mate. The Federal Government had worked the problem by the Rule of False.

At dawn of the thirteenth, Lee left the lines of Cold Harbour and, passing the Chickahominy, bivouacked that night between White Oak Swamp and Malvern Hill. The next day and the next the Army of Northern Virginia crossed the James by pontoon at Drewry's Bluff, and pressed south to the Appomattox and the old town of Petersburg. Here was Beauregard, and here, on the fifteenth, Butler, by Grant's orders, had launched an attack from Bermuda Hundred, heroically repulsed by the small grey force at Petersburg. Now on the sixteenth and the seventeenth came Lee and the Army of Northern Virginia, entering the lines of Petersburg while drum and fife played "Dixie." Of the Army of the Potomac the Second and Ninth Corps were up and in position, the Fifth upon the road. Face to face again were Hector and Achilles, Army of Northern Virginia, Army of the Potomac, but the first again held the inner line. South of Richmond as north of Richmond, Grant found Lee between him and Richmond.

There was a garden behind the kinsman's house in Richmond. Cleave and Judith, coming from the house, found it empty this afternoon save for its roses and its birds. A high wall, ivy-covered, cloistered it from the street. Beneath the tulip tree was a bench and they sat themselves down here. He leaned his head back against the bark and closed his eyes. It was several days before the lifting of the warring pieces across the river. With the Second Corps he was on his way to the Valley. "I did not know," he said, "that I was so tired. I have not slept for two nights."

"Sleep now. I will sit here, just as quietly —"

He smiled. "It is very likely that I would do that, is it not?" Bending his head, he took her hands and pressed his forehead upon them. "Judith — Judith — Judith —"

The birds sang, the roses bloomed. From the south came a dull booming, the cannon of Beauregard and of Butler, distant, continuous, like surf on breakers. The two paid it no especial attention.

Life had been set now for a long while to such an accompaniment. There was something at least as old as strife, and that was love; as old and as strong and as perpetually renewed.

The shadows lengthened on the grass. There came a sound of bugles blowing. The lovers turned and clung and kissed, then in the violet light their hands fell apart. Cleave rose. "They are singing, 'Come away!'" he said.

There were stars in a wreath now upon the collar of his coat. She touched them, smiling through tears. "*General Cleave.* . . . It comes late but it comes well. . . . Oh, my general, my general!"

"Little enough of the Stonewall Brigade remains," he said. "For the most part what was not killed and was not captured at Spottsylvania has been gathered into Terry's brigade, and goes, too, to the Valley. But the Sixty-fifth goes with me and the Golden Brigade. The Golden Brigade cares for me because I am Warwick Cary's kinsman."

"Not alone for that," she said, "but for that also . . . Oh, my father — my father!"

From the street outside the garden wall came a sound of marching feet. Above the ivy showed, passing, the bayonet points. It was sunset and the west was crimson. Swallows circled above the house and the gold cups of the tulip tree. The marching feet went on, and the gleaming bayonet points. There came a flag, half visible above the ivy, silken, powder-darkened, battle-scarred. Cleave raised his hand in salute. The flag went by, the sound of the marching feet continued. High in the tree, against the rosy sky, a bird with a lyric throat began to sing, piercing sweet and clear.

"Judith," said Cleave, "before I go, there is a thing I want to tell you. Two days ago I was riding by A. P. Hill's lines. There was a marshy place, on the edge of which the men were raising a breast-work. Judith, I am certain that I saw Stafford. He has done as I did — done what was and is the simple, the natural thing to do. Whether under his own name or another, he is there, heaping breast-works as a private soldier."

"He could not do as you did! You went clear and clean, and he—"

"I do not know that there is ever any sharp line of difference. It is a matter of degree. I have come," said Cleave simply, "to understand myself less and other people more. I did not show that I recognized him, for I could not tell if he would wish it . . . I thought that you should know. It is not a time now for enmities."

"God knows that that is true," said Judith, weeping.

CHAPTER XXIX

LITTLE PUMPKIN–VINE CREEK

THE log cabin looked out upon a wooded world, a world that rolled and shimmered, gold-green, blue-green, violet-green, to horizons of bright summer sky. In the distance, veiled with light, sprang Lost Mountain and the cone of Kennesaw. Far or near there were hamlets—Powder Spring, Burnt Hickory, Roxanna—north, there was the village of Allatoona, and south, that of Dallas; but from the log cabin all were sunk in a sea of emerald. New Hope Church was somewhere near, but its opening, too, was hardly more than guessed at. But Pumpkin-Vine Creek might be seen in its meanderings, and the rippling daughter stream that the soldiers called "Little Pumpkin-Vine" flashed by the hill on which stood the cabin.

It was a one-room-and-a-lean-to, broken-down, deserted, log-and-clay thing. Whoever had lived in it had flown, leaving ashes on the hearth, and a hop-vine flowering over a tiny porch. A monster pine tree, scaled like a serpent, sent its brown shaft a hundred feet in air. Upon the sandy hilltop grew pennyroyal. Pine and pennyroyal, the intense sunshine drew out their strength. All the air was dryness and warmth and a pleasant odour.

Steadying himself by the lintel Edward Cary rose from the log that made the doorstep. A stick leaned against the wall. He took this, and proceeded, slow-paced, to make his way to the pine tree and the low brink of the hill above the creek. The transit occupied some minutes, but at last he reached the pine, tired but happy. There was a wonderful purple-brown carpet beneath. He half sat, half reclined upon it, and leaning forward watched Désirée on her knees before a little shallow bay of the creek. It was washerwoman's day. There were stepping-stones in the clear brown water, and she was across the stream, her head downbent, very intently scrubbing.

"O saw ye bonny Lesley," —

sang Edward, —

> "As she gaed o'er the Border?
> She's gane like Alexander,
> To spread her conquests further."

Désirée straightened herself. "How did you come there? I left you asleep. Ah, a wicked patient — a malingerer!"

"The cabin was cold, so I came out into the sun."

She rose from her knees, took up the small heap of her washing, and, stepping lightly from stone to stone, came to his side of the water. Here, in a square of absolute gold, she spread the washing out to dry. Her sleeves were rolled up to her shoulders, her thick and beautiful hair hung braided to her knee, she looked in that quaint place like an enchanted princess out of a rosy fairy tale.

> "O my Luve's like a red, red rose," —

sang Edward, —

> "That's newly sprung in June:
> O my Luve's like the melodie,
> That's sweetly played in tune! —"

Désirée turned, came up the pennyroyal bank, and sat beside him on the pine-needle carpet. Bending, he pressed his lips on her bare arm.

> "As fair art thou, my bonnie lass,
> So deep in luve am I —"

In the distance they heard the sound of axes against the trees. Breastworks and rifle-pits were in the making over there. Light curls of smoke told where were camp-fires. Not far away the creek was crossed by a wood road. Now a score of horses with three guardian men came down to the ford to drink. Somewhere a bugle sounded. Brown and black and grey, the horses pricked their ears; then, satisfied that it was not battery bugle, dropped again to the cool water. Out of the forest across Little Pumpkin-Vine came a steady, dreamy humming — voices of the Army of Tennessee, encamped here, encamped there, in this region south of the Etowah.

"I should like to die on a day like this," said Désirée. "Just such a day — and life so strong and sweet! To touch, taste, smell, hear, see, feel, and know it all — and then to go, carrying the flavour with you!"

"With which to set up housekeeping again?"

"With which to set up housekeeping again — in a larger, better house."

"But with old comrades?"

She let the pine needles stream through her hands. "Certainly with old comrades. Father . . . Louis . . . People who used to come to Cape Jessamine, people I have known elsewhere. . . . All people, in fact, and all in better, larger houses . . . all old comrades" — she turned and kissed him — "and one lover."

"In a better, nobler house," said Edward. "But don't die, Désirée — not yet — not yet —"

The creek murmured, the wind whispered, the wild bees hummed above the flowers. Somewhere down the stream was an army forge. *Clink! clink!* went hammer against iron. On some hidden road, too, guns were passing — you heard the rumble and the whinnying of the horses. In another direction wagons were parked; there was a sense, through vague openings in a leafy world, of the white, bubble-like tops. More horses came to the ford to be watered. The sun grew brighter and brighter, climbing the sky, the pine and penny-royal more pungently alive, the voices in the wide woods distincter, less like a dreamy wash of the sea. The hazel bushes across the stream parted and two men appeared with water-buckets. They dipped for their mess, adjusted their heavy wet burdens and went away, sociably talking.

"'T was while we was fighting at Cassville. Jake thought he was killed, but he was n't! Funny fellow, but you can't help liking him!"

"That's so! He's got converted. Converted last meeting. Says he don't know but one prayer and was kind of surprised he remembered that. Says it now before every little fight we go into. Says —

> "'*Now I lay me down to sleep,*
> *Pray the Lord my soul to keep —*'"

"Sho! Everybody remembers that! Taught it to us most before we could talk!

> "'*Now I lay me down to sleep,*
> *Pray the Lord my soul to keep,*
> *If I should die before I wake*
> *Pray the Lord my soul to take —*'"

The hazel bushes closed and the voices died like a ripple out of water. The light grew more golden, the shadows shorter. Late May in Georgia was more hot than a Northern midsummer, but to-day a crisp breeze made the heat of no moment. The air was very dry, life-giving. A soldier with a fishing-pole made his appearance. He came along beneath the bank and the pine tree, chose a deepish pool and a rock to sit on, placed a tin cup with bait beside the latter, and had baited his hook and cast the line before he observed his neighbours. He rose and saluted, then made a movement to take up his bait-cup and proceed downstream.

"No, no!" said Edward. "Fish ahead! But are there any fish there?"

The fisherman sat down upon the rock. "I'm not really expecting any. But catching fish is not all there is in fishing."

"Quite true," said Edward, and lay back upon the purple-brown carpet. Désirée sat with her hands about her knee, her eyes upon a vast castle of cloud, rising pearl-bright, into the azure sky.

The fisherman fished, but caught nothing. "I expect," he said, "that there is good fishing in the Etowah. Looked so the day we crossed it."

"That was a hard crossing," said Désirée.

"Hard enough!" answered the fisherman. "But Old Joe got us across. I am not one of the grumblers."

"There was n't much grumbling."

"That's so! Army of Tennessee's a right fine body of men." He cast again. "It's quieter than Sleepy Hollow this morning! There was a considerable rumpus yesterday. They say, too, that General Wheeler got in on their rear and beat a brigade and captured two hundred and fifty wagons. I reckon we'll hear raindrops on the roof before night!"

"I should n't be surprised."

"These pesky little battles," said the fisherman. "I've stopped counting them — Thought I had a bite!"

"Many a little makes a mickle."

"That's true! We've been fighting for a month, and we're walking round to-day like a game-cock looking at his spurs. Army of Tennessee and Joseph E. Johnston."

He bent his eyes upon his pole. The wind sung in the pine tree, *clink! clink!* went the forge downstream. The pearly cloud castle rose higher. Off on the left, where was Hardee's corps, a bugle trilled as sweetly as a bird. There were a million forest odours, with the pine, played upon by the sunshine, for dominant. The dry pure air was life-giving.

"I gather," said the fisherman, "that there are, on our side, two theories as to the conduct of this war. The one wants great crashing battles that shall force the foe to cry, 'Hold, enough!' — 'Fight him on sight, and without regard to odds.' The other says, 'We have n't got many men, and when they 're gone, we have no more. There 's only one set of chessmen in this establishment. So spare your men. We 've got a Goliath to fight. Well, don't rush at him! — Fence with him; maybe you 'll prove the better fencer. Don't strike just to be striking; strike when you see an advantage to follow! You can't thrash him outright; he 's too big. But you may *wear* him out. Giants sometimes lack a giant patience. This one has a considerable clamour for peace behind him at home. Save your men, strike only when there 's sense in striking, and take Time into your councils! You may not win this way, but you certainly won't the other way.' The first 's the Administration and a considerable part of the press, and the last 's Joseph E. Johnston."

" 'There was a general named Fabius,' " said Edward. — "You 're a good observer."

"I 'm a better observer than I am a fisherman," said the disciple of Walton.

Désirée stepped down the bank into the square of gold and gathered up her washing. With it over one arm she returned and gave her hands to Edward. They said good-day to the fisherman, and went away, up the slight hill, Edward doing well with his stick and an arm over her shoulder. They laughed like children in the sunshine.

They had what she called "tisane" for dinner — "tisane" with hard-tack crumbled in. A drummer-boy, straying by, was given his share. They sat on billets of wood underneath the hop-vine, ate and drank and were happy. The boy was fourteen and small for his age. He had a shock of sunburnt hair and a happy, freckled face, and he said that he hoped the war would never stop. When every crumb and drop was gone, he volunteered to "wash up," and went whistling down to Little Pumpkin-Vine with the tin cups and spoons and small, black kettle.

Other soldiers strayed past the cabin. An orderly appeared, sent by officers' mess of the ——th Virginia. He bore, together with enquiries and messages, to-morrow's rations. A picket detail went marching over the hilltop. About three o'clock came a clattering of horses' hoofs. The hill was a fair post of observation, and here was the commanding general with his staff. All stopped beneath the pine; Johnston pointed with his hand, now here, now there; his chief of staff beside him nodding comprehension.

Then the General, dismounting, came over to the cabin. "No, no! don't stand!" he said to Edward. "I only want to ask Mrs. Cary for a cup of water. How is the wound to-day?"

"Very much better, sir. I'll report for duty presently."

"Don't hurry," said Johnston, with kindness. "It's a mistake to get well too quickly." He had much warm magnetism, tenderness with illness, an affectionate deference always toward women. He took the cup of water from Désirée, thanked her, and said that evidently the campaign had not harmed her. "Women always were the best soldiers."

General Mackall had ridden up. "There's many a true word said in jest," he remarked.

"I did n't say it in jest, sir," said Johnston. He mounted and gathered up the reins, an erect and soldierly figure. "General Hood," he said, "is moving from Allatoona, and I have ordered Hardee's corps back from the Dallas and Atlanta road. There may come a general battle on this ground. If it arrives, my dear," — he spoke to Désirée, — "you apply for an ambulance and leave this cabin!"

Off he rode in the golden light. At sunset came marching by the ——th Virginia, going toward New Hope Church. The road ran behind the cabin. Désirée helped Edward out to it, and they stood in a little patch of sunflowers and greeted the regiment. The regiment to a man greeted back. The colonel stopped his horse and talked, the captains smiled and nodded, the men gave the two a cheer. It was one of the friendly, sunshiny moments of war. The regiment was like a dear and good family; everywhere in and out ran the invisible threads of kindliness. The regiment passed, the rhythmic beat of feet dying from this stretch of the road. Désirée and Edward went back to the cabin through the languorous, Southern dusk, with the lanterns of the fire-flies beginning, and the large moths sailing by. There was a moon, and all night, in the wood behind the cabin, a mocking-bird was singing.

The next day and the next and the next there was fighting — not "a great, crashing battle," but stubborn fighting. It waxed furious enough where Hooker struck Stewart's division of Hood's at New Hope Church, and where, on the twenty-eighth, Cleburne and Wheeler met and forced back Palmer and Howard; but when calm came again only a couple of thousand of each colour lay dead or wounded around New Hope Church.

The calm fell on Sunday. Edward and Désirée, sitting beneath the pine tree, marked the cannons' diminuendo. It was a hot and heavy day and the dead and wounded were on their hearts. Yet to them, too, it was fearfully an everyday matter. The time to visualize what will fall under the harrow of war is before the harrow is set in motion. Afterwards comes in Inevitableness with iron lips, and Fatalism with unscrutinizing gaze, and Use with filmed eyes, and Instinct with her cry, "Do not look too closely, seeing one must keep one's senses!" and Old Habit with her motto, "True children do as their fathers did." — And so at last, on both sides, from the general to the drummer-boy, from the civil ruler to the woman scraping lint, no one looks very closely at what falls beneath the harrow. Madness lies that way, and in war one must be very sane. No one escaped the taint of not looking, not even the two beneath the pine tree.

Off in the horizon clouds were piling up. Presently there was heard a mutter of thunder. Edward and Désirée watched the sky darken and the big pine begin to sway. In the distance there was yet an occasional boom of cannon. "That is toward Dallas," said Edward. "Earth thunder and heaven thunder."

The lightning flashed. The earth voices began to lose out, the aërial ones to gather strength. A wind lifted the dust and the small dry débris of grass and herb. The old pine cones came shaking down. The thunder began to peal. Désirée rose. "We must go indoors. It has the right of way now — the old, old storm."

As they reached the cabin the thunder grew loud above them.

The dust of the earth went by in a whirlwind. Rain was falling, in heavy pellets like lead, but as yet it had not lightened the oppression. The two leaned against the doorway and watched. A blinding flash, a sound as of falling battlements of the sky, and the pine tree was blasted before them.

CHAPTER XXX

KENNESAW

THE blue army was massed beyond Noonday Creek, in front of Pine Mountain, and on the Burnt Hickory road. The grey held a line from Gilgal Church to a point beyond the Marietta and Ackworth road. It was the fourteenth of June — news just received by way of Atlanta of Grant's movement toward the James. On the crest of Pine Mountain was a grey outpost — Bates's Division of Hardee's corps. At Gilgal Church, Johnston, on his chestnut horse, was in conversation with that churchman-militant with a Spartan name — Lieutenant-General Leonidas Polk. Hardee rode up. "General, I should be grateful if you would come with me to the top of the mountain yonder. Bates there is too exposed."

The three, Johnston with Hardee and Polk, rode through the thick brush, by a narrow and rough bridle-path, up to the crown of the low mountain. Dismounting in the rear of Bates's works they went forward on foot, the men saluting where they lay behind heaped logs. Overhanging the slope was a parapet, and the three walked here, opening their field-glasses as they walked. Before them stretched the wooded country, and full in sight, the heavy lines of the foe. Not a thousand feet away a field-battery held a hilltop.

"Wait till nightfall," said Johnston, "then let Bates join you at Gilgal."

He lowered his field-glass. Out of the mouth of one of the blue cannon on the hilltop came a puff of white smoke. The shot cut away a bough of the oak under which the three were standing. "Certainly this parapet is too exposed," said Hardee. "Come this way, General." As they moved diagonally across the spur, the blue guns opened full pack. A shot passed through the breast of Leonidas Polk, sometime Bishop of Louisiana. He fell, lying at full length upon the summit, dead, with a pleasant look upon his face.

On the sixteenth, grey left and blue right shifted positions, coming again to face each other. There was skirmishing and cavalry fighting. On the nineteenth, the two fencers again changed ground. The grey left, Hardee, now stretched across the Lost Mountain and Marietta road; the grey right, Hood, lay beyond the Canton road; and Loring, who had succeeded Polk, held flank and crest of Kennesaw Mountain. At once, grey and blue, the interminable entrenching began again, the grey throwing up earthworks and defences, the blue making lines of approach. Throughout the latter half of June, hour after hour, day after day, night after night, there was fighting. The first half of the month it had poured rain. Torrent after torrent had successfully interfered with man's operations. Under streaming skies, with the earth semi-liquid, the roads bottomless, the unending forest like oozy growths of an ocean floor, entrenching, manœuvres for advantage of position, attack and parry — one and all had been attended with difficulties. General Rain and General Mud had as usual put their unrecorded fingers into the current of events. But now, though sun and cloud still fought, the roads were drying and there was fighting every day.

Up on the crest of Kennesaw, Edward Cary, lying with his men behind a work of earth and logs, saw the sun rise and the sun set, and often in the dead of night the solemn pomp of stars. All around him, beneath the stars, were the shadowy forms of sleeping men. The footfall of the pickets could be heard, that and the breathing of the sleepers. Slowly came on the grey dawn; reveille sounded and the day's work was before you. Night came again and the stars and the shadowy forms of men — though not all, who were breathing the night before, breathed now where they slept.

Cary's mind ranged far from the comfortless top of Kennesaw. First of all and oftenest it looked southward, across the forest, to where, in a farmhouse near Smyrna Church, Désirée slept or waked. It paused there, suspended, watching her where she lay, then passed from the quiet room and swept in widening circles around the core of life. . . . This Georgian battle-ground! Fifty days now of a great strategic campaign — Dalton and the spring-time far behind — Atlanta and the pitched battle that must toss victory into this camp or into that drawing nearer. The Army of Tennessee, stanch and cheerful even in the rain-filled rifle-pits on Kennesaw; gaunt, heroic, like its brother the Army of Northern Virginia. . . . Not the Georgia battle-grounds alone; — all battle-fields — all the South one battle-field, fringed and crossed with weary, weary, weary marches! Suddenly he saw how red were the rivers and how many houses were blackened ruins. There was a great loneliness, and he thought he saw children straying, lost, across the plain. Edward sat up and rested his forehead on his hands. "What is it all for?" he thought. "It is absurd." The sky was clear to-night. He looked up at the Great Bear and the Dragon. "We are in a world of contradictories. There is the heroic, the piteous, and the beautiful, there is a loud and sweet music, — and yet it is all in the service of the King of the Dwarfs, of a gnome with a gnome's brain. . . . How to change the service?"

In the cold hour before the dawn, he slept, to be presently awakened by the sound of the pickets' pieces and a night attack. Half an hour's fighting rolled it back, down Kennesaw, but when it was done the men were kept awake lest the wave should return.

They talked, behind the breastworks, while the stars faded. "Wish it was a false alarm! Wish I'd wake up and find myself asleep."

"O God, yes! In my bed at home."

"Talking about false alarms — Did you ever hear about Spaulding?"

"What Spaulding? — No."

"It was in Mississippi; — Grant somewhere near, but nobody knew how near; — all of us scattered over a few hills and marshes, keeping pretty good lookout, but yet knowing that nobody could be within a day's march of us. In comes Spaulding in haste to headquarters, to the general's tent. In he comes, pale and excited, and he brings a piece of news that was indeed alarming! He had been on a hill overlooking the river — I forget its name — there's such an infinity of rivers in this country! Anyhow he had seen the most amazing thing, and that was what he had come like lightning back to the camp to tell the general about. A column of the enemy was crossing the river — they had laid pontoons and they were crossing by them and by a ford as well. It was a large force — a division undoubtedly, possibly a corps. Artillery was crossing as he looked. The ford was black with infantry, and there was cavalry on the farther bank. A man on a great black horse was directing. On this

side was a man on a very tall grey horse, a man with a bloody handkerchief tied round his head under his hat. The troops saluted him
as they came out of the water. All were crossing very silently and
swiftly. Spaulding had run all the way from the hill; he had to put
his hand to his side as he talked, he was so breathed. — Well, immediately there was activity enough at headquarters, but still activity with a doubt, it was so amazing! What were the pickets doing
— to say nothing of the cavalry? Well, the long roll was beaten, and
everybody scurried to arms, and off went two aides at full speed to
the hilltop to examine that thief in the night-time crossing, and
Spaulding went behind the one on the strongest horse. He was just
as calm and sure. 'Yes, it's amazing, but it's so! I think the man
on the black horse is Grant. I could n't see the face of the man on
the grey horse—only the bloody cloth around his head.' Well, they
got there, all the fuss behind them of the regiments forming — they
got to the hilltop and there was the river sure enough before them,
just as the aides knew it would be. 'Now, you see!' says Spaulding,
for he had been hurt by the way everybody, even the general, said,
'Impossible!' — 'See what?' say the aides. 'Are you mad?' asks
Spaulding impatiently. 'The bridge and the ford and the crossing
guns and infantry, the man on the black horse and the man on the
grey with the cloth around his head.' — One of the aides rides down
the hillside toward the river and finds a picket. 'Have you seen anything unusual up or down or across the river?' 'No,' says the picket,
or words to that effect. 'Have you?' —Well, that aide goes back
and he takes Spaulding by the shoulders and shakes him. And then
the two, they stand on either side of him, and the one says, 'Look
now, and pretty quick about it, and tell us what you see!' — 'You
damned fools,' says Spaulding, 'I see a column crossing, infantry
and artillery, a man on a black horse directing, and a man on a grey
horse with a bloody cloth —' And then he stopped speaking and
stared, the colour going out of his face and his eyes starting from
his head. And presently he just slipped like water down between
them and sat upon the earth. 'Great God!' he said, 'there is n't
anything there!' — So they took him back to headquarters, the
drums still beating and everybody getting into ranks —"

"What did they do to him?"

"Well, if he'd been a drinking man he'd have been drumhead

court-martialled and shot. But he was n't — he was a nice, clean, manly kind of young fellow, a great mathematician, and the boys all liked him, and his officers, too. And he was so covered with confusion 't was pitiful. The general's a mighty good man. He said those things happened sometimes, and he quoted Shakespeare that there are more experiences in heaven and earth — or words to that effect. Spaulding was put under arrest, and there was enquiry and all that, but at the last he was given a caution and sent back to his regiment. But he kind of pined away and took to mooning, and in the next battle he was killed — and killed, that was the funny thing, by a pistol shot from a man on a grey horse with a bloody handkerchief tied round his head! He shot Spaulding through the brain."

The sun pushed a red rim above the eastern horizon. The day's work began. Fighting—and fighting — and fighting again on Kennesaw and over the rolling country from which Kennesaw arose! On the twentieth, Wheeler with a thousand horsemen crashed against and drove a force of blue cavalry. On the twenty-second, on the Powder Spring road, Hood struck Schofield and Hooker. The divisions of Hindman and Stevenson were engaged here, advancing with heroism under a plunging fire, musketry and artillery, and driving the blue from their first to their second line of entrenchments. The ground was fearfully difficult. The blue had everywhere epaulements from which they brought to bear upon the charging grey a terrible raking fire of grape and canister. Stevenson's men fell thick and fast; when night laid her stilling hand upon the guns, he had lost in killed and wounded eight hundred and seventy men. On the twenty-fourth, the blue came in line of battle against Hardee, and were repulsed. On the twenty-fifth, they again struck Stevenson, and were repulsed. All day the twenty-sixth there was bitter skirmishing. On the twenty-seventh, upstormed the battle of Kennesaw Mountain.

It began in the early morning with all of Sherman's guns. They shelled the crest and sides of Kennesaw; roaring, they poured fierce death into the air, hoping that he would find many victims. He found many, though not so many as the blue hoped. The atmosphere rocked and grew smoky; it was a fierce, prolonged cannonade. During the furious overture, behind the tall, fretted screen of smoke, the blues were forming in two lines of battle, long and thick.

The grey position was exceedingly strong. The grey said as much, contemning the shells that shrieked and dropped.

"We're pretty well fixed! W. T. Sherman'll find there ain't no buried treasure on Kennesaw! General Joe's going to win out on this campaign."

"We're going to have a battle here. But I don't think it's going to be the big battle. I think the big battle's going to be at Atlanta."

"Maybe so. Anyhow he'll win out, and that's all I'm caring about! — This place's a regular sea-beach for shells."

There were in the company a father and son — a tall, lean, lantern-jawed, silent man of sixty and a tall, lean, lantern-jawed, silent man of thirty-five. Except that they messed and foraged together they did not seem to have much to say to each other. They were near Edward where he stood behind the rifle-pit.

"I reckon," said the elder, "that the cotton air blooming mighty pretty, 'long about now."

"I reckon it air," said the younger.

The cannonading did not cease, but now, while all the guns thundered, the blue pushed forward a thick line of skirmishers. Behind them showed, between the trees, wide and long and dark, two bands of infantry. The grey batteries that had been sparing ammunition now ceased to spare it. They opened full cry. Grey and blue, the noise was appalling.

"I reckon," said the elder tall man, "that the mill wheel air turning to-day."

"I reckon it air," said the younger.

The blue moved forward to the assault, — Schofield and McPherson and Thomas. They came on boldly and well, cheering, with waved banners, now lost amid the trees, now seen as clearly as aught could be seen under and in the sulphurous battle-cloud. They were striking right and left and centre. On they came — larger — larger — Full in their faces sprang the fire of the trenches.

The attack just here was desperate. The blue swarmed through the felled trees, seized an advanced breastwork, swarmed on toward the second and stronger line. This line beat them back, burst from the trenches, rushed forward and down, retook the captured work, struck a flag there upon the parapet, and, hurrying on, fell upon the backward-sinking foe. There followed hand-to-hand fighting, with much carnage. The two tall men were in front. A minie ball cut the father down. He lay across a hummock of earth from behind which two or three grey men were firing. The son fought on above the dead body. The face looked at him each time he brought rifle to shoulder. The plain gravity of it, living, was gone; now it was contorted like a gargoyle. A third line of blue came shouting up to reinforce the other two; there ran a grey order to fall back to the earthworks. The tall, lean man, his musket yet in hand, stooped, put his arms under the elder's body, lifted it, and with it across his shoulder started up the mountain-side. An officer ordered him to put the body down, but he shook his head. "I could n't do that, sir. It's father." Just outside the breastwork an exploding shell killed him, too.

Up and over the slopes of Kennesaw rushed another charge. The grey clutched with it, locked and swayed. Down it went, down the slopes of Kennesaw. Mountain and surrounding foot country were wrapped in smoke. For three hours the clamour held; — with onslaught and repulse and heavy loss to the blue. At last, in the hot and heavy noon, the North drew sullenly back, beaten on Kennesaw.

The ——th Virginia moved from the line it had successfully held to a point on the southern face it was ordered to entrench and hold. Moving so, it passed over ground where lay many dead and injured. This had been the rear of the position. Shells had not spared it. They had exploded among ammunition wagons and ambulances, setting afire and consuming the hut that had been division headquarters, injuring various noncombatants, working wrack and ruin here as among the trenches. The regiment halting for a moment, Edward had time to observe the corpse of a drummer-boy, lying in the briar and grass beneath a splintered tree. The shell had struck it full in the breast, tearing the trunk asunder. Above the red ghastliness rose a young face round and freckled. Edward knew it for that of the drummer-boy who wanted the war never to stop.

Two men in the rank nearest him were talking of money. "You have paper money and you have war, and in war you always over-issue. We did it in the old Revolution — and there were the French *assignats* — and Great Britain did the same thing when she was fighting Napoleon. You over-issue and over-issue and the whole

thing depreciates. Sometimes it's slow and sometimes it's hand
over hand. And then you can't redeem, and the whole bottom
drops out —"

The regiment moved forward. The woods on Kennesaw were
afire.

That night, from the house near Smyrna Church, Désirée watched
the line of flame. She stood with three women in a cotton-field and
watched. One of the women was old, and her sons were there where
the flame was. She rocked herself to and fro, and she beat her hands
together and she cursed war. One of the women had a babe in her
arms. It wailed, and she opened her dress, and put her breast to its
mouth. The wind loosened her hair. It blew about her, framing her
brooding young face. Simple and straight she stood amid the cotton,
giving life more life, while her dark eyes were filled with the image
of death. The wind blew the smoke over the cotton-fields; to the
women's ears it brought alike the groaning.

Two days later, Sherman in Georgia, like Grant in Virginia, re-
sorted again to a turning movement. South and east he pushed his
right, until it threatened to crook between Johnston and Atlanta.
Johnston lifted the Army of Tennessee from Kennesaw and set it
down at Smyrna Church. In its rear now was the Chattahoochee,
its bridges covered by the Georgia militia. A very few miles behind
the Chattahoochee was Atlanta, fairly fortified. Smyrna Church
and Station saw heavy, continued skirmishing. On the fourth, Sherman pushed Schofield and McPherson yet farther south, curving like
a scimitar upon the Smyrna position. His advance thrust the Georgia
militia back to Nickajack Ridge, baring the approach to the river.
That night Johnston moved from Smyrna and took up position on
the north bank of Chattahoochee. Here were works prepared in advance, and here for several days the hours were filled with skirmishing. Sherman had brought up, hot foot, the remainder of the blue
army from Kennesaw. "We ought," he says, "to have caught
Johnston on this retreat, but he had prepared the way too well."

The Chattahoochee was a fordable stream. On the eighth, some
miles above the grey entrenchments, Sherman crossed over two
army corps. On the ninth, the Army of Tennessee crossed the Chattahoochee, and took up position behind Peach Tree Creek, a bold

affluent of that river. The ground was rough, seamed with ravines.
It was high and convex to the foe. Behind it was a fortified town, fit
base for a culminating battle. "About the middle of June," says
Joseph E. Johnston, "Captain Grant, of the Engineers, was instructed to strengthen the fortifications of Atlanta materially, on
the side toward Peach Tree Creek, by the addition of redoubts and
by converting barbette into embrasure batteries. I also obtained
promise of seven seacoast rifles from General D. H. Maury, to be
mounted on that front. Colonel Presstman was instructed to join
Captain Grant with his subordinates, in this work of strengthening the defences of Atlanta, especially between the Augusta and
Marietta roads, as the enemy was approaching on that side. For
the same reason a position on the high ground looking down into
the valley of Peach Tree Creek was selected for the army, from
which it might engage the enemy if he should expose himself in the
passage of the stream. The position of each division was marked
and pointed out to its staff officers." "And," says the Federal
General Howard, "Johnston had planned to attack Sherman at
Peach Tree Creek, expecting just such a division between our wings
as we made."

For a week Sherman made feints and demonstrations. The end
of that time found the two armies actually confronted. Behind the
two there had fallen into the abyss of time seventy days of hard and
skilful fencing. Each had felt the rapier point, but no vital spot
had been reached. Each had lost blood; thousands lay quiet forever
in the dark woods and by the creeks of that hundred and twenty
miles. Each had been at odd times reinforced; the accession in
strength had covered the loss. On the last day of June the Federal "effective strength for offensive purposes" is given as one
hundred and six thousand, nine hundred and seventy men. On
the same day Johnston's effective strength is given as fifty-
four thousand and eighty-five men. General Sherman states that
throughout the campaign he knew his numbers to be double those
of Johnston. He could afford to lose two to one without disturbing
the relative strength of the armies.

On the evening of the seventeenth of July there was delivered
to the commander of the Army of Tennessee a telegram from
Richmond. It read, —

"Lieutenant-General J. B. Hood has been commissioned to the temporary rank of general under the late law of Congress. I am directed by the Secretary of War to inform you that, as you have failed to arrest the advance of the enemy to the vicinity of Atlanta, and express no confidence that you can defeat or repel him, you are hereby relieved from the command of the Army and Department of Tennessee, which you will immediately turn over to General Hood.

"S. COOPER, *Adjutant and Inspector-General.*"

Hardee, coming presently to headquarters, was shown the telegram. Johnston sat writing. Several of his staff were in waiting, one with pale face and set lips, another with eyes that winked back the tears.

Hardee read. "I don't believe it," he said.

"A thing may be both unbelievable and a fact," said Johnston, writing. "Well, I've got my wound. It's pretty deep — so deep that I scarcely feel it."

He rose from the table and going to the window stood looking out at Antares, red in the heavens. "I have sent out the orders transferring the command," he said. "It's a strange world, Hardee."

"Sometimes I think it's a half-crazy one, sir," said Hardee, with a shaking voice. "I know what the army's going to think about it —"

"I wish as little said as possible," said Johnston. "It is the only way to take — wounds."

He came back to the table, sat down, and began to write. "There are certain memoranda of plans —" Through the window came a sound of horses stopping at the door, followed by a noise of steps in the hall. "Here is General Hood," said Johnston, and rose.

One of his colonels, in his official report, speaks as follows: "On the seventeenth of July the commanding general published an address to the army and announced that he would attack General Sherman's army so soon as it should cross the Chattahoochee. It was understood that the enemy was crossing at Roswell Factory beyond the right flank of the army and east of Peach Tree Creek. . . . The order of battle was received with enthusiasm and the most confident spirit prevailed. Next day, the eighteenth, while we were forming to march from our bivouac to the right, a rumour prevailed that General Johnston had been removed from command, and after we had marched some distance on the road to Atlanta a courier handed me a circular order from General Hood, announcing General Johnston's removal and assuming command. Shortly after, the farewell address of General Johnston was received and read to the regiment. It is due to truth to say that the reception of these orders produced the most despondent feeling in my command. The loss of the commanding general was felt to be irreparable. Continuing the march and passing by his headquarters, Walker's division passed at the shoulder, the officers saluting, and most of the latter and hundreds of the men taking off their hats. It had been proposed to halt and cheer, but General Johnston, hearing our intention, requested that the troops pass by in silence."

"The news," said Fighting Joe Hooker, — "the news that General Johnston had been removed from the command of the army opposed to us was received by our officers with universal rejoicing."

"Heretofore," said Sherman, "the fighting has been as Johnston pleased, but now it shall be as I please."

CHAPTER XXXI

THUNDER RUN

Yes, Mr. Cole," said Christianna, in her soft, drawling voice; "it's just like you say. Life's dead."

Sairy, sitting in the toll-house door, threaded her needle. "You an' Tom, Christianna, air awful young yet! Life ain't dead. She's sick, I'll allow, but, my land! she's stood a power of sicknesses!"

"It seems right dead to me," said Christianna.

She leaned her head against the pillar of the toll-house porch, her sunbonnet fallen back from her fair hair. The wild-rose colour still clung, but her face had a wistfulness. The little ragged garden was gay with bloom, but it was apparent that there had been no gardening for a very long time. The yellow cat slept beneath the white phlox. Thunder Run Mountain hung in sunshine, and Thunder Run's voice made a steady murmur in the air. Tom, with his trembling old hands, folded a newspaper and put it beneath the empty toll-box. He knew every word of it; there was no use in going over it any more.

"They don't go into details enough," said Tom; "I want to know how the boys look, and what they're saying."

"New Market!" said Sairy. "All them children. I can't get New Market out of my head."

"I've been down to Three Oaks for a day," spoke Christianna. "Mrs. Cleave wouldn't talk about New Market, but it seemed like Miss Miriam couldn't keep away from it. Lexington — an' the cadets marchin' at dawn — marchin' with their white flag with Washington on it — marchin' so trim down the Valley Pike —"

"Fawns fighting for the herd," said Tom.

"An' General Breckinridge welcomin' them — an' some troops that wanted to make fun singin', '*Rock-a-bye, baby, on the tree-top*' — an' Sunday mornin' comin', an' the battle —"

"And that was a hard field," said Tom, "to plough on a Sunday morning."

"Mrs. Cleave said that once before there was a Children's Crusade an' that no good came of it. She said that when the old began to kill the young Nature herself must be turning dizzy. An' Miss Miriam read every paper an' then lay there, lookin' with her big, burnin' eyes."

Sairy rose, went into the kitchen, and returned with a pan of apples which she began to pare. The sun was over the shoulder of Thunder Run Mountain and in its heat and light the flowers in the garden smelled strongly, the mountain-head lay in a shimmering haze, and a pool of gold touched Christianna's shoe. It was late in May, the Wilderness and Spottsylvania over — Cold Harbour not yet — in Georgia the armies lying about New Hope Church.

"Mother came up the mountain yesterday," said Christianna.

"I hope she's well?"

"Yes, ma'am, she's real well. Mother's awful strong. It's one of the hospital's half-empty times, so she's come home for a week. She's cuttin' wood this mahnin'. It's mighty good to have her home — she's so cheerful."

"That's where she shows her strong mind."

"Yes, ma'am. She says that when summer comes you don't have smallpox, and when winter comes, typhoid eases off. Mrs. Cleave says the soldiers all like mother."

"Allan," remarked Sairy, — "Allan always said Mrs. Maydew was an extraordinary woman. Talkin' of Allan —"

A lean, red-brown hand came over the gate to the latch. The yellow cat rose, stretched himself, and left the path. The hand opened the gate and Steve Dagg, entering, limped the thirty feet between gate and porch.

"Mornin', folks!" he said, with an ingratiatory grin.

"Mornin'."

Steve sat down upon the step, carefully handling, as he did so, the treasure of his foot. "It's awful hard to be lamed for life! But if you're lamed in a good cause, I reckon that's all you ought to ask!"

Sairy eyed him with disfavour. "Land sake, Steve, the war ain't goin' to last that long!"

"We were talking about New Market," said Tom. "Since Monday there ain't any news come from Richmond way."

"That's so," said Steve, "but I reckon we're fightin' hard somewhere 'bout the Chickahominy. Gawd knows we fought there in '62 like lions of the field! Did I ever tell you about Savage Station, 'n' a mountain o' dirt 'n' stuff the Yanks had prevaricated the railroad with — 'n' how we cleared it away — me 'n' an artilleryman of Kemper's 'n' some others — so that what we called the railroad gun could pass —"

"Yes, you've told it," said Tom, "but tell it again."

"'N' the railroad gun — that was a siege-piece on a flatcar, Miss Christianna — come a-hawkin' 'n' a-steamin' up 'n' I 'n' the others piled on. Gawd! it was sunset 'n' the woods like black coal ag'in' it . . . 'n' we came on the railroad bridge 'n' the Yanks began to shell us." Steve shivered. "Them shells played on that gun like the rain on Old Gray Rock up there; 'n' jest like Old Gray Rock we looked at 'em 'n' said, 'Play away!' — 'n' we rumbled 'n' roared off the bridge, 'n' got into position on top of an embankment, 'n' three batteries begun to shell us, 'n' we shelled back; 'n' those of us who were n't at the guns, we took off our hats 'n' waved 'n' hurrahed —"

"If there ain't any top to truth," said Sairy, *sotto voce*, "neither air there any bottom to lyin'.'"

"'N' I reckon we saved the day for General Magruder! The artilleryman was a cowardly kind of fellow, 'n' he left us pretty soon, but the rest of us — Gawd! we 'n' that railroad gun did the business! Naw," said Steve mournfully, "they may think they're fightin' hard down 'roun' Richmond, but it ain't like it used to be! We ain't never goin' to see fightin' ag'in like what we fought in '62. The best men in this here war air dead or disabled. — Of course, of course, Mrs. Cole, thar air exceptions!"

"A man from Lynchburg passed this way yesterday," said Sairy. "He was tellin' us that Crook and Averell air certainly goin' to join Hunter at Staunton an' that Lynchburg's right uneasy. He said there was a feelin' in the air that this end of the Valley was n't going to be spared much longer. He said that General Smith at Lexington told him that the storm was comin' this way, and in that case Thunder Run might hear some thunder that was n't of the Lord's manufacturing! Of course, if we do," said Sairy, "we'll have the benefit of your experience an' advice an' aid."

Christianna spoke in her drawling voice. "Mother says there's talk of maybe havin' to move the hospital. She says they all say

Hunter's one of the worst. He's one of the burnin' kind, an' he's got a lot of men who can't understand what you say to 'em — Germans."

"I think we ought to be organizing a Home Guard," said Tom. "There's your grandpap, Christianna, and the doctor and Charley Key and the boy at the sawmill —"

"An' Steve," said Sairy.

Steve squirmed upon the step. "I've seen a lot of Home Guards," he said gloomily, "'n' they don't do a danged bit of good! They're jest ridden over! Gawd! Thunder Run ain't got a reception of what war is! General Lee oughtter send a corps —"

"Maybe he will," said Tom hopefully. "Maybe he'll send the Second Corps!"

"The Second Corps!" Steve grew pale. "He can't send the Second Corps — it was all cut to pieces at Spottsylvania Court-House — Johnson's division was, anyhow! The Second Corps ain't — ain't the fightin' corps oncet it was. He'd better send the First or the Third. . . . Ouch! Do you mind ef I just loosen my shoe for a bit, Mrs. Cole? My foot's awful bad this mornin'."

"You'd better telegraph him about the corps," said Sairy, "right away. Otherwise he might think 't was good enough for us — Valley men an' all, an' some of them even livin' on Thunder Run. I could ha' guessed without bein' told that your foot was bad this mornin'."

Steve blinked. "I don't want you to think, Mrs. Cole, that Steve Dagg wouldn't be glad to see the division 'n' the brigade 'n' the Sixty-fifth — what's left of them. I'd be glad enough to cry. It's funny how fond soldiers get of each other — marchin' 'n' sufferin' 'n' fightin' together 'n' helpin' each other out of Devil's Holes 'n' Bloody Angles 'n' Lanes 'n' such. No, 'm, 't is n't that. I'd be jest as glad to see the boys as I could be. I was jest a-thinkin' of the good of us all, 'n' them Marse Robert could spare 'n' them he could n't." He rose, holding by the sapling that made the porch pillar. "I reckon I'll be creepin' along. Old Mimy at the sawmill's makin' me a yarb liniment."

He went. Tom took for the twentieth time the newspaper from beneath the toll-box. Christianna sat absently regarding the great, sun-washed panorama commanded by Thunder Run Mountain. The yellow cat came back to the path.

Sairy sighed. "It was always a puzzle to me what the next world does with some of the critturs it gets!"

"It don't seem noways anxious to get Steve," said Tom, and began to read again about Spottsylvania.

An hour later Christianna in her blue sunbonnet went up the mountain road toward the Maydew cabin. Rhododendron was in bloom; pine and hickory and walnut and birch made a massive shadow through whose rifts the sun cast bright sequins. Thunder Run, near at hand now, was uttering watery violences. The road, narrow and bad for wheels, was pleasant under the foot of a light walker, untrammelled, elastic, moving with delicate vigour. Christianna loosened her sunbonnet, and the summer wind breathed upon her forehead and ruffled her hair. She was dreaming of city streets and houses, of Richmond, and the going to and fro of the people there. Old Grey Rock rose before her to the right of the road. As she came abreast it, Steve Dagg rose from behind one of its ferny ledges.

He grinned at her violent start. "Laid an avalanche for you, did n't I? You ain't really frightened? Did you think it was a bear?"

"No! I thought it was a snake an' a cat-o-mount an' a — a monkey!" said Christianna, with spirit. "Friendly an' polite people don't do things like that!"

Steve's whine came into his voice. "Why don't you like me, Miss Christianna? I don't see why —"

"If you don't see that, you won't never see anything!" said Christianna. "An' I'd like to walk home in peace an' quietness, Mr. Dagg!"

Steve kept beside her. "I got a good cabin — thar ain't any better on the mountain! I got" — his voice sank — "I got a little money, too, 'n' it ain't Confederate money that's worth jest about as much as so many jimson leaves! *It's gold.* I've got it hid." He glanced about him. "I did n't mean to tell that. You won't mention it, Miss Christianna?"

"No," said Christianna; "it ain't worth mentionin'."

Steve touched her sleeve with persuasive fingers. "I never loved a lady like I love you. Gawd! we'd be jest as happy —"

Christianna walked faster. Ahead, in the light and shadow, a wild turkey crossed the road. Pine and hemlock showed dark and thick against the intense mid-day sky. Thunder Run, now much below the road, spoke with a lessened voice. Butterflies fluttered above wild honeysuckle in bloom, and high in the blue a hawk was sailing. Steve, keeping beside her, tried to put his arm around her waist. She broke from him and ran up the road. Long-legged and light of weight he ran after her, caught up with her, and began afresh to press his suit.

"Why don't you like me, Miss Christianna? Lots of women in the Valley 'n' down about Richmond have! There was one up near Winchester that was so fond of me I could n't hardly git away. — There ain't no reason that I kin see — I'd be jest as good to you as any man on this mountain. Most of the men have died off it, anyway, 'n' I'm *here!* Why don't you *try* to like me? Ain't Daggs as good as Maydews? 'N' as for Allan Gold, if you're thinkin' of him —" ,

Christianna turned. "From now right on I'm goin' to bear witness that there is n't a crittur on Thunder Run that uses its feet any better or faster than Steve Dagg can! You can walk an' you can run, an' when the army comes this-a-way I'm goin' to bear witness that you can march! I'm goin' to stand up just the same as in an experience meetin' an' bear witness! An' if the army takes you away with it —"

Steve gasped. "It can't! I got a doctor's certificate. — It ain't any way from Grey Rock, 'n' love made me run. It was jest a moment 'n' I'll pay for it to-morrow. I could n't march on that foot if Glory itself was there, hollerin' me on! — Who'd believe you, either? A woman's word ain't countin' much. Besides," — he grinned, confidence returning, — "besides, you would n't tell the regiment I'd run after you 'n' — 'n' kissed you —" His arm darted around her again. Christianna smote him on the cheek, broke away, and fled up the mountain.

Around a turn of the road appeared, pacing stately, Mrs. Maydew. She was tall and strong, and she carried an axe in the hollow of her arm.

Christianna stopped short with a sound between a sob and a laugh. She looked back. "Are n't you comin' on to the cabin, Mr. Dagg?"

"Naw," said Steve, "not to-day," and, turning, went, elaborately limping, down the mountain.

Some days later, being at the unworked sawmill at the foot of the mountain, he heard news. Crook and Averell had made a junction with Hunter at Staunton. Hunter had now an army of eighteen thousand men. Hunter was marching up the Valley, burning and destroying as he came. Hunter certainly meant to strike Lexington. Hunter —

"Reckon we'd better rest right quiet here, don't you?" asked Steve. "Even if they came into the county, they would n't be likely to take a road this-a-way?"

"I would n't put it beyond them," said the sawmill man darkly. "There's a lot of valuable property on this mountain."

Steve grew profoundly restless. Each day now for a long time there was news. Breckinridge was at Rockfish Gap barring with a handful of troops Hunter's direct road to Lynchburg. Hunter thereupon came on up the Valley with the intent to cross the Blue Ridge and pounce on Lynchburg from the west. He was a destroyer was Hunter and a well-hated one. The country was filled with sparks from his torches and with an indignant cry against his mode of warfare. Breckinridge marched to Lynchburg, but he detached McCausland with orders to do the best he could to harry and retard the blue advancing host. Down upon the Chickahominy, Lee was about to send Early, but days of fighting and burning must elapse before Early could reach Lynchburg. On the twelfth of June Hunter came to Lexington.

CHAPTER XXXII

HUNTER'S RAID

VIRGINIA Military Institute cadets were younger than they used to be. To suit the times the age of admittance had been dropped. Even so, steadily from the beginning there was a road of travel from the V. M. I. to the battle-fields. Out upon it went many a cadet in his trig white and grey, never to return. In May, 1864, the entire two hundred and fifty had travelled it, travelled down the Valley to New Market to help Breckinridge fight and win that battle. In dead and wounded, V. M. I. lost sixty boys. Now after a time of wild and blissful excitement the lessened corps was back in Lexington, back at the V. M. I., back to the old barracks, the old parade ground, the old studying. To the cadets it seemed hard lines.

Hunter and his eighteen thousand came up the pike from Staunton, thirty-five miles away. McCausland and a cavalry brigade, drawn across his front at Midway, did all that could be done in the way of skirmishes for delay. Breckinridge was guarding Lynchburg, an important centre of communications, a place of military stores and hospitals, and filled with refugees. Early and the Second Corps were yet in Tidewater Virginia. There was no help anywhere. V. M. I. received orders to withdraw from Lexington.

McCausland had the bridge across North River lined with hay, saturated with turpentine. An alley through was left for his men when, at the last, they must fall back before the blue advance. The night of the eleventh passed, the people of Lexington sleeping little, the cadets under arms all night. Dawn came up in rose and silver. House Mountain had a roof of mist; all the lovely Rockbridge country was as fresh and sweet as any Eden. Out the Staunton road came a burst of firing; then with a clattering of hoofs, with shouts, with turning in saddles and emptying of pistols and carbines, McCausland and his troopers appeared, pressed back upon the bridge. They crossed, horsemen and a section of artillery, then struck a torch into the turpentine-soaked hay. Up roared a pillar of flame, reddening the water. With a great burst of noise Hunter's vanguard appeared. They galloped up and down the north bank of the river shouting and firing. McCausland answered from the hills across. The bridge burned with a roaring noise and a great cloud of smoke. A Federal battery coming up got into position on a great rise of ground commanding the town, and from it began to shell the most apparent mass of buildings. This was the Virginia Military Institute.

The grey and white cadets were drawn up on the parade ground. They stood there with their colours, with their tense young faces. The first shell struck the hall of the Society of Cadets, struck and exploded, working ruin. After this there began a bombardment of the corner towers, and a heavy rain upon the parade ground.

"Attention! Right face! Forward! March!"

Drum and fife played "Dixie." Away from the old V. M. I., coming down in ruin about them, marched the cadets. They marched to a fierce bright music, but their faces were flushed and quivering. It needed all their boy pride to keep the tears away. Lexington, anxious-hearted, saw them go. Behind them the batteries were thundering, and Hunter's thousands were gathering like locusts. Colonel Shipp and the cadets took the Balcony Falls road — Balcony Falls first and then Lynchburg, and active service somewhere if not at Lexington. . . .

They came to a high hill, several miles south of the town. *"Halt!"* and the two hundred and fifty halted, and resting on their pieces looked back. The Virginia Military Institute was on fire. Tower and turret, arsenal, mess hall, barracks, houses of the professors, all were burning down.

Hunter made no long tarrying in Lexington. He waited but to burn the house of the Governor of Virginia and swept on toward the pass in the Blue Ridge he had in mind. His line of march brought him and his thousands into a country as yet uncharred by war.

At Three Oaks there was a wounded soldier — a kinsman of Margaret Cleave's, wounded in a skirmish in southwest Virginia and brought in an ambulance by his servant back to his native county. Here he found his own home closed; his mother gone to

Richmond to nurse another son, his sister in Lynchburg with her husband. The ambulance took him on to Three Oaks, and here he had been for some days. Exposure and travel had not been good for him, and though his wound was healing, he lay in a low fever. He lay in Richard's room, nursed by Margaret and an old, wrinkled, coloured woman.

Tullius was at Three Oaks. Cleave had sent him back, months before, to be a stay to the place. Now Margaret, coming through the hall, found him on the back porch, standing on the step between the pillars like a grave old Rameses. It was a hot June day, with clouds that promised a storm.

"What is it, Tullius?" asked Margaret. She took an old cane-seat chair and faced him. There were threads of grey in her hair. The old man noticed them this morning.

"Miss Miriam ain' nowhere 'roun', is she?"

"No. She is out with her book under the oaks. What is it?"

"They've flowed over Buchanan, Miss Margaret. I done took the horse an' went down as far as Mount Joy. I met a man an' he say they tried to cross by the bridge, but General McCausland done burn the bridge. Hit did n't stop 'em. They marched up the river to the ford an' crossed, an' come hollerin' an' firin' down on the town. An' a house by the mouth of the bridge caught an' a heap of houses were burnin', he say, when he left. An' he say that some of the Yankees were those foreigners that can't understand a word you say, an' a lot of them were drunk. I saw the smoke an' fire an' heard the shoutin'. An' then I come right home."

"Do you think that they will march this way?"

"There ain't any tellin', Miss Margaret. They've got bands out, 'flictin' the country."

Margaret rested her forehead upon her hands. "Captain Yeard-ley — it will put his life in danger to move him . . . and then, move him where? Where, Tullius, where?"

"Miss Margaret, I don' know. Less 'n 't was somewhere in the woods or up on the mountain-side."

Margaret rose. "Get the wagon, then. We 'll make a bed for him, and do all we can, and then pray to God. . . . You 'd better go by the old Thunder Run road and turn off up one of the ravines."

"Miss Margaret, Jim's got a good head, an' he kin tek the Captain away an' tek care of him. I'se gwine stay at Three Oaks. I'se gwine stay with you an' Miss Miriam."

Miriam's startled voice came through the hall from the front porch. "Mother! mother, come here! Here's a boy who says the Yankees are burning Mount Joy!"

She did not wait for her mother, but came down the hall, at her heels a white-lipped, wild-eyed youngster of twelve. News came from him in gulps, like water from a bottle. He had been taking his father's horse to be shod, and down near Mount Joy he had seen the Yankees coming up the road in time to get out of their way. He had gone through a gate into an orchard and had got down and hidden with the horse below a bank with elder growing over it. From there he had seen how the Yankees came through the big gate and over the garden and to the house. . . . After a while, when it was all on fire and there was a lot of noise and he could n't see much for the smoke, a little coloured girl had come creeping through the orchard grass. She told him the Yankees said they were going to burn every house in the country they could get at. And she said he had a horse, and why did n't he go and tell people, so's they could get their things out — and he thought he'd better, and so he had been telling them —

How long since he had left the orchard?

He did n't know — he thought about three hours.

Mahalah came running in. "O my Lawd, Miss Margaret! O my Lawd, de Yankees comin' up de big road lak er swarm o' bees! O my Lawd, dey kills an' eats you!"

"Nonsense, Mahalah! Be quiet! Tullius, go upstairs to the east room window and see how near they are."

Tullius returned. "They've got a mile an' a half yit, Miss Margaret, an' they ain't marchin' fast. Just kind o' strollin'."

"How many?"

"Hundred or two."

"Get the wagon as quickly as you can. If Jim can get down the farm road to the woods without their seeing him, the rest may be done. Tell Jim to hurry. Then you and he come and lift Captain Yeardley."

She turned and went upstairs toward Richard's room. Going,

she spoke over her shoulder to her daughter. "Miriam, get everybody together and make them take it quietly. Tell them no one's going to harm them!"

"Everybody" was not hard to get together. Counting out Tullius and Jim, there were only Aunt Ailsey and Mahalah, old Peggy, Martha and young Martha, William and Mat and Rose's Husband. They were already out of cabin and kitchen and in from the home fields. Miriam gathered them on the side porch. They all adored her and she handled them with genius. Her thin cheeks had in each a splash of carmine, her eyes were unearthly large, dark and liquid. All that she said to them was that it was good manners to do so and so — or not to do so and so — in a contingency like the present. Ladies and gentlemen keep very quiet and dignified — and we are ladies and gentlemen — and that is all there is about it. "And here is the wagon, and now we'll see Captain Yeardley off, and wish him a good journey, and then *we'll forget that he has ever been here*. That's manners that every one of us must show!"

Tullius and Jim brought the wounded officer downstairs on his mattress and laid him in the wagon. Old Patsy followed to nurse him, and they placed beside him, too, his uniform and hat and sword. He was flushed with fever and light-headed.

"This is no way to do it!" he insisted. "Inconsiderate brutes to take advantage! — Ladies, too! Must stay and protect. — Lovely day for a drive! See the country at its best! — New fashion, driving lying down! driving in bed! — Time for new fashions, had old fashions long enough! — Bring the ladies home something pretty — scarf or feather! — saw a man once show the white feather — it was n't pretty. — Pretty, pretty —

'Pretty Polly Watkins —'"

Jim drove him away, trying to sing. It was not far to where the farm road dipped into a heavy woodland. The rumble of the wagon died from the air.

Mother and daughter turned and looked at each other. Margaret spoke. "The hair trunk with Will's things in it, and the portraits and silver and your great-grandfather's books and letters — we might hide them in the hollow behind the ice-house. No one can see it for the honeysuckle."

"Very well. I'll get the books and papers."

Tullius and Mat carried out the small hair trunk and took down the two or three oil portraits and the Saint Memin. Miriam, with Peggy to help, laid a sheet on the floor and heaped into it a treasured shelf of English poetry, essay, philosophy, and drama, old and mellow of binding, with quaint prints, and all annotated in her great-grandfather's clear, firm writing. To them she added a box filled with old family, Revolutionary, and Colonial letters. William and Rose's Husband took up the bundle, Martha and young Martha and Mahalah filled their aprons with the silver. All hurried through the flower garden, between the sweet william and canterbury bell and hermosa roses, to the mossy-roofed ice-house and a cavity, scooped by nature in the bank behind and veiled by a mass of vines. Will and Miriam had always used it when they played Swiss Family Robinson. Now they leaned the portraits against its damp walls and set the hair trunk and the silver and the books and papers on the earth that glistened where snails had traversed it. The honeysuckle did not hide the place perfectly, but it would take a deliberate search and sharp eyes to discover it, and beggars must not be choosers. The movements of all had been swift; they were back through the flower garden to the house in the shortest of times. As mother and daughter reëntered the hall they heard through the open front door a hum of voices and a sound of oncoming feet.

"We had best meet them here," said Margaret.

"I am going upstairs to get my amethysts," said Miriam. "I am going to put them around my neck, inside my dress."

Three Oaks was burned. Porch and pillars, doors and windows, hall and chambers, walls and chimneys submitted, since they could not help it, to a shroud of fire, and crumbled within it. The family was allowed to take nothing out. Matters that they prized were taken out, indeed, but not by them nor for them. At the eleventh hour soldiers, searching the garden, found the little cavern and its contents. The silver was reserved, but the hair trunk, the portraits, books and papers were thrown into the flames.

Margaret Cleave and her daughter and the coloured people watched destruction from the knoll beneath the three oaks. It was home that was burning — home that had been long lived in, long loved. The outdoor kitchen and the cabins also caught — all Three

Oaks was burning down. In the glare moved the band of the foe sent out to do the work. The sun had set and the night was at hand — at hand with storm. Already the lightnings were playing, the thunder pealing. Three soldiers came up to the cluster beneath the oaks. They rolled in their gait like sailors.

"Look here! Rebel women ain't got any need of watches and rings! If you've got any on, hand them over!"

"Miss Margaret," demanded Tullius, "what'll I do?"

Margaret looked at him with her beautiful, friendly eyes. "Nothing in the world, Tullius. Stay perfectly still!" — She explained to the soldiers. "I gave my watch and some rings that I had to the Confederacy long ago. My daughter has neither."

"She's got a chain around her neck this minute. If you don't want —"

"Exactly. Give the gentleman the necklace, Miriam."

Miriam unclasped and gave it. The three looked at Mahalah's hoop earrings, but at that moment an officer came up and they perforce fell back. "The men are — er — exhilarated, and not well in hand," he said. "I would advise you ladies to leave the place."

They went, Margaret and Miriam leading, Tullius and the others pressing behind them. Save for the lightnings it was dark when they passed through the big gate out upon the open road. Behind them the three oaks stood up like giant sea fans in an ocean of fire. A moment later the storm broke in a wild clamour of wind and rain.

CHAPTER XXXIII

BACK HOME

EIGHT thousand strong the Second Corps, Jubal Early at its head, left the region of the Chickahominy on the thirteenth of June, marched eighty-odd miles in four days, boarded at Charlottesville the Orange and Alexandria and so came south to Lynchburg. Here, Breckinridge being wounded, D. H. Hill, brought to this town on some duty, was found in command. He had earthworks and a motley force — Breckinridge's handful, cavalry ready to fight dismounted, home guard, hospital convalescents, V. M. I. cadets. Noon of seventeenth in came Early with Ramseur's division, Gordon's following.

Hunter, having burned and harried Rockbridge and a corner of Botetourt, crossed the Blue Ridge and swept through Bedford toward Lynchburg, Imboden and McCausland skirmishing with him at New London, and again and heavily at the Quaker Meeting-House. From this point, cavalry fell back to Lynchburg, where with Breckinridge's men they held the Forrest road. On came the eighteen thousand and found breastworks across their path, and Ramseur and Gordon with artillery. Hunter halted, deployed, brought up artillery and thundered for an hour, then, night appearing in the east, went into camp over against the grey front. The next day and the next there was thunder of cannon and cavalry skirmishing, but no battle. Suddenly, on the night of the nineteenth, Hunter broke camp, and, facing about, marched away to the westward. His army doubled in numbers the grey force in his front. Why he went so hastily after nothing but a glancing blow or two the grey could not tell — though Gordon states, "If I were asked for an opinion as to this utterly causeless fright and flight I should be tempted to say that conscience was harrowing General Hunter, and causing him to see an avenger wrapped in every grey jacket before him." Be that as it may, Hunter was gone at midnight, and the grey column took up the pursuit at dawn, moving by the Liberty turnpike. Behind the Second Corps lay the giant labour, giant weariness of Wilderness to Cold Harbour, and on this side of that the forced marching from Tidewater, and now, rolling on in a dream of weariness, the pursuit after Hunter, sixty miles in two days and a half.

It was a weary dream and yet it had its interest, for this was new country to the Second Corps, thrown this way for the first time in all the war. It knew much of Virginia so exceedingly well — and here was a new road and the interests of a new road! Here and there in column it was not new country, it was to soldiers here and there land of old time, their part of Virginia. Some had had furloughs and had come back to it, once or twice or thrice; others had missed furloughs, had not seen these mountains and waters for so long a time that now they looked at them wistfully as we look with closed eyes at the landscapes of childhood. The thickness of a life seemed to lie between them and the countryside; one could not reckon all that had happened since they had marched from these blue mountains and these sunny fields — marched to end in one battle the trouble between North and South!

Richard Cleave rode at the head of the Golden Brigade. There were now no full grey brigades, no complete grey regiments. All were worn to a wraith of their former seeming. They took not a half, often not a third, of the space of road they once had covered. The volume of sound of their marching was diminished, the flags were closer together. Had the dead come to life, taken their old places, there would have passed on the Liberty pike a very great army. But scattered like thistledown from the stem lay the dead in a thousand fields.

The living Sixty-fifth moved with jingle and clank through the heat and dust and glare. It had men and officers who were at home in this landscape seen through clefts in the dust cloud. What was left of the old Company A were all from the rolling hills, the vales between, the high blue mountains now rising before the column. Thunder Run men pointed out the Peaks of Otter; there ran a low talk of the James, of North Mountain and Purgatory, of Mill Creek and Back Creek and Craig Creek, of village and farm and cabin, smithy and mill. Company A did not feel tired, it was glad when the halts were ended, glad to hear the *Column forward!*

Matthew Coffin had been home twice since First Manassas; other men of the region had been home, Thunder Run had seen a furlough or two, but many of the living of Company A had not returned in four years' time. Allan Gold had not been back nor Dave and Billy Maydew.

The column was moving rapidly. Hunter had a few hours' start, but this was the "foot cavalry" that was pursuing him. The road was rough, the dust blinding, the heat exhausting, but on pressed the "foot cavalry." "*Hot! Hot! Hot!*" said the rapid feet, so many of them half-shoeless. "Heat and dust! Heat and dust! There used to be springs in this country, — springs to drink and creeks to wade in. . . . Then we were boys — long ago — long ago —"

Mouth furred with dust, throat baked with dust and cracked with thirst, much ground to cover in short time, the column for the most part kept its lips closed. It went steadily, rhythmically, bent on getting its business done, no more forever aught but veterans, seasoned, grey, determined. But in the short halts granted it between long times it spoke. It lay on the ground beside welcome waters and babbled of heaven and earth. That portion of the Sixty-fifth whose shores these were spoke as soldiers immemorially speak when after years the war road leads past home. The rests were short. *Fall in! Fall in!* — and on after Hunter swung the Second Corps.

In the hot June dusk, in the small town of Liberty, twenty-five miles from Lynchburg, they found his rear guard. Ramseur charged and drove it through the place and out and on into the night. There sprang a sudden shriek of shells, rear guard joining main body, and the batteries opening on the grey, heard coming up in the night. The grey line halted; grey and blue, alike exhausted with much and sore travel, fell upon the warm earth and slept as they had been dead, through the short summer night. Grey was in column as the candles of heaven were going out — on before them they heard the blue striking the flints on the Liberty and Salem turnpike.

The sun came up hot and glorious. Full before the column rose the Blue Ridge. The men, moving in a huge dust cloud, talked only between times. "Hunter's a swift Hunter or he wants to get away mighty bad! 'Burner' Hunter!" — "I could get right hot of heart — but what's the use?" —"I don't bother about the use. You've got to have a heart like a hot coal sometimes, with everything blowing upon it!" — "That's so! Life's right tragic." — *Press forward, men!* — "Peaks of Otter! Boys from hereabouts say there's an awful fine view from the top." — "Awful fine view? Should think there was! When you're up there — if you go alone — you feel like you're halfway upstairs to God! Don't do to go with anybody — they make a fuss and enjoy it." — "We're going straight into the mountains." — "Yes, straight into the mountains. Thunder Run Mountain's over there."

The road was now a climbing road. The column moved upon it like a gleaming dragon — the head in thick woods lifting toward the heights, the rear far back in the rolling green land just north of Liberty. The Golden Brigade was near the head. The Sixty-fifth felt the world climb beneath its feet. Allan and Billy were thinking of Thunder Run; Matthew Coffin was thinking of the pale blue letter-paper girl. Allan's vision was now the toll-gate and now the school-house, and now, and at last persistently, the road up Thunder Run Mountain and Christianna Maydew walking on it. Blended with this vision of the road was a vision of the hospital in Richmond after Gaines's Mill. He lay again on a blanket on the floor in a corner of the ward, thirsty and in pain, with closed eyes, and Christianna came and knelt and gave him water. . . .

The road climbed steeply. Above ran on to the sky long, wooded, purple slopes. At one point showed a break, a "gap." "That's where we're going! That's Buford's Gap!" On and on and up and up — *Halt!* rang out from the head of the column, and *Halt! — Halt! — Halt!* ran from segment to segment of the mounting length.

Hunter, a week before, had not appeared on Thunder Run Mountain. No torch came near its scattered "valuable property." The few men left upon the mountain were not pressed or shot or marched away to Yankee prisons. Thunder Run Mountain saw burning buildings in the valleys below and heard tales of devastation, even heard wind of a rumour that Hunter's line of march lay across it, in which case it might expect to be burned with fire and sowed with salt. It was this rumour that sent Steve Dagg on a visit to a long-forgotten kinswoman in Bedford. . . . And then the line of march had proved to be by the kinswoman's house!

Steve broke from a band of Federals speaking German and somewhat blindly plunged into the woods toward the Peaks. "Gawd! I reckon they ain't comin' to the top of Apple Orchard!"

With occasional descents to a hermit's cabin for food he lay out on Apple Orchard until he had seen the last horseman of the Federal column disappear, Lynchburg direction. It was warm and pleasant on Apple Orchard and the hermit was congenial. Steve stayed on to recuperate. And then, with suddenness, here again in the distance appeared the head of the Federal column — coming back! Steve felt the nightmare redescending.

The hermit, who was really lame, went to the nearest hamlet and returned with news. "We got army at Lynchburg — big army. Hunter's beaten stiff and running this way! He'll cross at Buford's again, and I reckon then he'll keep to the woods and go west. You'd better wait right here —"

"Thank you, I thought I would," said Steve. "A man can have a fightin' temper, 'n' yet back off from a locomotive —"

Hunter's thousands disappeared, the last rear guard horseman of them. Steve was content. And then of a suddenness, there burst a quarrel with the hermit. He had a gun and a dog and Steve found it advisable to leave. It came into his head, "The Yanks ain't goin' to make any stop this side of Salem, if there! 'n' if the Second Corps comes along, it's goin' to hurry through. If it's after Hunter it won't have no time to come gallivantin' on Thunder Run! Old Jack would ha' rushed it through like greased lightning, 'n' I reckon Old Dick or Old Jube, or whatever darn fool's riskin' his skin leadin', 'll rush it through too! — I'll go back to Thunder Run."

He began to put his intention into execution, moving across miles of woodland with a certain caution, since there might just possibly be blue stragglers. He found none, however, and came in good spirits to a high point from which he could discern distances of the Liberty pike running southeast to Lynchburg. Upon it, quite far away, was a moving pillar of dust, moving toward him. Steve knew what it was well enough. "Second Corps," he grinned. "*Yaaih! Yaaaihh!* Reckon I'll be travelling along!"

So sure was he that the road before him was clear, and he was in such good spirits from the consideration that the "foot cavalry" would hurry incontinently after Hunter, that he quite capered along the road that now climbed toward Buford's Gap. It was afternoon, warm, with a golden light. And then, suddenly, being almost in the gap, he observed something which gave him pause. It was nothing more or less than trees cut away from a rocky height overhanging the gorge through which passed the road, and some metal bores projecting from the ledges. Steve's breath came whistlingly. "Gawd! Yankee battery!" In a moment he saw another, perched on a further ledge and masked by pine boughs. Steve panted. "Avalanche! Another minute 'n' they'd ha' seen me."

He was already deep in the woods beside the road, his face now turned quite away from his projected path. Indeed, when he came to himself he found that he was moving southward, and due, if he kept on, to meet that dust cloud and the Second Corps. His heart beating violently, he drew up beneath a hemlock, the vast brown trunk and a mile or so of blue air between him and the cannon-fringed crags. Here he slid down upon the scented earth and fell to thinking, his hand automatically beating to death with a small stick a broken-winged moth creeping over the needles. Steve thought at first with a countenance of blankness, and then with a strange, watery smile. His eyes lengthened and narrowed, his lips widened. "I got an idea," he whispered. "Make 'em like me."

Sitting there he rolled up his trouser leg, removed a rotten shoe and ragged sock, then took a knife from his pocket and after a shiver of apprehension scraped and abraded an old, small wound and sore until it bled afresh. Out of his pocket he took a roll of dirty bandage kept against just such an emergency as this. Having first carefully stained it with blood, he rolled it around foot and shin, pinned it with a rusty pin, donned again sock and shoe, stood up and gave three minutes to the practice of an alternate limp and shuffle. This over he broke and trimmed a young dogwood for a staff, and with it in hand he went southward a considerable distance through the woods, then crossed to the road. Behind him, a good long way off, showed the gap where was planted the "avalanche." Before him came rolling the road from Liberty. The dust cloud on it was rapidly growing larger. Steve, leaning heavily on his stick, limped to meet it.

Cavalry ahead took his news, halted and sent back to Jubal Early. That commander spurred forward. "'Avalanche?' What d'ye mean? Guns? Where? Up there? — — ——! All right. Two can play at that game — *Battery forward!*"

Steve conceived himself to be neglected. Carefully propped by his stick and a roadside boulder he hearkened to orders and marked manœvres until he was aweary. He had saved the Second Corps and it was n't noticing him! He grew palely dogged. "They got ter notice me. Gawd! I've seen a man thanked in General Orders 'n' promoted right up for less 'n I've done!" In addition to a sense of his dues a fascination kept him where he was. The unwonted feeling of superiority protected him from fear; no army would too closely question its saviour! The rag about his foot, as he assured himself every now and then with a glance, was good and bloody. So well fixed and with such a vantage-point, he gave way to a desire just to see how the boys looked after so long a time. Vanguard and artillery had gone forward; down the road he saw coming at a double an infantry brigade; further back the main body had been halted. He gathered from a comment of officers passing that there was a conviction that it was only Hunter's rear guard before them in the pass. Cavalry scouts spurring back, clattering down dangerous paths from adjoining crests, justified the conviction. The Federal main body was pressing on upon the Salem road while the rear guard gained time. And here the blue rear guard, observing from its crags that the ambuscade had been discovered, opened fire. The grey guns now in battery on a knoll of hemlocks answered. The Blue Ridge echoed the thunders.

It was near sunset and the brigade coming up was bathed in a slant and rich light. With a gasp Steve recognized the horse and rider at its head. He raised and bent his arm and hid his face, only looking forth with one frightened eye. Cleave and Dundee went by without recognizing him, without, as far as he could tell, glancing his way. Steve chose again to feel injury. "Gawd, Colonel! if I did try to get even with you once, ain't you a general now, 'n' ain't I jest saved your life 'n' all your men? — 'n' you go by without lookin' at me any more 'n if I was dirt! If you'd been a Christian 'n' stopped, I could ha' told you you were goin' home to find your house burned down 'n' your sister dyin'! I jest saved your life 'n' you don't know it! I jest saved this army 'n' don't any one know it. . . . O Gawd! here's the Sixty-fifth!"

Steve could not stand it. "Howdy, boys!" he said. "Howdy, howdy!" The water came into his eyes. He saw through a mist the colours and the slanted bayonets and the ragged hats or no hats and the thin, tanned faces. A drop gathered and rolled down his cheek. There was a momentary halt of the Sixty-fifth, the last rank abreast of the boulder by the road. *Forward!* and the regiment moved on, and Steve marched with it. "Yaas, you did n't know it, but I jest saved you boys 'n' the army! I was comin' along the road — I got a sore foot — 'n' I looked up 'n' seed the guns —"

The sun went down and the night came, with the guns yet baying at one another, and the well-posted blue yet in possession of the rocks above the gorge. But in the middle of the night the blue withdrew, hurrying away upon the Salem road. McCausland, pursuing, captured prisoners and two pieces of artillery. But the great length of Hunter's column, wheeling from Salem toward Lewisburg, plunged into the mountains of western Virginia. From the grey administration's point of view it was better there than elsewhere. Early, under orders now for the main Valley, rested in Botetourt for one day, then took the pike for Staunton.

One day! Matthew Coffin spent it with the blue letter-paper young lady. Allan Gold and Billy and Dave Maydew covered with long strides the road to Thunder Run. Making all speed up and down, they might have the middle of the day for *home-at-last.* Richard Cleave rode to Fincastle and found in a house there his mother and sister. Miriam was sinking fast. She knew him, but immediately wandered off to talk of books, of Hector and Achilles and people in the " Morte d'Arthure." He had but two hours. At the end he knelt and kissed his sister's brow, then came out into the porch with his mother and held her in a parting embrace. She clung to him with passion. "Richard — Richard! — All is turned to iron and clay and blood and tears! Love itself is turning to pure pain —"

Riding back to his troops he went by Three Oaks. There was only a great blackened chimney stack, a ragged third of a wall, a charred mass behind. He checked Dundee and stood long in the ragged gap where the gate had been and looked, then went on by the darkening road to the Golden Brigade.

Up on Thunder Run, throughout the morning, there was great restlessness at the toll-gate. Tom knew they could n't come this way — yes, he knew it. Their road lay along other mountains — he wished that he had the toll-gate at Buford's. Yes, he knew they

would n't be likely to stop — he knew that, too. He did n't expect
to see any one. He could have borrowed the sawmill wagon and
gone down the mountain and over to the Salem road and seen them
pass just as well. — No, he was n't too weak. He was n't weak at
all — only he wanted to see the army and Allan. He had n't ever
seen the army and now he did n't reckon he would ever see it. Yes,
he could imagine it — imagine it just as well as any man — but he
did n't want to imagine it, he wanted to see it! And now he would n't
ever see it — never see it and never see Allan.

"Sho! you will," said Sairy. "You'll certainly see Allan."

But Tom did not believe it, and he wanted intensely to see the
army. "I see it when I dream, and I see it often and often when
I'm sitting here. I see it marching, marching, and I see it going into
battle, and I see it bivouacking. But it won't look at me, and though
sometimes I take the boys' hands there ain't any touch to them, and
I can see the drums beating, but they don't give any sound —"

Sairy looked away, out and over the great view below the toll-
gate. "I know, Tom. Sometimes in the night-time I sit up an' say,
'That was a bugle blowing.' An' I listen, but I can't hear it then.
— But the Lord tells us to be content, an' you'd better let him see
you're tryin' to mind him! What good'll it do Allan or the army if
I have to set up with you to-night an' your heart gives out? You'd
better save yourself so's to see him when he does come home. My
land! the lot of things he'll have to tell, settin' on the porch an' the
war over, an' school takin' in again —"

"Sairy," said Tom wistfully, "sometimes I get an awful fear that
we ain't going to beat —"

"Sho!" said Sairy. "If we don't beat one way we will another!
I ain't a-worryin' about that. Nothing's ever teetotally beaten, not
even eggs when you make cake. It's an awful safe universe."

"It ain't your day," said Tom, "for a clean apron, but you've
got one on."

"I ain't never denied that there was a Sunday feel in the air! We
may n't see the army and we may n't see Allan, but they're only a
few miles from us."

"What's that I smell? — It's gingerbread baking!"

"I had a pint of molasses saved away an' a little sugar. I just
thought I might as well make gingerbread. If Allan came he'd like

it, an' if he did n't we could eat it talkin' of him an' sayin' we were keepin' his birthday."

She went into the kitchen. Tom rested his forehead on the knob of his cane. His lips moved. The wind rustled the leaves of the forest, the sun shone. Thunder Run sang, the bees hummed above the old blush roses, the yellow cat came up the path and rubbed against Tom's ankle. The smell of the gingerbread floated out hot and strong, a redbird in a gum tree broke into a clear, high carolling.

"O Lord, I'm an old man," whispered Tom. "I ain't got much fun or pleasure before me —"

Sairy, coming back to the doorstep, stood a moment, then struck her hands together. "Allan's coming up the road, Tom!"

An hour of happiness had gone by. Then said Allan: "I've two hours yet and the last part of it I'm going to spend telling about the Wilderness and Spottsylvania and Cold Harbour. But now I want to go up the mountain and say 'how d' ye do' to the Maydews."

"Yes, I reckon you'd better," said Tom. "Only don't stay too long. They've got Billy and Dave."

"Bring Christianna down the mountain with you," said Sairy. "Billy and Dave can tell her good-bye here just as well as there."

Up on the mountain Mrs. Maydew made a like suggestion. "Allan, I'd like to talk to you, but I've got to talk to Billy an' Dave. Violetta and Rosalinda they're gettin' somethin' for those boys to eat, they look so thin an' starved, an' grandpap an' the dawgs air jest sittin' gazin' for pure gladness! — Christianna, you entertain Allan."

"I've got time," said Allan, "to go look at the school-house. That 's what I'd like to do."

The school-house was partly fallen down and the marigolds and larkspur that Allan had planted were all one with the tall grass, and a storm had broken off a great bough of the walnut tree. Allan and Christianna sat on the doorstep, and listened to a singing that was not of Thunder Run.

Allan took her hand. "Christianna, I was the stupidest teacher—"

That night the Second Corps lay by the James, under the great shadow of the Blue Ridge, but at dawn it took the road for Staunton and thence for the lower Valley. It went to threaten Washington and to clutch with Sheridan, who was presently sent to the Valley with orders to lay it waste — orders which he obeyed to the letter.

CHAPTER XXXIV

THE ROAD TO WASHINGTON

STEVE had had no intention whatever of rejoining the army. And yet here he was, embodied again in the Sixty-fifth, and moving, ordinary time, on Staunton! How it had happened he could hardly have related. Weariness of life on Thunder Run, where of late he had begun to dislike even Christianna Maydew, — uncertainty as to whether the Yankees might not return and sweep it clean, in which case his skin might be endangered, — a kind of craving hunger for company and variety and small adventure, coupled with memories of much of the same, — a certain pale homesickness, after all, for the regiment, — a conviction that battles were some distance off, probably clear to the other end of the Valley, and that straggling before such an event was only a matter of watching your opportunity, — all this and a ragged underweb of emotionalism brought Steve again to follow the drum. It is doubtful, however, if anything would have done so had he not by purest accident encountered his sometime colonel.

Cleave, riding along the forming brigade in the first light, reached the Sixty-fifth. The regiment cheered him. He lifted his hat and came on down the line, an aide behind him. Steve, on the rim of a camp-fire built by recruits of this year who knew not the Sixty-fifth of the past, tried to duck, but his general saw him. He spoke to the aide. "Tell that man to come here."

Steve limped forward with scared eyes, a cold dew upon hands and forehead. And after all, all that the general said was, "You are nettle and dock and burr by nature and anger has no meaning in dealing with you! Are you coming again with the Sixty-fifth?"

"Gawd, General! not if you think I'd better not, sir,—"

"I?" said Cleave, "I will speak to your colonel about you. For the rest you can fire a musket." He smiled grimly. "Still that sore foot? Has it been sore all this time?"

"General, it's been sorer!—'n' if you'd tell the men that they

shan't act some of them so cold 'n' some of them so hot toward me?—
'n' I saved the life of them all only day before yesterday," Steve
whimpered, "'n' yours, too, General."

"Thank you," said Cleave with gravity. "Fall in, now — and
remember that your Captain's eye will be on you."

Fall in! — Fall in! — Fall in! . . . Column forward!

Down the Valley Pike marched the Second Corps. Lexington —
Staunton — Harrisonburg — on and on upon the old, familiar road.
"Howdy, Valley Pike," said the Second Corps. "Howdy, Old
Lady! Missed us, have n't you? We've missed you. We've
thought of you — thought of you in all kinds of tight places! —

> "'Should auld acquaintance be forgot
> And days of auld lang syne —'"

"Don't seem to us you're looking well — ragged and lonely and
burned up and hewed down — cheer up!

> "'We'll take a cup of kindness yet —'"

Miles and miles and miles of old-time heat and dust and thirst!
Tramp, tramp! — Tramp, tramp! Miles and miles. "There never
were enough springs and streams on this road and old Miss War's
done drunk those up! — O Lord, for a river of buttermilk! —"

The dust weighted down pokeberry and stickweed, alder, blackberry and milkweed. The old trim walls bounding the Valley Pike
were now mere ruinous heaps of stones. The thousands of marching
feet, the wheels, the hoofs furred these with dust. There were no
wooden fences now of any description; there were few wayside trees,
few wayside buildings. There were holes where the fence posts had
been, and there were stumps of trees and there were blackened
foundations where houses had been, and all these were yellowed
and softened with dust. A long, thick, and moving wall, the dust
accompanied the Second Corps.

The Second Corps was used to it, used to it in its eyes, its throat,
down its neck, in its shoes, all over. The Second Corps was used to
poor shoes and to half shoes — used to uniforms whose best day was
somewhere in past ages — used to hunger — used to thirst, thirst,
thirst — used to twenty miles, twenty miles in heat and glare, or in
mud and rain, or in ice or snow — used to the dust cloud, used to

the storm, used to marching and marching, used to battling, used to a desperate war in a desperate land, used to singing, used to joking, used to despairing, used to hoping — used to dusty marches! It was a long time since the dusty march by Ashby's Gap across to First Manassas. New Market, Mount Jackson, Edenburg, Woodstock, Strasburg, Middletown, Kernstown — on the second of July they came to Winchester. Sigel was at Martinsburg beyond.

Winchester was haggard, grey, and war-worn. How many times she had changed hands, passed from grey lover to blue master, it would be hard to tell. They were very many. Winchester had two faces, a proud and joyful and a depressed and sorrowful face. To-day she wore the first.

On through Winchester, out upon the Pike to Martinsburg! There was skirmishing and Sigel quit the place, leaving behind him a deal of stores. That night he retired across the Potomac, to Maryland Heights by Harper's Ferry, and the next day he burned the railroad and pontoon bridges at that place. The fifth and sixth of July the Second Corps crossed the river at Shepherdstown, crossed with loud singing.

> "Come! 'T is the red dawn of the day,
>   Maryland!"

Steve was with the Sixty-fifth still. He had meant to leave before they got to Martinsburg, but the occasion did not arise and the Sixty-fifth swept him on. He had meant to hide in Martinsburg and soberly wait until the Second Corps had disappeared in the direction of the Potomac, when he would emerge and turn his face homeward. But in Martinsburg were the stores that Sigel had abandoned. Coffee, sugar, canned goods, wheat bread — Steve supped with the regiment on the fat of the land. But it was his intention not to be present at roll-call next morning, and in pursuance of it he rolled, in the dark hour before dawn, out of the immediate encampment of the Sixty-fifth, down a little rocky lane and under the high-built porch of a small house of whitewashed stone. Here he lay until the first light. . . . It showed through the lattice of his hiding-place an overturned sutler's wagon. Steve, creeping out, crept across and with his arms that were lean and long, felt in the straw. The wagon had been looted and the tears nearly came to his eyes on finding it so. And then he came upon a bottle fallen from a case that had been taken away. It was champagne.

Reveille sounding, the Sixty-fifth rose in the dim light and while making its cursory toilette thought of breakfast with coffee — with coffee — with coffee! Mess-fires burst into saffron bloom, the good smell of the coffee and of the sizzling bacon permeated the air, the Sixty-fifth came most cheerfully to breakfast. It sat down on the dewy earth around the fires, pleasant at this hour of the morning, it lifted its tin cups, blew upon the scalding coffee, sipped and sipped and agreed that life was good. Everybody was cheerful; at roll-call which immediately followed, everybody was present, in a full, firm tone of voice. Steve Dagg, filled with French courage, was most present.

French courage was still unevaporated when the column moved forward. Then, with a shock, it was too late — he could n't get away — they were crossing the Potomac —

"I hear the distant thunder-hum,
Maryland!
The Old Line bugle, fife, and drum,
Maryland!"

"Gawd!" thought Steve. "They got me at last! I can't get away — I can't get back 'cross the river! Why'd I drink that stuff that was like cider 'n' whistled me back jest as easy? Why'd I leave Thunder Run? They got me in a trap —"

Maryland Heights was strongly fortified, too strongly for Breckinridge and Gordon, demonstrating against it, to drive out the blue forces. After a day Early swept on through the passes of South Mountain, toward Frederick, east and south of which town runs the Monocacy. On this stream there formed to meet the grey a portion of the blue Eighth Army Corps and Rickett's division of the Sixteenth Corps, six thousand men under General Lew Wallace.

There were earthworks and two blockhouses and they overfrowned the two bridges that crossed the Monocacy. Beyond these and on either side the blue lines, strongly seen in the clear, hot forenoon, were fields with board fences and straw stacks, much stout fencing and many and closely ranged straw stacks. Through these fields ran the clear road to Washington, blocked now at the river by Wallace and his men.

Jubal Early sent McCausland across, who dismounted his caval-rymen and with them fell so furiously on the enemy's left flank that it broke. It gathered again and pushed McCausland back, where-upon Early sent across by the same ford Breckinridge with Gordon's division, Ramseur in the mean time skirmishing on the western bank with the blue's advanced front. Gordon attacked with his usual gallantry, King's and Nelson's artillery supporting. The blue cen-tre broke and rolled back from the banks of Monocacy. Ramseur and Rodes now crossed with a shout, and at a double all grey troops swept forward.

Steve crossed Monocacy because he must, and climbed several fences because he saw that if he did n't he would be trampled. But in the straw field he fell, groaning. "Hit?" asked the man beside him and was immediately gone, the regiment rushing forward.

Steve drew himself well behind a great straw stack, splitting the advance like a spongy Gibraltar. Here he found a more or less like-minded private from one of the Georgia regiments. This one had quite deeply burrowed, and Steve, noting the completeness of his retirement, tore out for himself a like cavern in the straw. Outside was shouting and confusion and smoke; in here was space at least in which to have a vision of the clear security of Thunder Run Moun-tain. "You wounded, too?" proffered from behind a straw parti-tion his fellow retirer.

"Yaas," answered Steve. "In the foot."

"I got hurt in the hip," said the other. "It's an old strain, and sometimes, when we're double-quicking, I'm liable to give out. The boys all know about it and make allowance. They all know I fight like the devil up to that point."

"Same here," said Steve. "I fight like a tiger, but now 'n' then comes along a time when a man's under a moral necessity not to. When your foot gives under you you can't go on charging — not if Napoleon Cæsar himself was there shoutin' about duty!"

"Them's my sentiments," said the other. "We're going to win this battle. I see it the way we looked going in. How do you feel about going on to Washington?"

"I've had my doubts," said Steve. "How do you feel?"

"It's powerful rich and full of things to eat and drink and wear. But there'd be awful fighting getting in."

"That's the way I feel," said Steve. "Awful fightin' 'n' I don't —"

An officer's sword invaded their dwelling-place. "Get out of here! What are you doing hiding here? Tie you in this rick and set fire to it, you damned skulkers! Get out and march ahead!" The flat of the sword descended vigorously.

Steve yelped and rubbed. "Gawd, Captain! don't do that! I got a hurt foot —"

Much later, having been carried on — the whole wagon train now crossing — in a commissary wagon travelling light, he rejoined his brigade and regiment. He found the Sixty-fifth in a mood of jubilation bivouacked in the dusk Maryland countryside, with a glow yet in the west and the fireflies tinselling all the fields. Steve came in for supper, and between slow gulps of "real" coffee related an adventure in the straw field, marvellous as the "Three Turks' Heads." His mess was one of "left-overs," seven or eight of the stupid, the ne'er-do-weel or the slightly rascally sort, shaken together in the regiment's keen sifting of human nature. Totally incredulous, save for a deficient one or two, the mess yet found a place for Steve, if it were only the place of a torn leaf from a rather sorry jest-book. The ne'er-do-weel and the slightly rascally, most of whom were courageous enough, began to describe for his benefit the *chevaux-de-frise* of forts around Washington. They made Steve shiver. He went to bed frightened, and arose under the stars, still frightened.

This day, the tenth of July, the Second Corps marched twenty miles. The day was one of the hottest of a hot summer. Not the lightest zephyr lifted a leaf or dried the sweat on a soldier's brow. The dust of the Georgetown Pike rose thick and stifling until it made a broad and deep and thick and stifling cloud. There was little water to be had throughout the day. The Second Corps suffered profoundly. That night it lay in the fields by the roadside near Rockville. The night was smoking hot, and the men lay feverishly, moving their limbs and sighing, troubled with dreams. The bugles sounded under a copper dawn and they rose to an eleventh of July, hot, dust-clogged, and thirsty as had been the tenth.

There were sunstrokes this day, exhaustion from heat, a trail of involuntary stragglers, men limping in the rear, men sitting, head on knees, beneath the powdered wayside growth, men lying motionless in the ditch beside the road. Horses fell and died. There were many delays. But through all heat, great weariness, and suffering, Early, shrill-voiced and determined, urged the troops on upon the road to Washington. The troops responded. Something less than eight thousand muskets moved in the great dust of the pike, forty guns, and ahead, the four small cavalry brigades of McCausland, Imboden, W. L. Jackson, and Bradley Johnson. "— —!" said Early. "If we can't take it, at least we can give it a quaking fit! — increase the peace clamour! It's worth while to see if we can get to the outer fortifications before they pour their — — numbers into them!"

The Second Corps marched fast, now by the Silver Spring Road, Imboden's cavalry ahead, Jackson's on the flank, full before them Fort Stevens, very visible in the distance, Washington. The men moistened their lips, talked, for all the dust in their throats, the blood beating in their temples, and the roaring in their ears. "Take it! Could we take it?" — " By supernal luck — a chance in a million — if they were all asleep or dazed!" — "Take it and end the war — O God, if we could!" — "Run up the Stars and Bars — Play 'Dixie' everywhere — Live! at last *live* after four years of being born!" — "Take Washington — eight thousand of us and the cavalry and the twelve-pounder Napoleons —" From the front broke out a long crackling fire. "Cavalry in touch — cavalry in touch." Rodes's division, leading, came into line of battle. As it did so rose in the south between Fort Stevens and the city a great dust cloud. "— —!" said Early. "There isn't a plan or a cannon numbers won't spike! — *Skirmishers to the front!*"

"Every prominent point," says a Federal officer, speaking of the Washington fortifications, — "every prominent point, at intervals of eight hundred to one thousand yards, was occupied by an enclosed field fort; every important approach or depression of ground, unseen from the forts, was swept by a battery for field-guns; and the whole connected by rifle trenches which were in fact lines of infantry parapets, furnishing emplacement for two ranks of men, and affording covered communication along the line, while roads were opened wherever necessary, so that troops and artillery could be moved rapidly from one point of the immense periphery to another, or under cover, from point to point along the line. The counterscarps were surrounded by abatis; bomb-proofs were provided in nearly all the forts; all guns, not solely intended for distant fire, placed in embrasures and well traversed. All commanding points on which an enemy would be likely to concentrate artillery . . . were subjected not only to the fire, direct and across, of many points along the line, but also from heavy rifled guns from points unattainable by the enemy's field-guns." There were twenty thousand blue troops, garrison and reserves, and in addition, at two o'clock of this day, began to arrive Ricketts's and Emory's divisions of the Sixth and Nineteenth Corps, sent by Grant.

The eleventh and the twelfth there was heavy skirmishing. During these days the Second Corps saw that it could not take Washington. The heat continued; now through quivering air, now through great dust clouds they saw the dome of the capitol. It was near, near! The Second Corps was closer to Washington than ever in this war had been the North to Richmond; it was very near, but there is the possible and there is the impossible, and it was not possible for the Second Corps to make entry. On the night of the twelfth it withdrew from before Washington and marching to the Potomac crossed by White's Ford into Loudoun County. Fifteen thousand blue troops pursued, but the grey crossed the river in safety. They crossed singing "Swanee River." It was the last sally of the beleaguered South forth upon the beleaguerer's ground. Henceforth, the battle thundered against the very inner keep of the fortress.

Marching through great dust and heat and glare and weariness back through Maryland to the Potomac, the Second Corps gathered up from the roadside and the byways and the hedges its stragglers, involuntary or otherwise. A dozen hours from Washington it gathered out of a cornfield Steve Dagg.

CHAPTER XXXV

THE CRATER

A T Petersburg, on the Appomattox, twenty miles south of Richmond, June went by in thunder, day and night, of artillery duels, with, for undersong, a perpetual, pattering rain of sharpshooters' bullets, torn across, at intervals, by a sharp and long sound of musketry. In the hot and sickly weather, under the hovering smoke, engineers of the Army of Northern Virginia, engineers of the Army of the Potomac worked like beavers. The grey line drawn by Beauregard early in the month was strengthened and pieced out. Over against it curved a great blue sickle of forts, with trenches and parapets between. Grey and blue alike had in the rear of their manned works a labyrinth and honeycomb of approaches, covered ways, pits, magazines, bomb-proofs, traverses. The blue had fearfully the advantage in artillery. Grey and blue, the lines, in part, were very close, so close that there would be little warning of assault. The Army of Northern Virginia, now, in numbers, not a great army, had to watch, day and night. It watched with an intensity which brought a further depth into men's eyes, deep enough now in all conscience, deep enough in the summer of 1864!

On the twenty-second, Grant attempted to extend his flank upon the left toward the Weldon Railroad. Lee sent A. P. Hill out against this movement. Hill, in his red battle shirt, strong fighter and prompt, swung through an opening left unaware between the two corps, the Second and Sixth, and, turning, struck the Second in the rear. After the fiercest fighting the blue, having lost four guns and several stands of colours, and seventeen hundred prisoners, drew back within their lines.

Grant dispatched two divisions of cavalry with orders to tear up the Lynchburg and Danville Railroad. They spread ruin south to the Staunton River, but here W. H. F. Lee, who had followed, attacked them at Blacks and Whites. Retiring they found themselves between two fires. Wade Hampton and Fitzhugh Lee, back from the fight at Trevillian's Station, fell upon the two divisions at Sapony Church. Infantry of Mahone's came up also and aided. After a running fight of a day and night, in which the blue lost, in killed and wounded and taken, fifteen hundred men, twelve guns, and a wagon train, they escaped over the Blackwater, burning the bridge, between them and the grey, and so returned to Grant at Petersburg.

On the first of July, General Alexander, Longstreet's Chief of Artillery, wounded and furloughed home, was driven, before quitting the lines, to Violet Bank, where were Lee's headquarters. About the place were small, much the worse for wear, Confederate tents. The commanding general himself had a room within the house. The wounded officer found him standing, with several of the staff, upon the porch steps. He had his field-glasses open, and he was listening to the report of a scout. When at last the man saluted and fell back, Alexander stated the conviction that was in him. He felt a certainty that the enemy was engaged in driving a mine under the point known as Elliott's Salient.

"Why do you think so, General?"

"Their sharpshooters keep up a perpetual, converging fire, sir, upon just that hand's-breadth of our line. On the other hand, they pay so little attention to the works to right and left that the men can show themselves with impunity. They are not clearing the ground for surface approaches — well, then, I think that they are working underground. If you were going from that side to explode a mine and assault immediately afterward, that would be the place you would choose, I think."

"That is true," said Lee. "But you would have to make a long tunnel to get under that salient, General."

"About five hundred feet, sir."

Mr. Francis Lawley, of the London *Times*, was of the group upon the steps. "In the siege of Delhi, sir, we drove what was, I believe, considered the longest possible gallery. It was four hundred feet. Beyond that it was found impossible to ventilate."

"The enemy," said Alexander, "have a number of Pennsylvania coal-miners, who may be trusted to find some means to ventilate. This war is doing a power of things that were not done at Delhi."

"I will act on your warning, General," said Lee.

The next day the grey began to drive two countermines. Later in the month they started two others. Pegram's battery occupied the threatened salient, with Elliott's troops in the rifle-pits. The grey miners drove as far and fast as they might, but they tunnelled outward from either flank of the salient, while the Pennsylvania coalminers, twenty feet underground, dug straight toward the apex. The days passed — many days.

On the eighteenth was received the news of the removal of Joseph E. Johnston from the command of the Army of Tennessee. Wade Hampton, being at headquarters, heard Lee's expression of opinion and wrote it to General Johnston. . . . "He expressed great regret that you had been removed and said that he had done all in his power to prevent it. He had said to Mr. Seddon that if you could not command the army we had no one who could." Later came the tidings of Hood's lost battle of Atlanta and all its train of slow disaster. On the twenty-fifth, news of Jubal Early's victory at Winchester the day before was cheered to the echo. In the last days of the month came news of Stoneman and McCook's raiding in Georgia and of the scattered fighting in Arkansas.

North and South, away from the camps, there was flagging of spirit and sickness of soul. In the North the war was costing close upon four millions of dollars a day. Gold in July went to two hundred and eighty-five. The North gained now its fresh soldiers by bounties, and those heavy. All the northern tier of states, great as they were, untouched by invasion, and the ocean theirs — all the North winced and staggered now under the burden of the war. But the South — the South was past wincing. Bent to her knees, bowed like a caryatid, she fought on in her fixed position.

At Petersburg, Grant meant to explode a great mine and to follow it, in the confusion, by a great and determined assault. Moreover, in order to weaken the opposition here and the more to distract and appall, he detached Hancock with twenty thousand men for a feint against Richmond. Hancock marched to Deep Bottom, where Butler, having ironclads on the river and a considerable force encamped on the northern bank, guarded two pontoon bridges across the James. Between this place and Richmond was Conner's grey brigade and at Drewry's Bluff, Willcox's division. Moving with Hancock was Sheridan and six thousand horse.

Lee, watchful, sent Kershaw's division to join with Willcox and Conner and guard Richmond. Hancock crossed on the twenty-seventh, and that morning Kershaw came into collision with Sheridan, losing prisoners and two colours. Lee further detached W. H. F. Lee's cavalry and Heth's infantry. The alarm bell rang rapid and loud in Richmond and all the home defences went out to the lines. But Hancock, checked at Deep Bottom, only flourished before Richmond; on the twenty-ninth, indeed, drew back in part to the Petersburg lines, in order to take part in the great and general assault. When the thirtieth dawned, with Willcox, Kershaw, Heth, and the cavalry away, Lee was holding lines, ten miles from tip to tip, with not more than twenty thousand men.

It was a boding, still night, hot in the far-flung wild tangle of trenches, pits, and approaches, hot in the fields, hot in Poor Creek Valley where the blue were massing, hot amongst the guns of Elliott's Salient. The stars were a little dimmed by dust in the air and the yet undissipated smoke from the artillery firing that had ceased at dusk.

In the blue lines there was between generals a difference of opinion as to what division should lead in the now imminent assault. Burnside advised the use of Ferrero's coloured division. Meade dissented, and the point was referred to Grant. He says: "General Burnside wanted to put his coloured division in front, and I believe if he had done so it would have been a success. Still I agreed with General Meade as to his objections to that plan. General Meade said that if we put the coloured troops in front (we had only one division) and it should prove a failure, it would then be said, and very properly, that we were shoving these people ahead to get killed because we did not care anything about them. But that could not be said if we put white troops in front."

This settled it, and Ledlie's division was given the lead. It formed behind earthworks full in front of Elliott's Salient, in its rear two supporting divisions; its objective Cemetery Hill, commanding the town; its orders, as soon as the mine should explode, to pass over and through the grey's torn line, take the hill, and pass into Petersburg. It was midnight when Ledlie's line was formed, the supporting divisions drawn up. The night was hot and exceedingly close; the men stood waiting, feverish, every sense alert. One o'clock —

two o'clock — three o'clock. Ledlie moved forward, taking position immediately behind the breastworks. Again a wait, every eye upon where, in the darkness, should be Elliott's Salient.

On the grey side there was knowledge that a mine was digging, but ignorance of the day or night in which it would be fired. Lee slept, or waked, at Violet Bank; far and near in its trenches the Army of Northern Virginia lay, well-picketed, in a restless sleep. The nights were hot, and there was much misery and frequent night firing. All sleep now was restless, easily and often broken. There were South Carolina troops in and about Elliott's Salient. Reveille would sound and the sun would rise shortly before five o'clock.

The stars began to pale. Ledlie sent to General Burnside to ask the cause of delay. The men had been in ranks for four hours. Burnside answered that the fuse had been lit at a quarter-past three but evidently had not burned the sufficient distance. A lieutenant and a sergeant had volunteered to enter the tunnel, find out what was the matter and relight the fuse. Ledlie's aide returned and reported, and the division stood tense, gazing with a strained intention. It was light enough now to see, beyond their own advanced works, the grey line they meant to send skyward. Beyond the line was Petersburg, that they meant to take; beyond Petersburg, a day's march, was Richmond.

The light strengthened, pallor in the north and south and west, in the east a cold, faint, upstreaming purple. Somewhere in the cavalry lines a bugle blew, remote, thin, of an elfin melancholy. As though it had been the signal, the mine exploded.

The morning light was darkened. The earth heaved so that many of the blue staggered and fell. A mass sprang into the air, mounted a hundred feet and spread out into an umbrella-shaped cloud. As it began to descend, it was seen that earth and rock might come upon the blue themselves. The troops gave back with shouts.

In that cloud of pulverized earth, smoke, and flame were mammoth clods of clay, one as large as a small cabin, timber of salient and breastworks, guns, carriages, caissons, sandbags, anything and everything that had been upon the mined ground, including some hundreds of human beings. The hole it left behind it was one hundred and seventy feet long, sixty wide, and thirty deep. Back into this now rained in part the lumps of earth, the logs of wood, the pieces of iron, the human clay. The trembling of the earth ceased, the sound of the detonation ceased. There came what seemed an instant of utter quiet, for after that rage of sound the cries of the yet living, the only partially buried in that pit, counted as nothing. The instant was shattered by the concerted voice of one hundred and fifty blue guns and mortars, prepared and stationed to add their great quota of death and terror. They brought into that morning of distraction one of the heaviest cannonades of all the war.

Through the rocking air, in the first slant beams of the sun the blue troops heard the order to advance. They moved. Before them were their own breastworks over which they must swarm, thus sharply breaking line. Beyond these, one hundred and fifty yards away, were curious heaps of earth, something like dunes. The air above was yet dust and smoke. On went the Second Brigade, leading. It came, yet without just alignment, to the crest of the dunes, and from these it saw the crater. . . . There was no pausing, there could be none, for the First Brigade, immediately in the rear, was pressing on. The blue troops slid down the steep incline and came upon the floor of the crater, among the débris and the horribly caught and buried and smothered men.

There followed a moment's hesitation and gasp of astonishment; then the blue officers shouted the brigade forward. It overpassed the seamed floor and reached the steep other side of the excavation. Behind it it heard, or might have heard if anything could have been heard in the roar of one hundred and fifty guns, the First Brigade slipping and stumbling in its turn down the almost perpendicular slope into the crater. The Second Brigade climbed somehow the thirty feet up to the level of the world at large. On this side the hole it was a grey world.

If the explosion had stunned the grey, they had now regained their senses. If the force of the appalling blue cannonade caused an end-of-the-world sensation, even in such a cataclysm there was room for action. The grey acted. Into the ruined trenches right and left of and behind the destroyed salient poured what was left of Elliott's brigade. Regiments of Wise and Ramseur came at a run. Lee, now with Beauregard at the threatened front, sent orders to Mahone to bring up two brigades with all speed. A gun of Davidson's battery in a salient to the right commanded at less than four hundred yards what had been Elliott's Salient and was now the crater. Wright's battery on the left, Haskell's Coehorn mortars fringing a gorge line in the rear, likewise could send death into that hollow. Infantry and artillery, the grey opened with a steady, rapid fire. And all the time, behind the blue Second Brigade, now forming for a rush on the greyward edge of the crater, came massing into that deep and wide and long bear-pit more blue troops, and yet more. And now the Second Brigade, checked and disconcerted by the unexpected strength of the resistance, wavered, could not be formed, fell back into the crater that was already too filled with men.

Here formation became impossible. An aide was sent in hot haste to General Ledlie, for his own fame somewhat too securely placed in the rear. Ledlie sent back word to Marshall and Bartlett, leading, that they must advance and assault at once; it was General Burnside's order. The aide says: "This message was delivered. But the firing on the crater now was incessant, and it was as heavy a fire of canister as was ever poured continuously upon a single objective point. It was as utterly impracticable to re-form a brigade in that crater as it would be to marshal bees into line after upsetting the hive; and equally as impracticable to re-form outside of the crater, under the severe fire in front and rear, as it would be to hold a dress parade in front of a charging enemy."

So far from the pit being cleared, it received fresh accessions. Griffin's brigade, coming up, tried to pass by the right, but entangled in a maze of grey earthworks, trenches, traverses, and disordered by the searching fire, it too fell aside and sank into the hollow made by the mine. "Every organization melted away, as soon as it entered this hole in the ground, into a mass of human beings clinging by toes and heels to the almost perpendicular sides. If a man was shot on the crest he fell and rolled to the bottom of the pit."

The blue Third Division, arriving, attacked the manned works to the left, took and for a little held them, then was driven back. Haskell's grey battery of sixteen guns on the Jerusalem Plank Road came greatly into action. Lee and Beauregard were watching from the Gee house. Mahone, of A. P. Hill's Corps, was coming up with three brigades, coming fast. . . .

The coloured division of the Ninth Army corps had a song, —

"We looks lak men er-marchin' on,
  We looks lak men ob war —"

They had sung it sitting on the ground around camp-fires the
night before when they had been told that they would lead the
charge — the great charge that was going to take Blandford Church
and Cemetery, and then Petersburg, and then Richmond, and was
going to end the war and make all coloured people free, and give
to every one a cabin, forty acres, and a mule, and the deathless
friendship of the Northern people.

"We looks lak men er-marchin' on,
  We looks lak men ob war —"

They had not led that grotesquely halted charge, but now they,
too, were required for victims by the crater. Burnside sent an order,
"The coloured division to advance at all hazards."

It advanced, got somehow past the crater and came to a bloody,
hand-to-hand conflict with the grey. The fighting here was brutal,
a maddening short war in which, black and white, the always animal struggle of war grew more animal yet. It was short. The coloured
division broke and fell back into the crater. . . . All the grey batteries, all the grey infantry poured fire into this place where Burnside's white and coloured troops were now inextricably mixed. At
ten o'clock up came Mahone with three brigades and swept the
place.

By two o'clock the Confederate lines were restored and the battle
of the crater ended. This day the blue had been hoist by their own
petard. The next day Grant sent a flag of truce asking a cessation
of hostilities until he could gather his wounded and bury the dead.
Lee gave four hours.

During this truce grey soldiers as well as blue pressed to the edge
of the crater to observe and wonder. They were used to massacre
and horror in great variety, but there was something faintly novel
here. They came not ghoulishly, but good-naturedly — "just want-
ing to see what gunpowder could do!" They fraternized with the
blue at work and the blue fraternized with them, for that was the
way the grey and blue did between hostilities. They spoke the same
language, they read the same Bible, they had behind them the same
background of a far island home, and then of small sailing-ships at

sea, and then of a new land, huge forests, Indians, wolves; at last towns and farms, roads, stages, packet-boats, and railway trains. They had to an extent the same tastes — to an extent like casts of countenance. The one used "I guess" and the other used "I reckon," and they differed somewhat in temperament, but the innermost meaning was not far from being the same. At the worst an observer from a far country might have said, "They are half brothers." So they fraternized during the truce, the grey this afternoon, the more triumphant, and the blue the more rueful. . . . "Hello, Yanks! You were going to send us to Heaven, were n't you? and instead you got sent yourselves!" — "Never mind! better luck next time! You certainly made a fuss in the world for once!" — "How many pounds of gunpowder? 'Eight thousand.' Geewhilikins! That was a sizable charge!" — "If you'd been as flush of gunpowder as we are, you might have made it twenty, just as easy!" — "There's a man buried over there — see, where the boot is sticking up!" — "Yes, you blew some of us into Heaven — twenty-two gunners, they say, and about three hundred of Elliott's men—just enough to show your big crowd the way!" — "That junk-heap over there's Pegram's guns." — "Such a mess! White men and black men and caissons and limbers." — "I thought that body was moving; but no, it was something else." — "Got any tobacco?" — "We'd like first-rate to trade for coffee." — "There's a man crying for water. Got your canteen?—mine is n't any nearer than a spring a mile away. I'll take it to him— know what thirst means— been thirsty myself and it means Hell!" — "Well, it was a fine mine, if it did go a bit wrong, and you deserve a lot of credit — though I don't think some of your generals do!" — "Yes, that's so! People stay what they always were, even through war. Lee stays Lee and Grant stays Grant, and Meade stays Meade, and A. P. Hill stays A. P. Hill. And some others stay what they always were, too, — more's the pity!" — "Here, we'll help cover this row." — "Did you see little Billy Mahone charging? Pretty fine, was n't it?" — "Saw your Colonel Marshall and General Bartlett when they were taken prisoner. They seemed fine men. Yes, that's so! We ain't got a monopoly, and you ain't got a monopoly."

The truce would last until full dark. Now, as the sun went down in a copper sky, most of the work was done. In great numbers the wounded had been lifted from the floor and sides of the crater; in great numbers the dead had been lowered into trenches, shallow trenches, the earth just covering the escaped from life. There were yet blue working-parties, a faint movement of blue and grey watchers, but the crater was lonely to what it had been. Only the wild débris remained, and the mounds beneath which life had gone out and been buried. There seemed a silence, too, heavy with the approaching night. A grey pioneer detail that had been engaged in repairing a work that flanked the vast excavation rested on spade and pick and gazed into the place. An infantry company of A. P. Hill's, marching to some assigned post, was halted for five minutes and allowed to break ranks. Officers and men desired to look at the big hole in the ground.

In groups or singly they peered over the edge or scrambled halfway down the loose earth of the sides. The sun's rim had dipped; the west showed a forbidding hue, great level washes of a cold and sickly colour. Steadily this slope of the great earth wheeled under, leaving the quenchless hearth of the sun, facing the night without the house of light. It was all but dusk. One of the soldiers of this company was Maury Stafford. He stood alone, his back to a great projecting piece of timber and looked into the pit and across to the copper west. "Barring prison," he thought, "for simple horror I have never seen a worse place than this."

CHAPTER XXXVI

THE VALLEY

EARLY's task in the Valley throughout this summer and autumn was to preserve a threatening attitude toward blue territory on the other side of the Potomac, to hinder and harass Federal use of the Chesapeake and Ohio Canal and the Baltimore and Ohio Railroad, and to render the Northern Capital so continuously anxious that it might at any time choose to weaken Grant in order to add to its own defences. In addition he had presently Sheridan to contend with, Sheridan strengthened by Hunter, returned now from the Kanawha Valley to the main battle-grounds.

Sheridan's task in the Valley was to give body to the Northern reasoning as to the uses, at this stage of the game, of that section. With war rapidly concentrating as it now was, the Northern Government saw the Valley no more as a battle-ground, nor as of especial use to the blue colour on the chessboard. But it was of use to the grey, especially that rich portion of it called the Shenandoah Valley. Moreover it was grey; scourge it well and you scourged a grey province. Make it untenable, a desert, and the loss would be felt where it was meant to be felt. Sheridan, with Hunter to aid, devastated as thoroughly as if his name had been Attila. McCausland made a cavalry raid into Pennsylvania and, in reprisal for Hunter's burnings, burned the town of Chambersburg. It did not stop the burnings across the river; they went on through the length and breadth of the Valley of Virginia. Over the mountains, in Northern Virginia, in the rolling counties of Fauquier and Loudoun, was "Mosby's Confederacy," where the most daring of all grey partisan leaders "operated in the enemy's lines." Mosby did what lay in man to do to help the lower Valley. He "worried and harassed" Sheridan by day and by night. But the burning and lifting went on. When late autumn came, with winter before it, a great region lay bare, and over it wandered a vision of drawn faces of women and a cry of small children.

Sheridan in person did not come until the first week in August. Late in July Early fought the Army of West Virginia, Crook and Averell, at Winchester — fought and won. Here the Golden Brigade did good service, and here the "Fighting Sixty-fifth" won mention again, and here Steve Dagg definitely determined to renounce the Confederate service.

Life had taken on for Steve an aspect of '62 in the Valley — only worse. In a dreadful dream he seemed to be recovering old tints, repeating old experiences from Front Royal to Winchester — but all darkened and hardened. In '62 the country was still rich, and you could forage, but now there was no foraging. There was nothing to forage for. Then the old Army of the Valley had been ill-clad and curiously confident and cheerful, with Mr. Commissary Banks double-quicking down the pike, before Old Jack! Now the Second Corps was worse-clad, and far, far from the ancient careless cheer. It still laughed and joked and sang, but less often, and always, when it did laugh, it was with a certain grimness as of Despair not far off. On night and day marches, you heard song and jest, indeed, but you heard heavy sighs as well — a heavy sighing in the night-time or the daytime, as the army moved on the Valley Pike. Now confident good cheer in others was extraordinarily necessary to Steve. When it flagged, it was as though a raft had sunk from beneath him. Yes, it was '62 over again, but a homesick, strange, far worse '62! Daily life grew to be for him a series of shocks, more or less violent, but all violent. Life went in magic-lantern slides — alternate blackness and frightful, vivid pictures in which blood red predominated. Steve developed a morbid horror of blood.

August came. At Moorefield occurred a cavalry fight, Averell against McCausland and Bradley Johnson, the grey suffering defeat. On the seventh came Sheridan with the Sixth and the Nineteenth Army Corps and Torbert's great force of cavalry. The blue forces in the Valley now numbered perhaps forty-five thousand, with some thousands more in garrison at Martinsburg and Harper's Ferry. Lee sent in this month Kershaw's division and Fitzhugh Lee's cavalry, but in a few weeks, indeed, Kershaw must be recalled to Petersburg, where they needed every man — every man and more! In the Valley August and the first third of September went by in marchings and counter-marchings, infantry skirmishing and cavalry raids. The third week of the latter month found the grey gathered behind the Opequon.

Mid-September and the woods by the Opequon turning red and gold. "Ah," said the Sixty-fifth, "we camped here after Sharps-burg, before we went over the mountains and fought at Fredericks-burg! But it is n't as it was — it is n't as it was —"

Gordon and Breckenridge and Ramseur and Rodes, with Fitz Lee's cavalry sent up from Tidewater, all camped for a time beside the Opequon. The stream ran with an inner voice, an autumn colouring was on the land. "But it is n't bright," said the men, "it is n't bright like it was that fall!" — "Is n't time yet for it to be bright. Bright in October." — "Yes, of course — but that fall it was bright all the time! The seasons are changing anyhow." — "What's that the Bible student 's saying? '*The lean kine and the lean ears of corn —*'" Opequon flowed on, brown and clear, but much of the woodland by Opequon had been hewed away, and the bordering lands were not now under cultivation. All were bare and sorrowful. There were no cattle, no stock of any kind. The leaves turned red and the leaves turned yellow and the wind murmured through the hacked and hewed forest, and the nights were growing chill. "Do you remem-ber," said the men, "the day that Heros von Borcke brought Old Jack the new uniform from Jeb Stuart?" — "Do you remember the revival here?"

"We're tenting to-night on the old camp-ground.
    Give us a song to cheer—"

The seventeenth and eighteenth all divisions moved nearer to Winchester. The nineteenth the battle of Winchester had its mo-ment in time, — a battle very fortunate for the Confederates early in the day, not at all so fortunate later in the day, — a fierce, drama-tic battle, in which the blue cavalry played the lion's part, — blue cavalry very different, under Sheridan in '64, from the untrained and weakly handled blue cavalry of the earlier years, — a battle in which Rodes was killed and Fitzhugh Lee wounded, in which killed and wounded and missing the blue lost upward of five thou-sand, and in killed and wounded and captured the grey lost as many — a bitter battle!

Steve had to fight — he could not get out of it. He was out on the

Berryville road — Abraham's Creek at his back. The Sixty-fifth was about him; it was steady and bold, and he got some warmth about his heart out of the fact. In the hopeful first half of the day, with a ruined stone wall for breastwork, with Nelson's and Braxton's guns making a shaken grey rag of the atmosphere, with Ramseur standing fast, with Gordon and Rodes sweeping to Ramseur's aid, with Breckenridge, the "Kentucky Gamecock," fighting as magnificently as he looked, with Lomax and Fitz Lee, with the storm and shouting, and the red field and blue and starry cross advanced, with about him the strength of the Golden Brigade and the untroubled look of the Sixty-fifth, Steve even fought as he had never fought before. He tore cartridges, loaded and fired, and he grinned when the wind blew the smoke, and the opposite force was seen to give way. When the Golden Brigade went forward in a charge, he went with it a good part of the way. But then he stumbled over a stone and fell with an oath as of pain. The Golden Brigade and the Sixty-fifth went on and left him there near a convenient cairn of stones with a reddened vine across it. His action had been largely automatic; he had no longer in such matters the agony of choosing; as soon as fear entered his heart his joints acted. Now they drew him more securely behind the heap of stones. Far ahead, he heard, through the thunder of the guns, the voice of the Golden Brigade, the voice of the Sixty-fifth Virginia charging the foe. He looked down, and to his horror he saw that he was really wounded.

This was high noon, and at high noon the grey thought with justice that they had the field, had it, despite the fall of Rodes, a general beloved. Now set in a level two hours of hard fighting to hold that field. . . . And then wheeled on the afternoon, and the tide definitely turned. Crook's corps, not until now engaged, struck the left on the Martinsburg Pike, and the blue cavalry, disciplined now and strong, came in a whirlwind upon the rear of this wing, pushing it and a cavalry brigade of Fitz Lee's back — back — back through Winchester — back on the centre and right, now furiously attacked by all three arms. The tide raced to its ebb with the grey. . . . Gordon found his wife in the street in Winchester, pleading with Gordon's men to go back and strike them anyhow. Her tears were streaming. "The first time I ever saw Confederate lines broken, and I hope it will be the last!"

They were broken. It was not wild panic nor rout, but it was a lost battle, known as such at last by even the most stubbornly determined or recklessly brave. By twilight the Second Corps was in retreat, moving in order up the Valley Pike, sullen and sorrowful, torn and decimated and weary, heartsick with the dead and wounded and captured left behind. Kernstown! They looked at the old field with unseeing eyes.

Steve, behind his cairn of stones, had viewed with agony a blue cavalry charge coming. It passed him in dust and thunder, the hoof of a great chestnut actually striking his shoulder. It passed, but the dust had not settled before infantry of Rodes, pressed this way, overran his fraction of the field, behind them another wild cavalry dash. It was sickening to see the horses ride men down, ride them down and strike them under! It was sickening to see the sabres flash, descend all bright and rise so red! It was sickening to hear cries, oaths, adjuration, and under all a moaning, moaning! And the smoke, so thick and stifling, and a horror even of taste and smell . . . Steve, with a flesh wound across his thigh where a bullet had glanced, got up and ran, dropping blood.

As he went he found about him the wildest confusion. Units and groups of cavalry, infantry, and artillery were shaken together as in a glass. Here infantry preponderated, here mad horses, larger than nature, appeared to rear in the smoke, and here panting men tried to drag away the guns. Here were the wounded, here were shouting and crying, here were officers, impassioned, rallying, appealing, coercing, and here were the half-sobbing answers of their men. "Lost, lost!" said in effect the answers of the men. "Lost, lost! You, the leaders, know it, and we know it. You would lead us to noble death, but we must keep to life if we can. We have fought very well, and now we are tired, and there is something to be said for knowing when you are beaten and trying another tack." — "Lost, lost!" said the shot and shell. "Lost, lost!" said the wind whistling from the sabres of Merritt's charging cavalry. "Lost, lost!" said the autumn night. "Lost, lost!" said the dust on the Valley Pike.

Steve tried to get taken on in an ambulance, but the surgeon in charge first laid practised fingers around his wrist, and then told him to go to hell — in short to walk to hell — and leave ambulances for hurt folks. "Gawd!" thought Steve, "'n' I saved this army on the road to Buford's!"

Night came on, night without and night within. The outer night was a night of stars. Myriads and myriads, they showed, star clouds in the Milky Way, and scattered stars in the darker spaces. The air was very clear, and the starshine showed the road — the long, palely gleaming, old, old, familiar road. Within, the night was dark, dark! and peopled with broken hopes. *Tramp, tramp!* on the Valley Pike. *Tramp, tramp!* with sore and tired feet, with hot and tired hearts. *Tramp, tramp!* and all the commands were broken, officers seeking for their men and men for their officers, a part of one regiment marching with a part of another, all the moulds cracked. *Tramp, tramp! Tramp, tramp!* and fathers were weeping silently for sons, and sons for their fathers, and brothers for brothers, and many for their country. *Tramp, tramp!* and there came a vision of the burning Valley, and of Atlanta burning, burning, for not one house, said the dispatches, had Sherman left standing, and a vision of the trenches at Petersburg, and a vision of Richmond, Richmond perhaps crashing down in ruin to-night, wall and pillar, and the flames going up. *Tramp, tramp!* and a flame of wrath came into the marching hearts, welcome because it warmed, welcome because anger and hate gave at least a strength, like a pale reflex of the strength of love, welcome because before it fled the shadows of weakness, and in it despair grew heroic. Now the men, exhausted as they were, would have turned, and gone back and struck Sheridan. *Tramp, tramp! Tramp, tramp!* and there came a firmness into the sound. Throughout the night, now it came and now it went, and now it came again.

The night went by, though it was long in going. Dawn came, though it was slow in coming. When it was light we saw Massanutten, and the north fork of Shenandoah, and Fisher's Hill. "This is a good place to stand," said Early, and began to build breastworks. In the afternoon up came Sheridan, something over twice as many-numbered as the grey, and all flushed with victory, and took his stand on Cedar Creek, several miles from Fisher's Hill. All day the twenty-first and part of the twenty-second he reconnoitred, and in the night-time of the twenty-first he placed Crook and the Army of West Virginia in the deep forest between Little North Mountain and the Confederate left. They stayed there hidden until nearly sundown of the twenty-second. Then he brought them out in a flank attack, so sudden and so swift! . . . And at the same moment all his legions struck against the centre.

Steve heard the cry, "Flanked! — We are flanked!" He witnessed the rush of arms, and then he waited not to see defeat — which came. He fled at once. Halfway to Woodstock he stopped at a Dunkard's house, where an old, long-bearded man gave him a piece of bread and asked no questions, but sat looking at him with dreamy, disapproving eyes. "Yes, the soldier could sleep here, although to be a soldier was to be a great sinner." Steve did not care for that. He slept very well for an hour on the floor of a small bare room above the porch. At the end of that time he was awakened by a sound upon the pike. He sat up, then went on all fours across to the window and put out his head. "Gawd! they're comin' up the pike — retreatin'!" He felt a wild indignation. "The Second Corps ain't any more what it used to be! Retreatin' every whipstitch like it's been doin'." *Tramp, tramp! Tramp, tramp!* He heard them through the dark, clear night, growing loud now upon the limestone pike. "Well, I ain't a-goin' along! I'm tireder than any dawg! — 'n' hurt besides." He lay down beneath the window and shut his eyes. But he could not keep the sound out, nor a picture of the column from winding through his brain. "They ain't got any shoes, 'n' they're gettin' so ragged, 'n' hunger-pinched. They're gettin' hunger-pinched. They've fought 'n' fought till they're most at a standstill. They've fought mighty hard. Ain't anybody ever fought any harder. But now they're tired — awful tired. No shoes, 'n' ragged, 'n' hunger-pinched — Coffin, 'n' Allan, 'n' Billy, 'n' Dave, 'n' Jim Watts, 'n' Bob White, 'n' Reynolds, 'n' all of them. Even Zip the coon's hunger-pinched. They've all got large eyes, 'n' they've fought most to a standstill, 'n' the flags are gettin' heavy to carry. . . ." *Tramp, tramp! Tramp, tramp!* He dozed and heard the gun-wheels in a half dream, crossing a bridge with a hollow sound. Wheels and wheels and a hollow sound. Memory played him a trick. He was lying in a miry, weedy ditch under a small bridge on the road between Middletown and Winchester. The guns were passing over his head, *rumble, rumble, rumble!* And then a plank broke and a gun-wheel came down and tried to knock him into Kingdom Come. . . . He woke fully with a violent start and the sweat cold upon his body. . . . The column was directly passing, — he heard voices, marching feet, officers' orders, wheels, hoofs, marching feet, voices, — all distant, continuous sound broken, become a loud, immediate, choppy sea. "Go on!" whispered Steve. "Go on! I ain't a-goin' with you."

The column went on, marching by the little dark and silent house, on up the pike, beneath the stars, toward Woodstock, and some pause perhaps beyond. It moved so near that Steve heard at times what the soldiers said. He gathered that Fisher's Hill was a word of gloom and would remain so. On it went, on it went, until from van to rear ten thousand men had passed. And then, as the sound of the sea was lessening, a knot of officers drew up almost beneath the window. They spoke in slow, tired, dragging voices. "Orders are no halt until we've passed Woodstock. — Six miles yet. Where then? I do not know. — Fight again? Yes, of course — fight to the bitter end! I don't suppose it's far off. — Here's Berkeley. Well, what's the news, Captain?"

"Sheridan's after us, sir. . . . Listen!"

They listened. "Yes. . . . Coming up the pike. . . . I should say he has thirty thousand infantry and as many horse as we have of all three arms. Well! let the curtain ring down. We've made good drama."

When they were gone, Steve rose and leaned cautiously out of the window. Yes, he could hear the Yankees, he could hear them coming. They were far off, but they were coming, coming.— A light burst forth in the night, in the north, then another and another. "They're firin' barns and houses as they pass." — Below him rose a final clatter of horses' hoofs, voices, curt orders, oaths — the grey rear guard drawing off, following the main body. Steve ran downstairs and out into the road. He stopped a horseman. "For Gawd's sake, comrade, take me on behind you! I marched with the boys till I just dropped, 'n' I said, 'Go on, 'n' maybe a horse or a wagon'll be good to me.' — I got a sore hurt in the leg —"

"All right," said the horseman. "Get up!" and they went on up the pike with the sky red behind them, and night before. "It's most the end, I reckon."

Woodstock — and a halt below at Narrow Passage — then on a windy, dusty day to New Market, while Sheridan paused and finally went into camp at Mount Jackson — then aside from the Valley Pike, eastward by the Port Republic road — then into the great shady amphitheatre of Brown's Gap — and here quiet at last, quiet and rest. Again it was an old, old camping-ground. The Second Corps stared, sombre-eyed, with faces that worked. "Old Jube is all right — but, O God, for Stonewall Jackson!"

Weeks went by. The woods changed, indeed. The leaves brightened and brightened, and now they began to fall in every wind. To and fro, forth from the gaps of the Blue Ridge and back to their shelter, moved the Army of the Valley, to and fro—to and fro. In these days came Kershaw, sent by Lee — twenty-seven hundred infantry and Cutshaw's battery. The Second Corps welcomed South Carolina. "You're the fiery boys! 'Come, give us a song to cheer!' — Never have forgotten how you taught us to cook rice! — in the first century, along about First Manassas. Never have forgotten, but the commissary's out of rice."

In these days Sheridan, keeping his main force between New Market and Woodstock, began with that great force of Torbert's cavalry to harry the Valley as it had not yet been harried. He wrecked the Central Railroad and burned bridges and sent the Confederate stores at Staunton up in flames. That was all right; that was understood — but Sheridan stopped there as little as would Attila have done. Before winter came, he swept the Valley bare as Famine's hand; he made it so bare that he said himself, "A crow, flying over the Valley of Virginia, would have had to take his rations with him."

A little past the middle of October Early determined to attack. With Kershaw and with Rosser's small reinforcement of cavalry, he could bring into the field a force little more than a third the size of the blue army now lined up behind Cedar Creek. But forage and supplies were gone; it was risk all or lose all. "'Beggars must not be choosers,'" said Early, and the Second Corps went back to the Valley Pike and marched toward Fisher's Hill. It marched through a country where all was burned, — houses, mills, barns, wheat and straw and hay, wagons and farm implements, smithies, country stores and hostelries, — all, all charred and desolate. It saw women and children, crouching for warmth against blackened chimney-stacks. It marched hungry itself and now with tattered clothing — all the small divisions, the small brigades, the small regiments — all the defenders of the Valley, taking now so little room on the Valley Pike. It marched with a fringe of stragglers, with a body of the sick and straggling bringing up the rear. Nowadays men straggled who had never done that before; nowadays men deserted who were not deserters by nature. And mostly these deserted because a cry, insistent and wild, reached them from home. "Starving! We are starving and homeless. I, your mother, am crying for bread! — I, your wife, am crying for bread! — We, your children, are crying for bread! We are sick — we are dying — we will never see you again—"

CHAPTER XXXVII

CEDAR CREEK

O N the eighteenth of October, the grey being again drawn up at Fisher's Hill, Gordon, with General Clement Evans and Jed Hotchkiss and Major Hunter of Gordon's staff, climbed Massanutten, overhanging the Confederate right. Up here, on the craggy mountain brow, high in the blue air, resting a moment amid red scrub oak and yellow hickory, they looked forth. They saw the wonderful country, the coloured forest falling, slope after slope, from their feet, the clear-flowing Shenandoah, Cedar Creek winding between hills, and on these hills they saw with their field-glasses Sheridan's army. "Not only," says Gordon, "did we see the general outlines of Sheridan's breastworks, but every parapet where his heavy guns were mounted, and every piece of artillery, every wagon and tent and supporting line of troops. . . . I could count, and did count, the number of his guns. I could see distinctly the three colours of trimmings on the jackets respectively of infantry, artillery, and cavalry, and locate each, while the number of flags gave a basis for estimating approximately the forces with which we were to contend in the proposed attack."

Down went Gordon and reported to Early. "We *can* turn his flank, sir. We can come with one spring upon his left and rear. Demonstrate right and centre where he is formed to repel us, but strike him on the left where he is n't! He thinks he's got there for shield an impassable mountain and a river."

Early swore. "Well, is n't the mountain impassable? It looks it. It's precipitous."

"No. There's a very narrow path. Start at nightfall and we can cross the corps, single-file, by dawn."

Early swore again, but in the end approved. "——! It's a desperate game, but then we're desperate gamesters! ——! All right, General! Get your men ready."

The red-gold day drew to a close. Through all the Second Corps there ran an undefined tremor, a beat of hope, a feeling as of, per- haps, — God knew! — better things at last! Supperless men looked almost fed. With the shining-out of the evening star the Second Corps began to move across the face of Massanutten. The way was narrow. Above sprang the mountain heights, below rolled the Shenandoah. Soldier followed in soldier's footsteps, very silently, sure-footed, under orders not to speak. Ragged and grey and silent, their gun-barrels faintly gleaming, they went along, high on the side of Massanutten, a long, thin, moving thread, moving all night in the autumn wind. Steve was of it, of it because he could not help him- self. He had tried — he certainly had tried hard, as he told himself with water in his eyes — but Dave Maydew had adopted him, and would n't let him out of his sight. Now he was moving between Dave and Jim Watts — and he was n't let to speak — and he heard Shenandoah brawling, brawling down below — and the world was lonesomer than lonesome! There were to-night a number of shoot- ing stars. There was something awful in the height of the sky and in the appearance and disappearance of these swift lights. Steve felt an imaginative horror. The end of the world began to trouble him, and a query as to when it was going to happen. " Maybe it's goin' to happen sooner 'n we think!"

Ahead, where there was a buttress of cliff, very evident from where the Sixty-fifth moved in a concave filled with shadow, occurred a gash across the footpath which made it dangerous. This side of the shoulder was well hidden from any blue picket across the water. A torch had been lighted and was now held close to the earth, so that eyes might read and feet might safely cross the gash in the way. The red, smoky, upstreaming light just showed each passing soldier. The Golden Brigade moved forward, regiment by regiment. The Sixty-fifth yet halted in the hollow of the mountain, recognized Cleave as he stood a moment bathed in the red light. There was a sound of satisfaction. "We're all right. We're going to win some more."

Over the face of Massanutten went the Second Corps — over in silence and safety — over and on to the woods beside Shenandoah. Here the divisions were halted, here they lay down on the fallen leaves and waited. They heard the river, they heard the voices of the blue vedettes upon the farther side. They waited — all the ragged grey troops — lying on the leaves, in the cold hour before the dawn. They were very hungry, very tired. Some of them slept; others lay and thought and thought, or looked at pictures in the dark. Steve still watched the shooting stars, still thought of the Judgment Day. He was conscious of a kind of exaltation. "I'm gettin' to be a fighter with the best of them!"

The lines of grey rose from the moss and leaves. A cold and pallid light was in the forest. Ahead broke out shouting, and then a rapid carbine firing. Payne and his cavalry were on the bank of Shenandoah, midstream in Shenandoah, — on the farther bank, — in touch, like lightning before the storm, with the blue vedettes and mounted supports! *Fall in! Fall in! — Forward!*

How cold was the water of Shenandoah! North Carolina and Georgia troops and Terry's brigade, that held within it most of the fragments of the old Stonewall Brigade, were the first to enter. Behind came all the others, the mass of the Second Corps. Cold was the October water, — cold, deep, and rushing fast to the sea. Over it, holding high every musket, went the Second Corps, and made no tarrying, formed in the thickening light in the woods where the blue outposts had been, formed and went forward at a run, led by the din of the cavalry ahead. Not only the cavalry, for now they heard Kershaw thundering upon the front. Everywhere noise arose and tore the solemn dawn. The woods opened, there came a sense of cleared spaces, and then a vision of a few breastworks, — not many, for Sheridan had not thought his army could be turned, — of serried tents, of a headquarters flag, of a great park of bubbly, white-topped wagons, of the rear, in short, of the Army of the Shenandoah. It showed a scene of vast and sudden confusion and noise; it buzzed like an overturned hive. "*Yaaihhh! Yaaiihhh! Yaaaaiiiihhh!*" rang the yell of the Second Corps.

It struck so fierce and it struck so fell, while in front Kershaw and Rosser aided so ably — the bees all left the hive and, save those who were struck to the ground and they were many, and those who were captured and they were many, streamed to the northward in a strange panic. They dashed from the tents where they had been sleeping; with the sleep yet in their eyes they poured across the fields. They left the wide camp, left arms, knapsacks, clothing, and their huge supplies. They "possessed not even a company organization," but crying, as the grey had cried, hereabouts, a month before, "Flanked! We are flanked!" the Eighth and Nineteenth Corps, taken with madness, hurried northward by the pike and by the fields. It was a rout that for a time savoured of the old, old First Manassas rout. The blue, as the grey, were brave enough, — no one by now in this war doubted blue courage or grey courage, — but to be flanked at dawn was to be flanked at dawn, and brave men or not brave men, and however often in this war you had outgazed her, smiled her from the field, Panic Fear was yet a giantess of might! Now or then, here or there, in a blue moon, she had her innings.

The Sixth Corps on the right stood fast. Gordon proposed to mass the grey artillery against it, then to attack with infantry. "At this moment," he says, "General Early came upon the field and said, 'Well, Gordon, this is glory enough for one day! This is the nineteenth. Precisely one month ago to-day we were going in the opposite direction.' . . . I pointed to the Sixth Corps and explained the movements I had ordered, which I felt sure would compass the capture of that corps — certainly its destruction. When I had finished, he said, 'No use in that. They will all go directly.' 'That is the Sixth Corps, General. It will not go unless we drive it from the field.' 'Yes, it will go, too, directly.'"

Down went Gordon's heart, down, down! "And so," he says, "it came to pass that the fatal halting, the hesitation, the spasmodic firing and the isolated movements in the face of the sullen, slow, and orderly retreat of the superb Federal corps, lost us the great opportunity."

Jubal Early thinks otherwise and says so. He says that the position of the Sixth Corps was very strong and not to be attacked on the left because the approach was over open, boggy ground, swept by the blue artillery. He did attack on the right, but just as Ramseur and Pegram were advancing to occupy an evacuated position, the enemy's great force of cavalry began to press heavily on the right, and Pegram was sent to the north of Middletown to take position across the pike and oppose this force. Kershaw and Gordon's commands were broken and took time to re-form. Lomax had not arrived. Rosser, on the left, had all he could do barely to hold in check the cloud of threatening cavalry. The enemy had taken up a new position north of Middletown. Early now, the morning advancing, ordered Gordon, he says, "to take position on Kershaw's left and advance with the purpose of driving the enemy from his new position — Kershaw and Ramseur being ordered to advance at the same time." He continues: "As the enemy's cavalry on our left was very strong, and had the benefit of an open country to the rear of that flank, a repulse at this time would have been disastrous, and I therefore directed General Gordon, if he found the enemy's line too strong to attack with success, not to make the assault. The advance was made for some distance, when Gordon's skirmishers came back reporting a line of battle in front behind breastworks, and General Gordon did not make the attack. It was now apparent that it would not do to press my troops farther. They had been up all night and were much jaded. In passing over rough ground to attack the enemy in the early morning their own ranks had been much disordered, and the men scattered, and it required time to re-form them. Their ranks, moreover, were much thinned by the absence of men engaged in plundering the enemy's camps. . . . The delay . . . had enabled the enemy to rally a portion of his routed troops, and his immense force of cavalry, which remained intact, was threatening both of our flanks in an open country, which of itself rendered an advance extremely hazardous. I determined, therefore, to try and hold what had been gained."

Now Gordon was a generous, chivalrous, bold, and devoted soldier. And Jubal Early was a bold and devoted man and a general of no mean ability. Which was right and which was wrong, or how largely both were right, will, perhaps, be never known. But hard upon Early's slur upon the conduct of the troops, his repeated statement that they were too busy plundering to go forward, there comes an indignant cry of denial. Says Clement Evans, "My command was not straggling and plundering." And General Battle, "I never saw troops behave better than ours did at Cedar Creek." And General Wharton, "It is true that there were parties passing over the field and perhaps pillaging, but most of these were citizens, teamsters, and persons attached to the quartermaster's and other departments, and perhaps a few soldiers who had taken the wounded to the rear. No, General; the disaster was not due to the soldiers leaving their commands and pillaging." And another officer, "The men went through a camp just as it was deserted, with hats, boots, blankets, tents, and such things as tempt our soldiers scattered over it, and after diligent enquiry I heard of but one man who even stopped to pick up a thing. He got a hat and has charges preferred against him." And one of the grey chaplains, who says that he was a free-lance that day, and all over the field from rear to front, "It is true that many men straggled and plundered; but they were men who in large numbers had been wounded in the summer's campaign, who had come up to the army for medical examination, and who came like a division down the pike behind Wharton, and soon scattered over the field and camps and helped themselves. They were soldiers more or less disabled and not on duty. This body I myself saw as they came on the battle-field and scattered. They were not men with guns. But there can be no doubt that General Early mistook them for men who had fallen out of ranks." And Gordon, "Many of the dead com-manders left on record their testimony; and it is true, I think, that every living Confederate officer who commanded at Cedar Creek a corps, or division, or brigade, or regiment, or company would testify that his men fought with unabated ardour, and did not abandon their places in line to plunder the captured camps."

So the Army of the Valley that is about to go down to defeat need not go there with any imputation of misconduct. Let us say instead that it continued to do well.

And now it stands there waiting for orders to advance, for orders to go into battle, to engage the Sixth Corps, and now the day is growing old, and now Crook and Wright, far down the Valley Pike, begin to check the fleeing masses of the Eighth and Nineteenth, to bring them into something more than company organization, and to force them to listen to talk of going back and retrieving . . . and now news comes to Sheridan himself who had slept the night of the eighteenth in Winchester.

As he mounted his horse there came a confused rumour of dis-aster; as, a hard rider, he thundered out of Winchester with twenty miles to make, the wind brought him faintly the din of distant battle. He bent to the horse's neck and used the spur. About nine o'clock, south of Winchester, "the head of the fugitives appeared in sight, trains and men coming to the rear with appalling rapidity." His followers did what they could to stop the torrent; he galloped on.

The day wore away, the grey under arms, but inactive, waiting

— waiting. Upon the top of Massanutten, in a wine-hued world above the smoke and clamour, was a grey signal station, and it signalled the Army of the Valley below. It signalled first, "The enemy has halted and is re-forming." It signalled second, "They are coming back by the pike and neighbouring roads." It signalled third, "The enemy's cavalry has checked General Rosser, and assumed the offensive." It signalled fourth, "The enemy, in heavy column, is coming up the pike."

The rallied Eighth and Nineteenth Corps, Sheridan at their head, came back and joined the steadfast Sixth. Together they gave battle to the grey who had waited for this strange hour. In it the tables were turned. Command after command, the grey were broken. There was a gap in the line, left who knew how? Through it like a river in freshet roared the blue.

It beat upon Steve's brain like waves of hell, that battle. The Sixty-fifth had held him like a vise; not for one moment had he escaped. In the midst of plenty he was not let to plunder; in the face of danger he was not somehow able to fall out, to straggle, or to malinger. All his talents seemed to desert him. Perhaps Dave Maydew had him really under observation, or perhaps he only fancied that that was the case. He was afraid of Dave. Through the forenoon, indeed, hope sustained him. The Yankees had run away, and though the Golden Brigade with others shifted its place, moving from left to right, and though, beside the first great onset, it came sharply several times into touch with the foe, it, too, under division orders, must end in waiting, waiting. Steve was convinced that the Yankees were too frightened to come back, and that presently there would be broken ranks and permission to the men to help themselves in moderation. The hope kept him cheerful, despite the grumbling of the Sixty-fifth. "Why don't we go forward? What are we waiting here for? We're losing time, — and losing it to *them*. Why don't we — What are they signalling up there on the mountain?" — And then burst the storm and hope went out.

The lantern slides shifted rapidly — now black, now fearful, vivid pictures. For what seemed an eternity Steve did tear cartridges, load and fire with desperation. A black ring came round his mouth; the sweat poured down, his chest heaved beneath his ragged shirt. *Fire! — Fire! — Fire! — Fire!* And all to right and left was the

Sixty-fifth, fighting grimly, and beyond, the balance of the Golden Brigade, fighting grimly. He saw Dave Maydew sink to his knees, and then forward upon his hands, and at last roll over and lie dead with a quiet face. He saw Sergeant Billy Maydew, passing down the line, pause just a moment when he saw Dave. "I reckon I'll be coming, too, directly, Dave," said Billy, then went on with his duty. He saw Allan, tall and strong and fair, set in a great smoke wreath firing steadily. *Fire! — Fire! — Fire! — Fire!* There rose a question of ammunition. Jim Watts was one of those who went for cartridges and brought them while the air was a shriek of shells. Steve saw the cartridge-bearers askance, coming, earnest-faced, through the cloud — then the cloud grew red-bosomed, and he saw them no more. He heard a voice, "*Fix bayonets!*" and he saw Cleave, dismounted, leading the charge. He went with the Sixty-fifth; he could not help it; he had in effect run amuck. He felt the uneven ground beneath his feet like a rhythm, and the shrieking of the minies became, for the first and only time in his life, a siren's song. Then through the smoke came a loom of forms; he saw the blue cavalry bearing down, many and fast. *Halt! — Left Face! Fire!* — but on they came, for all the emptied saddles. A thousand cymbals clashed in the air, a thousand forms, gigantic in the reek, towered before the vision; there came a chaos of voices, appalled or triumphant, a frightful heat, a pressure, a roaring in the brain. Steve saw Richard Cleave where he fell, desperately wounded, he saw the Golden Brigade, he saw the Sixty-fifth Virginia broken and dashed to pieces. With the cry of a Thunder Run creature in a trap, he caught at the reins of the horse that reared above him, red-nostrilled, with eyes of fire. Its rider, a tall and powerful man with yellow mustaches, bending sideways, cut at him with a sabre. Steve, a gash across each arm, dropped the bridle. The horse's hoof struck him on the forehead, and the world went down in a black and roaring sea.

When he came to himself it was dark. The smoke hung heavy and there was the taste and scent of the battle-field. At first there seemed no noise, then he heard the groaning and the sighing. The greater noise, the thunder and shouting, had, however, rolled away. He raised himself on his elbow, and then he sat up and rested his head on his knees. He was deadly sick and shivering. As little by little his wits came back, he began to draw conclusions.

There had been a battle — now he remembered — and the army was beaten. . . . He listened now in reality and he heard, far up the pike and across the fields, in the darkness, the sound of retreat and pursuit. It made a wall of sound, stretching east and west, rolling southward, going farther and farther away, dwindling at last into a hollow murmur, leaving behind it the bitter, pungent night, and the sounds as near at hand as crickets in the grass. *Water — water — water — water . . . O God! — O God! — O God!*

Steve rose uncertainly. His tongue, too, was swollen with thirst. He saw lights wavering over the field, and here and there a flare where camp followers had built themselves a fire. There reached his ears a burst of harsh laughter, then from some quarter where there was pillaging a drunken quarrel. The regularly moving lights were, he knew, gatherers of the wounded. A shrill crying from a hollow where was a red glare proclaimed a field hospital. But the gatherers of the wounded were clothed in blue. They would touch no grey wounded until their own were served, and then, if events allowed them to minister, they would prove but lifters and forwarders to Northern prisons. Steve, swaying as he stood, stared at the bobbing lights. He was dead from hunger, tortured with thirst, and his head ached and ached from the blow of the horse's hoof. A thought came to him. If he told the bobbing lights that he loved the North and would fight for it in a blue coat, then, maybe, things would happen like a full canteen and a handful of hard-tack and a long and safe sleep beside one of those camp-fires. He started toward the lights. *Water! — Water! — Water! — Water!* cried the plain. *Ahhhh! Aaahhh! Water!*

Somewhere out of starveling and poor soil there pushed upward in the soul of Steve, came into a murky and muddy light, and there flowered, though after a tarnished and niggard sort, a something that first stayed his steps, then turned them away from the bobbing lights. It was not a strong growth, but the flower of it rubbed his eyes so that he saw Thunder Run rather than Northern plenty, and the haggard, fleeing grey army rather than a turned coat. He did not feel virtuous as he had done when he saved the army from the "avalanche," he only felt homesick and wretched and horribly suffering. When at a few paces he came to a deep gully and slipped and slid down its side to the bottom, where he was safe from the lights and from the thrust of some plunderer of the dead,—or the wounded whom they often, as safest, made the dead,—he found here beside him his old companion, Fear. Before this, on the day of Cedar Creek, from dawn to dusk, he had hardly once been afraid. Now he was — he was horribly afraid. There was long grass at the bottom of the gully, and he hoped for a runlet of some sort. He dragged himself along, hands and breast, until he felt mud, and then more and more moisture, until at last there came a puddle out of which he drank and drank as though he would never stop. It was too dark to see how bloody it was, and not even after moving his arm a little to the left and encountering the body of a soldier, did he cease to drink. His own arms were yet bleeding from the sabre cut and he was so dizzy that even here, with the lanterns all left behind, there were lights in the night like will-o'-the-wisps.

But the water, such as it was, put some spirit into him. Hands and knees, he crept down the floor of the gully until it deepened and widened into a ravine. Finally it led him to the creek side. Here, half in, half out of the water, was something that he put his foot upon for a log, but discovered to be the body of a man. Having reasoned that in this locality it would not improbably be the body of a blue vedette, Steve took it by the legs and drew it quite out upon the miry bank. He was correct, and there was a haversack, and in it bread and slices of meat. Steve, squatting in the mire, ate it all, then drank of the creek. He was dead for sleep; there had been none the night before, clambering along the face of Massanutten, and not too much the night before that; dead for sleep, and more tired than any dog. . . . He stood up, gazing haggardly into the night beyond the creek, then shook his head, and dropped upon the soft earth beside the dead vedette. It seemed to him that he had hardly closed his eyes when he heard a bugle and then the sound of trotting horse. "Cavalry comin' this way — Damn them to hell!" He staggered to his feet and down into the stream, crossed it somehow, and went up the farther bank, and on through forest and field, over stock and stone. He went away from the pike. "For I never want to see it again. It's ha'nted."

He went westward toward the mountains, and he walked all night over stock and stone and briar. Day broke, wan and sickly. It showed him a rough country, rising steeply to the wilder mountains, rough and so sparsely inhabited that he did not see a house. He went on, swaying now in his gait, and presently by the rising sun he saw a sloping field, ragged and stony and covered with a poor stand of corn, and at the top a fairish log cabin set against a pine wood. A curl of smoke was coming from the chimney.

Steve stumbled up the hillside and through a garden path to a crazy porch overhung by a gourd vine. Here a lean mountain woman met him. "Better be keerful!" she said. "The dawg's awful fierce! Here, dawg!"

The dog came, bristling. Steve retreated a few steps. "I ain't nothin' but a poor Confederate soldier! — 'n' I'm jest about dead for hunger 'n' tiredness. There's been an awful big battle 'n' I got my wounds. If you'd jest let me rest a bit here, ma'am, 'n', for God's sake, give me somethin' to eat —"

"Well," said the woman, "you kin rest, an' then you kin pay by helpin' me stack the corn. My husband was killed over in Hampshire, bushwhackin', an' the dawg an' I an' a gun air livin' together."

Steve slept all day in the lean-to, beneath a quilt of bright patchwork. He had cornbread and a chicken for supper, and then he wrapped himself luxuriously in the quilt again and slept all night. The next day he helped the mountain woman stack the corn.

"You live so out of the way," he said, "I don't reckon Sheridan'll never come burnin' 'n' slayin' up here! You got chickens 'n' a cow 'n' the fat of the land."

"It air a peaceful mountain," agreed the woman. "I ain't never seen a Yankee an' I don't know as I want to. Thar's a feud on between the folks in the Cove an' the folks on Deer Mountain, but my husband was a Hampshire man, an' I'm out of it. Don't nobody give me any trouble an' I get along. Yaas, the cow's a good milker an' I got a pig an' plenty of chickens."

"Don't you get lonesome, livin' this way by yourself — 'n' you a fine-lookin' woman, too?"

"Am I fine-lookin'?" said the mountain woman. "I never knew that before."

They stacked the corn all day, and at dark Steve had another chicken and more cornbread and an egg for supper.

"Tell me about your folks," said the woman, "an' how life's done you, an' about soldiering."

They sat on either side of the hearth, for the night was cold, and while the hickory log blazed, and the mountain woman used snuff, Steve indulged in a rhodomontade that did him credit. "But I ain't sure I'll go soldierin' any more," he closed. "Savin' the army 'n' all's enough. I got a honourable discharge."

The mountain woman dipped a bit of hazel twig again into the small round tin box of snuff. She was not much older than Steve, and, in a gaunt way, not bad-looking. "An' you ain't married?"

"Naw. I ain't never found any one to suit me—at least, till recently I thought I had n't."

In the lean-to, when he had rolled himself in the rising-sun quilt, he lay and looked out of the open door at the stars below the hilltop. "The army's beaten," he thought, "'n' the war's ended, or most ended. Anyhow it's fightin' now without any chance of anything but dyin'." He sat up and rested his chin on his knees. "I ain't ready to die . . . Sheridan's drivin' the Second Corps, 'n' the Sixty-fifth's all cut to pieces 'n' melted away, 'n' Grant's batterin' down Petersburg 'n' gettin' ready to fall on Richmond. We're beaten, 'n' I know it, 'n' I ain't a-goin' back; 'n' I ain't a-goin' back to Thunder Run neither — not yet awhile! An' she's strong 'n' a good worker, 'n' she's got property, 'n' I've seen a plenty worse-lookin'. Lucinda Heard was worse-lookin'."

The next day they gathered apples, for the mountain woman said she would make apple butter. It was beautiful weather, mild and bright. Steve lay on the porch beneath the gourd vine and watched his hostess hang the kettle over the outdoor fire and bring water in a bucket from the spring and fill it. While the fire was burning she came and sat down on the porch edge. "When air you goin' away?"

Steve grinned propitiatively. "Gawd knows I don't want to go away at all! I like it here fust-rate. — You ain't never told me your name?"

"My name's Cyrilla."

"That's an awful pretty name," said Steve. "It's prettier 'n Christianna, 'n' Lucinda, 'n' a lot others I've heard."

After supper they sat again on either side of the hearth, with a blazing hickory log between, and the mountain woman dipped snuff and Steve nursed his ankle.

"It's this-a-way," he remarked after a silence in which the crickets chirped. "I've kind of thought it out. War kills men off right along. When they're brave they get killed all the quicker, or they just get off by the skin of their teeth like I done. No matter how strong, 'n' brave, 'n' enterprisin', 'n' volunterin' they are, they get killed, 'n' killed. Killed off jest the same's the bees sting the best fruit. 'N' then what becomes of the country? It ain't populated 'less 'n the rest of us — them that got off by the skin of their teeth like I did, 'n' them that ain't never gone in like some bomb-proofs I know — 'less 'n the rest of us acts our part! That's what war does. It 'liminates the kind that pushes to the front 'n' plants flags. 'N' then — as Living don't intend to drop off — what's the rest of us that's left got to be? We got to be what I heard a preacher call 'seed-corn 'n' ancestors.' We got to marry 'n' people the earth. We ain't killed." Steve ceased to nurse his ankle, straightened his lean red body, and widening his lips until his lean red jaws wrinkled, turned to his hostess. "*Cyrilla.* — That's a mighty pretty name. . . . Why should n't you 'n' me marry? You got a house 'n' I got a house, over in Blue Ridge on Thunder Run Mountain, 'n' I got a little real money, too! When the war's over we can go get it. — What d' ye say?"

Cyrilla screwed on the top of the snuff-box. "I been right lone-some," she admitted. "But ef I marry you, you got to promise not to go bushwhackin'! You got to stay safe at home, 'n' you got to do what I tell you. I ain't goin' to have two husbands killed fightin' Yankees."

grew stronger — a winter light, cold and steel-like upon
river and the moving stream of men. *Fall in! Fall in!*
geants, and the men about the fires left the red warmth,
ranks waiting to move down to the water. "— —!
ngs of rivers! — —! Seeing that men have always
I reckon are always going to war, I don't see why Na-
d — if Nature's got a god — did n't make the earth a
d battlefield where enemies could clinch just as easy
inched till one or the other went over the edge of all
vent down, down, past whatever stars were on that side!
use of scooping rivers and heaping mountains in the
a nice, smooth, black, eternal plain — with maybe one
carry the blood away —"

rs, breaking step, crossed and crossed by the pontoon
e Duck River! — Quack! quack! — Franklin's on the
"Benjamin Franklin or Franklin Pierce?" — "Benja-
eaceful kind of fellow for a revolutionary — did n't be-
! Neither did Jefferson. Not on general principles.
arbarous. Fought on necessity, but believed in making
cur more rarely. Perfectly feasible thing! Necessity's
malleable than we think. When we don't want it war
cessary." — "Want it! Do you reckon any one wants
rd, yes! until they've got it. — Of course there's some
even after they've got it — but they're getting scarce."
know. Sometimes it's necessary, and sometimes it's
— "Yes. A hard necessity and a savage pastime.
There's a bigger phrase — 'Mother Earth and Fellow
olumn forward!
h the leafless country marched the somewhat tattered,
oeless Army of Tennessee. Tramp of feet and roll of
p of feet and roll of wheels . . . "Listen! Firing ahead!
est!" The marching Army took up the praise of For-
st! Forrest's like Stonewall Jackson — always in front
onal observations." — "Forrest! If I was a company
d rather see Forrest coming on King Phillip than King
Angel Gabriel!" — "Forrest! Did you ever see Forrest
n? Draws a pistol and shoots a retreating colour-
es the colours and says 'Come on!'" — "Forrest's had

CHAPTER XXXVIII

THE ARMY OF TENNESSEE

ON August the thirty-first Hood fought and lost the battle of
Jonesboro. On September the first he evacuated Atlanta,
besieged now for forty days, bombarded and wrecked and
ruined. On the second, with hurrahing, with music of bands and
waving of flags, Sherman occupied the forlorn and shattered place.

Forty thousand men, Hood and the Army of Tennessee lingered
a full month in this region of Georgia, first around Lovejoy's
Station, then at Palmetto. On the first of October they crossed the
Chattahoochee. Four days later was fought the engagement of
Allatoona. On northward went Hood over the old route that had
been travelled — though in an opposite direction — in the spring
and the early summer-time. Toward the middle of the month he
was at Resaca, and a day or two after he captured a small garrison
at Dalton. Behind him came, fast and furious, a blue host. He
made a forced march west to Gadsden on the Coosa. He was now
in Alabama and presently he marched past Decatur to Florence
on the Tennessee. Sherman sent by rail Schofield and two army
corps to Nashville, where was already George Thomas and his
corps. The blue commanding general had now sixty thousand men
in Tennessee, and sixty thousand in Georgia. To oppose these last
there was left Wheeler's cavalry and Cobb's Georgia State troops.
On the last day of October Hood crossed into Tennessee. Before
him and his army lay now the thirtieth of November and the fifteenth and sixteenth of December — lay the most disastrous battles
of Franklin and Nashville.

About the middle of September Sherman evicted the inhabitants
of Atlanta. "I take the ground," he states upon the occasion, with
the frankness that was an engaging trait in his character, "I take
the ground that Atlanta is a conquered place, and I propose to
use it purely for our own military purposes, which are inconsistent
with its inhabitation by the families of a brave people. I am ship-

ping them *all*, and by next Wednesday the town will be a real military town, with no women boring me every order I give."

In mid-November, quitting the place, he burned it before he went. "Behind us," he remarks, "lay Atlanta, smouldering and in ruins, the black smoke rising high in air and hanging like a pall over the ruined city. . . . The men are marching steadily and rapidly with a cheery look and a swinging pace."

Of his March to the Sea upon which he was now entered, he says, "Had General Grant overwhelmed and scattered Lee's Army and occupied Richmond he would have come to Atlanta; but as I happened to occupy Atlanta first, and had driven Hood off to a divergent line of operations far to the west, it was good strategy to leave him to a subordinate force and with my main army join Grant at Richmond. The most practicable route to Richmond was nearly a thousand miles in distance, too long for a single march; hence the necessity to reach the seacoast for a new base. Savannah, distant three hundred miles, was the nearest point, and this distance we accomplished from November 12th to December 21st." And he telegraphs to Grant that he will send back all his wounded and worthless and, with his effective army, "move through Georgia, smashing things to the sea." He kept his word. They were thoroughly smashed.

The men, marching "with a cheery look and a steady pace" listened to a General Order directing them to "forage liberally on the country," and "generally to so damage the country as to make it untenable to the enemy." They obeyed and made it untenable to all, including women and children, the sick and the old. They heard that their commander meant "to make Georgia howl," and they did what they could to further his wish. He states indeed — in a letter to his wife — that "this universal burning and wanton destruction of private property is not justified in war," and "I know all the principal officers detest the infamous practice as much as I do," but the practice went on — and he was commander. He left behind him, from north to south of a great State a swathe of misery, horror, and destruction fifty miles wide. There were good and gallant men in his legions, good and gallant men by the thousand, but "Sherman's bummers" went unchecked, and so far as is known, unrebuked. The swathe was undeniably there, and the insult and the agony and

the horror. Georgia was "mad
Sherman, and is qualified to kn

In the mean time Hood had cr
weather and was moving northw
weather cleared and there came
glow. The sun shone bright thou
recalled in this month from Mi
then came the corps of Stephen
A. P. Stewart, and of Cheatham.
Hardee himself, irreconcilably
transferral, had been sent to tak
South Carolina, Georgia, and Fl
thousand men, cavalry, infantry,
essee pursued the late Novemb
depleted army, but it could and

Lawrenceburg — Mt. Pleasant
River to cross. The night of the
the pontoon bridge. At dawn of
to cross — slow work as always
turn around fires on the river ban
cold like everything else. Wish
time I had a cup of coffee —" —
story before! Somebody tell a go
Tell about the mule and the dark

Down to the water and over t
dawn went the companies and the
blazed high, the soldiers talked.
Ridge." — "Missionary Ridge!" -
sionary Ridge was the place good m
ran hard in hell, but we fought h
fought hard — " "Up on Lookout
ground — D'ye remember how th
"A year ago! It was awful long w
mas to Christmas — but the lengt
thing awful!" — "That's so! It's
pens. I've seen men grow old fron
I've seen men grow old from At
place across the river? Franklin?

The ligh
the flowing
cried the s
and stood
These cro
warred an
ture and
smooth ro
and keep
things, an
What's t
way? Ju
wide rive

The so
bridge.
Harpeth.
min was
lieve in
Thought
necessity
much m
won't b
it?" —
that like
— "I d
good fu
'Patriot
Men."

On t
somewh
wheels,
That's
rest. "
making
in trou
Arthur
rally b
bearer

twenty-five horses killed under him." — "Did you ever hear him address his men? He's an orator born. It gets to be music. It gets grammatical — it gets to be great sonorous poetry." — "Yes, it does. I've heard him. And then an hour after I've heard him tell an officer 'Yes, that mought do' and 'It's got to be fit.' — And I've heard him say he never saw a pen but he thought of a snake." — "Forrest? You fellows talking about Forrest? Did you hear what Forrest said about tactics? Said he'd 'give more for fifteen minutes of bulge than for a week of tactics.'" — "Don't care! He's right good at tactics himself. Murfreesboro and Streight's Raid and other places and times without number! 'Whenever you see anything blue,' he says, 'shoot at it, and do all you can to keep up the scare!' Somebody told me he said about Okalona, 'Saw Grierson make a bad move, and then I rode right over him.' Tactics! Says it's his habit 'to git thar first with the most men.' That's tactics! — and strategics — and bulge — and the art of War!" — "Old Jack himself did n't know more about flanking than Forrest does." — "Did you hear what the old lady said to him at Cowan's Station?" — "No. What did she say?" — "Well, he and his men were kind of sauntering at a gallop through the place with a few million Yankees at their heels. The old lady did n't like men in grey to do that-away, so out she runs into the middle of the street, and spreads her skirts, and stops dead short, unless he was going to run over her, a big grey horse and a six-feet-two cavalryman with eyes like a hawk, and a black beard and grey head.—'Why don't you turn and fight?' — she hollers, never noticing the stars on his collar. 'Turn and fight, you great, cowardly lump! turn and fight! If General Forrest could see you, he'd take out his sword and cut your head off!'"

The firing ahead continued — the Tennessee men said that it was near Spring Hill — and Spring Hill was twelve miles from Franklin. "Going to be a battle?"—"Yes, think so. Understand Thomas is at Franklin behind breastworks." — "All right! 'Rock of Chickamauga' is one of the best — even if he is a Virginian!" — "Thomas is n't there himself — he's at Nashville. It's Schofield." — "All right! We'll meet Schofield." — "Column halted again! — Firing getting louder — Franklin getting nearer — the wind rising — Smoke over the hill-tops —" —"Who's this going by? — Give him a cheer! — Patrick Romayne Cleburne!" — *Column forward!* —

"Did you notice that old graveyard back there at Mt. Pleasant — a beautiful, quiet place? Well, General Cleburne rode up and looked over the wall, and he said, says he, 'If I die in this country, I should like to be buried here.' " — *Column forward!*

Spring Hill — Spring Hill at three o'clock, and Schofield's troops scattered through this region, concentrating hurriedly, with intent to give battle if needs be, but with a preference for moving north along the pike to Thomas at Franklin. What they wished was granted them. Here and there through the afternoon musketry rolled, but there was no determined attack. Hood says Cheatham was at fault, and Cheatham says General Hood dreamed the details and the orders he describes. However that may be, no check was given to Schofield that day, and in the dark night-time, he and his trains and troops went by the sleeping Confederate host and escaped, all but unmolested, to Franklin — and henceforth the Tennessee campaign was lost, lost!

Dawn and marching on Franklin — red dawn and the great beech trees of the region spreading their leafless arms across the way — sunrise and a cold, bright day — *Column forward! — Column forward!* — Hood "the fighter" at the head, tall and blue-eyed and tawny-bearded — S. D. Lee and Stewart and Cheatham — the division commanders, Patrick Cleburne and "Alleghany" Johnson and Carter Stevenson and Clayton and French and Loring and Walthall and Bate and Brown, and the artillerymen and the rumbling guns, and, *tramp, tramp, tramp, tramp!* the infantry of the Army of Tennessee. Eighteen hundred of these men were to die at Franklin. Four thousand were to be wounded. Two thousand were going to prison. A division commander was to die. Four brigade commanders were to die, others to be wounded or taken. Fifty-three commanders of regiments were to be among the killed, wounded, and captured. The execution was to take place in three or four hours of a November afternoon and a moonless night. *Tramp, tramp, tramp, tramp!* under the leafless beeches on the Franklin Pike. *Close up, men — close up! Column forward!* "What is that place in the distance with the hills behind it? — That's Franklin on the Harpeth."

The battle opened at four o'clock, and the sun set before five. There was an open, quite unobstructed plain running full to an

abatis and long earthworks, and behind these were the divisions of
Cox and Ruger and Kimball. Wood's division was over the
Harpeth and a portion of Wagner's occupied a hill a short distance
from the front. There were twenty-six guns mounted on the works
and twelve in reserve. "At four o'clock," says a Federal officer,
"the whole Confederate line could be seen, stretching in battle
array, from the dark fringe of chestnuts along the river bank, far
across the Columbia Pike, the colours gaily fluttering, and the muskets gleaming brightly, and advancing steadily, in perfect order,
dressed on the centre, straight for the works."

At first Success, with an enigmatical smile, rode with the grey.
The ——th Virginia yelled as they rode with her. Cheatham's men,
Stewart's men, Cleburne's famed veteran division yelled. *Yaaaihhh!*
Yaaaaihhh! Yaaaaaiiihhh! rang the Rebel yell, and echoed from
beyond the Harpeth and from the Winstead hills. They yelled and
drove Wagner's brigades and followed at a double, on straight to
the gun-crowned works. As the sun dipped came a momentary halt.
Cleburne was at the front of his troops, about him his officers, behind him his regiments waiting. It was growing cold and the earth
in shadow. A man, a good and gallant soldier, was sitting on a
hump of earth trying to tie a collection of more or less blood-stained
rags around his bare, half-frozen feet. He worked patiently, but
just once he uttered a groan. Cleburne heard the sound and turned
his head. Sitting his good horse he regarded the soldier for a moment
with a half-wistful look, then he dismounted, and without saying
anything to any one, drew off his boots. With them in his hand he
stepped across, in his stockinged feet, the bit of frosty earth to the
soldier. He held out the boots. "Put them on!" he ordered. The
man, astonished, would have scrambled up and saluted, but
Cleburne pushed him back. "Put them on!" he said. "It's an order.
Put them on." Stammering protests, the soldier obeyed. "There!
they seem to fit you," said General Cleburne. "You need them
more than I do." He moved back to his horse, put his stockinged
foot in the stirrup and mounted.

There sounded the charge. In went the corps of Stewart and
Cheatham, in went Cleburne's division with the blue flag, Alabama,
and Mississippi, Arkansas and Texas, a great veteran division,
"General Pat" leading. In the winter dusk came the whirlwind.

There was a cotton-gin in an open field — there were breastworks — every gun had opened, every musket was blazing, Casement's brigade was using magazine breech-loaders. There grew a welter, a darkness, a shrieking. General Adams, of Loring's division, sprang, bay horse and all, across a ditch and to the top of a parapet. Above him flared in the dark a flag. His hands were upon the staff. "Fire!" said the colour-guard, and their bullets killed him and the bay horse. Gist and Strahl were killed, Granbury was killed. And Patrick Romayne Cleburne was killed, and lay in his stockinged feet a few yards in front of the breastwork across which was stretched Adams's horse.

Thirteen times the grey charged. There was no wind to blow the smoke away. It lay like a level sea, and men fought in it and beneath it, and it would have been dark even in daytime. As it was, night was here, and it was dark indeed, save for the red murder light.

The ——th Virginia fought with the same desperation that its fellow regiments displayed. A wild energy seemed to inform the entire grey army. Edward Cary, rushing with his men to the assault, staggering back, going forward again, felt three times the earth of the breastworks in his hands.

He fought, since that was the business in hand, as though he loved it. He did not love it, but he was skilful, poised, and sure, and he knew no fear. His men had a strange love for and confidence in him. They never put it into words but "He comes from a sunrise land and knows more than we" was what they meant. He called half-gods by their names and had that detachment which perforce men honour. Now, sword in hand, striving to overmount the breastworks at Franklin, rallying and leading his men with a certain clean efficiency, he acted an approved part in the strife, but kept all the time a distance in his soul. He could not be all savage again and exult or howl. Nor was he merely civilized, to feel weakness and horror and repugnance before this blood and dirt and butchery, and yet for pure pride, fear of disgrace, and confusion of intellect, to call on every coarser fibre of the past, and exalt in the brain all the old sounding, suggestive words, the words to make you feel and not to think! He did not call upon the past though he acted automatically as the past had acted. He put horror and pity and cold distaste and a sense of the absurd to one side and did the work, since it still seemed to him that on the whole it must be done, with a kind of deadly calm. Had he been more than a dawn type, had he been a very little nearer to the future which he presaged, he might not have been there, somehow, in that dusk at all. He might have declined solutions practised by boar and wolf, and died persuading his kind toward a cleaner fashion of solving their problems. As it was, he hated what he did but did it.

Again and again the grey wave surged to the top of the breast-works. There it was as though it embraced the blue — blue and grey swayed, locked in each other's arms. Oh! fire and smoke and darkness, and a roaring as of sea and land risen each against the other — then down and back went the grey sea, down and back, down and back. . . . At nine o'clock the battle rested.

Long and mournful looked the line of camp-fires. There lay on the groaning field beneath the smoke that would not rise well-nigh as many dressed in blue as dressed in grey. But all loss now to the grey, with never a recruiting ground behind it, was double loss and treble loss. Every living man knew it, and knew that the field of Franklin was vain, vain! Another artery had been opened, that was all. The South was bleeding, bleeding to death.

There fell upon the Army of Tennessee a great melancholy. Reckless daring, yes! but what had reckless daring done? Opportunity at Spring Hill lost — Franklin, where there was no opportunity, lost, lost! — Cleburne dead — So many of the bravest and best dead or laid low or taken, so many slipped forever from the Army of Tennessee — cold, hunger, nakedness, Giant Fatigue, Giant Lack-of-Confidence, Giant Little-Hope, Giant Much-Despair — a wailing wind that like an æolian harp brought a distant crying, a crying from home. . . . Not Atlanta, not Missionary Ridge, not Vicksburg, — not anything was so bad as the night and day after Franklin, Tennessee.

The night of the thirtieth, Schofield, leaving his dead and wounded, fell back from Franklin to Thomas at Nashville a few miles to the north. Now there were at Nashville between fifty and sixty thousand men in blue. On the second of December Hood put his army into motion, and that evening saw it drawn up and facing Thomas. Returns conflict, but he had now probably less than thirty thousand men. The loss on the field had been great, and the straggling was great and continued so. Also, now at last, there was an amount of desertion.

The weather changed. It became cold winter. For fourteen days Hood who so despised breastworks, dug and entrenched. "The only remaining chance of success in the campaign at this juncture," he says, "was to take position, entrench about Nashville, and await Thomas's attack, which, if handsomely repulsed, might afford us an opportunity to follow up our advantage on the spot and enter the city on the heels of the enemy." — But George Thomas was a better general though not a braver man than Hood, and he had two men to Hood's one, and his men were clothed and fed and confident. He had no better lieutenants than had Hood, and his army was no braver than the grey army and not one half so desperate — but when all is weighed and allowed for his advantage remains of the greatest. And as at Franklin so at Nashville, the grey cavalry was divided and Forrest was fatally sent on side expeditions.

It began to snow, and as the snow fell it froze. The trees and the country side were mailed in ice and the skies hung grey as iron and low as the roof of a cavern. The Army of Tennessee, behind its frozen earthworks, suffered after a ghastly fashion. There was little wood for fires, and little food for cooking, and little covering for warmth. On the thirteenth there set in a thaw, and the fifteenth dawned, not cold, with a winter fog. Through it the 'Rock of Chickamauga' moved out in force from Nashville, and with his whole strength struck fair and full the Army of Tennessee.

Two days the two armies fought. In the slant sunshine of the late afternoon of the second day, the Federal commander brought a great concentration of artillery against the Confederate centre, and under cover of that storm of shot and shell, massed his troops and charged the centre. It broke. The blue poured over the breastworks. At the same moment other and dire blue strokes were delivered against the right and left. The grey army was crumpled together like a piece of cloth. Then in a torrent of shouting and a thunder of guns came the rout. The grey cloth was torn in strips and fled like shreds in a high wind. Beside the killed and wounded the grey left in the hands of the enemy fifty-four guns and four thousand five hundred prisoners. Night came down; night over the Confederacy.

Ten days and nights the shattered army fell back to the Tennessee, moving at first through a hail-storm of cavalry attacks. Forrest beat these off, Forrest and a greatly heroic rear guard under Walthall. This infantry command and Forrest saved the remnant of the army.

The weather grew atrocious. The country now was hilly, wooded, thinly populated. Snow fell and then sleet, and the ground grew ice and the rail fences and the trees were mailed in ice. The feet of the men left blood-marks on the ice, the hands of the men were frozen where they rested on the gun stocks. Men lay down by the roadside and died or were gathered by the blue force hard on the heels of the rear guard. The ambulances bore their load, the empty ammunition and commissary wagons carried as many as they might, the caissons were overlaid with moaning men, the mounted officers took men up behind them. Others, weak, ill, frozen, shoeless did their piteous best to keep up with the "boys." They fell behind, they sank upon the roadside, they drew themselves into the gaunt woods and lay down upon the frozen snow, arms over eyes. *Tramp, tramp, tramp, tramp!* went the column on the road. *Close up, men, close up — close up!* "It's the end, it's the end!" said the men. "For God's sake, strike up Dixie!"

> "'Way down South in the land of cotton,
> Old times there are not forgotten —"

XXXIX

COLUMBIA

THE bells of the South had been melted and run into cannon, and yet there seemed a tolling of bells. Everywhere they tolled — louder and louder! — tolled the siege of Savannah, tolled Hatcher's Run in Virginia, tolled Fort Fisher in North Carolina and the blue bombarding ships — tolled solemnly and loudly, "*The End is come!*"

Forrest guarding, the haggard remnant of the Army of Tennessee crossed the river on the twenty-seventh of December. There was a council of war. Where to go to rest — recoup — reorganize? Southwest into Mississippi? Southwest they marched and on the tenth of January came to Tupelo. Hood asked to be relieved from command and was relieved, A. P. Stewart succeeding him. Later the army, now a small, war-worn force, went to fight in North Carolina. But Stevenson's division and a few other troops were sent into South Carolina to Hardee who, with less than fifteen thousand men, mostly in garrison at Charleston, was facing Sherman and his sixty thousand, flushed from that March to the Sea which is described as "one long, glorious picnic," from the capture of Savannah, from the plaudits of the Northern press and the praise of Government. Now the idea that he should join Grant at Petersburg having been laid aside, Sherman proposed to march northward through South Carolina.

The bells tolled loud in the South, tolled for the women in the night-time, tolled for the shrunken armies, tolled for the cities that waited, a vision before their eyes of New Orleans, Atlanta, Savannah, tolled for the beleaguered places where men watched in the trenches, tolled for the burned farmhouses, the burned villages, the lonely, blackened country with the gaunt chimneys standing up, tolled for famine, tolled for death, tolled for the broken-hearted, tolled for human passions let loose, tolled for anger, greed and lust, tolled for the shrunken good, tolled for the mounting ill, tolled for war! Through the South they tolled and tolled.

Beauregard took command in South Carolina. It was not known whether Sherman would move north and west upon Augusta, just over the Georgia line, or east to Charleston, or almost due north to Columbia. Late in January he moved from Savannah in ruins, crossed the flooded Savannah River by pontoon, entered South Carolina, and marched northward toward Columbia the capital of that state. It being a rainy season, and swamp and river out of bounds, he made not more than ten miles a day.

At this time one of his staff officers writes, "The actual invasion of South Carolina has begun. The well-known sight of columns of black smoke meets our gaze again." And another Federal officer, "There can be no doubt of the assertion that the feeling among the troops was one of extreme bitterness toward the people of South Carolina. It was freely expressed as the column hurried over the bridge at Sister's Ferry, eager to commence the punishment of the original Secessionists. Threatening words were heard from soldiers who prided themselves on conservatism in house-burning while in Georgia, and officers openly confessed their fears that the coming campaign would be a wicked one. Just or unjust as this feeling was toward the country people in South Carolina, it was universal. I first saw its fruits at Purisburg, where two or three piles of blackened bricks and an acre or so of dying embers marked the site of an old, Revolutionary town; and this before the column had fairly got its hand in. . . . The army might safely march the darkest night, the crackling pine woods shooting up their columns of flame, and the burning houses along the way would light it on. . . . As for the wholesale burnings, pillage, devastation, committed in South Carolina, magnify all I have said of Georgia some fifty-fold, and then throw in an occasional murder, 'just to bring an old hard-fisted cuss to his senses,' and you have a pretty good idea of the whole thing."

General Sherman testifies that "the whole army is burning with insatiable desire to wreak vengeance on South Carolina. I almost tremble at her fate."

And one of his captains remarks of the situation several weeks later. "It was sad to see this wanton destruction of property which

. . . was the work of 'bummers' who were marauding through the country committing every sort of outrage. There was no restraint except with the column or the regular foraging parties. We had no communications and could have no safeguards. The country was necessarily left to take care of itself, and became a howling waste. The 'Coffee-coolers' of the Army of the Potomac were archangels compared to our 'bummers' who often fell to the tender mercies of Wheeler's cavalry, and were never heard of again, earning a fate richly deserved."

Winter is not truly winter in South Carolina, but in the winter of '65 it rained and rained and rained. All swamps and streams were out, low-lying plantations were under water, the country looked like a flooded rice-field. The water-oaks and live-oaks and magnolias stood up, shining and dark, beneath the streaming sky; where the road was corduroyed it was hard to travel, and where it was not wheels sank and sank. All the world was wet, and the canes in the marshes made no rustling. When it did not rain the sky remained grey, a calm grey pall keeping out the sun, but leaving a quiet grey-pearl light, like a dream that is neither sad nor glad.

"It is," said Désirée, "the air of Cape Jessamine that winter you came."

"Yes. The road to Vidalia! We passed at nightfall a piece of water with a bit of bridge. I helped push a gun upon it, and the howitzer knocked me on the head for my pains. I fell down, down into deep water, forty fathoms at the least, and blacker than ebony at midnight. . . . And then I waked up in Rasmus's cabin, and we had supper, and water came under the door, and we circumvented the bayou, and went to the Gaillard place which was called Cape Jessamine. And there I found a queen in a russet gown and a soldier's cloak. The wind blew the cloak out and made a canopy of it in the light of torches and bonfires. She stood upon the levee and bitted and bridled the Mississippi River — and I fell in love, deep, deep, forty thousand fathoms deep —"

"Two years. . . . You were so ragged and splashed with mud — And my heart beat like that! and said to me 'Who is this that comes winged and crowned?' — Listen!"

They were on a road somewhat to the southeast of Columbia, Désirée in an open wagon driven by a negro boy, Edward — major

now of the ——th Virginia — riding beside her on a grey horse. Ahead,
at some distance, they just saw the regiment, marching through a
gloomy wood, bound for a post on the Edisto. The sound of its
going and the voices of the men came faintly back through the damp
and quiet air. But what they heard was nearer, a passionate weeping amid the trees at a cross-road. Coming to this opening they found
a spacious family carriage drawn by two ancient plough horses, a
cart with a mule attached, and two or three negro pedestrians. The
whole had stopped the moment before and with reason. A white-
haired lady, stretched upon the cushions of the carriage laid cross-
wise, had just breathed her last. The weeping was her daughter's,
a dark, handsome girl of twenty. Two negro women lamented also,
while the coachman had gotten down from the box and stood staring, with a working face. There were some bags and pillows and
things of little account heaped in the cart, and on these a small
negro boy was profoundly sleeping.

Edward dismounted and Désirée stepped down from the wagon.
"What could they do? How sad it was! — Was there any help? — "
Désirée lifted the girl from her mother's form, drew her away to a
roadside log, and sitting there, held her close and let her weep.
Edward saw the oldest negro woman, murmuring constantly to herself, close the eyes of the dead mistress, straighten her limbs and fold
her hands. The other woman sat on the earth and rocked herself.
The plough horses and the mule lowered their heads and cropped
what green bush and grass there was. The little black boy slept
on and on. Edward talked with the coachman. "Yaas, marster, dat
so! — 'Bout thirty miles south from here, sah. *Bienvenu* — er
Lauren's place. En de Yankees come hollerin' en firin' en hits daid
of night en old Marster en young Marster wif Gineral Lee. — One
officer, he say git away quick! en he give me er guard en I hitches
up, en we lif' ol' Mistis out of her bed where she 's had pneumonia,
en Miss Fanny en her mammy en Julia dar wif her boy, we teks de
road."

Désirée and Edward saw the forlorn cortège proceed on its way
with hopes of a village or some country house. They stood a moment watching it disappear, then Désirée rested her hand upon his
arm and mounted again into the wagon, and he sprang upon his
horse that was named Damon, and the negro boy touched the mule

drawing the wagon with his whip, and they all went on after the regiment. They found it at twilight, encamped in the hospitable houses and the one street of a tiny rain-soaked hamlet. Headquarters was the parsonage and here was a room ready for the Major's wife. From colonel to cook the ——th Virginia loved the Major's wife. Romance dwelled with her, and a queenliness that was never vanquished. Her presence never wearied; she knew when to withdraw, to disappear, how not to give trouble, and how, when she gave it, to make it seem a high guerdon, a princess's favour. Sometimes the regiment did not see her for weeks or even months on end, and then she came like a rose in summer, a more golden light on the fields, a deeper blue in the sky. She made mystics of men.

Now the parson's wife made her welcome, and after a small supper sat with her in a clean bedroom before a fire. The parson's wife was full of sighs, and "Ah, my dears!" and ominous shakings of the head. "South Carolina's bound down," she said, "and going to be tormented. What you tell me about that dead woman and her daughter is but the beginning. It's but a leaf before the storm. We're going to hear of many whirled and trodden leaves."

"Yes," said Désirée, her eyes upon the fantastic shapes in the hollow of the fire. "Whirled and trodden leaves."

"I have a sister," said the parson's wife, "in Georgia. She got away, but will you listen to some of the things she writes?"

She got the letter and read. Désirée, listening, put her hands over her eyes and shivered a little for all the room was warm. "I should not have said such things could happen in a Christian land," she said.

"They happen," said the parson's wife. "War is a horror, and a horror to women. It has always been so and always will be so. And now I must go see that there is covering enough on the beds."

At cock-crow the regiment was up and away. Still the same pearly sky, the same quietude, the same stretches of water crept under the trees, the same heavy road, and halts and going on. The regiment took dinner beneath live oaks on a little rise of ground beside a swamp become a lake. Officers' mess dined a little to one side beneath a monster tree. All wood was wet and the fires smoked, but soldiers grow skilful and at last a blaze was got. Sherman was yet to the southward; this strip of country not yet overrun and provisions to be had. Officers' mess to-day sat down under the live oaks to what, compared to many and many a time in its existence, appeared a feast for kings. There were roasted ducks and sweet potatoes, rice and milk and butter. Officers' mess said grace devoutly.

Désirée said grace with her friends, for they had sent back to urge her wagon forward and to say they had a feast and to beg her company. She sat with Edward over against the Colonel, and the captains and lieutenants sat to either side the board. They made a happy dinner, jesting and laughing, while off in the grove of oaks was heard the laughter of their grey men. When dinner was over, and half an hour of sweet rest was over, into column came all, and took again the swampy road.

That evening headquarters was a fine old pillared house, set in a noble garden, surrounded in its turn by the fields and woods of a great plantation. Here there was a large family, an old man and his married daughters and their daughters and little sons. These made the men welcome where they camped beside fires out under the great trees of the place, and the grey officers welcome indoors, and Désirée welcome and gave her and Edward a room with mirrors and chintz curtains and a great four-poster bed and a light-wood fire. A little after the regiment, came up also a small troop of grey cavalry returning from a reconnoissance to the southward. Infantry and the plantation alike were eager for Cavalry's news. Its news was ravage and ruin, the locusts of Egypt and a grudge against the land. There were sixty thousand of the foe and it seemed determined now that Sherman meant Columbia.

"What are the troops at Columbia?"

"Stevenson's twenty-six hundred men, a few other scattering commands, Wheeler's cavalry — say five thousand in all."

"Could not General Beauregard bring troops from Charleston?"

"General Hampton thinks he might. — Evacuate Charleston — concentrate before Columbia. But I don't know — I don't know! There are not many thousands even at Charleston."

"It's the end."

"Yes. I suppose so. But fight on till the warder drops!"

There were the young girls and young married women in the great old house. There was a polished floor, and negro fiddlers had not left the plantation. Cavalry and infantry officers were, with some exceptions, young men — and this was South Carolina. "Yes, dance!" said the old gentleman, the head of the house. "To-morrow you may have neither fiddlers nor floor."

They danced till almost midnight, and at the last they danced the Virginia Reel. The women were not in silks or fine muslins, they were in homespun. The men were not dressed like the young bloods, the University students, the dandies of five years back. Their grey uniforms were clean, but very worn. Bars upon the collar, or sash and star took the place of the old elaboration of velvet waistcoat and fine neckcloth. Spurs that would have caught in filmy laces did not harm the women's skirts of linsey. The fiddlers fiddled, the lights burned. Up and down and up again, and around and around. . . .

Edward and Désirée, resting by a window, regarded the room, at once vivid and dreamy. "We were dancing," he said, "the Virginia Reel at Greenwood the night there came news of the secession of Virginia."

"Much has happened since then."

"Much."

The fiddlers played, the lights burned, they took their places. At midnight the revel closed, and they slept in the chamber with the mirrors and the fire, until the winter day showed, smoked-pearl, without the windows. At breakfast-time came a courier from Columbia, ordering the ——th Virginia back to that place.

The weather cleared and grew colder. The roads drying, the regiment made good pace. But for all the patches of bright sky there seemed to hang a pall over the land. The wind in the woods blew with a long, mournful, rushing sound. Désirée sat in the wagon with bowed head, her hands in her lap. Edward was ahead, to-day, with the regiment. The wagon went heavily on, the wind rushed on either side like goblin horsemen. At intervals during the morning the negro boy was moved to speech. "Yass 'm. All de ghostes are loose in de graveyards. Dey tel' erbout hit in de kitchen las' night. Dey been to er voodoo woman, en she say all de ghostes loose, high en low, out er ebery graveyard, en she ain't got no red pepper what kin lay them. She say time past she had ernough, but she ain't got ernough now."

"What are they doing — the ghosts?"

"Dey're linin' up in long lines like de poplars, en wavin' dere arms en sayin', 'De end's come! De end's come!' En den dey rises from de ground en goes erroun' de plantation in er ring, 'twel you almos' think hits jus' er ring ob mist. But dey keep er-sayin', 'De end's come! De end's come!' Yass'm, dey're all out, en dere ain't nothin' what kin lay them!"

Moving now as they were on a main road to Columbia they this day passed or overtook numbers of people, all going their way. These people looked distracted. "What was happening to the southward?" "Ruin!" they answered. Some talked quickly and feverishly as long as they might to the soldiers; others dealt in monosyllables, shook their heads and went on with fixed gaze. Shortly before this time General Sherman had written to General Halleck: "This war differs from European wars in this particular — we are not only fighting hostile armies but a hostile people; and must make old and young, rich and poor, feel the hard hand of want, as well as their organized armies." These on the road to Columbia were the unorganized — the old and very young and the sick and a great number of women.

The soldiers were troubled. "Sherman's surely coming to Columbia, and how will five thousand men hold it against sixty thousand? You poor people ought n't to go there!"

"Then where should we go?"

"God knows!"

"We are from Purisburg. There is n't a house standing."

"We are from Barnwell. It was burning when we left. Our home was burned."

"I am from toward Pocotaligo. It is all a waste. All black and burned."

On they streamed, the refugees. The regiment gave what help, what lifts upon the way it could. As for Désirée, coming on in her wagon, she took into it so many, that presently she found no room for herself, but walked beside the horse. And so, at last, on a dull, soft day, they came into Columbia.

It was the sixteenth of February. The Capital of South Carolina was by nature a pleasant, bowery town, though now it was so heavy of heart and filled with forebodings. Of the five thousand who formed its sole defence some portion was in the town itself, but the greater part lay outside, on picket, up and down the Congaree. The ——th Virginia, coming in, was quartered in the town until it was known what was to be done. Orangeburg was not many miles below Columbia, and the head of Sherman's column had reached Orangeburg. There was a track of fire drawn across the country; Columbia saw doom coming like a prairie-fire.

Edward found a room for Désirée and he came to her here an hour before dusk. They stood together by a window looking down into the street. "They are leaving home," she said. "I have seen women and children going all afternoon. I have seen such sad things in this pretty street."

"Sad enough!" he answered. "Désirée, I think that you must go too."

"No, no!" she said. "No, no! There is nowhere to go."

"There is Camden and the villages in the northern part of the State. It is possible that Sherman means when he has done his worst here, to turn back toward Charleston. There is no knowing, but it is possible. If he does that, Camden and those other places may escape."

"And you?"

"There are no orders yet. We may stay or we may march away. O God, what a play is Life!"

"Those women who are parting down there — saying good-bye to all they love — they do not at all know that they are going into safety, and those who are parting from them do not know. It might be better for them to stay in this large town. They are going away in the dark night, and the enemy may have parties out where they are going. I had rather stay here. I think that it is safer."

"Désirée, Désirée! If a man could see but ever so little of the road before him! If we are marched away in haste as we may be, you cannot go with us this time. Then to leave you here alone —"

"There is an Ursuline convent here," she said. "They will not burn that. If you leave me and evil comes near I will go there."

"You promise that?"

"Yes, I promise it."

It was in the scroll of their fate that he should leave her and that evil should come nigh. She waked in a strange red dawn to hear the tramp of feet in the street below. Instantly she was at the window. Grey soldiers were passing below — a column. In the south broke suddenly a sound of cannon. She saw a shell, sent from the other side of the river, explode in the red air above the city roofs. There came a feeling of Vicksburg again.

A hand was at her door. She opened it and Edward took her in his arms. "I have but an instant," he said. "If we go it may be better for this city than if we stayed. The mayor will surrender it peaceably, and it may be spared destruction. For you, Désirée — for you — God bless you, God keep you till we meet again!"

She smiled back at him. "That will be shortly."

"No man can tell, nor no woman. You will go to the Ursuline convent ? "

"Yes, I will go."

He strained her to him; they kissed and parted. The soldiers went by in the red dawn, out of the town, toward Winnsboro' to the northward. This day also Charleston was evacuated, Hardee with his men moving north to Cheraw on the Pedee. At Columbia the mayor and aldermen went out between eight and nine in the morning and, meeting the Federal advance, surrendered the town, and asked for protection for the non-combatants within its walls. How it was given let history tell. Several days later Sherman writes to Kilpatrick: "Let the whole people know that war is now against them, because their armies flee before us and do not defend their country or frontier as they should. It is pretty nonsense for Wheeler and Beauregard and such vain heroes to talk of our warring against women and children. If they claim to be men they should defend their women and children and prevent us reaching their homes."

Perhaps Wheeler and Beauregard and the other vain heroes would have prevented it if they could. Since, however, it lay in their hard fortune that they could not, there remained in General Sherman's mind no single reason for consideration.

Désirée went truly to the Ursuline convent, passing swiftly through the windy streets on a windy day, choosing small back streets because the principal ones were now crowded with soldiers, keeping close to the walls of the houses and drawing a scarf she wore more fully about head and face, for even through the side streets there were now echoing drunken voices. She came to the convent door, rang, and greeting the sister who came told how alone she was in the city. The door opened to admit her of course, and she only wished that Edward might see her in the convent garden or in the little room where the nuns said she might sleep that night.

But no one slept in the convent that night. It was burned. The nuns and the young girls, their pupils, and the women who had come for refuge stayed the night in the churchyard. It was cold and there was a high wind. The leafless branches of the trees clattered in it, and below, on their knees, the nuns murmured prayers, their half-frozen hands fingering their rosaries. The young girls drew together for warmth, and the Mother Superior stood, counselling and comforting. And the convent burned and the city burned, with a roaring and crackling of flames and a shouting of men.

CHAPTER XL

THE ROAD TO WINNSBORO'

SHE was a wise as well as a fair woman, and yet, the day after the burning of Columbia, she took a road that led northward from the smoking ruins. In the cold morning sunlight Sherman himself had come to the churchyard, and hat in hand had spoken to the Mother Superior. He regretted the accidental burning of the convent. Any yet standing house in town that she might designate should be reserved for her, her nuns and pupils. She named a large old residence from which the family had gone, and walking between files of soldiers the nuns and their charges came here. "We learned," says the Mother Superior, "from the officer in charge that his orders were to fire it unless the Sisters were in actual possession of it, but if even 'a detachment of Sisters' were in it, it should be spared on their account. Accordingly we took possession of it, although fires were already kindled near and the servants were carrying off the bedding and furniture, in view of the house being consigned to the flames."

All morning the burning, the looting and shouting went on. Smoke rolled through the streets, the wind blew flames from point to point. The house was crowded to oppression; there came a question of food for so many. Some one was needed to go to the mayor with representations, which might in turn be brought before the Federal commander. Désirée volunteered and the distance not being great, went and returned in safety. Not far from the door that would open to receive her was a burned house and before it an ancient carriage, and in the carriage two ladies and a little girl. There were soldiers in the street and to be seen through smoke beyond the fallen house, but here beside the carriage was an officer high in command and order prevailed. The officer was speaking to the ladies. "If there is any trouble, show your pass. I won't say that you are wise to leave this place, sad as it is! These are wild times, and there are more marauders than I like. Even if you make your way to your brother's house, you may find it in ashes. And if you overtake the rear of your army, what can that help? We will be sweeping on directly and the rebels — I beg your pardon, General Beauregard's army — will have to fall back before us or surrender. I think you had better stay. General Sherman will surely issue rations to the place."

"We prefer to go on," said the eldest of the two women. "We may find friends somewhere, and somewhere to lay our heads. We do thank you for the pass."

"Not at all!" said the officer. "As I told you, your father and my father were friends."

As he moved from the carriage door Désirée saw that there was an empty seat. "Oh," she thought, "if I might have it!"

Her face, turned toward the carriage, showed from out her hood. The younger of the women saw her, started and uttered an exclamation. "Désirée Gaillard!" she cried.

Lo! it was an acquaintance, almost a friend, a girl who had been much in New Orleans, with whom she had laughed at many a party. "Go with them! — yes, indeed, she might go with them." She ran to the house that was now the convent, gave the Mayor's message and thanked the Sisters for the help they would have given, then out she came to the smoke-filled street and took her place in the carriage. It had a guard out of town; the officer had been punctilious to do his best. It was understood that there were Federal troops on the Camden road, but they were going toward Winnsboro'. When the burning city lay behind them and the quiet winter fields around, when the guard had said a gruff "You're safe enough now! Good-day!" and turned back, when the negro driver said, "Git up, Lance! Git up, France!" to the horses, and the carriage wheels turned and they passed a clump of cedars, they were on the road that the grey troops had travelled no great chain of hours before.

They drove on and on, and now they overtook and passed or kept company with for a while mournful folk, refugees, people with the noise of falling walls in their ears. They had tales to tell and some were dreadful enough. Then for a time the road would be bare, a melancholy road, much cut to pieces, with ruts and hollows. Now and then in dropped haversack, or broken bayonet, or torn shoe, or blood-stained rag were visible tokens that soldiers had passed.

They had a little food and they ate this, and now and then they talked in low voices, but for the most part they sat silent, looking out on the winter landscape. The little girl was restless, and Désirée told her French fairy stories, quaint and fragrant. At last she slept, and the three women sat in silence, looking out. In the late afternoon, turning a little from the main road, they came to the country house for which they were bound.

The welcome was warm, with a clamour for news. *"Columbia burned! — oh, well-a-way!* . . . No Yankees in this part as yet. Our troops went by yesterday on the Winnsboro' road. It's said they'll wait there until General Hardee gets up from Charleston and they can make junction. There's a rumour that General Johnston will be put in command. Oh, the waiting, waiting! One's brain turns, looking for the enemy to come, looking for the South to fall — worse and worse news every day! If one were with the Army it would not be half so bad. Waiting, waiting here's the worst!"

In this Désirée agreed. It was away in a wood and upon a creek like the Fusilier place. The army was no great distance further on, and halted. In a day or two it would move, away, away! Her whole being cried out, 'I cannot stay here! If it comes to danger, this lonely place will be burned like the others. I were safer there than here. And what do I care for danger? Have I not travelled with danger for two years?"

That night when, exhausted, she fell asleep, she had a dream. She was back in Dalton, in the house with the lace-handkerchief dooryard. She was on her knees, cording a hair trunk, and the old negro Nebuchadnezzar and his horse Julius Cæsar were waiting. Somebody — it was not the two sisters who lived in the house — but somebody, she could not make out who it was — was persuading her to stay quietly there, not to take the road to Resaca. At first she would not listen, but at last she did listen and said she would stay. And then at once she was at Cape Jessamine and the house was filled with people and there was dancing. Everything was soft and bright and a myriad of wax candles were burning, and the music played and they talked about going to New Orleans for Mardi-gras and what masks they should wear. And she was exceedingly happy, with roses in her hair and an old gold-gown. But all the time she was trying to remember something or somebody, and it troubled her that she could not bring whatever it was to mind. And then, though she still danced, and though there stayed a gleaming edge of floor and light and flowers and moving people, the rest rolled away into darkness and a battlefield. She saw the stars above it and heard the wind, and then she left the dancers and the lights and they faded away and she walked on the battlefield, but still there was something she could not remember. She was unhappy and her heart ached because she could not. And then she came to a corner of the field where were dark vines and broken walls, and a voice came to her out of it, "Désirée! Désirée!" She remembered now and knew that Edward lay there, and she cried, "I am coming!" But even so the dream turned again, and she was back in the house with the lace-handkerchief yard, and the hair trunk was being carried back into the house and up the stairs, and the wagon at the gate turned and went away without her. Then there was darkness again, and the cave at Vicksburg, and a cry in her ears, "*Désirée! Désirée!*"

She waked, and, trembling, sat up in bed. "If I had not gone from Dalton," she said, "he would have died." She rose, crossed the room to a window and set it wide. It looked across the wood toward the road they had left, the Winnsboro' road. She stood gazing, in the night wind, the winter wind. There was a faint far light upon the horizon. Rightly or wrongly, she thought it was the camp-fires of the grey army. Another night and they would be further away perhaps, another night and further yet! Sooner or later there would be the battle, and the dead and the wounded left on the field. The wind blew full upon her, wrapping her white gown closely about her limbs, lifting her dark hair. "*Désirée! Désirée!*" The dream cry was yet in her ears, and there on the horizon flamed his camp-fires.

When morning came she begged a favour of her new friends in this place. Could they let her have a cart and a horse, anything that might take her to Winnsboro'? They said that if she must go she should have the carriage and horses and the old driver of yesterday, but surely it was not wise to go at all! News was here this morning that the ravage north of Columbia had begun. All this country would be unsafe — was perhaps unsafe at this moment and henceforth! No one expected this house to be spared — why should it be, more than another? — but at least it was not burned yet, and it was better to face what might come in company than alone! "Stay with us, my dear, stay with us!" But when she would go on, they understood. It was a time of wandering and of much travel under strange and hard conditions. As for danger — when it was here and there and everywhere what use in dwelling on it? No one could say with any knowledge, "Here is safety," or "There is danger." The shuttle was so rapid! What to-day seemed the place of safety was to-morrow the very centre of danger. What was to-day's field of danger might become to-morrow, the wave rushing on, quiet of foes as any desert strand! — Désirée kissed her friends and went away in the old carriage toward the Winnsboro' road.

The morning was dull and harsh with scudding clouds. The side road was as quiet as death, but when they came upon the broader way there grew a difference. The old negro looked behind him. "Dere's an awful fuss, mistis, en er dust! des lak de debbil got loose!"

"Drive fast," said Désirée. "If you come to a lane turn into it."

But the road went straight between banks of some height, without a feasible opening to either hand. Moreover, though the driver used the whip and the horses broke into something like a gallop, the cloud of dust and the noise behind steadily gained. There came a round of pistol shots. "They are firing at us," said Désirée. "Check the horses and draw the carriage to the side of the road."

Dust and noise enveloped them. A foraging party, twenty jovial troopers, drew rein, surrounded the carriage, declined to molest or trouble the lady, but claimed the carriage-horses in the name of the Union.

They cut the traces and took them, Désirée standing by the roadside watching. These men, she thought, were much like schoolboys, in wild spirits, ready for rough play but no malice. She was so used to soldiers and used to seeing in them such sudden, rough and gay humour as this that she felt no fear at all. When a freckled, humorous-faced man came over and asked her if she had far to travel, and if she really minded walking, she answered with a wit and composure that made him first chuckle, then laugh, then take off his cap and make her a bow. The troop was in a hurry. When it had the horses and had joked and laughed and caracoled enough, off it prepared to go in another cloud of dust. But the freckled man came back for a moment to Désirée. "If I may make so bold, ma'am," he said, "I'd suggest that you don't do much walking on this road, and that as soon as you come to a house you ask the people to let you take pot-luck with them for a while! The army's coming on, and we've got plenty of bands out that don't seem ever to have had any good womenfolk to teach them manners. If you'll take a friend's advice you'll stop at the nearest house — though of course, in these times, that ain't very safe neither!"

The carriage had the forlornest air, stranded there in the road, beneath a sky so cloudy that now there threatened a storm. The negro driver was old and slightly doddering. Moreover, when she said, "Well, Uncle, now we must walk!" he began to plain of his rheumatism. She found that it was actual enough; he would be able to walk neither fast or far. She looked behind her. A league or two back lay the turning that would lead to the house she had quitted. . . . But she shook her head. She had made her choice.

A mile from where they left the carriage they found at a cross-roads the cabin of some free negroes — a man and a woman and many children. Here Désirée left her companion. If she took the narrower road, where, she asked, would it lead her? Could she reach Winnsboro' that way? — Yes, if she went on to a creek and a mill, and if then she took the right-hand road. No, it wasn't much out of the way — three or four miles.

"And a quiet, safe road?"

"Yaas, ma'am. Jus' er-runnin' along quiet by itself. Hit ain't much travelled."

"But it will bring me to Winnsboro'?"

"Yaas, ma'am. Quicker'n de main road wif all dese armies hollerin' down it."

"Those men who went by a little while ago — were they the first to pass to-day?"

"No, ma'am, dat dey was n't! En *dey* was sober, Lawd!"

"And they've all kept on the main road?"

"Yaas, ma'am. All taken de main road."

She looked down the road she had come — the main road. Here was another cloud of dust; she heard a faint shouting. She had with her some Confederate notes, and now she put one of a large denomination into the hand of the old driver, nodded good-bye, and turned into the narrow way, that seemed merely a track through the forest. Almost immediately, as she came beneath the arching trees, the cabin, the negro family, the gleaming, wider road sank away and were lost.

She walked lightly and swiftly. She might have been wearied. For a month now she had known that she carried life beneath her heart. But she did not feel wearied. She felt strong and well and deathless. The miles were not many now before her. With good luck she might even reach her goal to-night. If not to-night then she would sleep where she might and go forward at dawn. Before another sun was high it would be all right — all right. The clouds began to lift, and though it was cold it did not seem so cold to her as it had been. At long intervals she passed, set back from the road, small farmhouses or cabins in ragged gardens. Most of these houses looked quite deserted; others had every shutter closed, huddling among the trees with a frightened air. As the afternoon came on the houses grew further apart. The road was narrow, untravelled of late — it seemed a lonely country. . . . At last she came to the promised creek and the mill. The mill-wheel was not turning, no miller and his men stood about the door, no horses with sacks thrown across waited without. There was no sign of life. But the miller's house was behind the mill, and here she saw a face at a window. She went and knocked at the door. An old woman opened to her. "Be the Yankees coming?" she said.

Désirée asked for a bit of bread, and to warm herself beside the fire. While she ate it, crouched in the warm corner of the kitchen hearth, the old woman took again her post at the window. "I keep a-watching and a-watching for them to come!" she said. "They've got a spite against mills. My father built this one, and when he died my husband took it, and when he died my boy John. The wheel turned when I was little, and when I was grown and had a lover, and when I was married and when there were children. It turned when there was laughing and when there was crying. The sound of the water over it and the flashing is the first thing I can remember. I used to think it would be the last thing I'd hear when I came to die, and I kind of hoped it would. I liked it. It was all mixed up with all kinds of things. But now I reckon before this time to-morrow it'll be burned. They've got a spite against mills. — Won't you stay the night?"

But there was an hour yet before sunset. The road to Winnsboro'? Yes, that was it, and it was only so many miles. The army? Yes, she thought the army was still there. Yesterday there had been what they called a reconoissance this way. A lot of grey soldiers had passed, going down to the Columbia road and back.

Désirée rose refreshed, gave her thanks and went her way. A wind bent the trees and tore and heaped the clouds. The low sun shone out and turned the clouds into purple towers, fretted and crowned with gold. The rays came to Désirée like birds and flowers of hope. For all the woe of the land her heart began to sing. She walked on and on, not conscious of weariness, moving as though she were on air, drawn by a great magnet. The clouds were enchanted towers, the sky between, a waveless sea; the wind at her back, driving her on, was welcome, the odour of woods and earth was welcome. On and on she went, steady and swift, an arrow meaning to pierce the gold.

Suddenly, with a shock, the enchantment went. The wind, blowing with her, brought a distant, confused sound. She turned. It was sunset, the earth was suddenly stern and dark. Above the woods, back the way she had come, rose thick smoke. She knew it for what it was, knew that some one of Sherman's roving bands was there at the mill, burning it down. She stood with knit brows, for now she heard men upon the road. The ground here rose slightly, the road running across a desolate, open field, covered with sedge, from which rose at intervals tall, slender pines. Their trunks and bushy heads outlined against the sky, that was now all flushed with carmine, gave them a curious resemblance to palm trees. West of the road, half way across the sedgy stretch, ran a short and ruined wall of stones, part of some ancient enclosure. Behind it showed again the darker, thicker wood. Désirée, leaving the road, went toward this, but she had hardly stepped from the trodden way into the sedge when behind her at the turn of the road appeared a man in uniform. She was above him, clear against the great suffusion of the sunset sky. He stared a moment, then turned his head and whooped, whereupon there appeared half a dozen of his fellows.

They caught up with her just as she reached the broken wall.

She saw that without exception they were drunk, and she set her back against the stones and prepared to fight.

Five thousand men could not meet in battle sixty thousand, but they could and did send out reconnoitring bodies that gathered news of Sherman, tarrying yet upon the Congaree, and gave some sense of protection to the country people and gave sharp lessons to the marauding parties that now and again they met with. By moving here and there they made a rumour, too, of gathering grey troops and larger numbers, of reinforcements perhaps from North Carolina, of at any rate grey forces and some one to play now protector, now avenger. So it was that on this winter afternoon the———th Virginia, three or four hundred muskets, with a small detachment of cavalry going ahead, found itself marching down the main road, fifteen miles toward Columbia. It knew by now of the burning of Columbia. "Everything in ashes — houses and stores and churches and a convent. The people with neither food nor shelter — going where they can." Grey cavalry and infantry asked nothing better than to meet its foes to-day. So great, around the blue army, was the fringe of foragers and pillagers and those engaged in "making the country untenable for the enemy," that the grey did meet to-day various bands of plunderers. When they did they gave short shrift, but charged, firing, cut them down and rode them over and chased them back toward Columbia and their yet stationary great force. The grey's humour to-day was a grim and furious humour.

The ———th Virginia passed a cross-roads, and a little later came to something that aroused comment among the men. It was an empty, old-fashioned carriage, standing without horses, half on the road, half over the edge. "Looks," said the men, "like the ark on Ararat!" — "Forlorn, ain't it?" — "Where's the horses and the people who were in it?" — "Reckon those Yanks before us took the horses. As for the people — I'd rather be a humming-bird in winter than the people in this State!"

Edward Cary rode across and checking his horse, leaned from the saddle and looked into the carriage — why, he hardly knew, unless it was that once in Georgia they had found a carriage stranded like this, and in it a child asleep. There was in this one nothing living. . . . Just as he straightened himself he caught a glint of something small and golden lying in a corner. He dismounted, drew the swinging door further open and picked it up. It was a locket, and he had had it in his hands before.

He remembered passing, a little way back, a negro cabin. After a word to the commanding officer he galloped back to this place. Yes, they could tell him, and did. "She took this road?" "Yaas, sah. Long erbout midday. We done tol' her erbout de creek en de mill en de right-han' road —"

"Has any one else gone by this road? Any soldiers?"

"Yaas, sah. Right smart lot ob soldiers. Dey ax where dat road go, en I say hit go to de mill. Den dey say dey gwine burn de mill, en dey goes dat way. I reckon hits been mo 'n three hours ergo, sah."

It was dusk when Edward Cary and twenty cavalrymen turned into this road, and it had been night for some time when they came to the reddened place where had stood the mill. It was all down now, though the flames were yet playing through the mass of fallen timbers. The mill-wheel was a wreck, the miller's house behind was burned. There were no soldiers here: they had destroyed and were gone. But out from some hiding-place came an old woman who seemed distraught. She stood in the flickering glow and said, "Yankees! Yankees!" and "They took an axe and killed the mill-wheel!"

Edward spoke to her, soothed her, and at last she drew her wits together, talked to him, and answered his questions. "Yes, a woman had been there and had left a little before sunset. Yes, dressed so and so — a beautiful woman. Yes, she had gone by that road, walking away alone. She said good-bye and then she had seen and heard nothing more of her. Then, in a little, little time, came the Yankees. Some of them were drunk, and she had run out of the house and hid within a brush heap. . . . And now the mill-wheel would never turn again."

"Which road did they take when they left — the Winnsboro' road or that one running south?"

She was not sure. She thought the one running south — but maybe some went one way, some another. She did not know how many there were of them. They were on foot and horseback, too. Her eyes strayed to where the wheel had been, and she fell again to plucking at her apron.

Cary and his men took the right-hand road. It lay quiet as death beneath the winter stars. They travelled it slowly, looking from side to side, but if there were signs that an enemy had been that way, in the darkness they could not read them. Neither did they see any sign of a solitary traveller. All was quiet, with only the sighing of the wind. At last, nearing Winnsboro', they came to their own picket-line. Camped by the road was a cavalry post. Edward spoke with the men here. "No. A quiet night — nothing seen and nothing heard out of the way. No one had passed — no, no woman."

Cary turned in his saddle and looked behind him. Clear night, and dark and still through all the few miles between this place which she had not passed and the mill which she had. . . . The men with him had been in the saddle since dawn. They were weary enough, and under orders to report that night at Winnsboro'. At the end he sent on upon the road well-nigh all the troop, then turned himself and with but three or four horsemen behind him, began to retrace the road to the mill. Light and sound of the picket post died behind him, there came only the quiet miles of a lonely country and the stars above.

The night was old when, suddenly, near again to the burned mill, there burst out of a by-path the men who had burned it. They had taken the southward running road, had burned two houses that lay that way, then encountering rough country and a swollen river, had elected, horse and foot, to march back the way they came. Now, emerging suddenly upon the wider road, they saw before them four horsemen, divined that they were grey, and with a shout joined battle.

"They are six to one, men!" cried Cary. "Save yourselves!"

There came the crash. He fired twice, emptying a saddle and giving a ball in the shoulder to the half-drunken giant who seemed to be leading. Then with oaths three pushed against him. His horse reared, screamed and fell, pierced by bullets. He leaped clear of the saddle and fired again, breaking a man's raised sabre arm. There was a blinding flash, a deafening sound — down, down he went into blackness and silence, into night deep as the nadir. . . .

When he came slowly, slowly back to feeling and consciousness he was alone. It was dawn, he saw that. For a long time there seemed nothing but the fact of dawn. Then he suddenly rested his hand on the earth and tried to lift himself. With the vain effort and the pain it brought came a troubled memory. He put his hand to his side and felt the welling blood. The wound, he presently saw, was deep and hopeless, deep enough to let death in. His head fell back against the bank behind him and he faced the dawn. He was lying at the edge of the road, his dead horse near. All noise and war and strife were gone, the three or four men who had been with him cut down, or taken prisoner, or fled, the blue triumphant band gone its way. There was an utter stillness, and the dawn coming up cool and pure like purple lilies. He slightly turned his head. About him was a field of sedge with scattered pines. The wind was laid, and it was not cold. He knew that his hurt was mortal. . . . Suddenly, as from another world, there came to him a very faint cry — half cry for help, half plaint to a heaven blind and deaf. He dragged himself to his knees, with his hand cleared the mist from his eyes and gazed across an half acre of sedge to a heap of ruined stones like a broken wall. The voice rose again, faintly. With a vast, illuminating rush came fully memory and knowledge, and like a dying leap of the flame, strength. He rose and crossed the sedge.

She was lying where her murderers had left her, beneath the ruined wall. She was dying, but she knew him when, with a cry, he fell beside her, stretched his arms above her. "Yes," she said. "I believed that you would come." Then, when she saw the blood upon him, "Are you going with me?"

"Yes, Love," he said. "Yes, Love."

The great dawn climbed stealthily, from tint to deeper tint, from height to height. The pine trees stood like dreaming palms, and the sedge spread like a floor of gold. "The river!" she said, "the great river that is going to eat us up at last! How it beats against Cape Jessamine!"

"When I saw Cape Jessamine go down, I thought only 'If I were there! If I were with her, together in the wave!'"

Their voices died to whispers. With a vague and fluttering hand she touched his brow and lips. "I wanted the child to live — I wanted that. But it was not to be — it was not to be —"

"Désirée! Désirée!"

A smile was on her lips — almost of derision. "War is so stupid," she said.

Upon the purple wall of the east a finger began to write in gold. The mist was stirring in the woods, the wind beginning. It lifted her dark, loosened hair, that was so wildly spread. It brought a drift of dead leaves across them where they lay. They lay side by side, like wreathed figures on a tomb. "Is it light?" she asked. "Can you see the light?"

"I can see it faintly. It is like the sound of the sea."

"It is very cold," she breathed. "Dark and cold."

"Yes. . . . Dark and cold."

"Give me your hand," she said. "Kiss me. We have been happy, and we will be so again. . . . Now I am going. . . . Dark, dark — dark —"

"Désirée —"

"I see light like a star. . . . Good-bye."

She died. With a last effort he moved so that his arms were around her body and his head upon her breast, and then, as the sun came up, his spirit followed hers.

CHAPTER XLI

THE BEGINNING OF THE END

IN this February the grey Congress at Richmond created the office of Commander-in-Chief of all the Confederate Armies, and appointed to it Robert Edward Lee. On the twenty-third Lee telegraphed to Johnston, then at Lincolnton, North Carolina:

"GENERAL J. E. JOHNSTON: —
Assume command of the Army of Tennessee and all troops in the Department of South Carolina, Florida, and Georgia. Assign General Beauregard to duty under you as you may select. Concentrate all available forces and drive back Sherman.
                                        R. E. LEE."

"All available forces" were not many, indeed they were very few, but such as they were Johnston drew them together, and with them, the middle of March, faced Sherman at Bentonville. "Drive back Sherman?" Once that might have deen done, with the old Army of Tennessee. It could not be done now with the handful that was left of that army. On the first of April General Sherman's effective strength is given for all three arms, as something over eighty-one thousand men. Infantry and artillery the grey had on this date sixteen thousand and fourteen men, with a little above four thousand cavalry. Bentonville saw, grey and blue, an almost equal loss. After Bentonville came some days of calm, the grey encamped at Smithfield, the blue at Goldsboro.

But through the pause came always the tolling of the bells, ringing loud and louder —

Early in February Lee at Petersburg wrote to the Secretary of War as follows. "All the disposable force of the right wing of the Army has been operating against the enemy beyond Hatcher's Run since Sunday. Yesterday, the most inclement day of the winter, the men had to be retained in line of battle, having been in the same condition the two previous days and nights. I regret to be obliged to state that under these circumstances, heightened by assaults and fire of the enemy, some of the men had been without meat for three days, and all were suffering from reduced rations and scant clothing, exposed to battle, cold, hail, and sleet. . . . The physical strength of the men, if their courage survives, must fail under this treatment. Our cavalry had to be dispersed for want of forage. Fitz Lee's and Lomax's divisions are scattered because supplies cannot be transported where their services are required. I had to bring W. H. F. Lee's division forty miles Sunday night to get him into position. Taking these facts in consideration with the paucity of our numbers, you must not be surprised if calamity befalls us." Bad in February, it was no better in March.

Back to the trenches before Petersburg came, because they were needed, sundry troops that had fought in the Valley. Back came what was left of the Golden Brigade, and what was left of the Sixty-fifth Virginia. But November and December and January, well-nigh all of that winter, Richard Cleave, carried across the mountains after Cedar Creek, lay at Greenwood, a desperately wounded soldier. In February he began to gather strength, but the latter half of that month found him still a prisoner in a large, high, quiet room, firelit and still.

On a grey afternoon, with a few flakes of snow in the air, turning from the window toward the fire, he found that Unity was his nurse for this twilight hour. She lifted her bright face from her hands. "That was a very sad sigh, Richard!"

He smiled. "Unity, I was thinking. . . . I have not been a very fortunate soldier. And I used — long ago — to think that I would be."

"Is there such a thing as a fortunate soldier?"

He smiled again. "That depends. — Is there such a thing as a fortunate war? I don't know."

His mother entered the room. "It's Cousin William, Richard. He wants to come in and talk a little while."

Cousin William appeared — seventy, and ruddy yet, with a gouty limb and an indomitable spirit. "Ha, Richard! that's more like! You're getting colour, and some flesh on your bones! When are you going back to the front?"

"Next week, sir."

Cousin William laughed. "Well, call it the week after that!" He sat by the couch in the winged chair. The firelight played through the room, lit the two women sitting by the hearth, and the two or three old pictures on the walls. Outside the snow fell slowly, in large, quiet flakes. "Have you had any letters?" asked Cousin William.

Unity answered. "One from Fauquier yesterday. None from Edward for some days. The last was just a line from Columbia written before the troops left the place and Sherman came and burned it. We can't but feel very anxious."

But Cousin William could not endure to see Greenwood downcast. "I think you may be certain they are safe. — What did Fauquier say?"

"Just that since Hatcher's Run there had been comparative inaction. He said that the misery in the trenches was very great, and that day by day the army was dwindling. He said we must be prepared now for the worst."

Cousin William flushed, leaned forward, and became violently optimistic. "You tell Fauquier — or I'll write to him and tell him myself — that that is no way to talk! It is no way for his father's son to talk, or his grandfather's grandson to talk! I am sure, Richard, that you don't feel that way!"

"Yes, sir, I do feel that way. We are at the end."

"At the end!" ejaculated Cousin William. "Absurd! We have held Grant eight months at Petersburg! — Well, say that General Lee eventually determines to withdraw from Petersburg! What will follow? Lee in Virginia and Johnston in Carolina have the inner lines. Lee will march south, Johnston will march north, they will join armies, first crush Sherman, then turn and destroy Grant! Richmond? Well, say that Richmond is given up, temporarily, sir — temporarily! We will take it again when we want it, and if they burn it we will rebuild it! Nothing can keep it from being our capital. The President and the Cabinet and offices can remove for a time. Who knows but what it may be very well to be free and foot-loose of defended cities? Play the guerilla if need be! Make our capital at mountain hamlet after mountain hamlet, go from court-house to court-house — A capital! The Confederacy has a capital in every single Southern heart —" Cousin William dashed his hand across his eyes. "I'm ashamed to hear you speak so, Richard! — But you're a sick man — you're a sick man!"

"God knows what should be done!" said Cleave. "I am not an easy giver-up, sir. But we have fought until there is little breath in us with which to fight any more. We have fought to a standstill. And it is the country that is sick, sick to death!"

"Any day England or France —"

"Oh, the old, old dream —"

"Say then it's a dream!" cried Cousin William angrily. "Say that is a dream and any outer dependence is a dream! The spirit of man is no dream! What have we got for dependence? We have got, sir, the spirit of the men and women of the South! We've got the unconquerable and imperishable! We've got the spiritual might!"

But Richard shook his head. "A fire burns undoubtedly and a spirit holds, but day by day and night by night for four years death has come and death has come! Half the bright coals have been swept from the hearth. And against what is left, sir, wind and rain and sleet and tempest are beating hard — beating against the armies in the field and against the country in the field. They are beating hard, and they will beat us down. They have beaten us down. It is but the recognition now."

"Then may I die," said Cousin William, "before I hear Virginia say, 'I am conquered!'" His eyes sparkled, his frame trembled. "Do you think they will let it rest there, sir! No! In one year I have seen vindictiveness come into this struggle — yes, I'll grant you vindictiveness on both sides — but you say that theirs is the winning side! Then I tell you that they will be not less but more vindictive! For ten years to come they will make us drink the water of bitterness and eat the bread of humiliation! *Virginia!* And that second war will be worse than the first!"

He rose. "I can't stay here and hear you talk like this! I suppose you know what you're talking about, but you people in the field get a jaundiced view of things! I'm going to see Noel. Noel and I worked it all out last night. — General Lee to cut loose from the trenches at Petersburg, Johnston to strike north, then, having the inner lines —" And so on.

When he was gone Richard laughed. Unity, the log in her hands with which she was about to replenish the fire, looked over her shoulder. "That's sadder than sighing!" she said. "Don't!"

"What shall we do?" he asked. "Go like pieces of wood for a twelvemonth — sans care, sans thinking, sans feeling, sans heart, sans — no, not sans courage!"

"No — not sans courage."

"I am not sad," he said, "for myself. It would be strange if I were, would it not, to-day? I have a great, personal happiness. And even this afternoon, Unity — I am saying good-bye, as one of the generality, to despair, and pain, and wounded pride, and foreboding, and unhappiness. I have been looking it in the face. Such and so it is going to be in the South, and perhaps worse than we know — and yet the South is neither going to die nor despair! — And now if there is any broth I surely could take it!"

Going downstairs Cousin William found the library and Miss Lucy. "I got too angry, I suppose, with Richard — but to lie there talking of surrender! *Surrender!* I tell you, Lucy, — but there! I can't talk about it. Better not begin."

"Richard is a strong man, William. He's not the weakly despairing kind."

"I know, Lucy, I know! But it's not so bad as he thinks. I look for a big victory any day now. . . . Well! let's talk of the wedding. When's it to be?"

"In three days. The doctor says he may come downstairs to-morrow. Corbin Wood will marry them, here in the parlour. Then, in a few days, Richard will go back to the front. . . . Oh, the sad and strange and happy so blended together. . . . We are so desperate, William, that the road has turned because we couldn't travel it so any longer and live! There's a strange kind of calm, and you could say that a quiet music was coming back into life. . . . If only we could hear from Edward!"

The sky was clear on Cleave's and Judith's wedding-day. The sun shone, the winds were quiet, there was a feeling in the air as of the coming spring. Her sisters cut from the house-plants flowers for Judith's hair; there fell over her worn white gown her mother's wedding-veil. The servants brought boughs of cedar and bright berries, and with them decked the large old parlour, where the shepherds and shepherdesses looked out from the rose wreaths on the wall as they had looked when Hamilton and Burr and Jefferson were alive. The guests were few, and all old friends and kinsfolk, and there were, beside, Mammy and Julius and Isham and Scipio and Esther and Car'line and the others, Tullius among them. A great fire warmed the room, shone in the window-panes and the prisms beneath the candles and the polished floor and the old gilt frames of the Cary portraits. Margaret Cleave sat with her hand shadowing her eyes. Her heart was here, but her heart was also with her other children, with Will and Miriam. Molly, who was Miriam's age, kept beside her, a loving hand on her dress. Cousin William gave away the bride. An artillery commander, himself just out of hospital, stood with Cleave. — Oh, the grey uniforms, so worn and weather-stained for a wedding party!

It was over — the guests were gone. The household, tremulous, between smiles and tears, went its several, accustomed ways. There was no wedding journey to be taken. All life was fitted now to a Doric simplicity, a grave acceptance of realities without filagree adornment. There was left a certain fair quietness, limpid sincerity, faith, and truth. . . . There was a quiet, cheerful supper, and afterwards a little talking together in the library, the reading of the Richmond papers, Unity singing to her guitar. Then at last goodnights were said. Judith and Cleave mounted the stairs together, entered hand in hand their room. The shutters were all opened; it lay, warmed by the glowing embers on the hearth, but yet in a flood of moonlight. His arm about her, they moved to the deep window-seat above the garden, knelt there and looked out. Valley and hill and distant mountains were all washed with silver.

"The moon shone so that April night — that night after you overtook the carriage upon the road — and at last we understood . . . I sat here all that night, in the moonlight."

"The garden where I said good-bye to you, a hundred years ago, the day after a tournament. . . . It does not look dead and cold and a winter night. It looks filled with lilies and roses and bright, waving trees — and if a bird is not singing down there, then it must be singing in my heart! It is singing somewhere! — Love is best."

"Love is best."

A week from this day he passed through Richmond on his way to the front. Richmond! Richmond looked to him like a prisoner doomed, and yet a quiet prisoner with a smile for children and the azure spaces in the winter sky. People were going in streams into the churches. The hospitals, they said, were very full. In all the departments, it was said, the important papers were kept packed in boxes, ready to be removed if there were need. No one any longer noticed the cannon to the south. They had been thundering there since June, and it was now March. There was very little to eat. Milk sold at four dollars a quart. And yet children played about the doors, and women smiled, and men and women went about the day's work with sufficient heroism. "Dear Dick Ewell" had charge of the defences of Richmond, the slightly manned ring of forts, the Local Brigade, Custis Lee's division at Chaffin's Bluff. In the high, clear March air, ragged grey soldiers passed, honoured, through the streets, bugles blew, or drums beat. One caught the air of Dixie.

Cleave rode out over Mayo's Bridge and south through the war-scored country to Petersburg and the grey lines, to division head-quarters and then to the Golden Brigade. The brigade and he met like tried friends, but the Sixty-fifth and he met like lovers.

The lines at Petersburg! — stretched and stretched from the Appomattox, east of the town, to Five Forks and the White Oak Road, stretched until now, in places, there was scarcely more than a skirmish line, stretched to the breaking-point! The trenches at Petersburg! — clay ditches where men were drenched by the winter rains, pierced by the winter sleet, where they huddled or burrowed, scooping shallow caves with bayonet and tin cup, where hands and feet were frozen, where at night they watched the mortar shells, and at all hours heard the minies keening, where the smoke hung heavy, where the earth all about was raw and pitted, where every muscle rebelled, so cramped and weary of the trenches! where there were double watches and a man could not sleep enough, where there were nakedness and hunger and every woe but heat, where the sharpshooters picked off men, and the minies came with a whistle and killed them, and the bombs with a shriek and worked red havoc, where men showed a thousand weaknesses and again a thousand heroisms! Oh, the labyrinth of trenches, forts, traverses, roads, approaches, raw red clay, and trampled herbage, hillock and hollow, scored, seamed, and pitted mother earth, and over all the smoke and noise, blown by the March wind! And Petersburg itself, that had been a pleasant town, was a place of ruined houses and deserted streets! A bitter havoc had been wrought.

The night of his return to the front Cleave stood with Fauquier Cary in an embrasure whence a gun had just been taken to strengthen another work, stood and looked first over the red wilderness of their own camp-fires, and then across a stripe of darkness to the long, deep, and vivid glow that marked the Federal lines. The night was cold but still, the stars extraordinarily bright. "For so long in that quiet room at Greenwood!" said Cleave. "And now this again! It has almost a novel look. There! What a great shell!"

"Fireworks at the end," answered Cary. "It is the end."

"Yes. It is evident."

"I have been," said Cary, "for a day or two to Richmond, and I was shown there certain papers, memoranda, and estimates. I wish you would listen to three or four statements out of many. — 'Amount needed for absolutely necessary construction and repair of railroads if they are to serve any military purpose $21,000,000.' — 'The Commissary debt now exceeds $70,000,000.' — 'The debt to various factories exceeds $5,000,000.' — 'The Medical Department asks for $40,000,000, at least for the current year.' — 'The Subsistence Bureau and the Nitre and Mining Bureau as well as other Departments are resorting to barter.' — 'Requisitions by the War Department upon the Treasury since '61 amount to $1,737,746,121. Of the requisition for last year and this year, there is yet unfurnished $160,000,000. In addition the War Department has a further arrearage of say $200,000,000.' — This was a letter from one of the up-river counties patriotically proposing the use of cotton yarn or cloth as specie — thus reducing the necessity for the use of Treasury notes to the smallest possible limit! Let us see how it went. — First it proposed the removal of all factories to safe points near the mountains, where the water-power is abundant and approach by the enemy difficult. Next the establishment of small factories at various points of like character. Around these, as centres, it goes on to say, 'the women of our country who have been deprived of all and driven from their homes by the enemy should be collected, together with the wives and daughters of soldiers and others in indigent circumstances. There they would not be likely to be disturbed by the enemy. Thus distributed they could be more easily fed, and the country be greatly benefited by their labours, which would be light and highly remunerative to them, thereby lessening the suffering at home and the consequently increasing discontent in the army. Cotton would be near at hand, labour abundant, and the necessity of the transportation of food and material to and from great centres of trade greatly reduced. We would furnish the women of the country generally with yarns and a simple and cheap pattern of looms, taking pay for the same in cloth made by them — ' et cætera! . . . How desperate we are, Richard, to entertain ourselves with foolery like this! — But the act to use the negroes as soldiers will go through. We have come to that. The only thing is that the war will be ended before they can be mustered in."

They turned in the embrasure and looked far and wide. It seemed a world of camp-fires. Far to the east, in the direction of City Point, some river battery or gun-boat was sending up rockets. Westward a blue fort began a sullen cannonade and a grey fort nearly opposite at once took up the challenge. "Fort Gregg," said Cary, "dubbed by our men 'Fort Hell,' and Fort Mahone called by theirs 'Fort Damnation.'"

For all that the night itself was so clear and the stars so high and splendid, there was a murk discernible everywhere a few feet above the earth, rising like a miasma, with a faint, distasteful odour. Through it all the fires lit by men shone blurred. The cannon continued to thunder, and above their salients gathered clouds of coppery smoke. A half brigade passed on its way to strengthen some menaced place, and a neighbouring fire showed in series its face and form. The men looked dead for sleep, hollow-eyed, hollow-cheeked. They dragged their limbs, their heads drooped, their shoulders were bowed. They passed like dull and weary sheep. Fort Hell and Fort Damnation brought more guns into action.

Cleave passed his hand before his eyes. "It's not," he said, "the way to settle it."

"Precisely not," answered Cary. "It is not, and it never was, and it never will be. And that despite the glamour and the cry of 'Necessity!'"

"Little enough glamour to-night!"

"I agree with you. The glamour is at the beginning. The necessity is to find a more heroic way."

The two went down from the embrasure and presently said goodnight. Cleave rode on — not to the house in which he was quartered, but to the portion of the lines where, he was told, would be found a command for which he had made enquiry. He found it and its colonel, asked a question or two, and at once obtained the request which he made, this being that he might speak to a certain soldier in such a company.

The soldier came and faced Cleave where the latter waited for him beside a deserted camp-fire. The red light showed both their faces, worn and grave and self-contained. Off in the night and distance the two forts yet thundered, but all hereabouts was quiet, the fires dying down, the men sinking to rest. "Stafford," said Cleave, "I have been lying wounded for a long while, and I have had time to look at man's life, and the way we live it. It's all a mystery, what we do, and what we do not do, and we stumble and stumble! . . ." He held out his hand. "Don't let us be enemies any longer!"

CHAPTER XLII

A CONFEDERATE soldier, John Wise, speaks of the General-in-Chief. "I have seen many pictures of General Lee, but never one that conveyed a correct impression of his appearance. Above the ordinary size, his proportions were perfect. His form had fullness, without any appearance of superfluous flesh, and was as erect as that of a cadet, without the slightest apparent constraint. No representation that I have ever seen properly conveys the light and softness of his eye, the tenderness and intellectuality of his mouth, or the indescribable refinement of his face. . . .

"There was nothing of the pomp or panoply of war about the headquarters, or the military government, or the bearing of General Lee. . . . Persons having business with his headquarters were treated like human beings, and courtesy, considerateness, and even deference were shown to the humblest. He had no gilded retinue, but a devoted band of simple scouts and couriers who, in their quietness and simplicity, modelled themselves after him. . . . The sight of him upon the roadside or in the trenches was as common as that of any subordinate in the army. When he approached or disappeared, it was with no blare of trumpets or clank of equipments. . . . He came as unostentatiously as if he had been the head of a plantation riding over his fields to enquire and give directions about ploughing or seeding. He appeared to have no mighty secrets concealed from his subordinates. He assumed no airs of superior authority. . . . His bearing was that of a friend having a common interest in a common venture with the person addressed, and as if he assumed that his subordinate was as deeply concerned as himself in its success. Whatever greatness was accorded to him was not of his own seeking. . . . But the impression which he made by his presence, and by his leadership, upon all that came in contact with him, can be described by no other term than that of grandeur. . . . The man who could so stamp his impress upon his nation . . . and yet die without an enemy; the soldier who could make love for his person a substitute for pay and clothing and food, and could, by the constraint of that love, hold together a naked, starving band, and transform it into a fighting army; the heart which, after the failure of its great endeavour, could break in silence, and die without the utterance of one word of bitterness — such a man, such a soldier, such a heart, must have been great indeed — great beyond the power of eulogy."

He had fifty thousand men to his opponents' hundred and odd thousand. His men were very weary, very hungry, very worn. He had a thirty-mile line to keep, and behind him the capital of his government of which he was the sole defence. For months there had come upon his ears, resoundingly, the noise of disaster, disaster in every ward of the one-time grey fortress of the South. For all victories elsewhere his opponent fired salutes, thundering across the winter air into the grey lines, listened to grimly, answered defiantly by the grey trenches. The victories in Georgia — Winchester and Cedar Creek — Franklin and Nashville — Fort Fisher — Savannah — Columbia — Charleston — the blue salvoes and huzzahs came with frequency, with frequency! And ever thinner and thinner grew the grey ranks.

. . . There was but one last hope untried, and that was slight indeed, slight as gossamer. Break away from these lines, cover somehow and quickly a hundred and forty southward-stretching miles, unite with Johnston, strike Sherman, turn and combat with Grant! How slight was the hope Lee perhaps knew better than any man. But he had accepted a trust, and hand and head served his cause to the last.

. . . To strike aside Grant's left wing, with a last deadly blow, and so pass out —

Fourteen thousand men, under Gordon, were given the attack upon Fort Stedman and the three forts on lifted ground beyond. On the twenty-fifth of March, at dawn, the assault was made — desperately made, and desperately repulsed. When the bitter day was over the blue had lost two thousand men, but the grey had lost twice as many.

A. P. Hill held the grey right from Hatcher's Run to Battery Gregg. Gordon had the centre. Longstreet held from the Appomattox to the White Oak Road. Now on the twenty-ninth of March, Grant planned a general attack. Sheridan was here from the Valley, to come in on the grey rear with thirteen thousand horse. Every corps of the Army of the Potomac had its appointed place and task in a great movement to the right. Lee, divining, drew from his threadbare, extended lines what troops he might and placed them at Five Forks, confronting the Second and Fifth blue Corps,— Fitz Lee's and W. H. F. Lee's cavalry, say four thousand horse, Pickett's division, thirty-five hundred muskets, Anderson with as many more. All the night of the twenty-ninth, troops were moving in a heavy rain.

Through the dripping day of the thirtieth sounded, now and again, a sullen firing. On the thirty-first the grey attacked — attacked with all their old élan and fury — and drove Sheridan back in disorder on Dinwiddie Court House. Night came down and made the battle cease. There dawned, grey and still, the first of April. All day there was fighting, but in the dim evening came the catastrophe. Like a great river that has broken its banks, the blue, advancing in force, overflowed Pickett's division. . . . The grey loss at Five Forks was five thousand.

With the morning light Grant began his general advance upon Petersburg. The grey trenches fought him back, the grey trenches that were now no more than a picket line, the grey trenches with men five yards apart. They gave him pause — that was all that they could do. All the South was an iron bell that was swinging — swinging —

General Lee telegraphed Breckinridge, Secretary of War. "It is absolutely necessary that we abandon our position to-night or run the risk of being cut off in the morning. I have given all the orders to officers on both sides of the river, and have taken every precaution I can to make the movement successful. Please give all orders that you find necessary in and about Richmond. The troops will all be directed to Amelia Court House."

This day was killed A. P. Hill.

In Richmond, twenty miles away, the second of April was a day bright and mild, with the grass coming up like emerald, the fruit trees in bloom, white butterflies above the dandelions, the air all sheen and fragrance. It was Sunday. All the churches were filled with people. The President sat in his pew at Saint Paul's, grave and tall and grey, distinguished and quiet of aspect. Here and there in the church were members of the Government, here and there an officer of the Richmond defences. Dr. Minnegerode was in the pulpit. The sun came slantingly in at the open windows, — sunshine and a balmy air. It was very quiet — the black-clad women sitting motionless, the soldiers still as on parade, the marked man in the President's pew straight, quiet, and attentive, the white and black form in the pulpit with raised hands, speaking of a supper before Gethsemane — for it was the first Sunday in the month and communion was to follow. The sun came in, very golden, very quiet. . . .

The sexton of Saint Paul's walked, on tiptoe, up the aisle. He was a large man, with blue clothes and brass buttons and a ruffled shirt. Often and often, in these four years, had he come with a whispered message or a bit of paper to this or that man in authority. He had come, too, with private trouble and woe. This man had risen and gone out for he had news that his son's body was being brought, into town; these women had moved gropingly down the aisle, because the message said father or brother or son or husband . . . Saint Paul's was used to the sexton coming softly up the aisle. Saint Paul's only thought, "Is he coming for me?" — "Is he coming for me?"

But he was coming, it seemed, for the President. . . . Mr. Davis read the slip of paper, rose with a still face, and went softly down the aisle, erect and quiet. Eyes followed him; many eyes. For all it was so hushed in Saint Paul's there came a feeling as of swinging bells. . . . The sexton, who had gone out before Mr. Davis, returned. He whispered to General Anderson. The latter rose and went out. A sigh like a wind that begins to mount went through Saint Paul's. Indefinably it began to make itself known that these were not usual summons. The hearts of all began to beat, beat hard. Suddenly the sexton was back, summoning this one and that one and the other. — "Sit still, my people, sit still, my people!" — but the bells were ringing too loudly and the hearts were beating too hard. Men and women rose, hung panting a moment, then, swift or slow, they left Saint Paul's. Going, they heard that the lines at Petersburg had been broken and that General Lee said the Government must leave Richmond — leave at once.

Outside they stood, men and women, dazed for a moment in the great porch, in the gay light of the sun. The street was filling with people, people in the green, climbing Capitol Square. It climbed to the building Jefferson had planned, to the great white pillars, beyond and between which showed the azure spring sky. The eyes of the people sought their capitol. They rested, too, on the great bronze Washington, riding his horse against the blue sky, with Marshall and Henry and Jefferson and Mason and Lewis and Nelson about him. Across from the church was a public building in which there were Government offices. Before this building, out in the street, a great heap of papers was burning with a light, crackling flame. "Government papers," said some one, then raised his eyes to the stars and bars above the white capitol and took off his hat.

All day the fevered city watched the trains depart, all day wagons and horsemen passed through the streets, all day there was a saying farewell, farewell — farewell to many things! All day the sun shone, all day men and women were conscious of a strange shock and dizziness, as of a violent physical impact. There was not much, perhaps, of conscious thought. People acted instinctively, automatically. Now and then weeping was heard, but it was soon controlled and it was not frequent. This was shipwreck after four years of storm, after gulfs of despair and shining shores of hope. It was taken quietly, as are many shipwrecks.

Night came. Custis Lee's troops at Chaffin's Bluff, eight miles below the city, began to withdraw, crossing the river by pontoons. There was now between Richmond and Manchester only Mayo's Bridge, guarded by a company or two of the Local Brigade. People were down by the river, many people. It seemed to give them company, swollen like their own hearts, rushing between its rocky islets, on and down to the boundless sea. Others wandered through the streets, or sat silent in the Capitol Square. Between two and three o'clock began the ordered blowing-up of powder magazines and arsenals and of the gunboats down the river. Explosion after explosion shook the night, terrific to the ear, crushing the heart. Up rushed the smoke, the water reddened, the earth trembled, shells from the arsenals burst high in air, lighting the doomed city. They wrought a further horror, for falling fragments or brands set afire first this building and then that. In a short while the whole lower part of the city was burning, burning down. Smoke mounted, the river was lit from bank to bank, there was born with the mounting flames a terrible splendour. On Cary Street stood a great Commissary depot, holding stores that the Government could not remove. Here, in the flame-lit street, gathered a throng of famished men and women. They broke open the doors, they carried out food, while the fire roared toward them, and at last laid hold of this storehouse also. Loud and loud went on the explosions, the powder, the ranged shells and cartridges, and now came the sound of the blowing up of unfinished gunboats. The smoke blew, red-bosomed, over the city. Through the murk, looking upward from the river, came a vision of the pillars of the Capitol, turned from white to coral — above, between smoke-wreaths, lit and splendid, the flag of the Confederacy. . . .

Dawn broke. The last grey troops passed over Mayo's Bridge, firing it behind them. There came a halt between tides, then, through the murk and roar of the burning city, in from the Varina and New Market roads a growing sound, a sound of marching men, of hurrahing voices, of bands that played now " Yankee Doodle" and now " The Star Spangled Banner."

Through the April country, miles and miles of springing verdure, miles and miles of rain-softened, narrow roads, marched the Army of Northern Virginia. It must guard its trains of subsistence. But so wet was the country where every streamlet had become a brook, and every brook a river, so deep were the hollows and sloughs of the unutterable road that many a wheel refused to budge. Supply and ammunition wagons, gun wheel and ambulance wheel must be dragged and pushed, dragged and pushed, over and over again. O weariness — weariness — weariness of gaunt, hardly-fed and over-worked horses, weariness of gaunt, hardly-fed, over-worked men! The sun shone with a mocking light, but never dried the roads. Down upon the trains dashed Sheridan's cavalry — fifteen thousand horsemen, thrice the force of the grey cavalry. Grey rear guard formed, brought guns into action, pushed back the assault, let the trains move on —and then in an hour, *da capo !* Horses fell in harness, wagons had to be abandoned, others, whirled against by the blue cavalry, were burned, there was no time that a stand could be made and rations issued — even had there been any rations to issue.

Amelia — There would be stores found at Amelia Court House. That had been arranged for. . . . But when on the fourth Longstreet reached Amelia, and after him Gordon and Ewell there were no stores found. Some one had blundered, something had miscarried. There were no stores.

On the fifth of April, Lee left Amelia Court House and struck westward, with a hope, perhaps, of Lynchburg and then Danville. Behind him was Grant in strength, Sheridan and Grant. . . . And still the bottomless roads, and still no rations for his soldiers. The Army of Northern Virginia was weak from hunger. The wounded were many, the sick and exhausted were more. There was now a great, helpless throng in and about the wagons, men stretched upon the boards, wounded and ill, stifling their groans, men limping and swaying alongside, trying to keep up. . . . And then, again and again, great cavalry dashes, a haggard resistance, a scattering, overturning, hewing-down and burning. . . . And still the Army of Northern Virginia drew its wounded length westward.

Sleep seemed to have fled the earth. Day was lighter and something warmer than night, and night was darker and more cold than day, and there seemed no other especial difference. The monotony of attack, monotonously to be repelled, held whether it were light or dark, day or night. Marching held. Hunger held. There held a ghastly, a monstrous fatigue. And always there were present the fallen by the road, the gestures of farewell and despair, the covered eyes, the outstretched forms upon the earth. And always the dwindling held, and the cry, *Close up! Close up! Close up, men!*

"Mighty cold April!" said the men. "Even the pear trees and the peach trees and the cherry trees look cold and misty and wavering — No, there is n't any wind, but they look wavering, wavering . . ." — "Dreamed a while back — sleeping on my feet. Dreamed the trees were all filled with red cherries, and the corn was up, and we had a heap of roasting ears . . ." — "Don't talk that-a-way! Don't tell about dreams! 'T is n't lucky! Roasting ears and cherries — O God! O God!" — "Talking about corn? I heard tell about a lady in the country. All the horses were taken and the plantation could n't be ploughed, and she wanted it ploughed. And so a battle happened along right there, and when it was over and everybody that could had marched away, she sent out and gathered two of the horses that were just roaming around loose. So she had plough-horses, but they were so hungry they were wicked, and she did n't have any fodder at all to give them. Not any at all. But women are awful resourceful. There were a lot of shuck beds in the quarter. She had the ticks ripped open and she took the shucks and soaked them in hot water and sprinkled them with a little salt and fed her plough-horses. If anybody stumbles on a shuck bed in this march I speak for it!" — *Close up! Close up! Close up, men!*

> " ' Maxwelton braes are bonny,
> Where early fa's the dew,
> And 't was there that Annie Laurie
> Gaed me her promise, true — ' "

And on they went — and on they went toward Appomattox.

In every company there was the Controversialist. Not cold nor hunger nor battle could kill the Controversialist. The Controversialist of Company A — the column being halted before a black and cold and swollen stream—appealed to Allan Gold. "I?" said Allan. "What do I think? I think that we were both right and both wrong, and that, in the beginning, each side might have been more patient and much wiser. Life and history, and right and wrong and minds of men look out of more windows than we used to think! Did you never hear of the shield that had two sides and both were precious metal? The traveller who said, ' This is a gold shield,' was right — half right. And the traveller who said, ' This is a silver shield,' was right — half right. The trouble was neither took the trouble to walk round the shield. So it is, I reckon, in most wars — this one not excepted! Of course, being in, we 've done good fighting — "

On moved the Army of Northern Virginia, through the cold river and up upon the farther side. *Column forward! Column forward!* Flowering fruit trees and April verdure and a clearing sky. On and on down a long, long vista. . . . *Tramp, tramp, tramp, tramp!*

> " ' Way down South in the land ob cotton,
> 'Simmon seed and sandy bottom — ' "

THE END

Library of Congress Cataloging-in-Publication Data

Johnston, Mary, 1870–1936.
  Cease firing / by Mary Johnston.
     p.   cm.
  A sequel to : The Long roll.
  ISBN 0-8018-5525-X (pbk. : alk. paper)
  1. United States—History—Civil War, 1861–1865—Fiction.
I. Title.
PS2141.C43   1996   96-27405
813'.52—dc20   CIP